Political Science

An Introduction

Political Science

An Introduction

FOURTEENTH EDITION

Michael G. Roskin
Lycoming College

Robert L. Cord
James A. Medeiros
Walter S. Jones

PEARSON

Boston   Columbus   Indianapolis   New York   San Francisco   Amsterdam   Cape Town
Dubai   London   Madrid   Milan   Munich   Paris   Montréal   Toronto   Delhi
Mexico City   São Paulo   Sydney   Hong Kong   Seoul   Singapore   Taipei   Tokyo

Editor-in-Chief: Dickson Musselwhite
Publisher: Charlyce Jones-Owen
Editorial Assistant: Laura Hernandez
Field Marketing Manager: Brittany
   Pogue-Mohammed
Program Manager: Rob DeGeorge
Project Manager: Carol O'Rourke
Senior Operations Supervisor: Mary
   Fischer
Operations Specialist: Mary Ann
   Gloriande

Cover Art Director: Maria Lange
Media Project Manager: Tina
   Gagliostro
Text Permissions Project Manager:
   Peggy Davis
**Full-Service Project Management,
Composition, and Design:** Integra
Printer/Binder: RRD, Crawfordsville
Cover Printer: Lehigh-Phoenix: Lehigh/
   Phoenix

Photo Credits p. 269: AP Photo/Pablo Martinez Monsivais; cover, p. 2, p. 28, p. 49, p. 68, p. 86, p. 109, p. 127, p. 148, p. 168, p. 187, p. 207, p. 228, p. 248, p. 291, p. 311, p. 331: Michael G. Roskin

Library of Congress Cataloging-in-Publication Data

Political science: an introduction/Michael G. Roskin, Robert L. Cord,
   James A. Medeiros, Walter S. Jones.— Fourteenth edition.
      pages cm
   ISBN 978-0-13-440285-7—ISBN 0-13-440285-5
   1. Political science.   I. Roskin, Michael G., 1939–
JA71.P623 2017
320—dc23

                                        2015030801

3   16

Student Edition
ISBN-13: 978-0-134-40285-7
ISBN-10:   0-134-40285-5

Instructor's Review Copy:
ISBN-13: 978-0-134-40989-1
ISBN-10:   0-134-40498-X

A La Carte Edition
ISBN-13: 978-0-134-40479-0
ISBN-10:   0-134-40479-3

PEARSON

Brief Contents

Contents

Preface

Political Science and Democracy

Some people say political science is impractical. It may be interesting, they add, but it really cannot be used for anything. Not so. Political science began as practical advice to rulers and still serves that function. Plato, Aristotle, Confucius, Machiavelli, Kautilya, and Ibn Khaldun, among others, aimed to give sound advice based on one or another theory. John Locke and the Baron de Montesquieu deeply influenced the framers of the U.S. Constitution. Political science has always entwined theoretical abstractions with applied reasoning. You may not become a political scientist, but you should equip yourself with the knowledge to make calm, rational choices and protect yourself from political manipulation.

One of the great questions of our day, for example, is whether democracy can and should be exported. China, the Middle East, and many other areas could benefit from democratic governance, but is it practical to push democracy on them? One of the original aims of the 2003 Iraq War was to install a democratic regime which would then inspire others in the region. Iraq, totally unready for democracy, turned from a brutal dictatorship into brutal chaos.

Even the United States, after more than two centuries of trying to apply a democratic constitution, is far from perfect. Reforms are badly needed—but blocked at every turn—in taxation, voting fairness, election campaigning, powerful lobbies, economic policy, and the inefficiency and complexity of government programs. By examining such problems, students see that democracy is a constantly self-critical and self-correcting process moved by open discussion and the admission of mistakes. It is always a work in progress.

Political science instructors may take some joy in the uptick of student interest in politics, although we cannot be sure how deep and durable this interest may be. Budgetary cliffhangers, spending cuts, and tax increases can provoke discussion. For some years, students were rather apolitical, a trend this book always tried to fight. We ask them, "Well, what kind of a country do you want? You'd better start developing your own rational perspectives now because soon you will have to make political choices."

Political Science: An Introduction seeks to blend scholarship and citizenship. It does not presume that freshmen taking an intro course will become professional political scientists. Naturally, we hope to pique their curiosity so that some will major in political science. This is neither a U.S. government text nor a comparative politics text. Instead, it draws examples from the United States and from other lands to introduce the whole field of political science to new students. Fresh from high school, few students know much of other political systems, something we attempt to correct.

The fourteenth edition continues our eclectic approach that avoids selling any single theory, conceptual framework, or paradigm as the key to political science. Attempts to impose a grand design are both unwarranted by the nature of the discipline and not conducive to broadening students' intellectual horizons. Instructors with a wide variety of viewpoints have no trouble using this text. Above all, the fourteenth edition still views politics as exciting and tries to communicate that feeling to young people new to the discipline.

New To This Edition

Instructor input, the rapid march of events, and the shift to digitalization brought some changes to the fourteenth edition:

- The old Chapter 2, Theories, has been merged into Chapter 1 to bring the total number of chapters down to seventeen, to better fit a semester.

- Jonathan Williamson of Lycoming College contributes to Chapter 1 with discussions of political theory and how political science contrasts with history and journalism.

- A new box in Chapter 3 explains Francis Fukuyama's three-step theory of the origins of political order.

- The 2015 *Charlie Hebdo* murders in Paris illustrate the problem of free speech as opposed to hate speech in Chapter 4.

- Recent Hong Kong protests now start Chapter 5, illustrating the struggle for democracy. Also new: Opportunism and corruption undermine Communist regimes.

- A new box in Chapter 6, "The Three Israels," shows how successive waves of immigrants brought distinctive political cultures to Israel.

- Jonathan Williamson, a pollster himself, updates Chapter 7 on public opinion.

- The rise of the Tea Party and super-PACs raises questions about the relevance of U.S. parties in Chapter 10.

- Nonwhite voters are increasingly important, and realignments may evolve more slowly than previously thought, explains Chapter 11.

- Incomprehensible, overlong legislation is now highlighted in Chapter 12.

- Chapter 13 now includes Fukuyama's thesis that uncorrupt, merit-based bureaucracies are the basis of good governance.

- Chapter 16 gives more emphasis to the mostly unhappy results of the Arab Spring and to ISIS and Islamic fundamentalism.

- Chapter 17 begins with the dangers of a new Cold War we face with Russia and China.

As ever, I am open to all instructor comments, including those on the number, coverage, and ordering of chapters. Would, for example, a textbook of fourteen chapters—one for each week of a typical semester—be a better organization?

REVEL™
Educational Technology Designed for the Way Today's Students **Read**, **Think**, and **Learn**

When students are engaged deeply, they learn more effectively and perform better in their courses. This simple fact inspired the creation of REVEL: an immersive learning experience designed for the way today's students read, think, and learn. Built in collaboration with educators and students nationwide, REVEL is the newest, fully digital way to deliver respected Pearson content.

REVEL enlivens course content with media interactives and assessments—integrated directly within the authors' narrative—that provide opportunities for students to read about and practice course material in tandem. This immersive educational technology boosts student engagement, which leads to better understanding of concepts and improved performance throughout the course.

Learn more about REVEL
www.pearsonhighered.com/REVEL

Features

The fourteenth edition merges old Chapters 1 and 2 (Theories) to give us seventeen chapters. The consolidation of twenty-one chapters into eighteen, more rationally arranged, received very positive instructor feedback in the eleventh and twelfth editions. We retain the introduction of methodologies early in an undergraduate's career. This does not mean high-level numbers crunching—which I neither engage in nor advocate—but a reality-testing frame of mind that looks for empirical verifiability. Where you can, of course, use valid numbers. As an instructor, I often found myself explaining methodologies in the classroom in connection with student papers, so I decided to insert some basic methodologies in boxes. Each of these boxes make one methodological point per chapter, covering thesis statements, references, quotations, tables, cross-tabulations, graphs, scattergrams, and other standard points, all at the introductory level. Instructors suggested that topics as important as "Key Concepts" should be integrated into the narrative, and I have done so. Boxes on Democracy, Theories, Classic Works, and Case Studies still highlight important political science ideas, provide real-world examples, and break up pages, making the text reader friendly.

The text boldfaces important terms and defines them in running marginal glossaries throughout the chapters. As an instructor, I learned not to presume students understood the key terms of political science. The definitions are in the context under discussion; change that context, and you may need another definition. There is a difference, for example, between the governing elites discussed in Chapter 5 (a tiny fraction of 1 percent of a population) and public opinion elites discussed in Chapter 7 (probably several percent). Italicized terms signal students to look them up in the glossary at the book's end.

Supplements

Pearson is pleased to offer several resources to qualified adopters of *Political Science* and their students that will make teaching and learning from this book even more effective and enjoyable. Several of the supplements for this book are available at the Instructor Resource Center (IRC), an online hub that allows instructors to quickly download book-specific supplements. Please visit the IRC welcome page at **www.pearsonhighered .com/irc** to register for access.

INSTRUCTOR'S MANUAL/TEST BANK This resource includes learning objectives, lecture outlines, multiple-choice questions, true/false questions, and essay questions for each chapter. Available exclusively on the Instructor Resource Center, **www.pearsonhighered/irc**.

PEARSON MYTEST This powerful assessment generation program includes all of the items in the instructor's manual/test bank. Questions and tests can be easily created, customized, saved online, and then printed, allowing flexibility to manage assessments anytime and anywhere. To learn more, please visit **www.mypearsontest.com** or contact your Pearson representative.

POWERPOINT PRESENTATION Organized around a lecture outline, these multimedia presentations also include photos, figures, and tables from each chapter. Available exclusively on the IRC.

ATLAS OF WORLD ISSUES (0-205-78020-2) From population and political systems to energy use and women's rights, the *Atlas of World Issues* features full-color thematic maps that examine the forces shaping the world. Featuring maps from the latest edition of *The Penguin State of the World Atlas*, this excerpt includes critical-thinking exercises to promote a deeper understanding of how geography affects many global issues. To learn more, please contact your Pearson representative.

GOODE'S WORLD ATLAS (0-321-65200-2) First published by Rand McNally in 1923, *Goode's World Atlas* has set the standard for college reference atlases. It features hundreds of physical, political, and thematic maps as well as graphs, tables, and a pronouncing index. Available at a discount when packaged with *Political Science: An Introduction*.

Acknowledgments

My special thanks to Jonathan Williamson of Lycoming College, who made many updates to this edition. Several people reviewed this and earlier editions, and I carefully considered their comments. For this edition, I wish to thank Maorong Jiang, Creighton University; Kimberly Turner, College of DuPage; Robert Porter, Ventura County Community College; John Sutherlin, University of Louisiana at Monroe; Ngozi Kamalu, Fayetteville State University; and Aaron Cooley, Johnston Community College. My thanks to Martha Beyerlein for her careful work throughout the production process.

Are further changes needed in the book, or have I got it about right? Instructors' input on this matter—or indeed on anything else related to the text or supplementary materials—is highly valued. Instructors may contact me directly at maxxumizer@gmail.com.

Michael G. Roskin

Part I
The Bases of Politics

Ch. 1 Politics and Political Science We study politics like a scientist studies bacteria, never getting angry at a fact but trying to understand how and why something happens. Political science focuses on power—how A gets B to do what A wants. We do not confuse our partisan preferences with the scholarly study of politics. Theories provide the framework for understanding the politics we study. Alternatives to the objective, theory-driven approach of political science include the emphasis on the unique taken by historians and journalists and the normative questions of political theorists.

Ch. 2 Political Ideologies Ideologies are plans to improve society. The classic liberalism of Adam Smith and classic conservatism of Edmund Burke and the modern versions of the same are still with us. Marx led to both social democracy and, through Lenin, to communism. Nationalism is the strongest ideology, sometimes turning into fascism. New ideologies include neoconservatism, libertarianism, feminism, environmentalism, and, currently a problem, Islamism. We study ideologies; we don't believe them.

Ch. 3 States Not all states are effective; many are weak, and some are failed. Aristotle's division of governments into legitimate and corrupt is still useful. Basic institutional choices can make or break a state. The territorial organization of states—unitary versus federal—and electoral systems—single-member versus proportional representation—are such basic choices. State intervention in the economy, or lack of it, may facilitate prosperity or stagnation.

Ch. 4 Constitutions and Rights These institutionalized documents formalize the basic structure of the state, limit government's powers, and define civil rights. Judicial review, the great U.S. contribution to governance, has over the years curbed sedition laws and expanded freedom of speech and freedom of press.

Ch. 5 Regimes Democracy is complex and must include accountability, competition, and alternation in power. In even the best democracies, elites have great influence but do not always trump pluralistic inputs. Totalitarianism is a disease of the twentieth century and has largely faded, but plenty of authoritarian states still exist. Democracy is not automatic but can fail in unprepared countries like Russia and Iraq.

Chapter 1
Politics and Political Science

 ## Learning Objectives

1.1 Evaluate the several explanations of political power.

1.2 Justify the claim that political science may be considered a science.

1.3 Evaluate the strengths and weaknesses of several theoretical approaches to political science.

1.4 Contrast normative theories of politics to political science.

When the Cold War ended, several thinkers held that democracy had won and would encompass the world. Soviet communism had collapsed and Chinese communism had reformed into state-managed capitalism. There were scarcely any other models for governance than Western-style capitalist democracy, argued some neo-conservatives. Even the Middle East, home to some of the worst dictators, would give way to democracy, argued Bush administration neo-cons as the United States invaded Iraq in 2003. The 2011 Arab Spring seemed to show the longing for democracy, aided by the new hand-held social media.

But we were too optimistic. Not everyone craved democracy; many, in fact, either feared it or wanted to use it for misrule. Russian democracy collapsed back into an autocracy that is now hostile to the United States. China's Communist chiefs oversaw dramatic economic growth but proclaimed that they would keep ruling. They jailed dissenters and also turned hostile to the United States. In the Middle East, elections produced undemocratic regimes (exception: Tunisia) and dangerous chaos. What had gone wrong? And what can political science tell us about why democracy did not spread as planned? Were these countries simply not ready for democracy, which seems to require a large, educated middle class and a tolerant, pluralist culture? Long-run, over several decades of economic and educational growth, is a march toward democracy likely to resume?

Questions like these make political science relevant and exciting. As its two-word name implies, political science is both a topic of study and a method for studying its topic. If we are studying politics, we need to start by thinking about what politics is. If we are studying it with science, we need to consider what makes the scientific method distinct from other ways to study politics.

What Is Politics?

1.1 **Evaluate the several explanations of political power.**

When you think of politics, you probably think of government and elections. Both are clearly political, but politics can happen in many more places. Politics happens in the workplace, in families, and even in the classroom. Consider the kid in class who asks too many questions and keeps the class late. What happens? Either the professor cuts the kid off, or his classmates express their disapproval to shape his behavior to achieve their goals. Either way, the kid's behavior is shaped by the politics of the classroom.

Politics is the ongoing competition between people, usually in groups, to shape policy in their favor. To do so, they may seek to guide policy indirectly by shaping the beliefs and values of members of their society. Notice this definition can encompass the politics of government, but it can also encompass the political dynamics in other contexts. While this text will largely focus on politics of governments, it is important to understand that politics is more fundamental than governments but occurs wherever human competitions play out.

Political Power

As Renaissance Florentine philosopher Niccolò Machiavelli (1469–1527) emphasized, ultimately politics is about power, specifically the power to shape others'
behavior. Power in politics is getting people to do something they wouldn't otherwise do—and sometimes having them think it was their idea.

political power

Ability of one person
to get another to do
something.

Some people dislike the concept of **political power**. It smacks of coercion,
inequality, and occasionally brutality. Some speakers denounce "power politics," suggesting governance without power, a happy band of brothers and sis-
ters regulating themselves through love and sharing. Communities formed on
such a basis do not last; or, if they do last, it is only by transforming themselves
into conventional structures of leaders and followers, buttressed by obedience
patterns that look suspiciously like power. Political power seems to be built into
the human condition. But why do some people hold political power over others?
There is no definitive explanation of political power. Biological, psychological,
cultural, rational, and irrational explanations have been put forward.

BIOLOGICAL   Aristotle said it first and perhaps best: "Man is by nature a political animal." (Aristotle's words were *zoon politikon*, which can be translated
as either "political animal" or "social animal." The Greeks lived in city-states
in which the polis was the same as society.) Aristotle meant that humans live
naturally in herds, like elephants or bison. Biologically, they need each other for
sustenance and survival. It is also natural that they array themselves into ranks
of leaders and followers, like all herd animals. Taking a cue from Aristotle, modern biological explanations, some of them looking at primate behavior, say that
forming a political system and obeying its leaders are innate, passed on with
one's genes. Some thinkers argue that human politics shows the same "dominance hierarchies" that other mammals set up. Politicians tend to be "alpha
males"—or think they are.

The advantage of the biological approach is its simplicity, but it raises a
number of questions. If we grant that humans are naturally political, how do

Classic Works

Concepts and Percepts

The great Prussian philosopher Immanuel Kant wrote
in the late eighteenth century, "Percepts without concepts are empty, and concepts without percepts are
blind." This notion helped establish modern philosophy
and social science. A percept is what you perceive
through your sensory organs: facts, images, numbers, examples, and so on. A concept is an idea in
your head: meanings, theories, hypotheses, beliefs,
and so on. You can collect many percepts, but without
a concept to structure them you have nothing; your
percepts are empty of meaning. On the other hand,
your concepts are "blind" if they cannot look at reality, which requires percepts. In other words, you need
both theory and data.

we explain the instances when political groups fall apart and people disobey authority? Perhaps we should modify the theory: Humans are imperfectly political (or social) animals. Most of the time, people form groups and obey authority but sometimes, under certain circumstances, they do not. This begs the question of which circumstances promote or undermine the formation of political groups.

PSYCHOLOGICAL Psychological explanations of politics and obedience are closely allied with biological theories. Both posit needs derived from centuries of evolution in the formation of political groups. Psychologists have refined their views with empirical research. In the famous Milgram study, unwitting subjects were instructed by a professor to administer progressively larger electric shocks to a victim. The "victim," strapped in a chair, was actually an actor who only pretended to suffer. Most of the subjects were willing to administer potentially lethal doses of electricity simply because the "professor"—an authority figure in a white lab smock—told them to. Most of the subjects disliked hurting the victim but rationalized that they were just following orders and that any harm done to the victim was really the professor's responsibility. They surrendered their actions to an authority figure.

Psychological studies also show that most people are naturally conformist. Most members of a group see things the group's way. Psychologist Irving Janis found many foreign policy mistakes were made in a climate of "groupthink," in which a leadership team tells itself that all is well and that the present policy is working. Groups ignore doubters who tell them, for instance, that the Japanese will attack Pearl Harbor in 1941 or that the 1961 Bay of Pigs landing of Cuban exiles will fail. Obedience to authority and groupthink suggest that humans have deep-seated needs—possibly innate—to fit into groups and their norms. Perhaps this is what makes human society possible, but it also makes possible horrors such as the Nazi Holocaust and more recent massacres.

CULTURAL How much of human behavior is learned as opposed to biologically inherited? This is the very old "nurture versus nature" debate. For much of the twentieth century, the cultural theorists—those who believe behavior is learned—dominated. Anthropologists concluded that all differences in behavior were cultural. Cooperative and peaceful societies raise their children that way, they argued. Political communities are formed and held together on the basis of cultural values transmitted by parents, schools, churches, and the mass media. Political science developed an interesting subfield, *political culture*, whose researchers found that a country's political culture was formed by many long-term factors: religion, child rearing, land tenure, and economic development.

Cultural theorists see trouble when the political system gets out of touch with the cultural system, as when the shah of Iran attempted to modernize an Islamic society that did not like Western values and lifestyles. The Iranians threw the shah out in 1979 and celebrated the return of a medieval-style religious leader, who voiced the values favored by traditional Iranians. Cultural theories can also be applied to U.S. politics. Republicans try to win elections by articulating the values of religion, family, and self-reliance, which are deeply ingrained into American culture. Many thinkers believe economic and political development depend heavily on **culture**.

culture

Human behavior that is learned as opposed to inherited.

The cultural approach to political life holds some optimism. If all human behavior is learned, bad behavior can be unlearned and society improved. Educating young people to be tolerant, cooperative, and just will gradually change a society's culture for the better, according to this view. Changing culture, however, is slow and difficult, as the American occupiers of Iraq and Afghanistan discovered.

Culture contributes a lot to political behavior, but the theory has some difficulties. First, where does culture come from? History? Economics? Religion? Second, if all behavior is cultural, various political systems should be as different from each other as their cultures. But, especially in the realm of politics, we see similar political attitudes and patterns in lands with very different cultures. Politicians everywhere tend to become corrupt, regardless of culture.

rational

Based on the ability to reason.

RATIONAL Another school of thought approaches politics as a **rational** thing; that is, people know what they want most of the time, and they have good reasons for doing what they do. Classic political theorists, such as Hobbes and Locke, held that humans form "civil society" because their powers of reason tell them that it is much better than anarchy. To safeguard life and property, people form governments. If those governments become abusive, the people have the right to dissolve them and start anew. This Lockean notion greatly influenced the U.S. Founding Fathers.

The biological, psychological, and cultural schools downplay human reason, claiming that people are either born or conditioned to certain behavior and that individuals seldom think rationally. But what about cases in which people break away from group conformity and argue independently? How can we explain a change of mind? "I was for Jones until he came out with his terrible economic policy, so now I'm voting for Smith." People make rational judgments like that all the time. A political system based on the presumption of human reason stands a better chance of governing justly and humanely. If leaders believe that people obey out of biological inheritance or cultural conditioning, they will think they can get away with all manner of deception and misrule. If, on the other hand, rulers fear that people are rational, they will respect the public's ability to discern wrongdoing. Accordingly, even if people are not completely rational, it is probably for the best if rulers think they are.

irrational

Based on the power to use fear and myth to cloud reason.

IRRATIONAL Late in the nineteenth century, a group of thinkers expounded the view that people are basically **irrational**, especially when it comes to politics. They are emotional, dominated by myths and stereotypes, and politics is really the manipulation of symbols. A crowd is like a wild beast that can be whipped up by charismatic leaders to do their bidding. What people regard as rational is really myth; just keep feeding the people myths to control them. The first practitioner of this school was Mussolini, founder of fascism in Italy, followed by

Hitler in Germany. A soft-spoken Muslim fundamentalist, Osama bin Laden, got an irrational hold on thousands of fanatical followers by feeding them the myth that America was the enemy of Islam.

There may be a good deal of truth to the irrational view of human political behavior, but it has catastrophic consequences. Leaders who use irrationalist techniques start believing their own propaganda and lead their nations to war, economic ruin, or tyranny. Some detect irrationalism even in the most advanced societies, where much of politics consists of screaming crowds and leaders striking heroic poses.

Power as a Composite

There are elements of truth in all these explanations of political power. At different times in different situations, any one of them can explain power. Tom Paine's pamphlet *Common Sense* rationally explained why America should separate from Britain. The drafters of both the U.S. Declaration of Independence and the Constitution were imbued with the rationalism of their age. Following the philosophers then popular, they framed their arguments as if human political activity were as logical as Newtonian physics. Historian Henry Steele Commager referred to the Constitution as "the crown jewel of the Enlightenment," the culmination of an age of reason.

But how truly rational were they? By the late eighteenth century, the thirteen American colonies had grown culturally separate from Britain. People thought of themselves as Americans rather than as English colonists. They increasingly read American newspapers and communicated among themselves rather than with Britain. Perhaps the separation was more cultural than rational.

Nor can we forget the psychological and irrational factors. Samuel Adams was a gifted firebrand, Thomas Jefferson a powerful writer, and George Washington a charismatic general. The American break with Britain and the founding of a new order were complex mixtures of all these factors. Such complex mixtures of factors go into any political system you can mention. To be sure, at times one factor seems more important than others, but we cannot exactly determine the weight to give any one factor. And notice how the various factors blend into one another. The biological factors lead to the psychological, which in turn lead to the cultural, the rational, and the irrational, forming a seamless web.

One common mistake about political power is viewing it as a finite, measurable quantity. Power is a connection among people, the ability of one person to get others to do his or her bidding. Political power does not come in jars or megawatts. Revolutionaries in some lands speak of "seizing power," as if power was kept in the national treasury and they could sneak in and grab it at night. The Afghan Taliban "seized power" in 1995–1996, but they were a minority of the Afghan population. Many Afghans hated and fought them. Revolutionaries think they automatically gain **legitimacy** and authority when they "seize power"—they do not. Power is earned, not seized.

legitimacy
Mass feeling that the government's rule is rightful and should be obeyed.

Is power identical to politics? Some power-mad people (including more than a few politicians) see the two as the same, but this is an oversimplification. We might see politics as a combination of goals or policies plus the power necessary to achieve them. Power, in this view, is a prime *ingredient* of politics. It would be difficult to imagine a political system without political power. Even a religious figure who ruled on the basis of love would be exercising power over followers. It might be "nice power," but it would still be power. Power, then, is a sort of *enabling device* to carry out or implement policies and decisions. You can have praiseworthy goals, but unless you have the power to implement them, they remain wishful thoughts.

Others see the essence of politics as a *struggle for power*, a sort of gigantic game in which power is the goal. What, for example, are elections all about? The getting of power. There is a danger here, however: If power becomes the goal of politics, devoid of other purposes, it becomes cynical, brutal, and self-destructive. The Hitler regime destroyed itself in the worship of power. Obsessed with retaining presidential power, President Nixon ruined his own administration. As nineteenth-century British historian and philosopher Lord Acton put it, "Power tends to corrupt; absolute power corrupts absolutely."

What Is Political Science?

1.2 Justify the claim that political science may be considered a science.

The study of politics can take many forms. Political science is a method of how to study politics. Political science ain't politics. It is not necessarily training to become a practicing politician. Political science is training in the calm, objective analysis of politics, which may or may not aid working politicians. Side by side, the two professions compare like this:

Politicians	Political Scientists
love power	are skeptical of power
seek popularity	seek accuracy
think practically	think abstractly
hold firm views	reach tentative conclusions
offer single causes	offer many causes
see short-term payoff	see long-term consequences
plan for next election	plan for next publication
respond to groups	seek the good of the whole
seek name recognition	seek professional prestige

Many find politics distasteful, and perhaps they are right. Politics may be inherently immoral or, at any rate, amoral. Misuse of power, influence peddling, and outright corruption is prominent in politics. But you need not like the thing

Classic Thought

"Never Get Angry at a Fact"

This basic point of all serious study sounds common-sensical but is often ignored, even in college courses. It traces back to the extremely complex thought of the German philosopher Hegel (1770–1831), who argued that things happen not by caprice or accident but for good and sufficient reasons: "Whatever is real is rational." This means that nothing is completely accidental and that if we apply reason, we will understand why something happens. We study politics in a "naturalistic" mode, not getting angry at what we see but trying to understand how it came to be.

For example, we hear of a politician who took money from a favor-seeker. As political scientists, we push our anger to the side and ask questions like: Do most politicians in that country take money? Is it an old tradition, and does the culture of this country accept it? Do the people even expect politicians to take money? How big are campaign expenses? Can the politician possibly run for office without taking money? In short, we see if extralegal exchanges of cash are part of the political system. If they are, it makes no sense to get angry at an individual politician. If we dislike it, we may then consider how the system might be reformed to discourage the taking of money on the side. And reforms may not work. Japan reformed its electoral laws in an attempt to stamp out its traditional "money politics," but little changed. Like bacteria, some things in politics have lives of their own.

you study. Biologists may study a disease-causing bacterium under a microscope. They do not "like" the bacterium but are interested in how it grows, how it does its damage, and how it may be eradicated. Neither do they get angry at the bacterium and smash the glass. Biologists first understand the forces of nature and then work with them to improve humankind's existence. Political scientists try to do the same with politics. The two professions of politician and political scientist bear approximately the same relation to each other as do bacteria and bacteriologists.

The Master Science

Aristotle, the founder of the **discipline**, called politics "the master science." He meant that almost everything happens in a political context, that the decisions of the *polis* (the Greek city-state and root of our words *polite, police,* and *politics*) governed most other things. Politics, in the words of Yale's Harold Lasswell (1902–1978), is the study of "who gets what." But, some object, the economic system determines who gets what in countries with free markets. True, but should we have a totally free-market system with no government involved? A decision to bail out shaky banks sparks angry controversy over this point. Few love the bankers, but economists say it had to be done to save the economy from collapse. Politics is intimately connected to economics.

Suppose something utterly natural strikes, like a hurricane. It is the political system that decides whether and where to build dikes or deliver federal funds to rebuild in flood-prone seacoast areas. The disaster is natural, but its impact on society is controlled in large part by politics. How about science, our

discipline
A field of study, often represented by an academic department or major.

Methods

Learning a Chapter

Read each chapter *before* class. And do not simply read the chapter; learn it by writing down the following:

A. Find what strikes you as the *three main points*. Do not outline; construct three complete sentences, each with a subject and predicate. They may be long and complex sentences, but they must be complete declarative sentences. You may find two, four, or six main points, but by the time you split, combine, and discard what may or may not be the main points, you will know the chapter. Look for abstract generalizations; the specifics come under the point C below, examples or case studies. Do not simply copy three sentences from the chapter. Synthesize several sentences, always asking what three sentences distilled from this chapter will most help me on the exam? These might be three main points from Chapter 1:

1. Study politics as a scientist studies nature, trying to understand reality without getting angry at it.
2. Political science combines many disciplines but focuses on power: who holds it and how they use it.

3. Politics can be studied objectively, provided claims are supported by empirical evidence and structured by theory.

B. List a *dozen vocabulary words*, and be able to define them. These are words new to you or words used in a specialized way. This text makes it easier with the boldfaced terms defined in the margins; for terms not in boldface, read with a dictionary handy.

C. Note specific *examples* or *case studies* that illustrate the main points or vocabulary words. Most will contain proper nouns (i.e., capitalized words). Examples are not main points or definitions; rather, they are empirical evidence that support a main point. The examples need not be complete sentences. These might be examples from Chapter 1:

Aristotle's "master science"
AIDS versus breast cancer research
West Germany's success story
Communist regimes in Eastern Europe
Afghanistan's chaos
Shah's regime in Iran erodes

bacteriologists squinting through microscopes? That is not political. But who funds the scientists' education and their research institutes? It could be private charity (the donors of which get tax breaks), but the government plays a major role. When the U.S. government decided that AIDS research deserved top priority, funding for other programs was cut. Bacteria and viruses may be natural, but studying them is often quite political. In this case, it pitted gays against women concerned with breast cancer. Who gets what: funding to find a cure for AIDS or for breast cancer? The choice is political.

Can Politics Be Studied as a Science?

Students new to science often assume it implies a certain subject for study. But science is a way to study nearly any subject. It is the method, not the subject. The original meaning of science, from the French, is simply "knowledge." Later, the natural sciences, which rely on measurement and calculation, took over the term. Now most people think of science as precise and factual, supported by experiments and data. Some political scientists have attempted to become like natural scientists; they **quantify** data and manipulate them statistically to validate **hypotheses**. The quantifiers make some good contributions, but usually they focus on small questions of detail rather than on large questions of meaning. This is because they generally have to stick to areas that can be quantified: public opinion, election returns, and congressional voting.

But large areas of politics are not quantifiable. How and why do leaders make their decisions? Many decisions are made in secrecy, even in democracies. We do not know exactly how decisions are made in the White House in Washington, the Elysée in Paris, or the Zhongnanhai in Beijing. When members of Congress vote on an issue, can we be certain why they voted that way? Was it constituents' desires, the good of the nation, or the campaign contributions of interest groups? What did the Supreme Court have in mind when it ruled that laying off schoolteachers based on race is unconstitutional but hiring them based on race is not? Try quantifying that. Much of politics—especially dealing with how and why decisions are made—is just too complex and too secret to be quantified. Bismarck, who unified Germany in the nineteenth century, famously compared laws and sausages: It's better not to see how they are made.

Does that mean that politics can never be like a natural science? Political science is an **empirical** discipline that accumulates both quantified and qualitative data. With such data we can find persistent patterns, much like in biology. Gradually, we begin to generalize. When the generalizations become firmer, we call them theories. In a few cases, the theories become so firm that we may call them laws. In this way, the study of politics accumulates knowledge, the original meaning of science.

The Struggle to See Clearly

Political science also resembles a natural science when its researchers, if they are professional, study things as they are and not as they wish them to be. This is more difficult in the study of politics than in the study of stars and cells. Most political scientists have viewpoints on current issues, and it is easy to let these views contaminate their analyses of politics. Indeed, precisely because a given question interests us enough to study it indicates that we bring a certain passion with us. Can you imagine setting to work on a topic you cared nothing about? If you are interested enough to study a question, you probably start by being inclined to one side. Too much of this, however, renders the study biased; it becomes a partisan outcry rather than a scholarly search for the truth. How can you guard against this? The traditional hallmarks of **scholarship** give some guidance. A scholarly work should be *reasoned, balanced*, supported with *evidence*, and a bit *theoretical*.

REASONED   You must spell out your reasoning, and it should make sense. If your perspective is colored by an underlying assumption, you should say so. You might say, "For the purpose of this study, we assume that bureaucrats are rational," or "This is a study of the psychology of voters in a small town." Your

quantify
To measure with numbers.

hypothesis
An initial theory a researcher starts with, to be proved by evidence.

empirical
Based on observable evidence.

scholarship
Intellectual arguments supported by reason and evidence.

basic assumptions influence what you study and how you study it, but you can minimize bias by honestly stating your assumptions. German sociologist Max Weber (1864–1920), who contributed vastly to all the social sciences, held that any findings that support the researcher's political views must be discarded as biased. Few attempt to be that pure, but Weber's point is well taken: Beware of structuring the study so that it comes out to support a given view.

BALANCED You can also minimize bias by acknowledging other ways of looking at your topic. You should mention the various approaches to your topic and what other researchers have found. Instructors are impressed that you know the literature in a given area. They are even more impressed when you can then criticize the previous studies and explain why you think they are incomplete or faulty: "The Jones study of voters found them largely apathetic, but this was an off-year election in which turnout is always lower." By comparing and criticizing several approaches and studies, you present a much more objective and convincing case. Do not commit yourself to a particular viewpoint or theory, but admit that your view is one among several.

SUPPORTED WITH EVIDENCE All scholarly studies require evidence, ranging from the quantified evidence of the natural sciences to the qualitative evidence of the humanities. Political science utilizes both. Ideally, any statement open to interpretation or controversy should be supported with evidence. Common knowledge does not have to be supported; you need not cite the U.S. Constitution to "prove" that presidents serve four-year terms.

But if you say presidents have gained power over the decades, you need evidence. At a minimum, you would cite a scholar who has amassed evidence to demonstrate this point. That is called a "secondary source," evidence that has passed through the mind of someone else. Most student papers use only secondary sources, but instructors are impressed when you use a "primary source," the original gathering of data, as in your own tabulation of what counties in your state showed the strongest Obama vote. Anyone reading a study must be able to review its evidence and judge if it is valid. You cannot keep your evidence or sources secret.

THEORETICAL Serious scholarship is always connected, at least a little, to a theoretical point. It need not be a sweeping new theory (that's for geniuses), but it should advance the discipline's knowledge a bit. At a minimum, it should confirm or refute an existing theory. Just describing something is not a theory, which is why Google or Wikipedia are seldom enough. You must relate the description to some factor or factors, supported, of course, with empirical evidence. The general pattern of this is: "Most of the time there is C there is also D, and here's probably why." Theory building also helps lift your study above polemics, an argument for or against something. Denouncing the Islamic State, which we all may do with gusto, is not scholarship. Determining why people join IS (studied by several scholars) would have important theoretical and practical impacts.

What Good Is Political Science?

Some students come to political science supposing it is just opinions; they write exams or papers that ignore all or some of the preceding points. Yes, we all have political views, but if we let them dominate our study we get invalid results, junk political science. Professional political scientists push their personal views well to one side while engaged in study and research. First-rate thinkers are able to come up with results that actually refute their previously held opinion. When that happens, we have real intellectual growth, an exciting experience that should be your aim.

Something else comes with such an experience: You start to conclude that you should not have been so partisan in the first place. You may back away from the strong views you held earlier. Accordingly, political science is not necessarily training to become a practicing politician. Political science is training in objective and often complex analysis, whereas the practice of politics requires fixed, popular, and simplified opinions.

Political science can contribute to good government, often by warning those in office that all is not well, "speaking Truth to Power," as the Quakers say. Sometimes this advice is useful to working politicians. Public-opinion polls, for example, showed an erosion of trust in government in the United States starting in the mid-1960s. The causes were Vietnam, Watergate, and inflation. Candidates for political office, knowing public opinion, could tailor their campaigns and policies to try to counteract this decline. Ronald Reagan, with his sunny disposition and upbeat views, utilized the discontent to win two presidential terms.

Some political scientists warned for years of the weak basis of the shah's regime in Iran. Unfortunately, such warnings were unheeded. Washington's policy was to support the shah, and only two months before the end of his rule did the U.S. embassy in Tehran start reporting how unstable Iran had become. State Department officials had let politics contaminate their political analyses; they could not see clearly. Journalists were not much better; few covered Iran until violence broke out. Years in advance, American political scientists specializing in Iran saw trouble coming. More recently, political scientists warned that Iraq was unready for democracy and that a U.S. invasion would unleash chaos, but Washington deciders paid no attention. Political science can be useful.

The Subfields of Political Science

Most political science departments divide the discipline into several subfields. The bigger the department, the more subfields it likely has. We will get at least a brief introduction to all of them in this text.

U.S. Politics focuses on institutions and processes, mostly at the federal level but some at state and local levels. It includes parties, elections, public opinion, and executive and legislative behavior.

Comparative Politics examines politics within other nations, trying to establish generalizations about institutions and political culture and theories of democracy, stability, and policy. It may be focused on various regions, as in "Latin American politics" or "East Asian politics."

International Relations studies politics among nations, including conflict, diplomacy, international law and organizations, and international political economy. The study of U.S. foreign policy has one foot in U.S. politics and one in international relations.

Political Theory, both classic and modern, attempts to define the good polity, often focused on major thinkers.

Public Administration studies how bureaucracies work and how they can be improved.

Constitutional Law studies the applications and evolution of the Constitution within the legal system.

Public Policy studies the interface of politics and economics with an eye to developing effective programs.

Comparing Political Science to History and Journalism

Understanding how others study politics shows what makes political science distinct. History and journalism have different goals from political science, but they share common features. History studies the past, and not all history focuses on politics. Journalism covers the present, and only some news stories are on politics. What they share, however is a focus on unique events. When a historian studies the French Revolution, she wants to tell the story of the people, the places, and the events to better understand what happened and put forward a thesis about why it happened. She is not interested in comparing the French to the American Revolution, as those are distinct, unique events that deserve separate study.

Similarly, a journalist reporting on a war will describe the events as they unfold. He interviews people affected by the conflict and chronicles a battle to explain why it was a turning point.

Political science approaches these tasks differently. Instead of focusing on one revolution, a political scientist might compare several revolutions to discover what links them together. What factors cause revolutions? Why do they sometimes succeed and sometimes fail? What are the consequences of revolution?

Similarly, a political scientist would not necessarily be interested in writing about today's battle or interviewing a war refugee. Instead, political scientists might be interested in what causes wars generally or why some small conflicts result in major wars and others do not. Under what circumstances do civil conflicts lead to genocide? What forms of aid are most successful when faced with large numbers of refugees?

generalize
Explaining the causes of consequences of a whole class of events.

Where historians or journalists often seek to explain the unique circumstances of a particular event, political scientists seek to **generalize**. What are the necessary and sufficient conditions that will lead to revolution, to war, or to other political outcomes? If decapitating the aristocracy happened only in the French Revolution, then a political scientist would dismiss it as a factor that explains revolution, whereas a historian might be very interested in guillotines. If a refugee suffered from war, the journalist might tell her story. A political scientist would focus on how a new strategy for the international response to a refugee crises led to a 50 percent increase in the number of refugees helped compared to the old strategy.

Political science ignores things that might appear important in one context but are irrelevant beyond that context. Instead, it can focus on the few factors that exist across similar contexts. Did a politician win an election because he ran an ad about his opponent who voted for an unpopular bill or because he spent $10 million to say so? Studying one campaign would not yield a definitive answer. Studying many campaigns could discover which was more important—negative advertising or campaign spending.

Theory in Political Science

1.3   Evaluate the strengths and weaknesses of several theoretical approaches to political science.

Schools in the United States typically ask students to accumulate knowledge—to know more stuff. Critics point out that knowledge is more than just accumulating facts because the facts will not structure themselves into a coherent whole. Gathering facts without an organizing principle leads only to large collections of meaningless facts, a point made by Kant. In science, theories provide structure that give meaning to patterns of facts. To be sure, theories can grow too complex and abstract and depart from the real world, but without at least some theoretical perspective, we do not even know what questions to ask. Even if you say you have no theories, you probably have some unspoken ones. The kinds of questions you ask and which ones you ask first are the beginnings of theorizing.

Theories are not facts. They are suggestions as to how the facts should be organized. Some theories have more evidence to support them than others. All theories bump into facts that contradict their explanations. Even in the natural sciences, theories such as the so-called Big Bang explain only some observations. Theories often compete with other theories. How can you prove which model is more nearly correct? Political scientists—really all scientists—test theories with observations of the world and adjust theories to better reflect what they see. The accumulation of knowledge through science is nearly always a slow incremental process. The following sections outline several theoretical frameworks political scientists have used to understand the political world.

Behavioralism

institutions

The formal structures of government, such as the U.S. Congress.

From the late nineteenth century through the middle of the twentieth century, American thinkers focused on **institutions**, the formal structures of government. This showed the influence of law on the development of political science in the United States. Woodrow Wilson, for example, was a lawyer (albeit unsuccessful) before he became a political scientist; he concentrated on perfecting the institutions of government. Constitutions were a favorite subject for political scientists of this period, for they assumed that what was on paper was how the institutions worked in practice. The rise of the Soviet, Italian, and German dictatorships shook this belief. The constitution of Germany's Weimar Republic (1919–1933) looked fine on paper; experts had drafted it. Under stress it collapsed, for Germans of that time did not have the necessary experience with or commitment to democracy. Likewise, the Stalin constitution of 1936 made the Soviet Union look like a perfect democracy, but it functioned as a brutal dictatorship.

positivism

Theory that society can be studied scientifically and incrementally improved with the knowledge gained.

The Communist and Fascist dictatorships and World War II forced political scientists to reexamine their institutional focus, and many set out to discover how politics really worked, not how it was supposed to work. Postwar American political scientists here followed in the tradition of the early nineteenth-century French philosopher Auguste Comte, who developed the doctrine of **positivism**, the application of natural science methods to the study of society. Comtean positivism was an optimistic philosophy, holding that as we accumulate valid data by means of scientific observation—without speculation or intuition—we will perfect a science of society and with it improve society. Psychologists are perhaps the most deeply imbued with this approach. **Behavioralists**, as they are called, claim to concentrate on actual behavior as opposed to thoughts or feelings.

behavioralism

The empirical study of actual human behavior rather than abstract or speculative theories.

Beginning in the 1950s, behaviorally inclined political scientists accumulated statistics from elections, public-opinion surveys, votes in legislatures, and anything else they could hang a number on. Behavioralists made some remarkable contributions to political science, shooting down some long-held but unexamined assumptions and giving political theory an empirical basis. Behavioral studies were especially good in examining the "social bases" of politics, the attitudes and values of citizens, which go a long way toward making the system function the way it does. Their best work has been on voting patterns, for it is here they can get lots of valid data.

By the 1960s, the behavioral school established itself and won over much of the field. In the late 1960s, however, behavioralism came under heavy attack, and not just by rear-guard traditionalists. Many younger political scientists, some of them influenced by the radicalism of the 1960s, complained that the behavioral approach was static, conservative, loaded with its practitioners' values, and irrelevant to the urgent tasks at hand. Far from being "scientific" and "value-free," behavioralists often defined the current situation in the United States as the norm and anything different as deviant. Gabriel Almond (1911–2002) and Sidney Verba (1932–) found that Americans embody all the good, "participant" virtues of the "civic culture." By examining only what exists at a given moment, behavioralists neglect the possibility of change; their studies may be time-bound. Behavioralists have an unstated preference for the status quo; they like to examine established democratic systems, for that is where their methodological tools work best. People in police states or civil conflicts know that honestly stating their opinions could get them jailed or killed, so they voice the "correct" views.

Perhaps the most damaging criticism, though, was that the behavioralists focused on relatively minor topics and steered clear of the big questions of politics. Behavioralists can tell us, for example, what percentage of Detroit blue-collar Catholics vote Democratic, but they tell us nothing about what this means for the quality of Detroit's governance or the kinds of decisions elected officials will make. There is no necessary connection between how citizens vote and what comes out of government. Critics charged that behavioral studies were often irrelevant.

By 1969, many political scientists had to admit that there was something to the criticism of what had earlier been called the "behavioral revolution." Some called the newer movement **postbehavioral**, a synthesis of traditional and behavioral approaches. Postbehavioralists recognize that facts and values are tied together. They are willing to use both the qualitative data of the traditionalists and the quantitative data of the behavioralists. They look at history and institutions as well as public opinion and rational-choice theory. They are not afraid of numbers and happily use correlations, graphs, and percentages to make their cases. If you look around your political science department, you are apt to find traditional, behavioral, and postbehavioral viewpoints among the professors—or even within the same professor.

postbehavioral
Synthesis of traditional, behavioral, and other techniques in the study of politics.

New Institutionalism

In the 1970s, political science partially pulled away from behavioralism and rediscovered institutions. In the 1980s, this was proclaimed as the "New Institutionalism." Its crux is that government structures—legislatures, parties, bureaucracies, and so on—take on lives of their own and shape the behavior and attitudes of the people who live within and benefit from them. Institutions are not simply the reflections of social forces. Legislators, for example, behave as they do largely because of rules laid down long ago and reinforced over the decades. Once you know these complex rules, some unwritten, you can see how politicians logically try to maximize their advantage under them, much as you can often predict when a baseball batter will bunt. It is not a mystery but the logic of the game they are playing. The preservation and enhancement of the institution becomes one of politicians' major goals. Thus, institutions, even if outmoded or ineffective, tend to rumble on. The Communist parties of the Soviet bloc were corrupt and ineffective, but they endured because they guaranteed the jobs and perquisites of their members.

Systems Theory

A major postwar invention was the "political systems" model devised by David Easton (1917–2014), which contributed to our understanding of politics by simplifying reality but in some cases departed from reality. The idea of looking at complex entities as systems originated in biology. Living organisms are complex and highly integrated. The heart, lungs, blood, digestive tract, and brain perform their functions in such a way as to keep the animal alive. Take away one organ and the animal dies. Damage one organ and the other components of the system alter their function to compensate and keep the animal alive. The crux of systems thinking is this: You cannot change just one component because that changes all of the others.

Political systems thinkers argued that the politics of a given country works as a feedback loop, a bit like a biological system. According to the Easton model (Figure 1.1), citizens' demands, "inputs," are recognized by the government decision makers, who process them into authoritative decisions and actions, "outputs." These outputs have an impact on the social, economic, and political environment that the citizens may or may not like. The citizens express their demands anew—this is the crucial "feedback" link of the system—which may modify the earlier decision. Precisely what goes on in the "conversion process" was left opaque, a "black box."

In some cases, the political systems approach fits reality. As the Vietnam War dragged on, feedback on the military draft turned negative. The Nixon administration defused youthful anger by ending the draft in 1973 and changing to an all-volunteer army. In the 1980s, the socialist economics of French President François Mitterrand produced inflation and unemployment. The French people, especially the business community, complained loudly, and Mitterrand altered

Figure 1.1 A model of the political system.

(Adapted from David Easton, A Systems Analysis of Political Life. *Chicago: University of Chicago Press, 1965, p. 32.)*

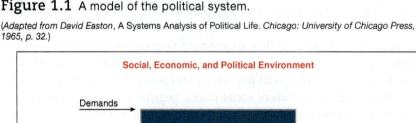

his policy back to capitalism. In these cases, the feedback loop worked. Feedback can also be split. The Obama administration saw healthcare reform as important and necessary, but half the U.S. population opposed it—a point the Republicans used in subsequent elections.

But in other cases, the systems model falls flat. Would Hitler's Germany or Stalin's Russia really fit the systems model? How much attention do dictatorships pay to citizens' demands? To be sure, there is always some input and feedback. Hitler's generals tried to assassinate him—a type of feedback. Workers in Communist systems had an impact on government policy by not working much. They demanded more consumer goods and, by not exerting themselves, communicated this desire to the regime. Sooner or later the regime had to reform. All over the Soviet bloc, workers used to chuckle: "They pretend to pay us, and we pretend to work." In the USSR, (botched) reform came with the Gorbachev regime, and it led to system collapse.

How could the systems model explain the Vietnam War? Did Americans demand that the administration send half a million troops to fight there? No, nearly the opposite: Lyndon Johnson won overwhelmingly in 1964 on an antiwar platform. The systems model does show how discontent with the war ruined Johnson's popularity so that he did not seek reelection in 1968. The feedback loop did go into effect but only years after the decision for war had been made. Could the systems model explain the Watergate scandal? Did U.S. citizens demand that President Nixon have the Democratic headquarters bugged? No, but once details about the cover-up started leaking in 1973, the feedback loop went into effect, putting pressure on the House of Representatives to form an impeachment panel.

Plainly, there are some problems with the systems model, and they seem to be in the "black box" of the conversion process. Much happens in the mechanism of government that is not initiated by and has little to do with the wishes of citizens. The American people largely ignored the health effects of smoking.

Theories

Models: Simplifying Reality

A model is a simplified picture of reality that social scientists develop to order data, to theorize, and to predict. A good model fits reality but simplifies it because a model as complex as the real world would be of no help. In simplifying reality, however, models risk oversimplifying. The problem is the finite capacity of the human mind. We cannot factor in all the information available at once; we must select which points are important and ignore the rest. But when we do this, we may drain the blood out of the study of politics and overlook key points. Accordingly, as we encounter models of politics—and perhaps as we devise our own—pause a moment to ask if the model departs too much from reality. If it does, discard or alter the model. Do not disregard reality because it does not fit the model.

Figure 1.2 A modified model of the political system.

(Adapted from David Easton, A Systems Analysis of Political Life. *Chicago: University of Chicago Press, 1965, p. 32.)*

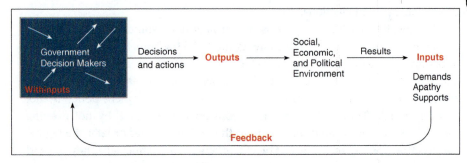

Only the analyses of medical statisticians, which revealed a strong link between smoking and lung cancer, prodded Congress into requiring warning labels on cigarette packs and ending advertising of cigarettes. It was a handful of specialists in the federal bureaucracy who got the anticigarette campaign going, not the masses of citizens.

The systems model is essentially static, biased toward the status quo, and unable to handle upheaval. This is one reason political scientists were surprised at the collapse of the Soviet Union. "Systems" are not supposed to collapse; they are supposed to continually self-correct.

We can modify the systems model to better reflect reality. By diagramming it as in Figure 1.2, we logically change little. We have the same feedback loop: outputs turning into inputs. But by putting the "conversion process" of government first, we suggested that it—rather than the citizenry—originates most decisions. The public reacts only later. That would be the case with the Afghanistan War: strong support in 2001 but fed up ten years later.

Next, we add something that Easton himself later suggested. Inside the "black box," a lot more happens than simply the processing of outside demands. Pressures from the various parts of government—government talking mostly to itself and short-circuiting the feedback loop—are what Easton called "within-puts." These two alterations, of course, make our model more complicated, but this reflects the complicated nature of reality.

Rational-Choice Theory

In the 1970s, a new approach, invented by mathematicians during World War II, rapidly grew in political science—rational-choice theory. Rational-choice theorists argue that one can generally predict political behavior by knowing the interests of the actors involved because they rationally maximize their interests. As U.S. presidential candidates take positions on issues, they calculate what will give them the best payoff. They might think, "Many people oppose the war in Afghanistan, but many also demand strong leadership on defense. I'd better just criticize 'mistakes' in Afghanistan while at the same time demand strong 'national security.'" The waffle is not indecision but calculation, argue rational-choice theorists.

Rational-choice theorists enrage some other political scientists. One study of Japanese bureaucrats claimed you need not study Japan's language, culture, or history. All you needed to know was what the bureaucrats' career advantages were to predict how they would decide issues. A noted U.S. specialist on Japan blew his stack at such glib, superficial shortcuts and denounced rational-choice theory. More modest rational-choice theorists immersed themselves in Hungary's language and culture but still concluded that Hungarian political parties, in cobbling together an extremely complex voting system, were making rational choices to give themselves a presumed edge in parliamentary seats.

Many rational-choice theorists backed down from their know-it-all positions. Some now call themselves "neoinstitutionalists" (see above section) because all their rational choices are made within one or another institutional context—the U.S. Congress, for example. Rational-choice theory did not establish itself as the dominant **paradigm**—no theory has, and none is likely to—but it contributed a lot by reminding us that politicians are consummate opportunists, a point many other theories forget.

Some rational-choice theorists subscribed to a branch of mathematics called game theory, setting up political decisions as if they were table games. A Cuban missile crisis "game" might have several people play President Kennedy, who must weigh the probable payoffs of bombing or not bombing Cuba. Others might play Soviet chief Nikita Khrushchev, who has to weigh toughing it out or backing down. Seeing how the players interact gives us insights and warnings of what can go wrong in crisis decision making. If you "game out" the 1962 Cuban missile crisis and find that three games out of ten end in World War III, you have the makings of an article of great interest.

Game theorists argue that constructing the proper game explains why policy outcomes are often unforeseen but not accidental. Games can show how decision makers think. We learn how their choices are never easy or simple. Games can even be mathematized and fed into computers. The great weakness of game theory is that it depends on correctly estimating the "payoffs" that decision makers can expect, and these are only approximations arrived at by examining the historical record. We know how the Cuban missile crisis came out; therefore, we adjust our game so it comes out the same way. In effect, game theory is only another way to systematize and clarify history (not a bad thing).

All these theories and several others offer interesting insights. None, however, is likely to be the last model we shall see, for we will never have a paradigm that can consistently explain and predict political actions. Every couple of decades, political science comes up with a new paradigm—usually one borrowed from another discipline—that attracts much excitement and attention. Its proponents exaggerate its ability to explain or predict. Upon examination and criticism, the model usually fades and is replaced by another trend. Political science tends to get caught up in trends. After a few iterations of this cycle, we

paradigm
A model or way of doing research accepted by a discipline.

learn to expect no breakthrough theories. Politics is slippery and not easily confined to our mental constructs. By acknowledging this, we open our minds to the richness, complexity, and drama of political life.

"Political Theory" versus Theory in Political Science

1.4 **Contrast normative theories of politics to political science.**

Departments of Political Science often house both political scientists and political theorists. Because they have the same departmental "home," the differences between how the two groups study politics is not obvious to most students. Where political scientists study politics by trying to understand how things *do* work, political theorists approach the study of politics from the perspective of how things *should* work.

The Normative Study of Politics

Some say Plato founded political science. But his *Republic* described an ideal *polis,* a normative approach rather than the objective approach of political science, which seeks to understand how things do work. Plato's student, Aristotle, on the other hand, was the first *empirical* political scientist and sent out his students to gather data from the dozens of Greek city-states. With these data, he constructed his great work *Politics* which combined both **descriptive** and **normative** approaches. He used the facts he and his students had collected to prescribe the most desirable political institutions. Political science in its purest form describes and explains, but it is hard to resist applying what is learned to normative questions and prescribing changes. Both Plato and Aristotle saw Athens in decline; they attempted to understand why and to suggest how it could be avoided. They thus began a tradition that is still at the heart of political science: a search for the sources of the good, stable political system.

Most European medieval and Renaissance political thinkers took a religious approach to the study of government and politics. They were almost strictly normative, seeking to discover the "ought" or "should," and were often rather casual about the "is," the real-world situation. Informed by religious, legal, and philosophical values, they tried to ascertain which system of government would bring humankind closest to what God wished.

Niccolò Machiavelli (1469–1527) introduced what some believe to be the crux of modern political science: the focus on power. His great work *The Prince* was about the getting and using of political power. He was a **realist** who argued that to accomplish anything good—such as the unification of Italy and expulsion of the foreigners who ruined it—the Prince had to be rational and tough in the exercise of power.

descriptive
Explaining what is.

normative
Explaining what ought to be.

realism
Working with the world as it is and not as we wish it to be; usually focused on power.

Although long depreciated by American political thinkers, who sometimes shied away from "power" as inherently dirty, the approach took root in Europe and contributed to the elite analyses of Mosca, Pareto, and Michels. Americans became acquainted with the power approach through the writings of the refugee German scholar of international relations Hans J. Morgenthau, who emphasized that "all politics is a struggle for power."

The Contractualists

Not long after Machiavelli, the "contractualists"—Hobbes, Locke, and Rousseau—analyzed why political systems should exist at all. They differed in many points but agreed that humans, at least in principle, had joined in what Rousseau called a **social contract** that everyone now had to observe.

social contract
Theory that individuals join and stay in civil society as if they had signed a contract.

Classic Works

Not Just Europeans

China, India, and North Africa produced brilliant political thinkers centuries ago. Unknown in the West until relatively recently, they were unlikely to have influenced the development of Western political theory with their ideas. The existence of these culturally varied thinkers suggests that the political nature of humans is basically the same no matter what the cultural differences.

In China, Confucius, a sixth-century B.C. advisor to kings, propounded his vision of good, stable government based on two things: the family and correct, moral behavior instilled in rulers and ruled alike. At the apex, the emperor sets a moral example by purifying his spirit and perfecting his manners. He must think good thoughts in utter sincerity; if he does not, his empire crumbles. He is copied by his subjects, who are arrayed hierarchically below the emperor, down to the father of a family, who is like a miniature emperor to whom wives and children are subservient. The Confucian system bears some resemblance to Plato's ideal Republic; the difference is that the Chinese actually practiced Confucianism, which lasted two and a half millennia and through a dozen dynasties.

Two millennia before Machiavelli and Hobbes, the Indian writer Kautilya in the fourth century B.C. arrived at the same conclusions. Kautilya, a prime minister and advisor to an Indian monarch, wrote in

Arthashastra (translated as *The Principles of Material Well-Being*) that prosperity comes from living in a well-run kingdom. Like Hobbes, Kautilya posited a state of nature that meant anarchy. Monarchs arose to protect the land and people against anarchy and ensure their prosperity. Like Machiavelli, Kautilya advised his prince to operate on the basis of pure expediency, doing whatever it takes to secure his kingdom domestically and against other kingdoms.

In fourteenth-century A.D. North Africa, Ibn Khaldun was a secretary, executive, and ambassador for several rulers. Sometimes out of favor and in jail, he reflected on what had gone wrong with the great Arab empires. He concluded, in his *Universal History*, that the character of the Arabs and their social cohesiveness were determined by climate and occupation. Ibn Khaldun was almost modern in his linking of underlying economic conditions to social and political change. Economic decline in North Africa, he found, had led to political instability and lawlessness. Anticipating Marx, Toynbee, and many other Western writers, Ibn Khaldun saw that civilizations pass through cycles of growth and decline.

Notice what all three of these thinkers had in common with Machiavelli: All were princely political advisors who turned their insights into general prescriptions for correct governance. Practice led to theory.

state of nature
Humans before civilization.

civil society
Humans after becoming civilized. Modern usage: associations between family and government.

Thomas Hobbes (1588–1679) imagined that life in "the **state of nature**," before **civil society** was founded, must have been terrible. Every man would have been the enemy of every other man, a "war of each against all." Humans would live in savage squalor with "no arts; no letters; no society; and which is worst of all, continual fear, and danger of violent death; and the life of man, solitary, poor, nasty, brutish, and short." To get out of this horror, people would—out of their profound self-interest—rationally join together to form civil society. Society thus arises naturally out of fear. People would also gladly submit to a king, even a bad one, for a monarch prevents anarchy.

John Locke (1632–1704) came to less harsh conclusions. Locke theorized that the original state of nature was not so bad; people lived in equality and tolerance with one another. But they could not secure their property. There was no money, title deeds, or courts of law, so ownership was uncertain. To remedy this, they contractually formed civil society and thus secured "life, liberty, and property." Locke is to property rights as Hobbes is to fear of violent death. Some philosophers argue that Americans are the children of Locke. Notice the American emphasis on "the natural right to property."

Jean-Jacques Rousseau (1712–1788) laid the philosophical groundwork for the French Revolution. In contrast to Hobbes and Locke, Rousseau theorized that life in the state of nature was downright good; people lived as "noble savages" without artifice or jealousy. (All the contractualists were influenced by not-very-accurate descriptions of Native Americans.) What corrupted humans, said Rousseau, was society itself. The famous words at the beginning of his *Social Contract*: "Man is born free but everywhere is in chains."

general will
Rousseau's theory of what a whole community wants.

But society can be drastically improved, argued Rousseau, leading to human freedom. A just society would be a voluntary community with a will of its own, the **general will**—what everyone wants over and above the selfish "particular wills" of individuals and interest groups. In such communities, humans gain dignity and freedom. If people are bad, it is because society made them that way (a view held by many today). A good society, on the other hand, can "force men to be free" if they misbehave. Many see the roots of totalitarianism in Rousseau: the imagined perfect society; the general will, which the dictator claims to know; and the breaking of those who do not cooperate.

Marxist Theories

Zeitgeist
German for "spirit of the times"; Hegel's theory that each epoch has a distinctive spirit, which moves history along.

Karl Marx (1818–1883) produced an exceedingly complex theory consisting of at least three interrelated elements: a theory of economics, a theory of social class, and a theory of history. Like Hegel (1770–1831), Marx argued that things do not happen by accident; everything has a cause. Hegel posited the underlying cause that moves history forward as spiritual, specifically the **Zeitgeist**, the spirit of the times. Marx found the great underlying cause in economics.

ECONOMICS   Marx concentrated on the "surplus value"—what we call profit. Workers produce things but get paid only a fraction of the value of what they produce. The capitalist owners skim off the rest, the surplus value. The working class—what Marx called the **proletariat**—is paid too little to buy all the products the workers have made, resulting in repeated overproduction, which leads to depressions. Eventually, argued Marx, there will be a depression so big the capitalist system will collapse.

proletariat
Marx's name for the industrial working class.

SOCIAL CLASS   Every society divides into two classes: a small class of those who own the means of production and a large class of those who work for the small class. Society is run according to the dictates of the upper class, which sets up the laws, arts, and styles needed to maintain itself in power. (Marx, in modern terms, was an *elite theorist*.) Most laws concern property rights, noted Marx, because the **bourgeoisie** (the capitalists) are obsessed with hanging on to their property, which, according to Marx, is nothing but skimmed-off surplus value anyway. If the country goes to war, said Marx, it is not because the common people wish it but because the ruling bourgeoisie needs a war for economic gain. The proletariat, in fact, has no country; proletarians are international, all suffering under the heel of the capitalists.

bourgeois
Adjective, originally French, for city dweller; later and current, middle class in general. Noun: *bourgeoisie*.

HISTORY   Putting together his economic and social-class theories, Marx explained historical changes. When the underlying economic basis of society gets out of kilter with the structure that the dominant class has established (its laws, institutions, businesses, and so on), the system collapses, as in the French Revolution and ultimately, he predicted, capitalist systems. Marx was partly a theorist and partly an ideologist.

Marxism, as applied in the Soviet Union and other Communist countries, led to tyranny and failure, but, as a system of analysis, Marxism is still interesting and useful. For example, social class is important in structuring political views—but never uniformly. Economic interest groups still ride high and, by means of freely spending on election campaigns, often get their way in laws, policies, and tax breaks. They seldom get all they want, however, as they are opposed by other interest groups. Marx's enduring contributions are (1) his understanding that societies are never fully unified and peaceful but always riven with conflict and (2) that we must ask "Who benefits?" in any political controversy.

One of the enduring problems and weaknesses of Marx is that capitalism, contrary to his prediction, has not collapsed. Marx failed to understand the flexible, adaptive nature of capitalism. Old industries fade, and new ones rise. Imagine trying to explain Bill Gates and the computer software industry to people in the 1960s. Marx also missed that capitalism is not just one system—it is many. U.S., French, Singaporean, and Japanese capitalisms are distinct from each other. Marx's simplified notions of capitalism illustrate what happens when theory is placed in the service of ideology: Unquestioning followers believe it too literally.

Both political science and political theory have their place. As a citizen looking to improve the world, you are thinking like a political theorist—how things should be. You will need to decide what actions to take to achieve the political change you desire. To do so, you need to understand how things actually work and why. You need the skills of the political scientist to see the world as it is. If you only wish the world to be, you may be attempting impossible change. Thus, in navigating through political life, we merge the objective lens of political science with the normative lens of political theory.

Review Questions

1. What does it mean to "never get angry at a fact"?

2. Why did Aristotle call politics "the master science"?

3. Is politics largely biological, psychological, cultural, rational, or irrational?

4. How can something as messy as politics be a science?

5. What did Machiavelli, Confucius, Kautilya, and Ibn Khaldun have in common?

6. How did Hobbes, Locke, and Rousseau differ?

7. What is the crux of Marx's theory?

8. What is rational-choice theory?

Key Terms

behavioralism, p. 16
bourgeois, p. 25
civil society, p. 24
culture, p. 6
descriptive, p. 22
discipline, p. 9
empirical, p. 11
generalize, p. 14
general will, p. 24

hypothesis, p. 11
institutions, p. 16
irrational, p. 6
legitimacy, p. 7
normative, p. 22
paradigm, p. 21
political power, p. 4
positivism, p. 16
postbehavioral, p. 17

proletariat, p. 25
quantify, p. 11
rational, p. 6
realism, p. 22
scholarship, p. 11
social contract, p. 23
state of nature, p. 24
Zeitgeist, p. 24

Further Reference

Clarke, Kevin A., and David M. Primo. *A Model Discipline: Political Science and the Logic of Representations.* New York: Oxford University Press, 2012.

Easton, David. *A Framework for Political Analysis.* Englewood Cliffs, NJ: Prentice Hall, 1965.

Fukuyama, Francis. *The Origins of Political Order: From Prehuman Times to the French Revolution.* New York: Farrar, Straus and Giroux, 2011.

Huysmans, Jeff. *What Is Politics? A Short Introduction.* New York: Columbia University Press, 2004.

Lane, Ruth. *Political Science in Theory and Practice: The "Politics" Model.* Armonk, NY: M. E. Sharpe, 1997.

Laver, Michael. *Private Desires, Political Action: An Invitation to the Politics of Rational Choice.* Thousand Oaks, CA: Sage, 1997.

Lipset, Seymour Martin. *Political Man: The Social Bases of Politics,* rev. ed. Baltimore, MD: Johns Hopkins University Press, 1981.

———, ed. *Political Philosophy: Theories, Thinkers, and Concepts.* Washington, DC: CQ Press, 2001.

Losco, Joseph, and Leonard Williams, eds. *Political Theory: Classic and Contemporary Readings,* 2nd ed., 2 vols. Los Angeles: Roxbury, 2002.

Morgenthau, Hans J., David Clinton, and Kenneth W. Thompson. *Politics Among Nations: The Struggle for Power and Peace,* 7th ed. Burr Ridge, IL: McGraw-Hill, 2005.

Naím, Moizés. *The End of Power: From Boardrooms to Battlefields and Churches to States, Why Being in Charge Isn't What It Used to Be.* New York: Basic Books, 2013.

Ryan, Alan. *On Politics: A History of Political Philosophy from Herodotus to the Present.* New York: Norton, 2012.

Shively, W. Phillips. *The Craft of Political Research,* 9th ed. New York: Pearson, 2012.

Theodoulou, Stella, and Rory O'Brien, eds. *Methods for Political Inquiry: The Discipline, Philosophy, and Analysis of Politics.* Upper Saddle River, NJ: Prentice Hall, 1999.

Tinder, Glenn. *Political Thinking: The Perennial Questions,* 6th ed. New York: Longman, 2003.

White, Stephen K., and J. Donald Moon, eds. *What Is Political Theory?* Thousand Oaks, CA: Sage, 2004.

Wilson, Edward O. *The Social Conquest of Earth.* New York: Norton, 2012.

Chapter 2
Political Ideologies

 Learning Objectives

2.1 Explain the difference between a political theory and an ideology.

2.2 Distinguish between classic and modern liberalism.

2.3 Contrast Burkean conservatism with its current variety.

2.4 Explain how socialism split into several varieties.

2.5 Trace the origins of nationalism until the present day.

2.6 List and define as many current ideologies as you can.

2.7 Evaluate the "end of ideology" argument.

In the last century, many political scientists thought ideological politics was over in the United States. **Pragmatic** politicians of both parties tended to stick to the political center and were willing to compromise. Recent elections, however, show strong and growing ideological divisions. Republicans denounce Democratic fiscal, healthcare, and finance reforms as "liberal" or even "socialist." Democrats denounce Republicans for trying to roll back necessary, progressive legislation and make rich people richer. There is little middle ground for moderation and compromise.

pragmatic
Using whatever works without theory or ideology.

America has experienced bouts of ideological politics before. Both main parties have ideological roots. Probably few Republicans knew it, but they were based on *classic liberalism*, harkening back to Adam Smith's 1776 admonition to get government out of the economy. Democrats, on the other hand, had long emphasized government solutions for financial crashes, poverty, health care, and education. They were *modern liberals*, quite distinct from the classic variety. Ideology is alive, well, and powerful in America.

What Is Ideology?

2.1 **Explain the difference between a political theory and an ideology.**

An ideology begins with the belief that things can be better; it is a plan to improve society. As economist Anthony Downs put it in 1957, ideology is "a verbal image of the good society, and of the chief means of constructing such a society." Political ideologies are not political science; they are not calm, rational attempts to understand political systems. They are, rather, commitments to *change* political systems. (An exception is classic conservatism, which aimed to keep things from changing too much.) **Ideologues** make poor political scientists, for they confuse the "should" or "ought" of ideology with the "is" of political science. **Ideologies** are often based on political and economic theories but simplified and popularized to sell to mass audiences, build political movements, and win elections. Ideologies might be called cheap theories.

ideologue
Someone who believes passionately in an ideology.

ideology
Belief system that society can be improved by following certain doctrines; usually ends in *ism*.

In politics, ideology cements together movements, parties, and revolutionary groups. To fight and endure sacrifices, people need ideological motivation, something to believe in. Americans have sometimes not grasped this point. With their emphasis on moderation and pragmatism, they fail to understand the energizing effect of ideology in the world today. Muslim *jihadis*, committed to a mix of *salafiyya*, tribalism, anticolonialism, and even a bit of socialism (see below), sacrificed their lives to kill Americans and fellow Muslims. We never understood the new, fanatic ideology—sometimes called *Islamism*—we faced in Afghanistan and Iraq.

We tend to forget that more than two centuries ago, Americans were quite ideological, too, and—imbued with a passion for freedom and self-rule, via the pens of John Locke and Thomas Paine—beat a larger and better-equipped army of Englishmen and Hessians who had no good reason to fight. Our Civil War was in part fought on ideological grounds over the definition of human freedom and the power of the states to go separate ways.

Be warned: Ideologies never work precisely the way their advocates intend. Some are hideous failures. All ideologies contain wishful thinking, which frequently collapses in the face of reality. Ideologues claim they can perfect the world; reality is highly imperfect. The **classic liberalism** of Adam Smith did contribute to the nineteenth century's economic growth, but it also led to great inequalities of wealth and recurring depressions. It was modified into modern liberalism. Communism led to brutal tyranny, economic failure, and collapse. China quietly abandoned Maoism in favor of rapid economic growth. Ideologies, when measured against their actual performance, fall far short. Is that because political rivals thwarted implementation of the ideology or because the ideas themselves were defective? It depends on whom you ask.

classic liberalism
Ideology founded by Adam Smith to keep government out of economy; became U.S. conservatism.

Theories

The Origins of Ideologies

Many ideologies stem from deeper political theories. Classic liberalism traces back to seventeenth-century English philosopher John Locke who emphasized individual rights, property, and reason. Communism traces back to early nineteenth-century German philosopher G. W. F. Hegel who emphasized that all facets of a society—art, music, architecture, politics, law, and so on—hang together as a package, all the expression of an underlying *Zeitgeist*.

The philosophers' ideas, however, are simplified and popularized. Ideologists want plans for action, not abstract ideas. Marx, for example, "stood Hegel on his head" to make economics the great underlying cause. Most ideologies have a large economic component, for it is economics that will improve society. Lenin later stood Marx on his head to make his ideas apply to a backward country where Marx doubted they should. Mao Zedong then applied Lenin's ideas to an even more backward country, where they did not fit at all. Ideologies become warped.

Ideologies can be classified—with some oversimplification—on a left-to-right spectrum that dates back to the meeting of the French National Assembly in 1789. To allow delegates of similar views to caucus and to keep apart strong partisans who

might fight, members were seated as follows in a semicircular chamber: Conservatives (who favored continuation of the monarchy) were on the speaker's right, radicals (who favored sweeping away the old system altogether in favor of a republic of freedom and equality) were seated to his left, and moderates (who wanted some change) were seated in the center.

We have been calling their ideological descendants left, right, and center ever since, even though the content of their views has changed. The left now favors equality, welfare programs, and government intervention in the economy. The right stresses individual initiative and private economic activity. Centrists try to synthesize and moderate the views of both. People a little to one side or the other are called center-left or center-right. Sweden's political parties form a rather neat left-to-right spectrum: a small Left Party (formerly Communist); a large Social Democratic Party; and medium-sized Center (formerly Farmers'), Liberal, Christian, and Conservative Parties.

One ideology gives rise to others (see figure on the following page). Starting with the classic liberalism of Adam Smith, we see how liberalism branched leftward into radical, socialist, and communist directions. Meanwhile, on the conservative side, it branched rightward.

Figure 2.1 How political ideologies relate to one another: key thinkers and dates of emergence.

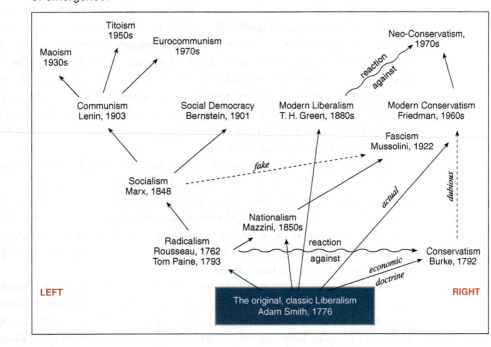

Liberalism

2.2   Distinguish between classic and modern liberalism.

Frederick Watkins of Yale called 1776 "the Year One of the Age of Ideology" and not just for the American Revolution. That same year Scottish economist Adam Smith published *The Wealth of Nations*, thereby founding classic laissez-faire economics. The true wealth of nations, Smith argued, is not in the amount of gold and silver they amass but in the amount of goods and services their people produce. Smith was refuting an earlier notion, called *mercantilism*, that the bullion in a nation's treasury determined its wealth. Spain had looted the New World of gold and silver but grew poorer. The French, too, since at least Louis XIV in the previous century, had followed mercantilist policies by means of government supervision of the economy with plans, grants of monopoly, subsidies, tariffs, and other restraints on trade.

Smith reasoned that this was not the path to prosperity. Government interference retards growth. If you give one firm a monopoly to manufacture something, you banish competition and, with it, efforts to produce new products and lower prices. The economy stagnates. If you protect domestic industry by tariffs, you take away incentives for better or cheaper products. By getting the government out of the economy, by leaving the economy alone (*laissez-faire*, in French), you promote prosperity.

But won't free competition unsupervised by government lead to chaos? No, said Smith; the market itself will regulate the economy. Efficient producers will prosper and inefficient ones will go under. Supply and demand determine prices better than any government official. In the free marketplace, an "unseen hand" regulates and self-corrects the economy. If people want more of something, producers increase output, new producers enter the field, or foreign producers bring in their wares. The unseen hand—actually, the rational calculations of myriad individuals and firms all pursuing their self-interest—microadjusts the economy with no government help.

This ideology took the name liberalism from the Latin word for "free," *liber*: Society should be as free as possible from government interference. As aptly summarized by Thomas Jefferson, "That government is best that governs least." Americans took to classic liberalism like a duck takes to water. It fit the needs of a vigorous, freedom-loving population with plenty of room to expand. Noneconomic liberty also suited Americans. Government should also not supervise religion, the press, or free speech.

But, you say, what you're calling liberalism here is actually what Americans today call conservatism. True. In the late nineteenth century, liberalism changed and split into modern liberalism and what we now call conservatism, which we discuss next. To keep our terminology straight, we call the original ideas of Adam Smith "classic liberalism" to distinguish it from the modern variety.

Modern Liberalism

By the late nineteenth century, it was clear that the free market was not completely self-regulating. Competition was imperfect. Manufacturers rigged the market—a point Smith himself had warned about. There was a drift to bigness and fewness: monopoly. The system produced a large underclass of the terribly poor (brilliantly depicted by Dickens). Class positions were largely inherited; children of better-off families got the education and connections to stay on top. Bouts of speculative investing led to recurring economic downturns—2008–2009 is just the most recent example—which especially hurt the poor and the working class. In short, the laissez-faire economy created some problems.

The Englishman Thomas Hill Green (1836–1882) rethought liberalism. The goal of liberalism, reasoned Green, was a free society. But what happens when economic developments take away freedom? The classic liberals placed great store in contracts (agreements between consenting parties with little government supervision): If you don't like the deal, don't take it. But what if the bargaining power of the two parties is greatly unequal, as between a rich employer and a poor person desperate for a job? Does the latter really have a free choice in accepting or rejecting a job with very low wages? Classic liberalism said let it be; wages will find their own level. But what if the wage is below starvation level? Here, Green said, it was time for government to step in. In such a case, it would not be a question of government infringing on freedoms but of government protecting them. Instead of the purely negative "freedom from," there had to be a certain amount of the positive "freedom to." Green called this *positive freedom*. Government was to step in to guarantee the freedom to live at an adequate level.

Classic liberalism expelled government from the marketplace; **modern liberalism** brought it back in, this time to protect people from a sometimes unfair economic system. Modern liberals championed wage and hour laws, the right to form unions, unemployment and health insurance, and improved educational opportunities. To do this, they placed heavier taxes on the rich than on the working class. They also regulated banking and finance to dampen the boom-and-bust cycle. This is the liberalism of the United States over the past century, the liberalism of Woodrow Wilson, Franklin D. Roosevelt, and Barack Obama; however, one strand of the old liberalism remains in the new: the emphasis on freedom of speech and press.

modern liberalism
Ideology favoring government intervention to correct economic and social ills; U.S. liberalism today.

Conservatism

2.3 **Contrast Burkean conservatism with its current variety.**

We should call the ideas of Edmund Burke (1729–1797) "classic conservatism," for his **conservatism** diverges in many ways from modern conservatism. Burke knew Adam Smith and agreed that a free market was the best economic system. Burke also opposed crushing the rebellious American colonists; after all, they were only trying to regain the ancient freedoms of Englishmen, said Burke. So far, Burke sounds like a liberal.

conservatism
Ideology of keeping systems largely unchanged.

But Burke strongly objected to the way liberal ideas were applied in France by revolutionists. There, liberalism turned into *radicalism*, influenced by philosopher Jean-Jacques Rousseau and, fresh from the U.S. revolution, Thomas Paine. As is often the case, an ideology devised in one place becomes warped when applied to different circumstances. Liberalism in America was easy; once the English and their Tory sympathizers cleared out, it fell into place without resistance. But in France, a large aristocratic class and a state-supported Roman Catholic Church had a lot to lose. The revolutionaries tried to solve the problem with the guillotine and swept away all established institutions.

This, said Burke, was a terrible mistake. Liberals place too much confidence in human reason. People are only partly rational; they also have irrational passions. To contain them, society over the centuries has evolved traditions, institutions, and standards of morality, such as monarchy and an established church. Sweep these aside, warned Burke, and man's irrational impulses burst out, leading to chaos, which in turn ends in tyranny far worse than the old system. Burke, in his 1792 *Reflexions on the Revolution in France*, predicted that France would fall into military dictatorship. In 1799, Napoleon took over.

Institutions and traditions that currently exist cannot be all bad, Burke reasoned, for they are the products of hundreds of years of trial and error. People have become used to them. The best should be preserved or "conserved" (hence the name conservatism). They are not perfect, but they work. This is not to say that things should never change. Of course they should change, said Burke, but only gradually, giving people time to adjust. "A state without the means of some change is without the means of its conservation," he wrote.

Burke was an important thinker for several reasons. He helped discover the *irrational* in human behavior: Humans are often guided by passion rather than by reason. He saw that institutions are like living things; they grow and adapt over time. And, most important, he saw that revolutions end badly, for society cannot be instantly remade according to human reason. Although Burke's ideas have been called an *anti-ideology*—for they aimed to shoot down the radicalism then engulfing France—they have considerable staying power. Burke's emphasis on religion, traditions, and morality has been taken over by modern conservatives. His doubts about applying reason to solve social problems were echoed by political scientist Jeane Kirkpatrick (1926–2006), President Reagan's UN ambassador, who found that leftists always suppose that things can be much better when in fact violent upheaval always makes things worse. In these ways, classic conservatism is very much alive.

Modern Conservatism

What happened to the other branch of liberalism, the people who stayed true to Adam Smith's original doctrine of minimal government? They are still very important, only today we call them conservatives. (In Europe, they still call them liberals or *neoliberals*, much to the confusion of Americans.) American conservatives got a big boost from Milton Friedman (1912–2006), a Nobel Prize–winning economist. Friedman argued that the free market is still the best, that Adam Smith was right, and that wherever government intervenes it messes things up. Margaret Thatcher in Britain and Ronald Reagan in the United States applied this revival of classic liberalism in the 1980s with mixed but generally positive results.

Modern conservatives worship the market more than Adam Smith ever did. Smith recognized that markets could be crooked and unfair. Today's conservatives contend that all markets are honest and self-correcting, certainly more so than government regulation, which they would roll back. Alan Greenspan, powerful chair of the Federal Reserve Board from 1987 to 2006, ignored warnings that the U.S. housing market was a bubble ready to pop. The huge banks would not be so greedy or foolish as to let that happen, he reasoned, so Fed action was unnecessary. (He later recanted.) Republicans and the Tea Party also assume that markets are more efficient than government programs and would privatize many functions, such as running health care only through private insurers. Critics call this "market fundamentalism," like a religious creed.

Modern conservatism also borrows from Edmund Burke a concern for tradition, especially in religion. American conservatives would put prayer into public schools, outlaw abortion and same-sex marriage, and support private and church-related schools. Modern conservatives also oppose special rights for women and minority groups, arguing that everyone should have the same rights. Modern conservatism is a blend of the economic ideas of Adam Smith and the traditionalist ideas of Edmund Burke.

Socialism

2.4   Explain how socialism split into several varieties.

Liberalism (classic variety) dominated the nineteenth century, but critics deplored the growing gulf between rich and poor. Unlike T. H. Green, some did not believe that a few reforms would suffice; they wanted to overthrow the capitalist system. These were the socialists, and their leading thinker was Karl Marx, who wrote less as a scholar than a promoter of revolution. He hated the "bourgeoisie" long before he developed his elaborate theories that they were doomed. An outline of his ideas appeared in his 1848 pamphlet *The Communist Manifesto*, which concluded with the ringing words: "The proletarians have nothing to lose but their chains. They have a world to win. Workers of all countries, unite!" Marx participated in organizing Europe's first socialist parties.

Marx's *Capital* was a gigantic analysis of why capitalism would be overthrown by the proletariat. Then would come socialism, a just, productive society without class distinctions. Later, at a certain stage when industrial production was very high, this socialist society will turn into *communism*, a perfect society without police, money, or even government. Goods will be in such plenty that people will just take what they need. There will be no private property, so there will be no need for police. Because government is simply an instrument of class domination, with the abolition of distinct classes there will be no need for the state. It will "wither away." Communism, then, was Marx's predicted utopia beyond socialism.

Marx focused on the ills and malfunctions of capitalism and never specified what socialism would be like, only that it would be much better than capitalism; its precise workings he left vague. This has enabled a wide variety of socialist thinkers to put forward their own vision of socialism and say it is what Marx really meant. This has ranged from the mild "welfarism" of social-democratic parties, to *anarcho-syndicalism* (unions running everything), to Lenin's and Stalin's hypercentralized tyranny, to Trotsky's denunciation of same, to Mao's self-destructive permanent revolution, to Tito's experimental decentralized system. All, and a few more, claim to espouse "real" socialism.

These different interpretations of socialism caused first the socialist and then the communist movement to splinter.

Social Democracy

By the beginning of the twentieth century, the German Social Democrats (SPD), espousing Marxism, had become Germany's biggest party. Marx had disparaged conventional parties and labor unions; bourgeois governments would simply crush them. At most, they could be training grounds for serious revolutionary action. But the German Social Democrats started succeeding. They got elected to the Reichstag and local offices; their unions won higher wages and better working conditions. Some began to think that the working class could accomplish its aims without revolution. Why use bullets when there are ballots?

Eduard Bernstein developed this view. In his 1901 *Evolutionary Socialism*, he pointed out the real gains the working class was making and concluded that Marx had been wrong about the collapse of capitalism and revolution. Reforms that won concrete benefits for the working class could also lead to socialism, he argued. In revising Marxism, Bernstein earned the name **revisionist**, originally a pejorative hurled at him by orthodox Marxists. By the time of the ill-fated Weimar Republic in Germany (1919–1933), the Social Democrats had toned down their militancy and worked together with liberals and Catholics to try to save democracy. Persecuted by the Nazis, the SPD revived after World War II and in 1959 dropped Marxism altogether, as did social democrats everywhere, and got elected more and more. They transformed themselves into center-left parties with no trace of revolution.

What, then, do **social democrats** stand for? They abandoned state ownership of industry. Only a few percent of Sweden's industry is state-owned, and much of that conservatives did long ago to keep firms from going under and creating unemployment. Said Olof Palme, Sweden's Social Democratic prime minister, "If industry's primary purpose is to expand its production, to succeed in new markets, to provide good jobs for their employees, they need have no fears. Swedish industry has never expanded so rapidly as during these years of Social Democratic rule." Instead of state ownership of industry, social democrats use *welfare* measures to improve living conditions: unemployment and medical insurance, generous pensions, and subsidized food and housing. Social democracies have become welfare states: *Welfarism* would be a more accurate term than *socialism*.

There's one catch—there's always at least one catch—and that is that welfare states are terribly expensive. To pay for welfare measures, taxes climb. In Denmark and Sweden, taxes consume half of the **gross domestic product (GDP)**, exactly the kind of thing Milton Friedman warned about. With those kinds of taxes, soon you are not free to choose how you live. U.S. liberalism is tinged with social democratic ideas on welfare. The left wing of our Democratic Party—for example, Elizabeth Warren and Bernie Sanders—resembles ideologically the moderate wings of European social democratic parties.

revisionist
Changing an ideology or view of history.

social democracy
Mildest form of socialism, promoting welfare measures but not state ownership of industry.

gross domestic product (GDP)
Sum total of goods and services produced in a given country in one year, often expressed per capita (GDPpc) by dividing population into GDP.

Communism

While the social democrats evolved into reformists and welfarists, a smaller wing of the original socialists stayed Marxist and became the Communists. The key figure in this transformation was a Russian intellectual, Vladimir I. Lenin (1870–1924). He made several changes in Marxism, producing *Marxism-Leninism*, another name for **communism**.

communism
Marxist theory merged with Leninist organization into a totalitarian party.

IMPERIALISM Many Russian intellectuals of the late nineteenth century hated the tsarist system and embraced Marxism as a way to overthrow tsarism. But Marx meant his theory to apply in the most advanced capitalist countries, not in backward Russia, where capitalism was just beginning. Lenin, in his seventeen-year exile in Switzerland, remade Marxism to fit the Russian situation. He offered a theory of economic imperialism, one borrowed from German revolutionary Rosa Luxemburg and English economist J. A. Hobson, who wondered why the proletarian revolutions Marx had predicted had not broken out in the advanced industrialized lands. They concluded that the domestic market could not absorb all the goods the capitalist system produced, so it found overseas markets. Capitalism had transformed itself, expanding overseas into colonies to exploit their raw materials, cheap labor, and new markets. Capitalism thus won a temporary new lease on life by turning into **imperialism**. With profits from its colonies, the mother imperialist country could also pay off its working class a bit to render it reformist rather than revolutionary.

imperialism
Amassing of colonial empires, mostly by European powers; pejorative in Marxist terms.

Imperialism had to expand, Lenin argued, but it was growing unevenly. Some countries, such as Britain and Germany, were highly developed, but where capitalism was just starting, as in Spain and Russia, it was weak. The newly industrializing countries were exploited as a whole by the international capitalist system. It was in them that revolutionary fever burned brightest; they were "imperialism's weakest link." Accordingly, a revolution could break out in a poor country and then spread into advanced countries. The imperialist countries were highly dependent on their empires. Once cut off from exploiting them, capitalism would fall. World War I, wrote Lenin, was the collision of imperialists trying to dominate the globe.

Lenin shifted the Marxian focus from the situation within capitalist countries to the global situation. The focus went from Marx's proletariat rising up against the bourgeoisie to exploited nations rising up against imperialist powers. Marx would probably not have endorsed such a redo of his theory.

ORGANIZATION Lenin's real contribution lay in his attention to organization. With the tsarist secret police always on their trail, Lenin argued, the Russian socialist party could not be like other parties—large, open, and trying to win votes. Instead, it had to be small, secretive, made up of professional revolutionaries, and tightly organized under central command. In 1903, the Russian Social Democratic Labor party split over this issue. Lenin had enough supporters at the party's Brussels meeting to win the votes of thirty-three of the fifty-one delegates present. Lenin called his faction *bolshevik* (Russian for "majority"). The losers, who advocated a more moderate line and a more open party, took the name *menshevik* ("minority"). In 1918, the Bolsheviks changed the party name to Communist.

Lenin's attention to organization paid off when Russia fell into chaos during World War I. In March 1917, a group of moderates seized power from the tsar, but they were unable to govern the country. In November, the Bolsheviks shrewdly manipulated councils (*soviets* in Russian) that had sprung up in the leading cities and seized control from the moderates. After winning a desperate civil war, Lenin called on all true socialists around the world to join in a new international movement under Moscow's control. It was called the Communist International, or *Comintern*. Almost all socialist parties in the world split; their left wings went into the Comintern and became Communist parties in 1920–1921. The resultant social democratic and Communist parties have been hostile to each other ever since.

How much Marxism-Leninism did Soviet rulers really believe? They constantly used Marxist rhetoric, but many argued they were cynical about ideology and just used it as window dressing. The Soviets never defined their society as Communist—that was yet to come; it was what they were working on. It is we in the West who called these countries "Communist." In 1961, Soviet party chief Nikita Khrushchev rashly predicted "communism in our generation," indicating that utopia would be reached by 1980. Instead, it declined, and at the end of 1991 the Soviet system collapsed.

MAOISM AND TITOISM In the 1930s, Mao Zedong concluded that the Chinese Communist Party (CCP) had to be based on poor peasants and guerrilla warfare. This was a break with Stalin's leadership, and after decades of fighting, the CCP took over mainland China in 1949. Mao pursued a radical course that included a failed attempt at overnight industrialization (the Great Leap Forward of 1958–1961), the destruction of bureaucratic authority (the Proletarian Cultural Revolution in 1966–1976), and even border fighting with the Soviet Union in 1969. After Mao's death in 1976, pragmatic leaders moved China away from his extremism, which had ruined China's economic progress. A few revolutionary groups stayed Maoist: Cambodia's murderous Khmer Rouge and India's Naxalites. **Maoism** is an ultraradical form of communism.

Maoism

Extreme form of communism, featuring guerrilla warfare and periodic upheavals.

Yugoslav party chief Josip Tito went the other way, developing a more moderate and liberal form of communism. Even though Tito's partisans fought the Germans in Stalin's name, Stalin did not fully control Tito, and in 1948 Stalin had Yugoslavia kicked out of the Communist camp. During the 1950s, the Yugoslav Communists reformed their system, basing it on decentralization, debureaucratization, and worker self-management. Trying to find a middle ground between a market and a controlled economy, Yugoslavia suffered economic problems in the 1980s. **Titoism** might have served as a warning to Communist rulers who wanted to experiment with "middle ways" between capitalism and socialism. The combination is unstable and worked only because Tito was undisputed ruler; when he died in 1980, Yugoslavia started coming apart until, by the early 1990s, it was a bloodbath.

Titoism

Moderate, decentralized, partially market form of communism.

Nationalism

2.5   **Trace the origins of nationalism until the present day.**

The real winner among ideologies—one that still dominates today—is **nationalism**, the exaggerated belief in the greatness and unity of one's country. Nationalism is often born out of occupation and repression by foreigners. "We won't be pushed around by foreigners any more!" shout Cuban, Palestinian, Chinese, and many other nationalists. Nationalism has triumphed over and influenced all other ideologies, so that, in the United States, conservatism is combined with American nationalism, and, in China, nationalism was always more important than communism.

nationalism
A people's heightened sense of cultural, historical, and territorial identity, unity, and sometimes greatness.

The first seeds of nationalism came with the Renaissance monarchs who proclaimed their absolute power and the unity and greatness of their kingdoms. Nationality was born out of **sovereignty**. *Nationalism*, however, appeared only with the French Revolution, which was based on "the people" and heightened French feelings about themselves as a special, leading people destined to free the rest of Europe. When a Prussian army invaded France in 1792, the "nation in arms" stopped them at Valmy; enthusiastic volunteers beat professional soldiers. The stirring "Marseillaise," France's national anthem, appeared that year.

sovereignty
A national government's being boss on its own turf, the last word in law in that country.

Later, Napoleon's legions ostensibly spread the radical liberalism of the French Revolution but were really spreading nationalism. The conquered nations of Europe quickly grew to hate the arrogant French occupiers. Spaniards, Germans, and Russians soon became nationalistic themselves as they struggled to expel the French. Basic to nationalism is resentment of foreign domination, be it by British redcoats, Napoleon's legions, or European colonialists. Nationalism blanketed Europe in the nineteenth century and in the twentieth century spread to Europe's colonies throughout the world. It is in the developing countries that nationalism is now most intense.

By the mid–nineteenth century, thinkers all over Europe—especially in Germany and Italy—defined the nation as the ultimate human value, the source of all things good. Italian writer Giuseppe Mazzini espoused freedom not for individuals—that was mere liberalism—but for nations instead. One achieved true freedom by subordinating oneself to the nation. Education, for example, had to inculcate a sense of nationalism that blotted out individualism, argued Mazzini.

Nationalism arises when a population, often led by intellectuals, perceives an enemy or "other" to despise and struggle against. In the twentieth century, this has often been a colonial power such as Britain, France, or the Netherlands, against whom, respectively, Indians, Algerians, and Indonesians could rally in their fight for independence. Nationalism holds that it is terribly wrong to be ruled by others. Thus, Bosnian Serbs did not consent to be ruled by Bosnian Muslims, Palestinians by Israelis, and Lithuanians by Russians. Some Chinese and Iranians, feeling they have been repressed and controlled by outside powers, lash out with nationalistic military and diplomatic policies. Even some Canadians, fearful of U.S. economic and cultural dominance, turn nationalistic.

Nationalism can lead to wars and economic isolation. "We won't let foreigners take over our economy!" say nationalists, but rapid economic growth needs foreign investment and world trade. Economic nationalists in the United States, for example, oppose exporting our newly abundant shale gas. It should be used by and for Americans! More than any of the previous ideologies, nationalism depends on emotional appeals. The feeling of belonging to a nation goes to our psychological center. What other human organization would we fight and kill for?

REGIONAL NATIONALISM In recent decades, the world has seen the rise of another kind of nationalism: regional nationalism, which aims at breaking up existing nations into what its proponents argue are the true nations. Militant Québécois want to separate from Canada, Basques from Spain, Tibetans from China, and Scots from Britain. Regional nationalism too is based on hatred of being ruled by unlike peoples.

Fascism

fascism
Extreme form of nationalism with elements of racism, socialism, and militarism.

In Italy and Germany, nationalism grew into **fascism**, one of the great catastrophes of the twentieth century. One sign of a fascist movement is members in uniforms; they crave military structure and discipline. Before World War I, Italian journalist Benito Mussolini was a fire-breathing socialist; military service changed him into an ardent nationalist. Italy was full of discontented people after World War I. "Maximalist" socialists threatened revolution. In those chaotic times, Mussolini assembled a strange collection of people in black shirts who wanted to end democracy and political parties and impose stern central authority and discipline. These Fascists—a word taken from the ancient Roman symbol of authority, a bundle of sticks bound around an ax (the *fasces*)—hated disorder and wanted strong leadership to end it.

Amid growing disorder in 1922, the king of Italy handed power to Mussolini, and by 1924 he had turned Italy into a one-party state with himself as *Duce* (leader). The Fascists ran the economy by inserting their men into all key positions. Italy looked impressive: There was little crime, much monumental construction, stable prices, and, as they used to say, "The trains ran on time." Behind the scenes, however, fascism was a mess, with hidden unemployment, poor economic performance, and corruption.

With the collapse of the world economy in 1929, however, some thought fascism was the wave of the future. Adolf Hitler in Germany copied Mussolini's fascism but had his followers wear brown shirts and added *racism*. For Hitler, it was not just Germans as a nation who were fighting the punitive and unfair Versailles Treaty and chaos of the Weimar Republic; it was Germans as a distinct and superior race. Hitler did not invent German racism, which went back generations, but he hyped it. The racist line held that a special branch of the white

Methods

Theses

Begin your paper with a clear, punchy **thesis**, a first sentence giving your main idea or claim, the point you are going to prove. A thesis that cannot be proved with empirical evidence is just speculation, not solid research. An initial attempt at a thesis is a *hypothesis*. If your evidence does not support your thesis, discard or change it. Your thesis paragraph should be about as long as this one.

The simplest thesis is that something is (or is not) happening: "More and more interest groups set up shop in Washington." Avoid trivial theses, anything well known or established: "The president is inaugurated on January 20 following the election." An interesting thesis explains how one thing relates to another: "White Protestant males vote strongly Republican." Gathering examples or case studies is often the initial step to developing a thesis. If you take the six counties in your state with the highest Obama vote, what generalizations can you make about them? Do not gently introduce your thesis (save that for your English class); move directly into it. A thesis is more definite than what the paper is "about." You left that behind in high school.

Next, you must support your thesis, like a lawyer making a case. Like a judge, your instructor decides if your evidence is valid and supports your point. In a short paper, you might back up your thesis with three to five supporting elements. You might want to use subheads, little titles in the middle of your paper, to separate your supporting arguments. Subheads help structure your ideas and make the paper easier to understand. If you cannot support your thesis with facts, numbers, quotes, or just plain reasoning, abandon or change it. As they say in the news business: "Back it up or back off."

Indirect
Television has a big impact on politics, and many critics feel that it is not always a good impact.

Unprovable
Democracy is the government of the people, by the people, and for the people.

Trivial
Tea Party supporters were unhappy with taxes and government.

Vague
This paper is about U.S. policy toward Iran over three decades.

Direct
U.S. television advertising makes viewers cynical and indifferent and leads to low voter turnout.

Provable
Better-off countries tend to be democracies, poor countries not.

Nontrivial
Tea Party supporters were mostly Republican voters angry over Obama's programs.

Clear
U.S. policy toward Iran failed to notice rising discontent against the shah.

Boldfaced and Centered

Boldface and center your subheads (like the above subhead) to make them stand out. A new subhead indicates you are moving on to another supporting element. A paragraph is one thought or point. Make about three of them per double-spaced page. A paragraph that rambles on for a whole page is hard to read. Have no more than one subhead per page. For example, if your thesis is that a sour economy hurts incumbent presidents in elections, you might make a subhead for each election: "The 2008 Elections," "The 2012 Elections," and so on. A five-page paper may have about three subheads, indicating you are supporting your thesis with three elements.

race, the Aryans, were the bearers of all civilization. A sub-branch, the Nordics, which included Germans, were even better. (Actually, Germans are of very mixed genealogy.) Nazis argued that the superior Nordics were being subjugated to the sinister forces of Judaism, communism, world capitalism, and even Roman Catholicism. This doctrine was the basis for the death camps.

thesis
A main idea or claim, to be proved by evidence.

Hitler was named chancellor (prime minister) in 1933 in a situation of turmoil and, like Mussolini, within two years perfected a dictatorship with majority German support. With Nazis "coordinating" the economy, unemployment ended and many working people felt they were getting a good deal with jobs, vacations, and welfare the regime provided. The Nazis' full name was the National Socialist German Workers Party, but the socialism was fake. Hitler's true aim was war, as war builds heroes. For a few years, Hitler dominated Europe and started turning the Slavic lands of Eastern Europe into colonies for Germans—*Lebensraum* (living space). Nazi death camps killed some six million Jews and a similar number of Christians who were in the way. Was Hitler mad? Many of his views were widely held among Germans, and he had millions of enthusiastic helpers. Rather than insanity, the Nazis demonstrated the danger of nationalism run amok.

The word *fascist* has been overused and misused. Some hurl it at everything they dislike. Spanish dictator Francisco Franco, for example, was long considered a fascist, but he was actually a "traditional authoritarian," for he tried to minimize mass political involvement rather than stir it up the way Mussolini and Hitler did. Brazilian President Getúlio Vargas decreed a fascist-sounding "New State" in 1937, but he was merely borrowing some fascist rhetoric at a time when the movement was having its heyday in Europe. Some right-wing American commentators denounce "Islamofascists" and "feminazis."

The Ku Klux Klan in the United States is sometimes called fascist, and its members wear uniforms. The Klan's populist racism is similar to the Nazis', but the Klan strongly opposes the power of the national government, whereas the Nazis and Fascists worshipped it. Now some European anti-immigrant and anti-EU parties are tinged with fascism. Hungary's Jobbik Party, which hates immigrants and Jews, parades in uniform.

Ideology in Our Day

2.6   List and define as many current ideologies as you can.

The Collapse of Communism

By the 1980s, communism the world over was ideologically exhausted. Few people in China, Eastern Europe, and even the Soviet Union believed it any longer. In the non-Communist world, leftists deserted Marxism in droves. Several West European Communist parties embraced "Eurocommunism," a greatly watered-down ideology that renounced dictatorship and state ownership of industry. Capitalism was supposed to have collapsed; instead, it was thriving in the United States, Western Europe, and East Asia. Many Communist leaders admitted that their economies were too rigid and centralized and that the cure lay in cutting back state controls in favor of market economies.

Reform-minded Soviet President Mikhail Gorbachev (who ruled 1985–1991) offered a three-pronged approach to revitalizing Soviet communism: *glasnost* (media openness), *perestroika* (economic restructuring), and *demokratizatzia* (democratization). Applied haltingly and half-heartedly, the reforms only heightened discontent, for now Soviets could voice their complaints. Starting in Eastern Europe in 1989, non-Communist parties took over. In the Soviet Union, a partially free parliament was elected and began debating change. Non-Communist parties and movements appeared. Gorbachev still could not make up his mind how far and fast reforms should go, and the economy, barely reformed, turned wildly inflationary. A 1991 coup failed, and by the end of the year the Soviet Union ceased to exist.

Neoconservatism

In the 1970s, a new ideology emerged in the United States: **neoconservatism**, much of it from disillusioned liberals and leftists. As neoconservative writer Irving Kristol put it, "A neoconservative is a liberal who's been mugged by reality." Neoconservatives charged that the Democratic Party had moved too far left with unrealistic ideas on domestic reforms and a pacifist foreign policy. Neoconservatives reacted against the Great Society programs introduced by Lyndon Johnson in the mid-1960s that aimed to wipe out poverty and discrimination. Some liberals said the Great Society was never given a chance because funds for it were siphoned away by the Vietnam War. But neocons said it worked badly, that many of the programs achieved nothing. The cities grew worse; educational standards declined; medical aid became extremely costly; and a class of welfare-dependent poor emerged, people who had little incentive to work. Neocons spoke of negative "unforeseen consequences" of well-intentioned liberal programs.

neoconservatism
U.S. ideology of former liberals turning to conservative causes and methods.

Especially bothersome to neocons: Affirmative action gave racial minorities preferential treatment in hiring, sometimes ahead of better-qualified whites. Many neoconservatives were horrified at the extreme relativism that had grown in the 1960s. Simplistic ideas—such as "It's all right if it feels good" and "It just depends on your point of view" and "multiculturalism"—drove many liberals to neoconservatism. Ironically, some neocons were college professors who had earlier tried to broaden their students' views by stressing the relativity of all viewpoints and cultures. Instead, students became vacuous.

In the younger Bush administration, highly placed neocons promoted war with Iraq both to protect the United States and to pull the Muslim world into democracy. Many old-fashioned conservatives, who express more isolationist ideas, despise the neocons, some of whom now advocate "getting tough" with Iran and China.

Libertarianism

Slowly growing since the 1960s is an ideology so liberal that it became conservative, or vice versa. **Libertarians** would return to the original Adam Smith, with essentially no government interference in anything. They would deliver what

libertarianism
U.S. ideology in favor of shrinking all government power in favor of individual freedom.

Republicans only talk about. They note that modern liberals want a controlled economy but personal freedom while modern conservatives want a free economy but constraints on personal freedom. Why not freedom in both areas? Libertarians oppose subsidies, bureaucracies, taxes, intervention overseas, and big government itself. As such, they plugged into a very old American tradition and gained respectability. Although no libertarian candidates won elections, their Cato Institute in Washington became a lively think tank whose ideas could not be ignored. (One Cato paper deplored cities building light rail systems when buses are better and cheaper. The paper's title: "A Desire Named Streetcar.") Some critics blame libertarian worship of unregulated markets for the reckless deals that produced the 2008 financial meltdown. Rep. Ron Paul (father of Sen. Rand Paul), who earlier ran for president earlier as a Libertarian, later attempted to gain the Republican nomination.

Feminism

feminism
Ideology of psychological, political, and economic equality for women.

Springing to new life in the 1960s with a handful of female writers, by the 1970s the women's movement had become a political force in the United States and Western Europe. **Feminist** writers pointed out that women were paid less than men, were not promoted, were psychologically and physically abused by men, were denied loans and insurance, and were in general second-class citizens.

The root problem was psychological, argued feminists. Women and men were forced into "gender roles" that had little to do with biology. Boys were conditioned to be tough, domineering, competitive, and "macho," and girls were taught to be meek, submissive, unsure of themselves, and "feminine." Gender differences are almost entirely learned behavior, taught by parents and schools of a "patriarchal" society, but this could be changed. With proper child rearing and education, males could become gentler and females more assertive and self-confident.

Feminists joined "consciousness-raising" groups and railed against "male chauvinist pigs." Feminism started having an impact. Many employers gave women a fairer chance, sometimes hiring them over men. Women moved up to higher management positions (although seldom to the corporate top). Working wives became the norm. Husbands shared in homemaking and child rearing. With more women going to college than men, many male-dominated professions—medicine, law, business—saw an influx of women.

Politically, however, feminists did not achieve all they wished. The Equal Rights Amendment (ERA) to the Constitution failed to win ratification by enough state legislatures. It would have guaranteed equality of treatment regardless of gender. Antifeminists, some of them conservative women, argued that the ERA would take away women's privileges and protections under the law, would make women eligible for the draft, and would even lead to unisex lavatories. Despite this setback, women learned there was one way they could count for a lot politically—by voting. In the 1980 election, a significant "gender gap" appeared, and now women generally vote more Democratic than do men.

Environmentalism

Also during the 1960s, **environmentalism** began to ripple through the advanced industrialized countries. Economic development paid little heed to the damage it did to the environment. Any growth was good growth: "We'll never run out of nature." Mining, factories, and even farms poisoned streams; industries and automobiles polluted the air; chemical wastes made areas uninhabitable; and nuclear power leaked radioactivity. To the credo of "growth," environmentalists responded with "limits." They argued, "We can't go on like this without producing environmental catastrophe." Love Canal, Three Mile Island, Chernobyl, and Beijing's air seemed to prove them right. The burning of fuels and forests increases CO_2 that may trap heat inside the earth's atmosphere and change climates.

The ecologists' demands were only partly satisfied with the founding of the Environmental Protection Agency (EPA) in 1970. Industrial groups argued that EPA regulations restricted growth and ate into profits; under Republican

environmentalism
Ideology to save an endangered nature through regulation and lifestyle changes.

Islamism
Muslim religion turned into a political ideology.

Case Studies

Islamism: A New Ideology with Old Roots

Islamism illustrates how an ideology can suddenly arise by combining older elements. *Salafiyya*, or Islamic fundamentalism, started in the thirteenth century with a call to return to the pure ways of the Prophet and is the founding and current faith of Saudi Arabia. Al Qaeda and ISIS are *salafi* movements. Islamism exploded in 1979 with the Iranian revolution and Soviet invasion of Afghanistan. Islamist parties—some moderate, some extremist—appeared in strength with the Arab Spring in Tunisia, Egypt, Libya, and elsewhere.

Islamism blends religion, nationalism, socialism, and a "rage against modernity" that had long been brewing in the Muslim world. With America in the lead, Islamists argue, the West erodes Islamic morals and culture, subjugates the region economically (oil), and steals Islamic holy land (Israel). Some of this traces back to centuries of antipathy between Christendom and Islam, some to the frustrations of modernization. Islamism grows with rapid population increases and high unemployment and in reaction to corruption and misrule in Muslim countries.

Islamism resembles nationalism, but in Islam the political was always intertwined with the religious. Mosque and state are to be one. The Prophet

Muhammad founded Islam as one giant community, the *umma*, that disdains nations as forms of idolatry. Accordingly, Al Qaeda and ISIS are uninterested in Palestinian or Iraqi nationalism except to use it on their march to a Muslim caliphate. They seek to oust U.S. influence, destroy Israel, and take over all Muslim countries and eventually the world. Then a purified Islam will share the wealth now concentrated in the hands of a few corrupt rulers, a sort of socialism. Fanatic and uncompromising, ISIS horrified the world with beheadings and immolations. Some Muslim countries—Pakistan and Saudi Arabia among them—fearing Islamist overthrow, attempt to buy them off.

Islamism has several weaknesses. First, it is split between *Sunni* and *Shia* branches of Islam. Sunni is mainstream Islam, accounting for some 85 percent of the world's Muslims, but Shias dominate Iran and parts of Iraq, Saudi Arabia, Lebanon, and elsewhere. Sunnis despise and mistrust Shias; ISIS aims to kill them. Second, Islamism has no economic plan and cannot put food on the table, something many Iranians now complain about. The extremists' killing of Muslims costs it support and allies. Long term, Islamism is likely to fade, but currently it forces us to consider military options.

presidents, the EPA was rendered ineffective. Energy production had to take first place over pristine environments, they argued.

Regulation was only part of the environmental credo. Many argued that consumption patterns and lifestyles in the advanced countries should change to conserve the earth's resources, natural beauty, and clean air and water. Americans, only about 4 percent of the world's population, consume a fourth of the world's manufactured goods and energy. In addition to being out of balance with the rest of the world, this profligate lifestyle is unnecessary and unhealthy, they argued. "Greens" urged public transportation and bicycles instead of cars, whole-grain foods and vegetables instead of meat, and decentralized, renewable energy sources, such as wind and solar energy, instead of fossil- or nuclear-fueled power plants.

Some environmentalists formed political parties, first the Citizens Party, then the Greens, but their main impact was within the two big parties, neither of which could ignore the environmental vote. In Western Europe in the 1980s, especially in Germany and Sweden, Green parties were elected to parliament, determined to end nuclear power, toxic waste, and war. Many young Europeans found the Greens an attractive alternative to the old and stodgy conventional parties. U.S. environmentalists promote renewable energy such as wind, solar, and biofuels and work to limit use of fossil fuels, such as a pipeline to bring

Democracy

Authoritarian Capitalism

Some thinkers see a new ideological challenge, "authoritarian capitalism," which allows a partial market economy under overall state control and has no intention of introducing democracy. This state is run by a single party with a small leadership group at its top—a group that claims to make wise economic decisions without the distraction and mess of democracy. A prime example is China, which abandoned Marx and Mao but aims to build its wealth and power. Russia runs along similar lines but with less success. Some people, especially in developing countries, are attracted to this authoritarian capitalist model.

China's power is concentrated in its seven-man Standing Committee at the top of the Communist Party. It lays down the main lines of economic control—where and how much to invest, ensure economic growth, and prevent inflation—mostly by means of huge state banks. For some decades, China enjoyed 10 percent annual growth (recently less) that impressed the world. The way Beijing sees it, the West, politically

paralyzed and economically stagnant, is played out. Look at the United States—so indebted and polarized it can barely pass a budget. Look at Europe—so indebted and splintered it cannot even manage its euro currency. China, goes the line, is well run by calm and bright leaders who have the Chinese people's interest at heart.

Skeptical observers doubt if authoritarian capitalism can serve as a long-term model. Difficulties mount—overinvestment, income inequality, corruption, and export dependency—that harm economic growth. Perhaps their biggest problem: succession crises with no stable way to move from one leader to the next. Both China and Russia have experienced difficulties with this. Discontent smolders in China and Russia with no democratic way to vent it. Authoritarian capitalism may follow the earlier rise and fall of totalitarian systems, which briefly offered some people hope during hard times but proved unworkable in the long run.

tar-sands oil from Canada. Environmentalists opposed the "fracking" of shale gas, which is cleaner than oil or coal but still pumps carbon into the atmosphere.

Is Ideology Finished?

2.7 **Evaluate the "end of ideology" argument.**

In 1960, Harvard sociologist Daniel Bell (1919–2011) argued that the century-long ideological debates were coming to a close. The failure of tyrannical communism and the rise of the welfare state were producing what Bell called the "end of ideology": There simply was not much to quarrel about. Henceforth, political debate would focus on almost technical questions of how to run the welfare state, said Bell, such as what to include under national health insurance.

In 1989, political scientist Francis Fukuyama went even further: Not only had the great ideological debate ended with the victory of capitalist democracy, but history itself could be ending. Fukuyama did not mean that time would stand still but rather that the human endpoint propounded by Hegel—free people living in free societies—was now coming into view. Not only had we beaten communism, suggested Fukuyama, there were no longer any other ideologies to challenge ours. With the end of ideology would come the end of history in the sense of the struggle of great ideas. (Life could get boring, sighed the puckish Fukuyama.)

A glance at today's news makes one doubt the Bell and Fukuyama theses. First, the collapse of communism in Europe by itself did not disprove Marx's original ideas, although now Marxists carefully distance themselves from the Soviet type of socialism. (We use socialism here to mean state control of industry, not welfarism, which is just a variation on capitalist democracy.) Socialists still debate the possibility of a benign socialism. New and dangerous ideological challenges emerged just as communism collapsed, especially Islamism and China's "authoritarian capitalism." And free democracy itself houses numerous ideological viewpoints: free market or government intervention, more welfare or less, a secular or religious state, and spreading democracy abroad or avoiding overseas involvement. Fukuyama need not worry about boredom.

Review Questions

1. Is it possible to be totally pragmatic, with no ideology?

2. How did classic liberalism turn into U.S. conservatism?

3. How close are modern liberalism and social democracy?

4. What changes did Lenin make to Marxism?

5. Why is nationalism the strongest ideology?

6. What are the main elements of fascism?

7. What is "Islamism," and why is it dangerous?

8. Do any ideologies attract today's students?

9. Could ideological politics die out?

Key Terms

classic liberalism, p. 30
communism, p. 37
conservatism, p. 33
environmentalism, p. 45
fascism, p. 40
feminism, p. 44
ideologue, p. 29

ideology, p. 29
imperialism, p. 37
Islamism, p. 45
libertarianism, p. 43
Maoism, p. 38
modern liberalism, p. 33
nationalism, p. 39

neoconservatism, p. 43
pragmatic, p. 29
revisionist, p. 36
social democracy, p. 36
Titoism, p. 38

Further Reference

Åslund, Anders, and Simeon Djankov, eds. *The Great Rebirth: Lessons From the Victory of Capitalism over Communism*. Washington, DC: Peterson Institute, 2014.

Baradat, Leon P. *Political Ideologies: Their Origins and Impact*, 11th ed. New York: Longman, 2011.

Cohen, G. A. *Why Not Socialism?* Princeton, NJ: Princeton University Press, 2009.

Fawcett, Edmund. *Liberalism: The Life of an Idea*. Princeton, NJ: Princeton University Press, 2014.

Frank, Thomas. *The Wrecking Crew: How Conservatives Rule*. New York: Metropolitan, 2008.

Frum, David. *Comeback: Conservatism That Can Win Again*. New York: Doubleday, 2009.

Grosby, Steven. *Nationalism: A Very Short Introduction*. New York: Oxford University Press, 2005.

Heilbrunn, Jacob. *They Knew They Were Right: The Rise of the Neocons*. New York: Doubleday, 2008.

Judt, Tony, and Timothy Snyder. *Thinking the Twentieth Century*. New York: Penguin, 2012.

Kristol, Irving. *The Neoconservative Persuasion: Selected Essays, 1942–2009*. New York: Basic Books, 2011.

Krugman, Paul. *The Conscience of a Liberal*. New York: Norton, 2007.

O'Hara, Kieron. *Conservatism*. Chicago, IL: University of Chicago Press, 2011.

Phares, Walid. *The War of Ideas: Jihadism against Democracy*. New York: Palgrave, 2007.

Sandle, Mark. *Communism*. New York: Longman, 2006.

Schmitt, Richard, ed. *Toward a New Socialism*. Lanham, MD: Lexington, 2007.

Sperber, Jonathan. *Karl Marx: A Nineteenth-Century Life*. New York: Liveright, 2013.

Tismaneanu, Vladimir. *The Devil in History: Communism, Fascism, and Some Lessons of the Twentieth Century*. Berkeley. CA: University of California Press, 2012.

Wolfe, Alan. *The Future of Liberalism*. New York: Knopf Doubleday, 2010.

Chapter 3
States

Learning Objectives

3.1 Explain with examples the institutionalization of power.

3.2 Distinguish between effective, weak, and failed states.

3.3 Contrast unitary and federal systems.

3.4 Explain the relationship between electoral systems and party systems.

3.5 Delineate the ways the state may relate to the economy.

The world is horrified at mass murder and abduction in northeast Nigeria. The demented Islamists of Boko Haram ("Western education is sinful") sold kidnapped schoolgirls into slavery. There was no easy way to crush this angry movement because corrupt and lawless Nigeria was too weak. Nigeria lacks the strong, cohesive governance that we take for granted. And Nigeria is not poor, but its vast oil revenues flow into the pockets of a powerful few. Large areas, including the impoverished northeast, get little or nothing. Nigeria illustrates the "weak state"—parts of it border on **anarchy**. In the oil-rich Niger Delta, unemployed young men join rebel-criminal bands because it is the best job they can get. Many countries around the world are weak states. Political scientists understand that the terms "state" or "nation" mask wide variations in actual ability to govern.

anarchy
Absence of government.

What are nations and states? A **nation** is a population with a certain sense of itself, a cohesiveness, a shared history and culture, and often (but not always) a common language. A **state** is a government structure, usually sovereign and powerful enough to enforce its writ. (Notice that here we use state in its original sense; the fifty U.S. states are not states in this sense of the word.) With the addition of South Sudan in 2011, there are 194 states in the world.

nation
Population with a historic sense of self.

state
Government structures of a nation.

Which came first, states or nations? Many suppose nations did, but in most cases states created their nations. The Zulus of South Africa, for example, are an artificially created nation put together from many clans and tribes two centuries ago by a powerful warrior, Shaka. Paris united many regions, mostly by the sword, to create France and inculcated Frenchness by education, language, and centralized administration. The French nation is an artificial creation of the French state. The United States was put together by a few men in Philadelphia from thirteen colonies. While assimilating tens of millions of immigrants, the United States developed a sense of nationhood based largely on the ideals of its founding documents and *political culture*. Nations do not fall from heaven but are created by human craftsmanship of varying quality.

Institutionalized Power

3.1 **Explain with examples the institutionalization of power.**

political institution
Established and durable pattern of authority.

Political institutions are the working structures of government, such as legislatures and executive departments. Institutions may or may not be housed in impressive buildings, although that can bolster their authority. The U.S. Supreme Court, even if it met in a tent, would be an important institution as long as its decisions were obeyed. It was not clear what the powers of the Supreme Court were to be when it began, but forceful personalities and important cases gave it power. Likewise, the Federal Reserve Board ("the Fed") evolved from calming bank panics, to fighting inflation, to arranging bailouts of financial giants. Congress could not do the job, so the Fed took on whatever new tasks were needed to stabilize the U.S. economy. Good institutions are flexible and evolve.

Authority—respect for political leaders—is a fluid thing and requires continual maintenance. A political institution is congealed or partly solidified authority. Over time, people have become used to looking to political institutions to solve problems, decide controversies, and set directions. Institutions, because they are composed of many persons and (if they are effective) last many generations, take on lives of their own apart from the people temporarily associated with them. The permanency of institutions beyond the individuals running them gives the political system stability; citizens know who is in charge and what is permissible.

Institutions are bigger than individual leaders. When President Nixon resigned under threat of impeachment in 1974, the institution of the presidency was scarcely touched. If there had been a series of such presidents, and if they had refused to resign, the institution itself would have been damaged. Some dictators try to make themselves into institutions, but they fail; the institutions they tried to build unravel upon their deaths. Josip Tito ruled Yugoslavia for thirty-five years and attempted to ensure his system would survive him, but it was based too much on himself. Eleven years after his death, Yugoslavia split apart in bloody fighting. Dictators seldom build lasting institutions; they rarely **institutionalize** their personal power.

Powerful inhabitants of an office can sometimes put their personal stamp on the institution. George Washington retired after two terms, and until FDR no president tried to serve longer. Washington institutionalized term limits into the presidency that were not codified into law until the Twenty-Second Amendment in 1951. West Germany's first chancellor, Konrad Adenauer, offered such decisive leadership that the chancellorship has been powerful ever since.

A basic way to study institutions is to locate the most powerful offices of a political system: Who's got the power? Constitutions may help but do not tell the whole story. The U.S. Constitution indicates the executive and the legislative powers are equal and in balance, but over two centuries power has gravitated to the presidency. The French constitution, set up by Charles de Gaulle in 1958, seems to give the presidency near-dictatorial powers. But French legislative elections sometimes produce parliaments of one party facing a president of another, "gridlock" in U.S. terms. The French president solved the problem by voluntarily letting an opposition prime minister take a bigger role, what the French call "cohabitation." Constitutions evolve in practice if not in wording.

A somewhat archaic question is the "form of state," whether a country is a **monarchy** or a **republic**. Almost all countries are now republics, which does not necessarily mean good or democratic. Figurehead constitutional monarchies still reign symbolically but do not actually rule in Britain, Norway, Sweden, Denmark, Spain, and Holland, which are happy with that status. Traditional, working monarchies are still found in the Arab world—Morocco, Saudi Arabia, Jordan, Kuwait, and others—but may be doomed unless they can turn themselves into limited constitutional monarchies. Failure to do so has led to the overthrow of traditional monarchies and their replacement by revolutionary regimes in Egypt, Iraq, Libya, Ethiopia, and Iran.

institutionalize
To make a political relationship permanent.

monarchy
Hereditary rule by one person.

republic
A political system without a monarch.

Classic Works

Aristotle's Six Types of Government

The earliest and most famous classification of governments was Aristotle's in the fourth century B.C. He distinguished among three legitimate kinds of government—where the ruling authority acts in the interests of all—and three corrupt counterparts—where government acts only in the interests of self.

A monarchy, according to Aristotle, is one person ruling in the interest of all. But monarchy can degenerate into tyranny, the corrupt form, under which the single ruler exercises power for the benefit of self. Aristocracy, Greek for rule of the best (*aristos*), is several persons ruling in the interest of all. But this legitimate rule by a fair and just elite can decay into oligarchy, the corrupt form, in which several persons rule in the interest of themselves.

Aristotle saw the *polity* (what we might call constitutional democracy) as the rule of many in the interests of all and the best form of government. All citizens have a voice in selecting leaders and framing laws, but formal constitutional procedures protect rights. Aristotle warned that polity can decay into the corrupt form, democracy, the rule of many in the interests of themselves, the worst form of government. Aristotle saw it happen in Athens, leading to the ruinous Pelopennisian War. Seduced by clever speeches in times of tension, the masses in a democracy fall under the sway of corrupt and selfish demagogues, who plunder citizens' property and lead the country to war. Aristotle's classification, which reigned for nearly 25 centuries, is still useful and can be summarized like this:

Who Governs	Legitimate Forms *Rule in the Interest of All*	Corrupt Forms *Rule in the Interest of Selves*
One	Monarchy	Tyranny
A few	Aristocracy	Oligarchy
Many	Polity	Democracy

Effective, Weak, and Failed States

3.2   **Distinguish between effective, weak, and failed states.**

Not all states really function as states; some hardly function at all. Just because a country has a flag and UN seat does not prove that it is a serious state. No world tribunal classifies states on the basis of their strength, but analysts see at least three categories:

Effective states control and tax their entire territory. Laws are mostly obeyed. Government looks after the general welfare and security. Corruption is fairly minor. Effective states tend to be better off, to collect considerable taxes (25 to 50 percent of GDP), and be democracies with free and fair elections. Effective states include Japan, the United States, and most European countries. Some put the best of these states into a "highly effective" category.

weak state

One unable to govern effectively, corrupt, and penetrated by crime.

Weak states are characterized by the penetration of crime into politics. You cannot tell where politics leaves off and crime begins. The government does not have the strength to fight lawlessness, drug trafficking, corruption, poverty, and breakaway movements. Justice is bought. Democracy is preached more than practiced, and elections are often rigged. Little is collected in taxation. Revenues from natural resources, such as Mexico's and Nigeria's oil, disappear into private pockets. Much of Asia, Africa, and Latin America are weak states.

Failed states have essentially no national government, although some pretend they do. Warlords, militias, and drug lords do as they wish. There is no law besides the gun. Territorial breakup threatens. Education and health standards plunge (as in the increase of HIV/AIDS). Many count Afghanistan, Libya, and Somalia as failed states. Pirates make their home in Somalia because there is no state power to stop them (and no jobs for young men). Only outside assistance and pressure keep these two countries from disappearing altogether. Some fear that Yemen, home to Islamist fighters, and the Central African Republic, wracked by Christian-Muslim war, are becoming failed states.

failed state
One incapable of even minimal governance, with essentially no national government.

Theories

Political Development in Three Stages

Stanford political scientist Francis Fukuyama advances an important theory why some countries are *failed states*. Despite our best efforts and billions of dollars, Afghanistan and Iraq are closer to anarchy than to democracy. They were in effect building second floors without first floors or foundations. A house without a foundation cannot stand.

Fukuyama sees three stages that cannot be skipped over. The first, long ago, is the establishment of the "state," usually by a monarch who gathers tribes and regions under him by the sword. Like Hobbes, Fukuyama doesn't require this king to be "good," just powerful enough to control or crush obstreperous elements. Many developing areas never established strong states.

The monarch soon requires bureaucrats to run the kingdom. The better this bureaucracy—loyal, literate, and relatively uncorrupt—the stronger the state. Without a good bureaucracy, the state is permanently flawed and weak. At first, bureaucratic jobs are sold; much later, they become impersonal and merit-based.

Next comes the more recent stage, the "rule of law" that all must obey. Churches, especially if they are outside of direct monarchical control, contribute by setting moral standards and inculcating a sense of right and wrong. Authoritarian system deliberately confuse rule of law with "rule by law" and "law of the ruler," hundreds of capricious laws to punish opponents and dissidents.

Once these two stages are firmly established, the system may be ready for the final stage, what Fukuyama calls "accountability" or more recently democracy, a fairly new thing. Parliament's trial and beheading of Charles I in 1649 for acting above the law showed the emergence of a pre-democratic accountability. The expansion of the franchise in the nineteenth century in the United States, Britain, and a few Continental countries brought democracy.

Now, if Fukuyama is right, what if you try to set up a democracy without a strong state or rule of law? It may try to look democratic for a while, with rigged elections and one-party rule but will collapse. Democracy may come too soon in the life of a nation, before the first two stages are established. This is what happened almost uniformly throughout Latin America until the 1980s. The neocons' attempt to establish democracy in Iraq had to fail; it had no foundation, not even a state.

Unitary or Federal Systems

3.3   **Contrast unitary and federal systems.**

An important and basic institutional choice is the territorial structure of the nation: unitary or federal. A **unitary system** accords its component areas little autonomy; most governance radiates from the capital city. The **first-order civil divisions**—departments in France, provinces in the Netherlands, counties in Sweden, prefectures in Japan—are largely administered by national authorities with only small local inputs. The first-order civil divisions of **federalism**—U.S. and Brazilian states, German *Länder*, and Swiss cantons—have considerable political lives of their own and cannot be legally erased or easily altered by the central power.

Unitary Systems

Unitary governments control local authorities and citizens' lives more than federal systems do. France's education ministry in Paris draws up school curricula in order to reduce regional differences in language and culture, which at one time were very strong. A century ago, a French education minister looked at his watch and proudly told an interviewer which Latin verbs were being conjugated all over France. Unitary states have national police forces and court systems, whose officers are appointed by the national government.

Center–periphery tensions or **regionalism** grew in several countries during the 1970s, and for several reasons. Economics was one. Local nationalists often claim that their region is poorer and shortchanged by the central government. The region may have a distinct language or culture that its people want to preserve. Many feel that important political decisions are not under local control, that they are made by distant bureaucrats. Often, regions harbor historical resentments at having long ago been conquered and forcibly merged with the larger nation. Iraqi Kurds feel this way about rule by Baghdad, which they ignore. Several unitary systems grope for solutions to the regional problem.

DEVOLUTION IN BRITAIN   The Celtic Scots and Welsh, pushed to the peripheries of Britain centuries ago by the invading Angles and Saxons, retain a lively sense of their differences from England. Many Scots and Welsh resent being ruled by London. During the 1970s, the Scottish and Welsh nationalist parties grew until they won several seats in Parliament. In 1997, the new Labour government of Tony Blair passed **devolution** bills that gave home-rule powers to Scotland, Wales, and Northern Ireland. The Scottish parliament, first elected in 1999, now has a government of "Scot Nats" with the power to tax and run Scotland's education, medical services, judicial system, and local government, somewhat like a U.S. state. Some say this makes Britain **quasi**-federal, but officially Britain is still unitary. A 2014 referendum, pushed by the Scot Nats, narrowly rejected breaking Scotland away from Britain. In 2015 national elections, the Scot Nats swept Scotand, bumping Labour out of its long-held dominance.

---

unitary system
Centralization of power in a nation's capital with little autonomy for subdivisions.

first-order civil divisions
Countries' main territorial components, such as U.S. states or Spanish provinces.

federalism
Balancing of power between a nation's capital and autonomous subdivisions, such as U.S. states.

center–periphery tension
Resentment of outlying areas at rule by nation's capital.

regionalism
Feeling of regional differences and sometimes breakaway tendencies.

devolution
Shifting some powers from central government to component units.

quasi
Nearly or almost.

Methods

Sources

Sources—where you get your facts, data, quotes, and ideas—are very important, the first things an instructor checks. Good sources are from specialized books, scholarly articles, or respected periodicals. Bad sources are ones that appear commonplace or dubious, such as textbooks (never use your current textbook as a source), encyclopedias (yes, even Wikipedia), dictionaries, and popular newsweeklies. To cite something, in parentheses and just before the period, put the author's last name followed (without comma) by the year (Smith 2010).

Google and Wikipedia are easy to use but seldom give a complete picture. They do not tell you what questions to ask. Many websites are advertising or propaganda. Most are so current or narrow that they fail to mention what happened last year or in another country; they lack historical and comparative perspective. For that, you still need books and articles.

Scholars divide sources into two types: primary and secondary. A primary source is direct material unfiltered through the mind of another. It might be a 2012 quote from Barack Obama (Jones 2013). It might be a statistical tabulation in a report (World Bank 2015, 274–275). It might be your own survey of college students.

A secondary source is another's synthesis, ideas, or opinions. It might be an article on a website about the U.S. policy toward Iran (Berry 2012). It might be a scholar's reading of the World Bank figures (Adams 2007). To use a football analogy, which is better: your personal observation of the game (primary source) or the sportscaster's description of it (secondary

source)? Instructors usually like primary sources. A paper might include as a primary source numbers from official documents, such as EPA budget cuts under Bush (Williams 2008). Williams's comments on the cuts, on the other hand, would be a secondary source (Williams). Just noting the same source twice does not make it two sources. A source means a different book or article.

Instructors are impressed if you have many good sources, say, ten in a five-page paper. If you cite a specific fact or quote, include the page number (Thompson 2001, 247). In the library's reference section, there are ways to get started fast, most on computer.

New York Times Index
Reader's Guide to Periodical Literature
Social Sciences Index
Public Affairs Information Service
CIA World Factbook
Facts on File
LexisNexis
Academic Index
First Search

For anything to do with executive-legislative relations (Congress, the White House, new laws, budgets), there's something so good it's almost cheating: *Congressional Quarterly*, which puts out a weekly, an annual, and a *Congress and the Nation* for each presidential term. For foreign countries, check the magazine *Current History* and the Country Study series of books published by the Library of Congress.

DECENTRALIZATION IN FRANCE   France was historically much more unitary than Britain. Everything is—or, until recently, was—run from Paris, a pattern that began with the absolutism of Louis XI in the fifteenth century. In the seventeenth century, Cardinal Richelieu centralized power in Paris by a system of provincial administrators, *intendants,* who reported back to him. The French Revolution, Napoleon, and republics that followed increased centralization. Now **prefects** report back from the **departments** to the interior ministry.

prefect
Administrator of a French department.

department
French first-order civil division.

Most of France's ninety-six *départements* were named after rivers to erase the historical memories of the old provinces. But France, like Britain, has distinctive regional subcultures: the Celtic Bretons (who fled from Britain centuries ago to escape the Saxons); the southerners of the Midi, whose speech is still flavored with the ancient *langue d'oc*; and the Corsicans, who speak an Italian dialect. Some Breton and Corsican separatists promote their cause with violence.

In 1960, to better coordinate economic development, President de Gaulle decreed twenty-two regions consisting of two to eight departments each. Starting in 1981, President Mitterrand instituted genuine **decentralization** that gave the regions certain economic-planning powers. The Paris-appointed prefects lost some of their powers to newly important departmental legislatures. France thus reversed five centuries of centralization.

decentralization
Shifting some administrative functions from central government to lower levels; less than *devolution*.

AUTONOMY IN SPAIN   Spain, too, decentralized. Here the problem was more urgent, for regional resentments, long buried under the dictatorial rule of Francisco Franco (1939–1975), came out with anger. Spain's regional problems were among the most difficult in Europe, second only to Yugoslavia (which disappeared). Basques and Catalans, in the north of Spain, have non-Castilian languages and distinctive cultures. In addition, many areas of Spain were granted *fueros* (local rights) in medieval times, which they treasured for centuries. Overriding regional diversity, Spanish centralizers attempted to plant a unitary system on the French model, producing great local resentment that appeared whenever Spain experimented with democracy. Breakaway movements appeared in 1874 and in the 1930s, only to be crushed by the Spanish army, which regards the unity of the country as sacred.

To appease regionalist feeling, which also appeared in more moderate forms in Catalonia, Galicia, Andalusia, and other areas, the new Spanish democracy instituted seventeen regional governments called **autonomías** with their own parliaments, taxation power, language rights, and control over local matters. A big problem lingered for decades in the Basque country in the northwest, where the terrorist ETA sought complete Basque independence with murder and bombing. Most Spaniards approve of the *autonomías*, but *center–periphery tensions*—especially in the Basque Country and Catalonia—over taxes and the sharing of revenues grew nasty during the crisis of the euro. Spain may again see breakaway movements.

autonomías
Spanish regions with devolved powers.

PROS AND CONS OF UNITARY SYSTEMS   Authority in unitary states can be absurdly overcentralized. Local government may not be able to install a traffic light or bus stop without permission from the capital. This leads citizens to ignore local affairs and produces political alienation. Centralization of power, however, can be an advantage in facing modern problems. Clear lines of authority without excess bickering among units of government can be useful. In unitary systems, the capital can marshal economic resources and coordinate planning and development. Taxation is nearly the same nationwide, so firms and individuals do not flee to low-tax states, as in the United States. Education standards can be high and uniform, as in Japan.

Case Studies

The Shaky Lives of Confederations

Theoretically, a third alternative to unitary and federal systems is the **confederation**. In a unitary system, power is concentrated in the national capital. In a federal system, power is balanced between the **center** and the components. In confederations, the component parts can override the center.

Confederations tend to have short lives; they either fall apart or become federations. This was the fate of the early United States under the Articles of Confederation.

Similarly, in the Confederate States of America, the states had such independence that they could not effectively wage the Civil War. Switzerland still calls itself a confederation (*Confoederatio Helvetica*)—which the Swiss proudly date to 1291—but it is now a federal system. The European Union (EU) started as a confederation, but with the growth of the powers of Brussels (its headquarters), especially with economic and monetary union (the euro currency), it is trying to become a federal system.

Japan gives a certain amount of autonomy to its subunits, but they, too, tug in a quasi-federal direction. An 1871 copy of the French system, Japan has forty-three **prefectures** plus its three largest cities and its thinly populated northernmost island, each with an elected governor and unicameral assembly. Their activities are still overseen and limited by the home affairs ministry in Tokyo, and they collect only about 30 percent of the taxes they need, what Japanese call "30 percent autonomy." Colorful, outspoken prefectural governors have recently been demanding more autonomy.

China is an in-between situation. Although unitary in form, it has decentralized administration to its twenty-three provinces and four biggest cities, which are instructed to do whatever it takes to grow the economy. Each provincial Communist Party chief structures administration as he wishes. The result is a legal patchwork that encourages violations of human rights, environmental degradation, and major corruption. Some liberal Chinese thinkers actually favor tighter central administration to promote uniform rule of law.

confederation
Political system in which components override *center*.

center
Nation's capital and its powers.

prefecture
Japanese first-order civil division.

Federal Systems

Federalism gives first-order civil divisions much autonomy while the central government runs areas that are inherently national. It is a difficult balancing act that varies among federal nations. Americans, with one of the first federal systems, sometimes urge federalism on other nations, such as Iraq, where recent hostility among Iraq's Shia, Sunni, and Kurds have led to major internal war. The Soviet Union and Mexico became so centralized that some wondered if they were still federal. The crux of a federal system is that the component states have some powers that cannot be easily overridden by the central government.

The components of a federal system are typically represented in an upper house such as the U.S. Senate or German Bundesrat. (Unitary systems do not really need upper houses, but most have them.) In federal systems, the central government has exclusive control over foreign, defense, and monetary policy. The states typically control education, police, highways, and other close-to-home affairs. Because the division of these powers is seldom clear or permanent, federalism rests on a delicate and changing balance between central power and local autonomy.

There are several reasons to form a federal union. The first is national security; small and weak states cannot defend themselves against powerful aggressors. (This was one of the main arguments of *The Federalist*.) The pooling of diplomatic and military resources of the states made Bismarck's Germany a major power. Federal unions serve economic purposes. U.S. prosperity is based in large part on its continent-wide market without trade barriers, a feat the European Union has copied. Federalism is often the only way to protect national unity. As Britain freed India in 1947, New Delhi set up a federal system that allowed such states as Bengal and Punjab to maintain their own languages and cultures while joining the Indian nation. Indian states would not have entered the federal union without a guarantee of local autonomy. Much of Latin America—especially the large countries of Argentina, Brazil, and Mexico—saw federalism as the only way to control their vast territories. Belgium in 1993 switched from a unitary to a federal system to give its two languages (French and Flemish) their own turf. The two still dislike each other, and Belgium could split apart.

PROS AND CONS OF FEDERAL SYSTEMS   Citizens are closest to their local governments, where they can influence officials and see how decisions are made. U.S. states have been called "laboratories of democracy" because they can experiment with new programs. If they work, they can be copied nationwide; if they fail, not much harm is done. On the other hand, local governments may lack the money to finance programs, and their officials are sometimes incompetent and corrupt. Local decision-making can lead to duplication of services and poor coordination.

The relationship of the states or provinces to other levels of government varies among federal systems. Each of Germany's sixteen Länder has its own constitution and government for **Land** affairs. The Landtag (state legislature) can even affect the national policy because it elects members of the Bundesrat (the upper house of the national legislature). India is unique among federal states because New Delhi can proclaim "president's rule" during disorder in a state and take over its government.

Land
German federal first-order civil division; plural *Länder*.

Each of America's fifty states can legislate in any area not delegated to the federal government or to the people. Usually, education, welfare, civil law, certain taxes, and licensing of professions are state functions. However, in the twentieth century, the federal government expanded in the areas of civil law, welfare, and economic regulation. The younger Bush moved education standards to the federal level with his No Child Left Behind Act, something that many states and traditional Republicans did not like. Dependent on federal grants and revenue sharing, the states must meet federal standards in many areas, even when the federal government cannot directly demand it. Washington, for example, threatened to withhold federal highway funds if states did not make 21 the legal drinking age. Most quickly did.

From the beginning, the United States has debated the proper role of the federal government and worried that "sectionalism" could pull the Union apart, which it did. Southern insistence on "states' rights"—the polite way to say slavery—led to secession and civil war. In the 1960s, controversial U.S. Supreme Court decisions prompted a campaign to curb the power of federal courts. Some insist that the concentration of power in Washington perverts American federalism and encroaches on individual freedoms. At the same time, local governments and citizens continue to rely on federal help in solving complex—and expensive—problems. Federalism is not an easy system to maintain and does not necessarily solve the problems of large and diverse countries. Consider the following.

EX-SOVIET FEDERALISM   On paper, the Soviet Union was a federation: Its fifteen **republics** even had the right to secede. In practice, under the tight control of the Communist Party—although usually staffed by local talent (Georgians ran Georgia, Uzbeks ran Uzbekistan, and so on)—they obeyed Moscow. Beneath a centralized veneer, however, lurked disunion. Gorbachev underestimated local nationalism, and when he allowed **glasnost** in the late 1980s, many Soviet republics went for independence, led by the Baltic states of Lithuania, Latvia, and Estonia, which Stalin had brutally annexed in 1940. With the collapse of the Soviet Union at the end of 1991, all fifteen republics proclaimed themselves independent. Now Russia aims to regain what it calls the "near abroad" either by economic ties or by military means, as in Georgia and Ukraine.

republic
In Communist Soviet Union and Yugoslavia, federal first-order civil division.

glasnost
Gorbachev's policy of media openness.

The bulk of the old Soviet Union continued as the Russian Federation, which is composed of eighty-nine autonomous republics, districts, regions, and even cities, most of which have signed a federation treaty with Moscow. Several areas, home to some of the hundred-plus ethnic groups within Russia, refused to sign and billed themselves as independent. The largely Muslim North Caucasus never liked being ruled by Moscow, and some areas now try to break away. Moscow, fearing that Chechen independence would encourage such demands elsewhere, brutally crushed Chechnya. Boston got a taste of Chechen terrorism in 2013. Putin reinstituted central control over unruly governors by creating seven super-regions headed by former colleagues from the security police.

Could the three Communist federations—the Soviet Union, Yugoslavia, and Czechoslovakia—have devised a more genuine federalism that would not have fallen apart? Or were these federations of unlike components doomed from the start? The Communists, by pretending to have solved the "nationalities question," merely suppressed it until it came out later.

EX-YUGOSLAV FEDERALISM Yugoslavia, founded only in 1918, was a new and somewhat artificial country whose components were rarely content. It fell apart once before, in World War II, when its German conquerors set up an independent Croatia with expanded territories. Croatian fascists murdered a third of a million Serbs and others, sowing hatred that erupted in the 1990s. The Communist Partisans who fought the Nazis thought federalism was the answer. Under the maverick Communist Tito, Yugoslav federalism let Yugoslavia's six republics run local affairs and sent equal numbers of representatives to both houses of parliament. Yugoslavia's collective presidency had one member from each republic.

This hyperfederal setup, however, did not calm local nationalism; it inflamed it. Each republic wanted its own railroads, steel mills, and control of its economy. Under Tito, the Communist Party and security police could hold Yugoslavia together, but after he died in 1980 the republics went their separate ways. Tito deserves blame for this, as he designed an unworkable system that had to fall apart. Yugoslavia is an example of poor institutional choices.

Slovenia, Macedonia, and Croatia declared their independence in 1991, followed by Bosnia in 1992. Serbian forces practiced "ethnic cleansing" and murdered thousands. A 1995 U.S.-brokered and NATO-enforced peace calmed Bosnia, but ethnic Albanians in Kosovo, a Serb province, moved for independence. In 1999, a U.S.-led bombing campaign prevented Serbia from wholesale massacre of Kosovars. Bosnia and Kosovo are, in effect, NATO protectorates. Even tiny Montenegro chose independence from Serbia in 2006.

centrifugal
Pulling apart.

CANADIAN FEDERALISM Canada is another federation with **centrifugal** tendencies. The British allowed the French-speaking Québécois to keep their language, and francophones became second-class citizens, poorer than other Canadians and discriminated against because almost all private and government business was in English. In the 1960s, the Parti Québécois (PQ) sprang up, dedicated to Quebec's independence from Canada. To appease them, the federal government in Ottawa in 1969 made Canada bilingual, with French and English having equal rights. The PQ wanted more and made French the only official language of Quebec. Trying to hold the federation—which came to look a bit like a confederation as the provinces overruled the center—together, Ottawa and the provincial governments laboriously developed two new federal accords, both rejected. The stumbling block was a separate status for Quebec as a "distinct society." Quebeckers said it did not go far enough; other Canadians said it went too far. Quebec's drive for sovereignty has receded, but Canadians still quarrel over federalism.

Federalism is difficult. These three cases remind us that federalism cannot cure everything. If the components are too different from one another—culturally, economically, linguistically, or historically—a federal system will not hold together. Shared language and culture, as in the United States, Australia, Brazil, and Germany, is a big help. With that as a foundation, the right balance must be found between central and state governments. The United States is still searching for its correct balance.

Electoral Systems

● **3.4**   **Explain the relationship between electoral systems and party systems.**

Electoral systems are also important institutional choices; they help determine the number of parties, the ease of forming a stable government, and the degree of citizen interest in politics. There are two general types of electoral systems with many variations.

Single-Member Districts

The simplest electoral system is the Anglo-American **single-member district**, wherein one member of Parliament or of Congress is elected to represent the entire district by winning a plurality (not necessarily a majority) of the votes. Called "single-member districts with plurality win" or "first past the post" (FPTP), this system pushes interest groups and political factions to coalesce into two big parties. If there were, say, four parties who received 25, 25, 24, and 26 percent of the vote, respectively, the last would win. Losing parties that are not far apart ideologically quickly recognize their advantage is to combine for the next election. Then this new party wins, forcing other small parties to combine. The message: Merge or lose. Woodrow Wilson won in 1912 only because Theodore Roosevelt split the Republican Party. FPTP countries tend to have two-party systems.

> **single-member districts**
> Electoral system that elects one person per district, as in the United States and Britain.

   Third parties exist in such systems but without much hope of winning. They may have an impact as protest and pressure groups on the big parties. The British Liberal Democrats can take as many as one vote in five, but because they are dispersed throughout the country, they win few seats. Single-member systems are unkind to third parties except in situations like Canada, Scotland, and India, where regional concentration of parties permits many to win seats.

ADVANTAGES OF SINGLE-MEMBER DISTRICTS   Politics in FPTP systems tend to the center of the political spectrum, for this is usually where the most votes are. This inhibits the growth of extremism. If leaders out of touch with mainstream views control the party, it will lose, and the losing leaders will likely be replaced. This is what happened with the Republicans after the conservative Goldwater in 1964, the Democrats after the liberal McGovern in 1972, and the Labour Party after two ineffective leaders, Gordon Brown in 2010 and Ed Miliband in 2015. Public opinion in most democracies forms a bell-shaped curve, with most people in the center. Parties that depart too far from the center penalize themselves. Some argue that the Republicans did that in 2012.

   Most FPTP systems also give a clear parliamentary majority to one party—thus they are called **majoritarian** systems—so coalitions are rarely necessary. Gains are magnified in single-member systems. In 2015, for example, the British Conservatives won only 37 percent of the vote but took 51 percent of the seats

> **majoritarian**
> Electoral system that gives more than half of seats to one party.

in Parliament. Remember, seats in FPTP systems are not proportional to votes. A relatively small swing of votes from one party to another can translate into many parliamentary seats, perhaps enough to form a parliamentary majority and a new government. The United States, with its constitutionally mandated separation of powers, muddies the advantage of this system by frequently giving the White House to one party and the Congress to another.

DISADVANTAGES OF SINGLE-MEMBER DISTRICTS   FPTP creates an artificial majority in parliament, which makes governing easier but does not fairly or accurately reflect public opinion or voting strength. In each district, the winner takes all. If there are two parties, the losing party, even if it received 49 percent of the vote, gets no representation. In some cases—including the United States—the party with the most votes nationwide fails to win a majority of seats, depending on how their votes are distributed across districts. Thanks to computers, most U.S. states are now so perfectly **gerrymandered**—some of the districts have bizarre shapes—that close to 400 out of 435 House seats are "safe" for one party or the other with few close or unpredictable races. This undermines democracy and builds extreme partisanship with little cooperation across party lines.

gerrymander
To draw electoral district boundaries to favor one party.

A single-member district that is competitive, where the election can go either way, pushes candidates to the political center and mutes partisanship. In such districts, the two big U.S. parties sometimes sound similar and centrist, resulting in voter boredom and low turnout. The European multiparty systems have higher voter turnouts, partly because voters can choose from a more interesting menu of parties.

Proportional Representation

proportional representation (PR)
Elects representatives by party's percent of vote.

Proportional representation (PR) systems are based on multimember districts; that is, each district sends several representatives to parliament, not just one. In the small countries of the Netherlands and Israel, the entire country is one big district. In Sweden the district is a county, in Spain a province. If the district is entitled to ten seats, each party offers voters a *party list* of ten candidates. Each voter picks one list, and the party gets seats in proportion to the votes it receives. If the party won 30 percent of the votes in a ten-member district, it would send the first three names on its party list to parliament. A party with 20 percent would send its first two names.

Rarely does the vote divide so neatly; one party might win 42 percent of eleven seats. Would it get 4.62 seats? How do you send a fraction of a person to parliament? The most common way to handle this is the d'Hondt mathematical formula, which slightly overrepresents the larger parties at the expense of smaller ones. Sweden "tops off" numerical discrepancies by using nationwide seats. Sweden's twenty-one districts elect only 310 of the Riksdag's 349 seats; the remaining thirty-nine seats are parceled out to rectify variances from the parties' national percentages.

To minimize the problem of splinter, nuisance, or extremist parties, PR systems require parties to win a certain percentage of the vote in order to obtain any seats at all. These are called "threshold clauses." In Germany and Poland, a party must win at least 5 percent of the vote nationwide; in Sweden and Italy, 4 percent; in Israel, 3.25 percent.

ADVANTAGES OF PROPORTIONAL REPRESENTATION PR means that the country's legislature more accurately reflects public opinion and party strength. Parties do not have to capture the big middle of the electoral spectrum as in Anglo-American systems and can thus articulate ideologies and principles more clearly because they do not try to please everybody. If a small part of the population really believes in something, they can run as a party and, provided they clear the electoral threshold, win seats. They are not forced to amalgamate into bigger parties and dilute their views, as in FPTP systems.

DISADVANTAGES OF PROPORTIONAL REPRESENTATION PR systems do little to fight party splintering, so they often lead to multiparty systems. This tendency, however, is waning, and two-plus party systems have emerged, even in PR systems. Sweden and Spain have two large parties plus a few smaller ones. Their political systems are not terribly splintered. Israel, on the other hand, is plagued by splinter parties; typically ten or more are elected to the Knesset. If the largest party falls short of half the seats in PR systems—usually the case— it must form a coalition with other parties. These coalitions are often unstable

majority
More than half.

plurality
The most, even if less than half.

mixed-member
Hybrid electoral system that uses both single-member districts and proportional representation.

Case Studies

French and German Variations

France uses single-member districts but with runoffs. Few candidates win a **majority** (more than 50 percent, not the same as the simple plurality in the Anglo-American system) on the first round, so those with at least an eighth of the vote go to a runoff a week later. Then a simple **plurality** suffices to win. By previous agreement between parties, some candidates withdraw and urge their supporters to vote for the candidate closest to them ideologically, so in most second-round contests, there are only two or three candidates. The first round in France is somewhat like a U.S. primary election.

The German system is basically half FPTP and half *proportional representation* (PR). On a split ballot, Germans vote in one column for an individual to represent their district; here plurality wins. In a second column, they vote for a party to represent their *Land* (state) in proportion to the votes received. Overall strength in the Bundestag is set by the second vote, the one for parties, so seats are proportional to votes. Half of the seats, though, are reserved for the 328 winners of the district contests. Germany's split representation system produced a *two-plus party system* and governing stability. The German system is a modification of the PR system and was designed after World War II to prevent a return to the weak and unstable Weimar system, which had proportional representation that treated the country as one big district. In the 1990s, Italy, New Zealand, and Japan adopted German-style **mixed-member** systems that combine single-member districts with PR for their parliamentary elections.

and unable to decide important issues. Where one party is big enough to govern alone, however, the system is quite stable. The Anglo-American systems mostly confer a majority and thus stability. When no party won a majority of seats in Britain in 2010, it too had to form a coalition (of Conservatives and Liberal Democrats, who did not get along). Italy, since World War II, exemplifies extreme instability. Its multiparty coalition governments on average last less than a year.

States and the Economy

3.5   **Delineate the ways the state may relate to the economy.**

Yet another way to classify governments is how they handle the economy. States face two questions: (1) How much of the economy should the state own or supervise? (2) How much of the nation's wealth should be redistributed to help the poorer sectors of society? The answers produce four basic approaches to promoting the general welfare: laissez-faire, statism, socialism, and the welfare state. These array themselves into a fourfold table (see Figure 3.1).

In a **laissez-faire** system, the government owns little or no industry and redistributes little in the form of welfare programs. These countries follow Adam Smith, seconded by Milton Friedman, who argued that government interference in the economy decreases growth and prosperity. The theory here is that private enterprise and individual initiative make a nation both free and prosperous.

A **welfare state** owns little or no industry but does redistribute wealth to the less well-off. Sometimes known as "social democracies," the welfare states of northwest Europe offer "cradle-to-grave" benefits in health insurance, child care, job training, and retirement funds. To pay for this, they charge the world's highest taxes—in Sweden and Denmark some 50 percent of GDP. Industry, though, is private and moneymaking.

Statism is an old system that predates laissez-faire. In its current form, as in Russia and China, it is called *state capitalism*. In these systems, the state

laissez-faire
French for "let it be"; economic system of minimal government interference and supervision; capitalism.

welfare state
Economic system of major government redistribution of income to poorer citizens.

statism
Economic system of state ownership of major industries to enhance power and prestige of state; a precapitalist system.

Figure 3.1 Statist, socialist, laissez-faire, and welfare-state approaches.

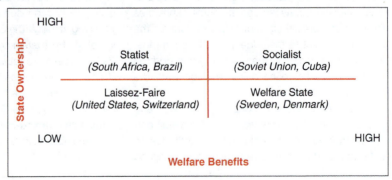

(meaning the national government) is the number-one capitalist, owning and running much major industry but providing few welfare benefits. Statism began when the French kings founded a powerful, centralized state that supervised industry for the sake of French wealth and power. Sometimes called by its French name *étatisme,* state capitalism typically includes state ownership of railroads, steel mills, banks, oil, and other big enterprises. Small and medium business is private and competitive. Statism caught on in much of Europe and Latin America. France, Brazil, Chile, and Mexico were statist systems but reformed in a free-market direction. Many developing countries followed statist models with the argument that only the government has the money, ideas, and talent to start up new industries. State-owned firms, however, are usually inefficient because they are run by bureaucrats and face little competition; often they operate at a loss and have to be subsidized by the national treasury. China's state-owned enterprises (SOEs) are a major drain on its banking system.

A **socialist** system practices both state ownership and extensive welfare benefits. Exemplified by the former Soviet Union, government owns nearly all the means of production, claiming it runs the economy in the interests of the society as a whole. However, the collapse of Communist regimes (which called themselves "socialist"; we called them "Communist") indicates they worked poorly. Today, only North Korea and Cuba remain as (negative) examples of socialism, and their systems seem ripe for change.

socialism
Economic system of government ownership of industry, allegedly for good of whole society; opposite of capitalism.

In actual practice, governments often combine elements of these four systems. Even the basically laissez-faire United States demands welfare measures and bailouts of financial giants deemed "too big to fail." Communist China and Vietnam, once strictly socialist, now have growing private, capitalistic sectors. These questions are never settled, and countries often change their combinations. In our day, we have seen a massive shift away from state-owned industry in Eastern Europe, France, and Latin America. Welfare states like Sweden, feeling the pinch of too-generous benefits and too-high taxes, have elected conservative governments.

A basic American attitude is that government should be kept small. In much of the rest of the world, however, state power is accepted as natural and good. In France, for example, Louis XI started a strong state in the fifteenth century, and Louis XIII and Cardinal Richelieu expanded it in the seventeenth century. This strong state implanted itself into French consciousness and later spread through most of Europe. The French-type **strong state** supervised the economy and education, collected taxes, built highways and canals, and fielded standing armies. A bureaucratic elite, trained in special schools, ran the country.

strong state
Modern form of government, able to administer and tax the entire nation.

These attitudes lasted well into the twentieth century and are still present. Defeated by Germany in 1870–1871, the French elite used the state as an *agent of modernization.* Paris tried to build a unified and cohesive population, to turn "peasants into Frenchmen." A centralized school system stamped out local dialects, broke stagnant rural traditions, and recruited the best talent for universities. State-owned industries turned France into an economic power. Beaten by Germany again in World War II, the French elite again used state power to modernize France.

Did it work? France did modernize greatly, but was this the fastest or most efficient way? Britain and the United States advanced further with minimal government supervision; competition within a free-market economy did the job faster and cheaper. (The comparison is not quite fair; Britain and the United States faced no powerful, expansionist Germany on their borders. If they had, the role of government would have been much bigger.)

Japan is another example of state-led modernization. With the Meiji Restoration of 1868, Tokyo assigned various branches of industry to samurai clans, provided funds, and told them to copy the best of the West. In one generation, Japan went from handicrafts to heavy industry under the slogan "Rich nation, strong army!" After World War II, the Ministry of Finance and Ministry of International Trade and Industry (MITI) supervised Japan's rapid economic leap by aiming bank loans to growth industries, keeping out foreign competition, and penetrating the world market with Japanese products. Before we say government supervision of the economy does not work, we must explain why it worked in Japan. The Japanese, of course, have an entirely different and more cooperative culture. An American MITI might not work in our economic and cultural context. And Japan's economic growth has stagnated since 1990; the formula no longer worked.

Should government attempt to supervise the economy by providing plans, suggestions, industry-wide cooperation, insurance, and loans? The traditional American answer is "No, it'll just mess things up." Europeans and Canadians are amazed at the bitter controversy surrounding U.S. national healthcare insurance, something they implemented decades ago. Even in America, however, the federal government has repeatedly pushed the U.S. economy forward by acquiring large territories, letting settlers homestead them, and giving railroads rights of way. In the 1930s, the Tennessee Valley Authority brought electricity and flood control to much of the American South, an area that was largely untouched by industrialization. Conservatives disliked the 2008 bailout of major financial institutions but most agreed it was necessary. America, too, has used the state as an agent of modernization and now has federal healthcare programs. One of the great questions of modern politics is how much state intervention do we want?

Review Questions

1. What is the difference between a nation and a state?

2. What are *weak states* and *failed states*?

3. What were Aristotle's six types of government?

4. What is the crux of a political institution?

5. What are the problems of unitary and federal systems?

6. What are the two main electoral systems and their advantages and disadvantages?

7. What is the difference between socialism and statism?

8. Is the U.S. preference for minimal government shared worldwide?

9. Can or should government attempt to modernize society?

Key Terms

anarchy, p. 50
autonomías, p. 56
center, p. 57
center–periphery tension, p. 54
centrifugal, p. 60
confederation, p. 57
decentralization, p. 56
department, p. 55
devolution, p. 54
failed state, p. 53
federalism, p. 54
first-order civil divisions, p. 54
gerrymander, p. 62

glasnost, p. 59
institutionalize, p. 51
laissez-faire, p. 64
Land, p. 58
majoritarian, p. 61
majority, p. 63
mixed-member, p. 63
monarchy, p. 51
nation, p. 50
plurality, p. 63
political institution, p. 50
prefect, p. 55
prefecture, p. 57

proportional representation
  (PR), p. 62
quasi-, p. 54
regionalism, p. 54
republic, pp. 51, 59
single-member district, p. 61
socialism, p. 65
state, p. 50
statism, p. 64
strong state, p. 65
unitary system, p. 54
weak state, p. 52
welfare state, p. 64

Further Reference

Acemoglu, Daron, and James A. Robinson. *Why Nations Fail: The Origins of Power, Prosperity, and Poverty*. New York: Crown, 2012.

Burgess, Michael. *Comparative Federalism: Theory and Practice*. New York: Routledge, 2006.

Dahl, Robert A., and Bruce Stinebrickner. *Modern Political Analysis*, 6th ed. Upper Saddle River, NJ: Prentice Hall, 2003.

Farrell, David M. *Electoral Systems: A Comparative Introduction*. New York: Palgrave, 2001.

Fukuyama, Francis. *Political Order and Political Decay: From the Industrial Revolution to the Globalization of Democracy*. New York: Farrar, Straus & Giroux, 2014.

Gallagher, Michael, and Paul Mitchell, eds. *The Politics of Electoral Systems*. New York: Oxford University Press, 2006.

Hueglin, Thomas O., and Alan Fenna. *Comparative Federalism: A Systematic Inquiry*. Decorah, IA: Broadview, 2006.

LaCroix, Alison L. *The Ideological Origins of American Federalism*. Cambridge, MA: Harvard University Press, 2010.

Lijphart, Arend. *Patterns of Democracy: Government Forms and Performance in Thirty-Six Countries*. New Haven, CT: Yale University Press, 1999.

Lindblom, Charles E. *The Market System: What It Is, How It Works, and What to Make of It*. New Haven, CT: Yale University Press, 2001.

McCabe, Neil Colman, ed. *Comparative Federalism in the Devolution Era*. Lanham, MD: Lexington, 2002.

Micklethwait, John, and Adrian Wooldridge. *The Fourth Revolution: The Global Race to Reinvent the State*. New York: Penguin, 2014.

Moreno, Luis. *The Federalization of Spain*. Portland, OR: F. Cass, 2001.

Stephens, G. Ross, and Nelson Wikstrom. *American Intergovernmental Relations: A Fragmented Federal Polity*. New York: Oxford University Press, 2006.

Van Creveld, Martin. *The Rise and Decline of the State*. New York: Cambridge University Press, 1999.

Zijderveld, Anton C. *The Waning of the Welfare State: The End of Comprehensive State Succor*. Piscataway, NJ: Transaction, 1999.

Chapter 4
Constitutions and Rights

 Learning Objectives

4.1 Distinguish between constitutions and statutes.

4.2 Explain the purposes of constitutions.

4.3 Explain the variety of "rights" in the modern world.

4.4 Explain how U.S. judicial review was a first among constitutions.

4.5 Trace the development of the U.S. right to free speech.

Americans have learned that the federal government massively surveys their phone calls and e-mails. The counterterrorist effort was old and passed as a series of laws, although Congress kept mum until an intelligence technician leaked to the media. The 1978 Foreign Intelligence Surveillance Act (FISA)—sponsored by Congressional liberals to *restrain* federal snooping on U.S. citizens, as Nixon had done—set up a secret FISA court that routinely grants sweeping warrants to collect information. After 9/11, Congress hastily passed the Patriot Act to monitor phone calls, e-mails, finances, credit cards, and Muslim citizens. With several amendments, laws now require phone and Internet carriers to give the National Security Agency their metadata on all communications. NSA supercomputers run algorithms of who contacts whom, for how long, and their location. The NSA claims it does not open messages but passes suspicious patterns on to the CIA or FBI, which can ask the FISA court for more intrusive warrants.

Although the laws aim at foreign threats, they open Americans to surveillance in possible disregard of Fourth Amendment guarantees against "unreasonable searches and seizures." Both liberals and conservatives fear invasion of privacy and rise of a Big Data police state. Defenders of the programs, both Republican and Democrat, say they infringe on no rights and are essential to fight terrorism. They deplore the outing of the programs and argue that all conform to law. Congress reauthorized FISA in 2012 with scarcely a murmur and claims it is kept informed. President Obama, a former professor of constitutional law, said: "You can't have 100 percent security and also then have 100 percent privacy and zero inconvenience. We're going to have to make some choices as a society." It was a perfect case for Supreme Court review.

The question of security and safety on one hand versus freedom and privacy on the other was not a new problem in U.S. history, which has seen similar restrictions on rights in other tense situations. Every political system has a problem establishing and limiting power, especially in times of stress. A fair balance between government powers and civil liberties is hard to strike and constantly shifting.

Likewise a balance between the wishes of the majority and the rights of the **minority** are not easy choices. For example, may states ban same-sex marriages, or does that deny homosexuals equal rights? For some, same-sex marriage violated their religious beliefs. In 2015, the Supreme Court ruled 5–4 that, based on equal protection of the laws, states could not refuse to marry same-sex couples. Some localities blocked construction of Muslim houses of worship, even though the Constitution guarantees freedom of religion. A handful argued that the First Amendment does not apply to Muslims.

minority
Subgroup distinct by background, viewpoint, or practice within the larger society.

These questions raise the issues of rights and political power. Most Americans would agree that a Supreme Court decision is law even if Congress and the states dislike it. We may disagree, though, over whether Muslims praying at the airport should be kicked off their flight on the suspicion that they might blow up the plane. Should special attention be paid to Middle Eastern–looking men who might, just might, be terrorists? And if they are not terrorists, do they have the right to sue their accusers? How do we determine the limits of political power and balance the needs of the majority with the rights of individuals and minorities? Some guidelines are provided by traditions, by **statutes**, and above all by national constitutions, which lay down the basic rules for governing.

statute

An ordinary law passed by a legislature, not part of the constitution.

Constitutions

4.1   Distinguish between constitutions and statutes.

constitution

Basic rules that structure a government, usually written.

In common usage, a **constitution** is a written document outlining the structure of a political system. Political scientists define "constitution" as the rules and customs, either written or unwritten, by which a government is run. Almost all nations have constitutions because they operate according to some set of rules. In chaotic, corrupt, or dictatorial systems, constitutions may not count for much. Afghanistan, divided by armed tribes and warlords, has not been able to implement its new constitution. In Congo (formerly Zaire), dictator Mobutu allowed nothing to limit his stealing of the country's wealth. And Stalin in 1936—precisely when he began his bloody purges—set up a Soviet constitution that looked fine on paper but was a trick to fool the gullible. A few countries like Britain and Israel have no single written document but still have constitutions. British customs, laws, precedents, and traditions are so strong that the British government considers itself bound by practices developed over the centuries. Thus, British government is constitutional.

Most constitutions now also specify individual rights and freedoms. Except for the U.S. Constitution, this has been a more recent thing. Canada got its Charter of Rights and Freedoms only in 1982. Britain got the equivalent only in 2000, when it adopted the European Convention on Human Rights. Before that, British rights and freedoms were not so clear.

Constitutions are supposed to establish the forms, institutions, and limits of government and balance minority and majority interests. Not all function that way. Political scientists study not only what is written but what is actually practiced. The Constitution of the United States, for example, is very short and leaves much unsaid. Its seven articles mostly define the powers of each branch of government; the subsequent twenty-seven amendments broadly define civil rights but leave much open for interpretation.

In contrast, most constitutions written since World War II have remarkable detail. The postwar Japanese constitution, which was drafted by the U.S. military government in five days in 1946 (they had been considering its elements for some time), contains forty articles on the rights and duties of the people alone, among them the right to productive employment, a decent standard of living, and social welfare benefits—a sharp contrast to the general values of "justice…domestic tranquility…common defense…general welfare…liberty" outlined in the American Preamble. Article I of the postwar German constitution (the Basic Law) also has a long list of rights, including not only fundamental legal and political freedoms but also social and economic safeguards, including state supervision of the educational system and public control of the economy.

The 1988 Brazilian constitution enumerates many rights—forty-hour work-week, medical and retirement plans, minimum wages, maximum interest rates, environmental protection, you name it—that Brazil's economy cannot afford. These rights can block needed economic reforms. Many now believe that detailed social and economic rights should not be put into constitutions; they should be passed later as *statutes* or left to the workings of the market. Rights that cannot be fulfilled are common in newer constitutions, whose idealistic drafters thought they could fix all social and economic problems.

Britain may be able to get by with no written constitution, although the British government is thinking about drafting one. The United States manages to function with a very general constitution. In both Britain and the United States, the details are filled in by usage over time. But most recently established nations commit themselves to long written constitutions that try to spell out everything in detail.

The Highest Law of the Land

4.2   Explain the purposes of constitutions.

Nations adopt constitutions for the same reason that the ancient Mesopotamian lawgiver Hammurabi codified the laws of Babylon: to establish a supreme law of the land. Constitutions state the fundamental laws of society and are not meant to be easily revised. They are yardsticks by which activities of the government or the people are measured. A legislature can pass a law one year and repeal it the next, but amending the constitution is made deliberately much harder. In Sweden, constitutional amendments must be passed by two successive legislatures with a general election in between.

Amending the U.S. Constitution is even more difficult. The most common procedure requires the approval of two-thirds of both the Senate and the House of Representatives, then ratification by three-fourths of the state legislatures. The fact that our Constitution has been amended only seventeen times since the adoption of the Bill of Rights in 1791 illustrates the difficulty of the amendment procedure. (The last, the Twenty-Seventh Amendment of 1992, specified no congressional pay raises without an election in between.) The Equal Rights Amendment failed to pass in 1983 because fewer than three-fourths of the state legislatures voted to ratify it. Republican proposals to alter the birthright clause of the Fourteenth Amendment to exclude "anchor babies" from citizenship would face a similar daunting challenge. Japan also requires two-thirds of each house plus a majority in a referendum. The prime minister in 2013 proposed lowering the two-thirds to simple majority in both houses, plus the referendum. This was controversial throughout Asia because it would make it easier to drop Article 9, by which Japan renounces the right to go to war.

Case Studies

The Dangers of Changing Constitutions

Beware the country that keeps introducing new constitutions; it is a sign of instability and indicates that no constitution has rooted itself into the hearts and minds of the people. France since the Revolution has had fifteen constitutions, not all of them put into practice. Brazil has had seven since independence in 1822. Yugoslavia under Tito came out with a new constitution every decade, each more dubious than the one before. The 1963 Yugoslav constitution provided for a legislature of *five* chambers. Such constant experimentation with the highest law of the land meant that no constitution was established and legitimate, one reason Yugoslavia fell apart in bloodshed in 1991. Constitutions are too important to experiment with.

The General Nature of Constitutional Law

Constitutions, no matter how detailed, cannot cover every problem that may arise, so most provide for a constitutional court to interpret the highest law in specific cases. This concept of judicial interpretation of a constitution is a fairly new thing worldwide; it was pioneered by the United States and has spread only in recent decades. Accordingly, many of our examples are American.

The U.S. Constitution says that "Congress shall make no law respecting an establishment of religion, or prohibiting the free exercise thereof" in Amendment I of the Bill of Rights. This is a very general statement, and how it is interpreted in a specific case—such as prayer in school or a satanic cult—depends on those in power at the time. Does it mean that prayer in public schools breaches the separation of church and state? Or that prayer in schools is part of the free exercise of religion? Or that prayer in schools is permissible if that is what most people in a given school district want?

Constitutional law must be interpreted for specific incidents. Who has the authority to decide what the general wording of a constitution means? Starting with the United States, now more than thirty nations give the power of **judicial review** to the highest national court. Such courts rule on the constitutionality of government acts and declare null and void acts they consider unconstitutional. This power is controversial. Many critics have accused the Supreme Court (most notably when Earl Warren was chief justice from 1953 to 1969) of imposing personal philosophies as the laws of the land. To a large extent, a constitution is indeed what its interpreters say it is, but the possibility of too subjective an interpretation is a necessary risk with judicial review.

The courts do not always interpret the constitution in a consistent fashion. The Warren Court exemplified **judicial activism**, which does not necessarily mean "liberal." It refers to a judge's willingness to strike down certain laws and practices. The opposite philosophy is **judicial restraint**, when a Supreme Court sees its job not as legislating but as following the lead of Congress. Justices Oliver Wendell Holmes and Felix Frankfurter, who counseled the Court on

judicial review
Ability of courts to decide if laws are constitutional; not present in all countries.

judicial activism
Judges' willingness to override legislatures by declaring statutes unconstitutional.

judicial restraint
Judges' unwillingness to overturn statutes passed by legislatures.

judicial restraint, are regarded as great liberals. The Roberts Court, on the other hand, struck down several laws but was considered conservative.

Likewise, Germany's Federal Constitutional Court is no stranger to controversy. Modeled after the U.S. Supreme Court—except that it has sixteen justices—the German court is mandated to make sure all laws conform to the **Basic Law**. In 1975, the German court found that a law permitting abortions conflicted with the strong right-to-life provisions of the Basic Law—enacted to repudiate the horrors of the Nazi era—and declared abortion unconstitutional. In 1995, it declared unconstitutional a Bavarian law requiring a crucifix in every classroom. In 2009, the German court warned that the European Union did not override German democracy and sovereignty. Not all nations give their highest court the power to declare something unconstitutional; some reserve that power for the legislature. The British Parliament largely determines what is constitutional.

Basic Law
(German *Grundgesetz*) Germany's constitution since 1949.

Constitutions and Constitutional Government

A constitution depends largely on the way it is interpreted. Two separate nations could adopt similar constitutions but have them work differently. Sweden and Italy have similar structures, but their **political cultures** are quite different—Swedes are obedient, Italians not so much—so written rules function differently. A constitution can be a fiction. The Soviet constitution set a government framework—a federal system with a bicameral legislature, with executive and administrative powers given to the cabinet-like Council of Ministers—and accorded to its citizens a long list of democratic rights. In actuality, the elite of the Communist Party controlled nearly everything, including individual rights.

political culture
The psychology of the nation in regard to politics.

Constitutionalism means that the power of a government is limited. We see its beginnings in the Magna Carta, which England's nobles forced King John to sign in 1215. The Great Charter does not mention democracy; it merely limits the king's power and safeguards the nobles' rights. Over the centuries, however, it was used to promote democracy and individual freedom in modern Britain, the United States, and Canada. In a constitutionally governed nation, laws and institutions limit government to make sure that the fundamental rights of citizens are not violated. In contrast, a totalitarian or authoritarian government is not limited by its constitution; individuals and minority groups have little protection against arbitrary acts of government, in spite of what the constitution may say. In the 1970s, the military regimes of Argentina and Chile "disappeared" (meaning tortured and killed) thousands of suspected leftists even though their written constitutions promised human rights. Currently, Chinese intellectuals struggle to get Beijing to enforce the rights already guaranteed by China's constitution. With true constitutionalism, they argue, many problems would be solved.

constitutionalism
Degree to which government limits its powers.

The United States is no stranger to violations of minority rights. In addition to slavery and the subsequent violation of the civil rights of African Americans in the American South, perhaps the next biggest was the 1942 internment of some 110,000 Japanese Americans on the West Coast under infamous Executive Order

9066, in the mistaken belief that they were enemy aliens (most were born in the United States). Robbed of their homes, businesses, and liberty without due process of law, they were sent to ramshackle, dusty camps surrounded by barbed wire and guard towers. Not one case of disloyalty was ever demonstrated against a Japanese American; they were victims of racism and wartime hysteria.

Even Secretary of War Henry L. Stimson, who signed the order, feared it "would make a tremendous hole in our Constitution." It did, but not until 1983 did a federal court overturn the legality of internment. The incident shows that even a well-established democracy can throw out its civil liberties in a moment of exaggerated and groundless panic. (A similar reaction flared after 9/11, aimed at Muslims.) The 442nd Regimental Combat Team, recruited from Japanese Americans, was the most decorated U.S. unit of World War II.

The Purpose of a Constitution

If some nations pay little heed to what is written in their constitutions, why do they bother to write a constitution at all? Constitutions do several things: They put in writing national ideals, formalize the structure of government, and attempt to justify the government's right to govern.

A STATEMENT OF NATIONAL IDEALS   The Preamble of the U.S. Constitution proclaims its dedication to six goals: to form a more perfect union, to establish justice, to ensure domestic tranquility, to provide for the common defense, to promote the general welfare, and to secure the blessings of liberty. The 1977 Soviet constitution proclaimed the Soviet Union to be a "developed socialist society" dedicated to building a classless utopia. The constitution of the Federal Republic of Germany, seeking to repudiate the Nazis, states its determination to "serve the peace of the world" and expressly proclaims that no group of people can be stripped of their German citizenship—a reaction to Hitler's Nuremburg Laws, which made hundreds of thousands of Germans noncitizens.

Preambles and lists of rights are symbolic statements: They indicate the values, ideals, and goals of those who draft the documents. Preambles are by nature very general and have dubious legal force. How are they interpreted? What does

Case Studies

Canada's New Constitution

Canada was in a curious situation. The British North America Act of 1867, passed by the British Parliament, gave Canada its independence, but as the British Dominion of Canada it could amend its constitution only by approval of the House of Commons in London.

Increasingly, this rankled Canadians, who demanded "patriation" of their constitution—that is, bringing it back to Canada. They got this only in 1982 along with something they had never had before, a Charter of Rights and Freedoms similar to the U.S. Bill of Rights.

the U.S. Constitution mean by a "more perfect union," "establish justice," or "promote the general welfare"? Constitutions state national ideals, but the interpretation of these goals and values requires some decisions.

FORMALIZES THE STRUCTURE OF GOVERNMENT   A constitution is also a blueprint, a written description of who does what in government, defining the authority and limiting the powers of each branch and providing for regularized channels through which conflict may be resolved. Articles I through III of the U.S. Constitution outline the duties of Congress, the president, and the judiciary. Congress may collect taxes and customs duties but is prohibited from taxing exports. The president is named commander in chief of the armed forces but must have the "advice and consent" of the Senate to conclude treaties. In a system in which there is **separation of powers**, the constitution divides authority and responsibilities among the various branches of government; it also limits the power of each branch.

No other constitution uses "checks and balances" like the American one; most, in fact, specify the unification of power, with no split between legislature and executive. Few other countries abhor the concentration of power the way the U.S. Founding Fathers did. The 1993 Russian constitution gives the executive far more power than the parliament, the **State Duma**, an imbalance that bothers few Russians, most of whom prefer a strong hand at the top to prevent anarchy and stabilize the economy. Again, political culture counts for a lot in how a constitution actually works.

Constitutions also outline the division of power between central and regional or local governments. In a federal system, powers and responsibilities are divided between one national government and several provincial or state governments. In the U.S. Constitution, this division is a general one; any powers not accorded to the central government are reserved for the states or the people. This division of power has become less clear-cut, especially in recent years, as the federal government has taken on a greater share of financing the operations of education, health, welfare, housing, and much else.

Most nations are unitary systems; that is, they do not divide power territorially but concentrate it in the nation's capital. Unitary systems do not seek to "balance" powers between central and provincial, but they may give a little autonomy to counties (Sweden and Ireland) or prefectures (Japan). They may also remake and even erase existing provinces and localities; this is not true with federal systems, which cannot easily erase or alter their component states, each of which has a legal existence.

ESTABLISHES THE LEGITIMACY OF GOVERNMENT   A constitution may also give a government the stamp of legitimacy, something both symbolic and practical. Some nations will not recognize a new state until it has a written constitution, which they take as a sign of permanence and responsibility. The U.S. Articles of Confederation and, subsequently, the U.S. Constitution symbolized American independence.

separation of powers
U.S. doctrine that branches of government should be distinct and should check and balance each other; found in few other governments.

State Duma
Russia's national legislature.

constituent assembly
Legislature convened to draft new constitution.

Most constitutions were written shortly after major changes of regime and try to establish the new regime's right to rule. A **constituent assembly** is a legislature meeting for the first time after the overthrow of one regime to write a new constitution. The Spanish parliament elected in 1977 turned itself into a constituent assembly to repudiate the Franco system with the new 1978 constitution. That job done, it turned itself back into the Cortes, the regular parliament. In 1990, Bulgaria elected a 400-member Grand National Assembly to write a new, post-Communist constitution. That done, in 1991 Bulgaria elected a regular parliament, the 240-member National Assembly. After ousting the Taliban regime, Afghan factions met in a *loya jirga,* a traditional constituent assembly, to produce a new constitution in 2004. The warlords and Taliban who run much of Afghanistan, however, ignore it.

Can Constitutions Ensure Rights?

4.3 Explain the variety of "rights" in the modern world.

Civil Liberties and Civil Rights

During World War II, Nazi concentration camps exterminated millions, and the Japanese army raped and pillaged China. In reaction, the world took steps to prevent such inhumanity. In 1948, the UN General Assembly adopted the Universal Declaration on Human Rights, a symbolic statement (with no real power of sanction) that establishes fundamental precepts and norms that most nations are reluctant to violate openly. Countries that do—Mao's 1958–1961 famine killed an estimated 36 million to 45 million Chinese, Saddam Hussein used poison gas against fellow Iraqis, Laurent Kabila condoned and covered up tribal massacres in the Congo—risk being isolated from world aid and trade. Charges of human-rights violations try to persuade Syria to cease killing its own citizens. Although not directly enforceable, the setting of norms for human rights made us more likely to seek them.

The Universal Declaration, patterned on the French Declaration of the Rights of Man and Citizen and on the American Declaration of Independence and the Bill of Rights, affirms the basic civil and human rights that government may not arbitrarily take away. These include the rights to life and freedom of assembly, expression, movement, religion, and political participation. The Universal Declaration also provides for many economic and cultural needs: the rights to work, to an education, to marry, to raise a family, and to provide for that family and the right to live according to one's culture. These rights are almost impossible to enforce, and few have tried. The fact is that rights and liberties are difficult to define, and all nations restrict civil liberties in some way. The problem of minority groups is worldwide. Europe's most serious civil-rights problem is with Gypsies, who are despised nearly everywhere.

Minority Groups and Civil Liberties

Few nations are homogeneous; most have citizens from several racial, ethnic, religious, cultural, or linguistic backgrounds, and their civil or cultural liberties are often compromised. Haitians living in Florida or Chicanos in California are at a disadvantage unless they speak English. Indians and Pakistanis in Great Britain, Algerians in France, and Turks in Germany are under pressure to conform to the dominant culture. But the Universal Declaration states that minorities have the right to preserve their cultural uniqueness. Can it—or should it—be enforced in these situations? The U.S. debate over "multiculturalism" hinges on this question. Should the United States abandon *e pluribus unum* in favor of preserving ethnic groups? Do the children of minority groups have the right to be schooled in their parents' language? Or should children receive the same schooling—the great school desegregation issue of postwar American politics? In 1957, President Eisenhower, in a tense standoff with segregationists, called up the Arkansas National Guard to integrate Central High School in Little Rock (photo on p. 68).

The Adaptability of the U.S. Constitution

4.4   **Explain how U.S. judicial review was a first among constitutions.**

Constitutions are modified by traditions, new usages, and laws. The U.S. Constitution does not mention political parties, yet our party system has become an established part of the American political process. Likewise, the U.S. Senate now needs sixty votes instead of fifty-one votes to pass almost anything. Without sixty votes to stop them, senators now routinely filibuster and block legislation. Nothing in the Constitution specifies this; it just happened as the chamber angrily polarized in recent years. Judicial precedents and government traditions, too, make up the fundamental laws of a society. Even the previously mentioned judicial review appears nowhere in the U.S. Constitution, The Supreme Court's authority to declare laws unconstitutional was first asserted in 1803 by the Court itself. Constitutions need some flexibility to adapt over time. The right to bear arms and freedom of expression illustrate the changing nature of the U.S. Constitution.

The Right to Bear Arms

In 2008, the Supreme Court ruled for the first time that the Second Amendment's "right to bear arms" is an *individual* right. The point has been and continues to be controversial. In 1939, the Court ruled in *United States v. Miller* against transporting sawed-off shotguns, and judges nationwide used Miller as the precedent to allow restrictions on gun ownership. But with *District of Columbia v. Heller*

Theories

What Is a Right?

Where do "rights" come from? Are they natural or artificial? Thinkers of a classic bent—including the U.S. Founding Fathers—took "natural rights" as a basis for **human rights**. Nature expresses God's intentions, which are not hard to discern. You know instantly and instinctively that it is wrong to crash a jetliner into a building. Life and liberty are natural; therefore, government may deprive people of these basic rights only for good cause. Human rights can generally be formulated in the negative as "freedom from," namely, from various forms of tyranny, the great concern of Thomas Jefferson.

Civil rights are newer and at a higher level; they grew up with modern democracy, in which citizens need the freedom to speak and vote. They are not as self-evident as human rights. Press freedom is probably a civil rather than a human right, although the two overlap. Those deprived of civil rights—such as the right to organize an opposition party—may soon also find themselves locked up by the dictatorial regime. In the United States, equal rights in schooling and voting became major civil-rights issues.

Economic rights are the newest—appearing in the nineteenth century with the early socialists—and shifting rights into the material realm. Advanced by liberals like Franklin D. Roosevelt, they are usually formulated in the positive as "freedom to," namely, to live adequately, have a job, and get an education and health care. Many of them cost lots of taxpayer money in government programs. Conservatives say these are not rights at all, merely desirable things demanded by various groups, such as oldsters demanding prescription drugs as a "right." Some fear a "rights industry" creating dubious rights without limit.

"Right," said English philosopher Jeremy Bentham, "is the child of law." Something becomes a right only when it is put into a constitution or statutes. Before the Medicare law, senior citizens had no right to federally funded health insurance. Now it is a right. All rights are more or less artificial or "socially **constructed**." Is something good and desirable automatically a right? Is everything an interest group demands really its right? Beware of overusing the term "rights."

human rights
Freedom from government mistreatment such as arrest, torture, jail, and death without due process.

civil rights
Ability to participate in politics and society, such as voting and free speech; sometimes confused with but at a higher level than human rights.

economic rights
Guarantees of adequate material standards of living; the newest and most controversial rights.

in 2008, the Court ruled that the District's strict gun law violated the Second Amendment. (Titles of U.S. court decisions are the italicized names of plaintiffs and defendants.)

The Founding Fathers wanted to prevent any concentration of power that might flow from a standing national army. The Constitution's "militia clauses" envisioned defense as largely in the hands of state "militias," which would disperse power among the states and citizen militia members. To bolster this, Amendment II of the Bill of Rights (adopted in 1791) says, "A well regulated Militia, being necessary to the security of a free State, the right of the people to keep and bear Arms, shall not be infringed." The militia concept of citizen-based defense never came to much (the states did not want to spend the money), so Washington eventually turned the militias into the National Guard.

But is there also an *individual* right, apart from belonging to a militia, to have guns? Liberals and gun-control advocates claimed there is not, that the right pertains only to militias. Accordingly, states and municipalities can restrict gun ownership. Washington, DC, for example, in 1976 outlawed private handguns, something that conservatives charged was unconstitutional. The Supreme Court in *Heller* decided 5–4 that handguns in the home for defense were legal. That instantly became the law of the land, and the National Rifle Association immediately brought suits to strike down similar laws nationwide.

Heller opened the door to numerous Second Amendment questions that will drag on for years. Does it mean Americans can own any gun without restriction? Outside of the home? Concealed? Machine guns? Sawed-off shotguns? Cop-killer ammunition? How about suspected terrorists or deranged youths? Or do states and municipalities still have the power to impose reasonable restrictions, such as preventing guns from being brought into public meetings? Both *Miller* and *Heller* illustrate that a two-century-old constitution will be reinterpreted in response to new conditions and cases, such as murderous rampages of mentally unbalanced people who have no trouble buying guns.

constructed
Something widely believed as old and hallowed but actually recent and artificial.

Freedom of Expression in the United States

4.5   **Trace the development of the U.S. right to free speech.**

"Congress shall make no law…abridging the freedom of speech, or of the press; or the right of the people peaceably to assemble, and to petition the government for a redress of grievances," says Amendment I of the U.S. Bill of Rights. We regard freedom of expression as a hallmark of any democratic nation. Citizens who think the government is bad or wrong may say so publicly. An antigovernment or antireligion artwork should draw no interference or investigation from a government agency.

Whereas U.S. law tilts strongly toward free speech, most countries outlaw "hate speech" in the interests of domestic calm. In most of Europe, it is illegal to deny that the Holocaust happened. The 2015 murder of twelve staffers of the Paris satirical weekly *Charlie Hebdo* by Muslim extremists raised the question of free speech versus hate speech. *Charlie* cartoons gleefully ridicule just about anything, including the Prophet Muhammad, something that offends Muslims worldwide. A million and a half people marched in Paris to proclaim the right of press freedom. Muslim crowds, however, raged against what they called hate speech. Which was it? We are reminded again of the cultural context of actions and of the difficulty of defining rights.

Free speech is not easy. Does it give a campus bigot the right to incite hatred of African American students? Does a newspaper have a right to publish information that might damage national security? Can a publicly funded museum reject artworks that offend some religious sensibilities? Americans believe in the right of free expression, but most agree that there are limits. As Justice Oliver Wendell Holmes argued, one cannot yell "Fire!" in a crowded theater unless there really is a fire. Does free speech include the right of a state to fly the Confederate battle flag? Such a symbol may push a seething racist to violence, such as the youth who killed nine African Americans in a Charleston, NC, church in 2015.

Before you decide that a case of offensive speech should or should not be protected by the First Amendment, remember the right to free speech would hardly be necessary to protect speech that offended no one. According to Justice Holmes, freedom of expression must also be restricted in cases in which statements or publications present a "clear and present danger" of bringing about "substantive evils," which Congress has a right to prevent. The Supreme Court in its 1925 *Gitlow v. New York* decision upheld the conviction of a radical who called for the violent overthrow of the government on the grounds that his words had represented a "bad tendency," which could "corrupt morals, incite crime, and disturb the public peace." That decision, during a "**red scare**," would likely have come out differently in tranquil times.

red scare

Exaggerated fear of Communist subversion, as in World War I and McCarthy periods.

First Amendment controversies are never-ending. In 1971, a multivolume, secret Defense Department study of the decisions that led to the Vietnam War was leaked to *The New York Times* and *The Washington Post*, both of which started publishing a series of sensational articles based on the study. The Nixon administration immediately got a court order blocking further publication on national-security grounds. In what became known as the *Pentagon Papers* case, the Supreme Court quickly and unanimously rejected the government's claim that official secrets had been compromised. By that time, most Americans were fed up with the war. The reasoning of Justice Hugo Black:

> Only a free and unrestrained press can effectively expose deception in government. And paramount among the responsibilities of a free press is the duty to prevent any part of the Government from deceiving the people and sending them off to distant lands to die of foreign fevers and foreign shot and shell.... [T]he newspapers nobly did precisely that which the founders hoped and trusted they would do.

Recently, some have argued that free speech has gone too far, especially if it deals in racism and pornography or if it throttles others' speech in the name of "political correctness." The Internet has opened vast new areas in this debate as it lets hate-filled, extremist messages circulate. The Islamic State successfully recruits online.

In 2010, federal courts overturned portions of campaign-reform laws designed to curb the influence of big money, partly because campaign contributions are seen by many as a form of free speech. Dollars, they argued, are like words; both should flow without restriction to support candidates and causes. Now millions go freely and directly to "super-PACs," which concentrate on negative campaigning, making U.S. elections dirtier than ever. Some fear rich corporations and individuals will simply buy elections.

Free Speech and Sedition

Sedition is heavy criticism of the government or officials aimed at producing discontent or rebellion. The U.S. government has used sedition laws to suppress radical expression several times since the adoption of the Bill of Rights. Congress passed the first Sedition Act in 1798, after the XYZ affair. It was aimed at the "Jacobins," as American defenders of the French Revolution were called, at a time when the United States was in an undeclared naval war with France. The Sedition Act was supposed to expire the day that President John Adams left office (which indicates that its true purpose may have been to influence the election). The act was controversial, but it lapsed without any test of constitutionality in the Supreme Court. The next Sedition Act came during the Civil War, when President Lincoln used his war powers to suppress Northern opponents of the war, who argued, among other points, "It's a rich man's war and a poor man's fight." The matter came before the Supreme Court, which declined to judge the legality of Lincoln's actions, so they went untested. After the Civil War, all "political prisoners" were pardoned.

sedition
Incitement to public disorder or to overthrow the state.

TWENTIETH-CENTURY SEDITION ACTS During World War I, the Espionage Act of 1917 produced Justice Holmes's "clear and present danger" doctrine. Socialists and pacifists were urging people to resist U.S. involvement in the war by refusing to serve in the army and to disrupt the war effort in other ways. The 1917 act prohibited any such attempts, and several were charged under it in 1919. In one case, the Supreme Court upheld the law on the grounds that free speech could be restricted if it created a "clear and present danger" to national security. Several hundred, including Socialist Party leader Eugene Debs, were imprisoned under the act, but most were pardoned as the war ended.

In the 1940s and 1950s, sedition acts were directed against Communists. The 1940 Smith Act, the most comprehensive sedition act ever passed, made it a crime to advocate the violent overthrow of the government, to distribute literature urging such, or to knowingly join any organization or group that advocated such actions. The Smith Act aroused much controversy but was not put to a constitutional test until 1951, when the Supreme Court upheld the convictions of the leaders of the American Communist Party even though they had not been charged with any overt acts of force against the government. "It is the existence of the conspiracy which constitutes the danger," ruled Chief Justice Vinson, "not the presence or absence of overt action." Since then, there have been other court rulings on the constitutionality of the Smith Act, and they have fluctuated. In *Yates v. the United States* in 1957, the Warren Court reversed the conviction of the Communist leaders on the grounds that there was no overt action, only abstract advocacy of rebellion. Four years later, in *Scales v. the United States*, the Court upheld the section of the Smith Act that makes membership in the Communist Party illegal—but this ruling also specified that it is active membership, involving the direct intent to bring about the violent overthrow of the government, that is criminal. The Court was careful to point out that membership per se was not made illegal by the Smith Act.

The most stringent legislation against Communist subversion was passed during the McCarthy era after World War II, another red scare. The McCarran Act of 1950 (the Internal Security Act) barred Communists from working for the federal government or in defense-related industries, established a Subversive Activities Control Board (SACB) to enforce the act, and required SACB-designated organizations to register with the attorney general. Critics of the McCarran Act charged that the law not only encroached on the rights of free speech and free assembly but also violated the self-incrimination clause of the Fifth Amendment. Although the Internal Security Act in its entirety has never been declared unconstitutional, every action by the SACB demanding specific organizational or individual registration with the attorney general's office has been declared unconstitutional. Finally, with the realization on all sides that the SACB accomplished nothing, it was abolished in 1973. Interestingly, the U.S. government did essentially nothing to stop criticism of the Vietnam War; opposition was too widespread, and there was no declaration of war.

Rights for Terrorists?

After 9/11, the Bush administration invented a new category for terrorist suspects who had been arrested: "unlawful enemy combatants." Evidence against them was often vague. They were in a limbo between criminal suspects and prisoners of war and lacked the rights of either. They were harshly interrogated by means such as "waterboarding," simulated drowning. No one knows if valid information was obtained, and statements obtained under duress are worthless in a court of law. Some were held in Guantánamo—because it was not on U.S. soil—without charge, trial, or time limit. Unquestionably many of them—but which?—were dangerous terrorists, but evidence against them was kept secret. In effect, they got life sentences without a trial.

After the 9/11 panic subsided, many wondered if this was constitutional. In 2004, the Supreme Court ruled that Guantánamo is effectively under U.S. laws. In 2006 and 2008, it ruled that suspected terrorists had **habeas corpus** rights. The court did not free any detainees or order any trials, but it did push the administration to decide whether they were criminal suspects or war prisoners. If the former, they get a trial; if the latter, they get treated under the Geneva Conventions. The law did not sit easily with the new category of "unlawful enemy combatant."

One fiery Islamist preacher in Yemen, who was born in the United States, used the Internet to encourage violence worldwide, and several answered his call, including a U.S. Army psychiatrist who killed thirteen fellow soldiers in 2009. A drone took out the preacher in 2011, raising questions of executing a U.S. citizen without due process.

habeas corpus
Detainee may protest innocence before a judge.

Methods

References

Whoever reads your paper should be able to look up your sources to make sure they are valid and in context. References are now usually put at the end. Shown here is the standard urged by the American Political Science Association, but this is not sacred. It is derived from that of the American Psychological Association ("psych style") and a variation of the *Chicago Manual of Style*. Your instructor may prefer the similar style of the Modern Language Association, and some may prefer the old-fashioned footnote style, which at least was consistent across disciplines. There is some variation in what is considered standard, especially with websites. In general, references give the reader a road map to your sources.

At the end of your paper, under the subhead "References" or "Works Cited," with hanging indents and in alphabetical order, give the author (last name first), the year, the article in quotation marks, the journal or book title italicized, and, if a book, the city and publishing house. If a journal, give the month and day at the end. Separate these elements with periods.

If there is no listed author, use the article's title or, especially with websites, the sponsoring agency's name. Here is what they look like:

Works Cited

Adams, Jonathan. 2007. *Development and the Environment*. Washington, DC: National Ecology Association.

Berry, Nicholas O. 2013. "Iran: Who Is Rational?" *Foreign Policy Forum*. May 21. foreignpolicyforum.com.

Jones, Robert. 2014. "Obama Announces Energy Program." *New York Press*. December 4.

Smith, Paul. 2015. "Obama and the Environment." *New Departure*. June 20.

Thompson, Earl. 2001. *George Bush and the Environment*. New York: Simple & Simon.

Williams, Charles. 2005. "The EPA Budget under Bush." *Ecology Quarterly* 17:417.

World Bank. 2009. *World Development Report 2008/2009*. New York: Oxford University Press.

The history of government actions to curb speech or arrest suspicious persons in the United States indicates that the guarantees of the Bill of Rights have been interpreted to mean different things over time. When Congress, the president, and the courts perceive danger and threat, they tend to be more restrictive, in other times more permissive. Rights are highly context-dependent. After the 9/11 terrorist attacks of 2001, few Americans worried about detaining hundreds of suspicious people without due process. A few years later, with examples of panicked overreaction in mind, some worried that the Patriot Act, passed in haste, should be modified to make sure it does not infringe on the Constitution or needlessly hassle travelers at airports. Warrantless wiretaps of that period were ruled unconstitutional.

We should remember this context dependency when we see legal restrictions on human and civil rights in other lands. Some regimes really are under siege; opponents want to overthrow them (often with good reason). And because elections are routinely rigged, the only way to overthrow such regimes is by extralegal means, which may include violence. In such situations, free speech may lead quickly to violent overthrow, which may be richly deserved. Governments of whatever stripe clamp down when they are scared, and they are scared because they know they may be overthrown. Myanmar (formerly Burma), South Korea, Indonesia, Egypt, Iran, South Africa, Argentina, and many other lands have imprisoned political opponents for speaking out. "Free speech" is not just a nice thing; it can be dynamite. Freedom of expression thrives best under long-established, legitimate governments in tranquil times. It is, in short, political.

Review Questions

1. What are constitutions and constitutionalism?

2. What makes something a "right"?

3. Should constitutions specify social and economic rights?

4. How can the very short U.S. Constitution still work in the modern age?

5. Do most constitutions have "checks and balances"?

6. How has the U.S. Constitution changed over time?

7. Should outlawing hate speech trump free speech?

8. Should terrorist suspects have any rights?

9. How did 9/11 alter the U.S. climate for rights? Has this happened before?

Key Terms

Basic Law, p. 73
civil rights, p. 78
constituent assembly, p. 76
constitution, p. 70
constitutionalism, p. 73
constructed, p. 78
economic rights, p. 78

habeas corpus, p. 82
human rights, p. 78
judicial activism, p. 72
judicial restraint, p. 72
judicial review, p. 72
minority, p. 69
political culture, p. 73

red scare, p. 80
sedition, p. 81
separation of powers, p. 75
State Duma, p. 75
statute, p. 70

Further Reference

Ackerman, Bruce. *Before the Next Attack: Preserving Civil Liberties in an Age of Terrorism.* New Haven, CT: Yale University Press, 2006.

Cornell, Saul. *A Well-Regulated Militia: The Founding Fathers and the Origins of Gun Control in America.* New York: Oxford, 2006.

Eisgruber, Christopher L., and Lawrence G. Sager. *Religious Freedom and the Constitution.* Cambridge, MA: Harvard University Press, 2007.

Fisher, Louis. *The Constitution and 9/11: Recurring Threats to America's Freedoms.* Lawrence, KS: University Press of Kansas, 2008.

Freeberg, Ernest. *Democracy's Prisoner: Eugene V. Debs, the Great War, and the Right to Dissent.* Cambridge, MA: Harvard University Press, 2009.

Herman, Susan N. *Taking Liberties: The War on Terror and the Erosion of American Democracy.* New York: Oxford University Press, 2011.

Howard, John. *Concentration Camps on the Home Front: Japanese Americans in the House of Jim Crow.* Chicago: University of Chicago Press, 2008.

Hunt, Lynn. *Inventing Human Rights: A History.* New York: Norton, 2007.

Levinson, Sanford. *Framed: America's Fifty-One Constitutions and the Crisis of Governance.* New York: Oxford University Press, 2012.

Lewis, Anthony. *Freedom for the Thought That We Hate: A Biography of the First Amendment.* New York: Basic Books, 2008.

Lichtblau, Eric. *Bush's Law: The Remaking of American Justice.* New York: Pantheon, 2008.

Maddex, Robert L., Jr. *Constitutions of the World,* 3rd ed. Washington, DC: CQ Press, 2007.

Mayer, Jane. *The Dark Side: The Inside Story of How the War on Terror Turned into a War on American Ideals.* New York: Doubleday, 2008.

Murphy, Walter F. *Constitutional Democracy: Creating and Maintaining a Just Political Order.* Baltimore, MD: Johns Hopkins University Press, 2007.

Nelson, Samuel P. *Beyond the First Amendment: The Politics of Free Speech and Pluralism.* Baltimore, MD: Johns Hopkins University Press, 2005.

Posner, Richard. *Not a Suicide Pact: The Constitution in a Time of National Emergency.* New York: Oxford University Press, 2006.

Risen, James. *Pay Any Price: Greed, Power, and Endless War.* Boston: Houghton Mifflin Harcourt, 2014.

Rosenfeld, Seth. *Subversives: The FBI's War on Student Radicals, and Reagan's Rise to Power.* New York: Farrar, Straus & Giroux, 2012.

Seidman, Louis Michael. *On Constitutional Disobedience.* New York: Oxford University Press, 2013.

Shipler, David K. *The Rights of the People: How Our Search for Safety Invades Our Liberties.* New York: Knopf, 2011.

Stevens, John Paul. *Six Amendments: How and Why We Should Change the Constitution.* New York: Little, Brown, 2014.

Stone, Geoffrey R. *Perilous Times: Free Speech in Wartime from the Sedition Act of 1798 to the War on Terrorism.* New York: Norton, 2004.

Wittes, Benjamin. *Law and the Long War: The Future of Justice in the Age of Terror.* New York: Penguin, 2008.

Chapter 5
Regimes

 Learning Objectives

5.1 Explain why representative democracy is the only feasible kind.

5.2 Contrast elitist and pluralist theories of democracy.

5.3 List the features attributed to totalitarianism.

5.4 Distinguish authoritarianism from totalitarianism.

5.5 Explain why new democracies often fail.

Hong Kong is a strange situation. A British colony since 1842, it was handed back to China in 1997 as a "special administrative region" with internal self-governance for fifty years. China, however, slowly chokes this off. Beijing fears the movement for Hong Kong democracy—which the British never implemented because Beijing told them not to—and takes steps to stifle it, lest it spread to the mainland. Beijing warns Hong Kong businesses and media that they will lose deals and advertising if they back the democracy movement. Hundreds of thousands of Hong Kongers, however, protest for democracy in the streets, and social media to demand open candidate nominations for the 2017 Hong Kong elections—not just those picked by a committee beholden to Beijing. Free Hong Kong elections would give mainlanders ideas about democracy.

Democracy is both contentious and contagious. It is not simple or easy. At the birth of the American Republic, many wondered if it would survive. They noted that Athenian and Roman democracy had both perished. In 1831–1832, French visitor Tocqueville took a close look and concluded U.S. democracy was admirable and viable. The rest of the world moved only slowly and grudgingly toward democracy in the late nineteenth and early twentieth centuries. Some countries tried democracy but slid backward. The Soviet, Italian, and German dictatorships evoked some admiration from Depression-wracked citizens of democracies.

The debate between dictatorship and democracy will likely continue. The two, however, are not simply black and white; in between are many variations. Classification is difficult; Table 5.1 is just an attempt. Some countries are pretend democracies, with controlled media, rigged elections, and obedient parliaments

Table 5.1 Main Regime Types

	Democratic *U.S., West Europe*	Transitional *Egypt, Russia*	Authoritarian *Iran, China*	Totalitarian *N. Korea, Cuba*
media	free	curbed	obedient	state-controlled
parties	several	one dominant	none or one	one
elections	competitive	flawed	rigged	fake or none
power	alternates among parties	rigid one man	in hands of small group	concentrated in one leader
ideology	many	limited range	none or pretend	one militant
constitution	restrains government	selectively interpreted	restrains individuals	worships state
civil liberties	protected	vulnerable	few	none
interest groups	many and autonomous	few and cowed	state-supervised	no autonomous ones
economy	market	partly market	partly state-run	state-run
military	subordinate to elected officials	plays a political role	intertwined with regime	controlled by ruling party
corruption	minor	widespread	pervasive	major

Table 5.2 Select Freedom House 2015 Rankings

United States	1	free
Canada	1	free
Brazil	2	free
India	2.5	free
Mexico	3	partly free
Bosnia	3.5	partly free
Colombia	3.5	partly free
Malaysia	4	partly free
Nigeria	4.5	partly free
Pakistan	4.5	partly free
Kuwait	5	partly free
Venezuela	5	partly free
Egypt	5.5	not free
Myanmar (Burma)	5.5	not free
Zimbabwe	5.5	not free
Iraq	6	not free
Afghanistan	6	not free
Ethiopia	6	not free
Iran	6	not free
Russia	6	not free
China	6.5	not free
North Korea	7	not free

SOURCE: Freedom House

and parties—like Russia and Iran. Many countries are in flux, shifting between more and less democratic and vice versa, what the table calls "transitional" regimes. Venezuela and Bolivia have taken on authoritarian hues, but Indonesia and Nigeria have moved in a democratic direction.

Freedom House annually ranks countries on a 1–7 scale and puts them into "free" (1 to 2.5), "partly free" (3 to 5), and "not free" (5.5 to 7) categories to indicate their degree of democracy (see Table 5.2). Some countries are borderline, some barely free (India), some move (Mexico was demoted from 2.5 to 3, Ethiopia from 5 to 6), and others at the upper end of not free (Myanmar and Zimbabwe at 5.5).

Representative Democracy

democracy

Political system of mass participation, competitive elections, and human and civil rights.

5.1 **Explain why representative democracy is the only feasible kind.**

Democracy has many meanings. Dictators misuse the word to convince subjects that they live in a just system. The Soviet Union used to claim it was the best democracy, and Libya's Muammar Qaddafi claimed he embodied the precise will of his people. Democracy does not always equal freedom. Elections, even free and fair ones as in Turkey and Egypt, can produce regimes that ride rough-shod over rights and freedoms, what is called **illiberal democracy**. Democracy is a complex and carefully balanced system that needs thoughtful citizens, limits on power, rule of law, and human and civil rights. Not every country that calls itself a democracy is one, and not every country is capable of becoming one. Egypt is a recent case in point.

illiberal democracy
Regimes that are elected but lack democratic qualities such as civil rights and limits on government.

Democracy (from the Greek *demokratía;* demos = "the people" and kratía = "rule") carried a negative connotation until the nineteenth century, as thinkers accepted the ancient Greeks' criticism of direct democracy as mob rule. A "true" democracy, a system in which all citizens meet periodically to elect officials and personally enact laws, has been rare: Athens's General Assembly, New England town meetings, and Swiss *Landsgemeinde* are among the few.

Some direct democracy continues in U.S. states through **referendums** on issues the legislature will not handle. Although referendums seem very demo-cratic, their sponsors can oversimplify and manipulate issues, as Californians see with the scores of measures—some contradicting others—they face on every ballot. French President Charles de Gaulle called referendums to build his own power and bypass conventional politicians. Pakistan's former president—a gen-eral who seized power in a 1999 military coup—had himself confirmed in office by a 2002 referendum. Few were fooled.

referendum
A mass vote on an issue rather than for a candidate; a type of direct democracy.

Direct democracy is difficult to carry out because of the size factor. As the Englishman John Selden noted in the early seventeenth century in arguing for a Parliament in London: "The room will not hold all." A national government that submitted each decision to millions of voters would be too unwieldy to function. **Representative democracy** evolved as the only workable system.

Modern democracy is not the actual setting of policy by the people. Instead, the people play a more general role. Democracy today is, in Lipset's words, "a political system which supplies regular constitutional opportunities for changing the governing officials, and a social mechanism which permits the largest possible part of the population to influence major decisions by choosing among contenders for political office." *Constitutional* means that the government is limited and can wield its authority only in specific ways. Representative democracy has several essential characteristics. Notice that it is not a simple system or one that falls into place automatically. It must be carefully constructed over many years. Attempts to thrust it onto unprepared countries like Russia or Iraq often fail.

representative democracy
One in which the people do not rule directly but through elected and accountable representatives.

Popular Accountability of Government

In a democracy, the policymakers must obtain the support of a majority or a plurality of votes cast. Leaders are accountable to citizens. Elected leaders need to worry that they can be voted out. No one has an inherent right to occupy a position of political power; he or she must be freely, fairly, and periodically elected by fellow citizens, either at regular intervals (as in the United States) or at certain maximum time spans (as in Britain). Most systems permit reelection, although some specify term limits. Reelection is the people's means both of expressing support and of controlling the general direction of government policy. Term limits may cast a shadow on popular accountability; if leaders know they cannot return for another term, they might be less responsive to the will of the citizenry.

Political Competition

Voters must have a choice, either of candidates or parties. That means a minimum of two distinct alternatives. In Europe, voters have a choice among several parties, each of which tries to distinguish its ideology and policies. One-party or one-candidate elections are fake. Americans are supposed to have a choice of two candidates, one for each major party, but most congresspersons run with little or no opposition, as campaign costs dissuade challengers from even trying. *Gerrymandering* by state legislatures guarantees most incumbents' reelection. Even the United States is less than fully democratic.

The parties must have time and freedom to organize and present their case well before elections. A regime that permits no opposition activity until shortly before balloting has rigged the election. Likewise, denying media access—especially by controlling television—stunts any opposition. Much of democracy depends on the political freedoms in the months and years before the actual balloting takes place. Physical balloting can still be a problem. In some places (such as Russia in 2012 and in old Chicago), reliable people "vote early and often," and votes are miscounted. Defective voting systems, such as Florida's punch-card ballots in 2000, may negate the popular will. Elections by themselves do not equal democracy. Supposing they do is a common mistake.

Alternation in Power

The reins of power must occasionally change hands, with the "ins" becoming the "outs" in a peaceful, legitimate way. No party or individual should get a lock on executive power. A system in which the ruling party stays in power many decades cannot really be democratic. Such parties say they win on popularity but often tilt the rules to ensure they stay in power. In 2015, Singapore's People's Action Party won its twelfth election in a row; it allowed only a short campaign and redrew constituency boundaries. Mexico's Institutional Revolutionary Party (PRI) won fourteen straight elections since the 1920s. In 2000, however, Vicente Fox of the National Action Party (PAN) won the presidency, and Mexico became more democratic. Likewise, Kenya in 2002 voted out the party that had ruled for thirty-nine years. Other African countries are also getting alternation in power—a good sign.

Harvard political scientist Samuel Huntington (1927–2008) proposed a "two-turnover test" to mark a stable democracy. That is, two electoral alternations of government indicate that democracy is firmly rooted. Poland, for example, overthrew its Communist regime in 1989 and held free and fair elections (called "founding elections"), won by the Solidarity coalition of Lech Walesa. Some Poles, however, hurt by rapid economic change, in 1995 voted in a president from the Socialists, a party formed out of the old Communist Party. But after a while, they did not like the Socialists either and in 1997 voted in a right-of-center party. Poland has had several turnovers and established its democratic credentials. Russia has never had a turnover.

One unstated but important function of alternation in power is control of corruption. An opposition party that hammers incumbents for corruption is a powerful corrective to the human tendency to misuse public office. Systems without alternation, such as Russia and China, are invariably corrupt.

Uncertain Electoral Outcomes

Related to alternation in power, democratic elections must have an element of uncertainty, fluidity, and individual vote switching. Voting must not be simply by groups, where 100 percent of a tribe, religion, social class, or region automatically votes for a given candidate or party. In such situations, the country may get locked in bitterness and intolerance. Some fear the U.S. *culture wars* are leading in that direction. A certain percent of the electorate must be up for grabs to keep politicians worried and attentive to the nation as a whole.

In Iraq, voting follows religion too closely. Sunnis and Shias mostly vote for different parties, making governance difficult and inviting uprisings. African voting, closely tied to tribe, does not produce democracy. In Zimbabwe, Robert Mugabe's majority Shona tribe reelected him for decades; he used his dictatorial powers to kill members of the minority Ndebele tribe with impunity. Some hope that enough Shonas will say, "I don't care if he's a Shona; he has ruined this country," and vote against his ZANU-PF party. Indians jest that "in India you don't cast your vote, you vote your **caste**." Indian elections can be partially predicted by knowing which castes favor which parties. Fortunately, Indian individualism often overrides caste, making Indian elections democratic and unpredictable.

caste
Rigid, hereditary social class or group.

Popular Representation

In representative democracies, the voters elect representatives to act as legislators and, as such, to voice and protect their general interest. Legislators usually act for given districts or groups. But how should they act? Some theorists claim legislators must treat elections as **mandates** to carry out constituents' wishes: What the voters want is what they should get. Other theorists disagree; constituents often have no opinion on issues, so representatives must act as **trustees**, carrying out the wishes of constituents when feasible but acting in the best interests of the whole. With opinion running against the 2008 and 2009 financial bailouts, U.S. congresspersons swallowed hard and voted for them, abandoning the mandate theory to act as trustees for the public good. As economist

mandate
A representative carrying out the specific wishes of the public.

trustee
A representative deciding the public good without a specific mandate.

Joseph Schumpeter (1883–1950) argued against the mandate theory: "Our chief problems with the classical (democratic) theory centered in the proposition that 'the people' hold a definite and rational opinion about every individual question and that they give effect to this opinion—in a democracy—by choosing 'representatives' who will see to it that the opinion is carried out."

Of course, few people hold definite opinions on every subject. If they were asked to vote on nitrous oxide limits or reckless bank lending, few would vote. Representative democracy, therefore, does not mean that the representative must become a cipher for constituents; rather, it means that the people as a body must be able to control the *general* direction of government policy. For example, the people may have a general desire to improve education, but they leave the means and details of achieving this goal to their legislators. It is this partnership between the people and the lawmakers that is the essence of modern democracy. Political scientist E. E. Schattschneider (1892–1971) summarized the case succinctly:

> The beginning of wisdom in democratic theory is to distinguish between the things that the people can do and the things the people cannot do. The worst possible disservice that can be done to the democratic cause is to attribute to the people a mystical, magical omnipotence which takes no cognizance of what very large numbers of people cannot do by the sheer weight of numbers. At this point the common definition of democracy has invited us to make fools of ourselves.

Majority Decision

On any important government decision, there is rarely complete agreement. One faction favors something; another opposes. How to settle the question? The simple answer is that the majority should decide, the procedure used in the democracies of ancient Greece. However, our more modern and practical concept of democracy is that the majority decides but with respect for minority rights. To uphold such rights, an independent judiciary, one not under the thumb of the regime, is a necessity.

Minority views are important. Probably every view now widely held was once a minority view. Most of what is now public policy became law as a result of conflict between majority and minority groups. Furthermore, just as it is true that a minority view may grow over time until it is widely accepted, so may a majority view eventually prove unwise, unworkable, or unwanted. If minority views are silenced, the will of the majority becomes the "tyranny of the majority," which is just as foreboding as executive tyranny.

Right of Dissent and Disobedience

Related to minority rights, people must have the right to resist the commands of government they deem wrong or unreasonable. This right was invoked in 1776 in the Declaration of Independence. Henry Thoreau (1817–1862), in his opposition to the 1846 war with Mexico, made probably the most profound American defense of **civil disobedience** when he declared, "All men recognize the right of revolution; that is, the right to refuse allegiance to, and to resist, the government, when its tyranny or its inefficiency are great and unendurable." The most celebrated advocate of civil disobedience was Indian independence leader Mahatma Gandhi, who read Thoreau. Both considered their method of resistance to be "civil"; that is, it was disobedience but it was nonviolent and did not exceed the general legal structure of the state. It was an attention-getting device that forced the authorities to rethink. Ultimately, Gandhi and his followers forced the British to leave India. The calls for armed violence from rightist militias are not "civil" disobedience.

civil disobedience
The nonviolent breaking of an unjust law to serve a higher law.

Some look on civil disobedience as an individual act of conscience, but others seek to organize it and mobilize it. The most prominent American organizer was the Reverend Martin Luther King, Jr., whose 1960s nonviolent civil-rights campaigns deliberately challenged racist local laws. He and others in his Southern Christian Leadership Conference were often arrested, but once the charges were brought before a federal court, the discriminatory law itself was usually declared unconstitutional. The long-range consequence of their actions changed both the laws and the psychology of America. Without civil disobedience, minority claims would have gone unheard; Congress would have reformed nothing.

Political Equality

In a democracy, all adults (usually now age eighteen and over) are equally able to participate in politics: "one person, one vote." In theory, all are able to run for public office, but critics point out that it takes a great deal of money—and often specific racial and religious ties—to really enter public life. Under the pressure of minority claims and civil disobedience, however, democracies tend to open up over time and become less elite in nature. Barack Obama's victories were examples.

Popular Consultation

Most leaders realize that to govern effectively, they must know what the people want and must be responsive to their needs and demands. Are citizens disturbed by foreign wars, taxes, unemployment, or the cost of gasoline? Intelligent leaders realize that they must neither get too far ahead of public opinion nor fall too far behind it. Leaders monitor opinion on a continuous basis. Public opinion polls are closely followed. The media can create a dialogue between people and leaders. At press conferences and interviews with elected officials, reporters ask "hot" questions. Editorials, letters to the editor, and "tweets" indicate citizens' views.

In recent years, several critics have noted that U.S. officials often rely heavily on the opinions of small segments of their constituencies because they are well-organized and highly vocal. Most Americans favor at least some gun control, but the National Rifle Association blocks firearms legislation. Washington typically listens to the finance community more than to ordinary citizens, which is why Congress bailed out giant banks in 2008.

Free Press

mass media
Modern means of communication that quickly reach very wide audiences. (The word *media* is plural; *medium* is the singular form.)

Dictatorships cannot tolerate free and critical **mass media**; democracies cannot do without them. One of the quickest ways to determine the degree of democracy in a country is to see if the media criticize government, tracked by Reporters Without Borders in its World Press Freedom Index. No criticism, no democracy. One current antidemocratic stunt: Use libel laws to block news reports of government corruption. The mass media provide citizens with facts, raise public awareness, and keep rulers responsive to mass demands. Without a free and critical press, rulers can disguise wrongdoing and corruption and lull the population into passive support. As China permitted a "democracy movement" in the late 1980s, the Chinese media became freer, more honest, and more critical. Beijing did not stand for that long; now critical journalists, doctors, lawyers, and activists are jailed. The new social media, which helped trigger the "Arab Spring," are hard to control, but China tries, shutting down thousands of blogs and tweets every year.

Some Americans argue that the U.S. media go too far, that they take an automatic adversarial stance that undermines government authority and weakens the nation. In some cases this may be true, but in a democracy there is no mechanism to decide what "too far" is. The checks on reckless reporting are competing journals, channels, and blogs that refute each other in what has been called "the marketplace of ideas." Then citizens, with no government supervision, can decide for themselves if charges are accurate. Only half in jest has the U.S. press been called "the fourth branch of government."

Democracy in Practice: Elitism or Pluralism?

5.2 Contrast elitist and pluralist theories of democracy.

elites
The "top" or most influential people in a political system.

pluralism
Theory that politics is the interaction of many groups.

Even if all these democratic criteria are met—no easy feat—political power will still not be evenly distributed; a few will have a lot, and many will have little or none. Political scientists see this unevenness of power as normal and unavoidable: **Elites** make the actual decisions, and ordinary citizens, the *masses*, generally go along with these decisions. The key dispute is how much elites are accountable to masses. Those who argue that elites are little accountable are *elite theorists;* those who argue that elites are ultimately accountable are **pluralists**.

One of the early thinkers on elites, Italian political scientist Gaetano Mosca (1858–1941), argued that government always falls into the hands of a few.

> In all societies—from societies that are very undeveloped and have largely attained the dawnings of civilization, down to the most advanced and powerful societies—two classes of people appear—a class that rules and a class that is ruled. The first class, always the less numerous, performs all of the political functions, monopolizes power, and enjoys the advantages that power brings, whereas the second, the more numerous class, is directed and controlled by the first, in a manner that is now more or less legal, now more or less arbitrary and violent.

German thinker Robert Michels (1876–1936) argued that any organization, no matter how democratic its intent, ends up run by a small elite; he called this the "Iron Law of Oligarchy." More recently, Yale political scientist Robert Dahl (1915–2014) held that "participatory democracy is not possible in large modern societies; government is too big and the issues are too complex.... The key political, economic, and social decisions...are made by tiny minorities.... It is difficult—nay, impossible—to see how it could be otherwise in large political systems." These three agree on the inevitability of elites, but Mosca and Michels, elite theorists, see elites as unaccountable, whereas Dahl, a pluralist, sees them as accountable.

Contrary to what one might suppose, modern elite theorists are generally not conservatives but radicals; they decry rule by elites as unfair and undemocratic. Columbia sociologist C. Wright Mills (1916–1962) denounced the "Power Elite" in which big business gives money to politicians, politicians vote massive defense spending, and top generals give lush contracts to big business. This interlocking conspiracy was driving the United States to war, Mills predicted.

Money and connections give elites access to political power, emphasize elite theorists. In 2004, Yale graduates Bush ('68) and Kerry ('66) were both members of the super-elite and secretive Skull and Bones society. In 2012, both Obama and Romney were Harvard Law School graduates. Members of Congress, half of whom are millionaires, earn about nine times what their constituents make. Elite, however, does not necessarily mean rich. Few rich people run for office, but they influence those who do by contributions. The "super-PACs" enable billionaires to freely give millions to influence elections. In return, they get favorable laws, policies, and tax breaks. The Bush administration gave the biggest of its 2001 tax cuts to the richest 1 percent and gave special deals to the oil industry, in which both Bush and Vice President Cheney had been executives. Big corporation money controls both major parties, charge critics. Massive campaign contributions make sure no important industry gets seriously harmed; witness the finance industry's ability to water down laws that regulate them. Critics detected a cozy club of top Wall Streeters and top federal officials. Elite theorists make their case with items like these.

Look again, argue pluralists. The Cold War, not a power elite, drove defense spending, which declined sharply after the Soviet threat disappeared.

Most politicians are of modest origins; few are from wealthy families (exceptions: both Roosevelts, JFK, the Bushes, and Romney). Politicians may take big contributions, but they are usually attuned to what wins votes. Big companies do get leaned on. The entire asbestos industry was closed down as a health hazard. Tobacco firms paid millions in lawsuits and face continual government pressure. Giant banks, much against their will, are regulated. Conservative billionaires lavishly funded pro-Romney super-PACs, which still lost the 2012 presidential election. According to elite theory, they should have won.

interest group
An association that pressures government for policies it favors.

Politics functions, say pluralists, through **interest groups**. Just about any group of citizens can organize a group to protest or demand something, and politicians generally listen. To be sure, if the group is wealthy and well-placed, it gets listened to more, but nobody has a hammerlock on the political system. U.S. oil companies are among the richest firms in the world, and they are pro-Arab. Why then does U.S. policy tilt toward Israel? Most American Jews and fundamentalist Christians are pro-Israel, and politicians need their votes and contributions. According to pluralists, interest groups are the great avenues of democracy, making sure government listens to the people. Many argue that only a pluralist society can be democratic. Efforts to found democracies in societies without traditions of pluralism are like trying to plant trees without soil, as we have seen in Russia, where the long Communist rule erased most naturally occurring interest groups.

The pure elite theorist views society as a single pyramid, with a tiny elite at the top. The pure pluralist views society as many billiard balls colliding with each other and with government to produce policy. Both views are overdrawn. A synthesis that more accurately reflects reality might be a series of small pyramids, each capped by an elite. There is interaction of many units, as the pluralists claim, but there is also stratification of leaders and followers, as elite thinkers would have it. (See Figure 5.1.) Robert Dahl called this a "polyarchy," the rule of the leaders of several groups who have reached stable understandings with each other.

Figure 5.1 Elite, pluralist, and polyarchy models.

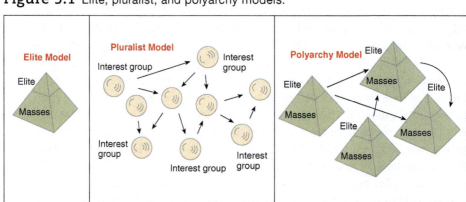

Arend Lijphart (1936–) called it "consociational democracy." The elites of each important group strike a bargain to play by the rules of a constitutional game and to restrain their followers from violence. In return, each group gets something; no one gets everything. Lijphart's example of where this has worked successfully is his native Netherlands, where the elites of the Catholic, Calvinist, and secular blocs reached an "elite accommodation" with each other. In Lebanon, by contrast, elite accommodation broke down, resulting in civil strife. Most stable countries have "conflict management" by elites. The United States shows an interplay of business, labor, ethnic, regional, and other elites, each delivering enough to keep their people in line, each cooperating to varying degrees with other elites. When elite consensus broke down, the United States, too, experienced a bloody Civil War.

Totalitarianism

5.3 **List the features attributed to totalitarianism.**

In **totalitarian** systems, elites are almost completely unaccountable; they lock themselves into power and are very difficult to oust, short of regime collapse, which we saw in Eastern Europe in 1989 and in the Soviet Union in 1991. There is now little totalitarianism left. Its emphasis on total control, brainwashing, and worship of the state and its leaders has proven mistaken and inefficient. Few people are now attracted to such political models. Only North Korea remains as a pristine example of totalitarianism, while China and Vietnam have opened up economically if not politically—a path Cuba may follow. Earlier in the twentieth

totalitarian
Political system in which the state attempts total control of its citizens.

Democracy

Dahl's "Influence Terms"

One of Robert Dahl's many contributions is his explication of the varieties of power, which Dahl defines as A getting B to do what A wants. Dahl prefers the more neutral "influence terms," which he arranged on a scale from best to worst:

- *Rational persuasion*, the nicest form of influence, means telling the truth and explaining why someone should do something, like your doctor convincing you to stop smoking.
- *Manipulative persuasion*, a notch lower, means lying or misleading to get someone to do something, the way politicians do in elections.

- *Inducement*, still lower, means offering rewards or punishments to get someone to do something, like bribery or vote buying.
- *Power* threatens severe punishment, such as jail or loss of job.
- *Coercion* is power with no way out; you have to do it.
- *Physical force* is backing up coercion with use or threat of bodily harm.

Thus, we can tell which governments are best: the democratic ones that use influence at the higher end of the scale. The worst use the unpleasant authoritarian forms of influence at the lower end.

century, though, with the regimes of Stalin, Mussolini, and Hitler, totalitarianism was riding high. Some thought it was the wave of the future, but it was a disease of the twentieth century. Most of our examples are historical, not current.

What Is Totalitarianism?

The twentieth-century phenomenon of totalitarianism is far removed from past autocracies. Peter the Great and Louis XIV were powerful despots but limited by the poor communications of the time. They could not closely control their subjects. Even Louis XIV, a kind of royal dictator, did not try to govern everything in France; average citizens lived their private lives. In contrast, totalitarian states of the twentieth century attempted to remold and transform every aspect of human life.

Totalitarianism began with Lenin's 1917 seizure of power in Russia. Mussolini in Italy in 1922 and Hitler in Germany in 1933 did the same. Note that all three countries had been deranged by World War I. Totalitarianism—a word coined by Mussolini's supporters in the 1920s—is a system in which one party holds total power and attempts to restructure society in accordance with party values. Freedom disappears. The old autocratic rulers kept their subjects quiet, but the totalitarian state insists on mass enthusiasm. Carl J. Friedrich (1901–1984) and Zbigniew Brzezinski (1928–) identified six features of totalitarian states. Four of them would have been impossible in preindustrial countries.

AN ALL-ENCOMPASSING IDEOLOGY Totalitarians push an official theory of history, economics, and future political and social development. The ideology portrays the world in black-and-white terms and claims to be building a perfect, happy society, so anyone against it is an "enemy of the people." All are supposed to believe and study the official ideology. Courses on Marxist-Leninist thought were required in all Communist states (and still are in China).

A SINGLE PARTY One party totally dominates politics, led by one man who establishes a cult of personality. Mussolini, Hitler, Stalin, and Mao had themselves worshipped. Party membership is controlled—usually less than 10 percent of the population—and is supposed to be an honor. Membership brings privileges, and in return members strongly support the party. **Hierarchically** organized, the party is either superior to or tied in with the formal institutions of government. Party functionaries hold all-important posts and impose at least outward conformity on all citizens.

hierarchy
Organized in a ranking of power from top to bottom, as if on a ladder.

ORGANIZED TERROR Security police use both physical and psychological methods to keep citizens obedient. The Nazi Gestapo, the Soviet NKVD under Stalin, and Mussolini's OVRA had no judicial restraints. Constitutional guarantees either did not exist or were ignored, thus making possible secret arrests, jailing, and torture. The security forces—sometimes called "secret police"—were often directed against whole classes of people such as Jews, landlords, capitalists, socialists, or clergy. The threat of the "knock at the door" cows most of the population. Mass arrest and execution show the state's power and the individual's helplessness. Not counting deaths in war, perhaps 40 million died under Mao (mostly by starvation), some 11 million under Hitler, and 6 million to 9 million under Stalin. Such terror doesn't work over the long run, however, and the Soviet Union abandoned the more ruthless tactics of Stalin, replacing them with more subtle forms of control and intimidation, such as loss of job or exile to a remote city.

MONOPOLY OF COMMUNICATIONS The media in totalitarian states are strictly censored to sell the official ideology and show the system is working well under wise leaders. Only good news appears. Sinister outside forces are portrayed as trying to harm the system and must be stopped.

MONOPOLY OF WEAPONS Governments of totalitarian nations have a complete monopoly on weapons, thus eliminating armed resistance.

CONTROLLED ECONOMY Totalitarian regimes control the economy. Stalin did so directly by means of state ownership and Hitler indirectly by means of party "coordination" of private industry. Either way, it makes the state powerful, for resources can be allocated to heavy industry, weapons production, or whatever the party wishes. Workers can be kept in line, and consumer needs or wants are unimportant. The Soviet Union was the first to send humans into outer space, for example, but fell far behind non-Communist countries in consumer products. Economic backwardness—they could not put food on the table—proved to be the great weakness of the Soviet Union and more recently of Cuba.

Image and Reality of Total Control

Just as there is no perfect democracy, neither is there perfect totalitarian dictatorship. Often outsiders were overly influenced by the image of total control projected by these states. Visitors to fascist Italy were impressed by the seeming law, order, cleanliness, and purposefulness of what they thought was one-man rule. Actually, many Italians quietly ridiculed Mussolini; his organizations and economic plans were a shambles; and he wasn't even in firm command of the country. In 1943, as the British and Americans overran southern Italy, Mussolini's own generals—who had been disobeying and lying to him for years—overthrew him in a coup. Then the king of Italy—Italy was technically a kingdom until 1946—fired Mussolini as prime minister. What kind of total control is that?

Since Stalin's death, every Soviet party chief denounced the bureaucracy, the deadening hand of routine, and the economic irregularities that impeded Soviet growth. But Khrushchev, Brezhnev, and Gorbachev couldn't touch the problem. Much of Soviet economic life ran by means of under-the-table deals and influence that defied centralized planning. Soviet workers stole everything from radios to locomotives and often showed up to work drunk or not at all. Where was the total control? The pages of *Pravda* and *Izvestia* thundered against these problems, but the government was unable to fix them.

Ruling Communist parties control jobs and career advancement, which increasingly attract not believers but opportunists, what Djilas called the "New Class." Young people join to get ahead and are privately cynical about party doctrine. Soon unlimited corruption reigns, damaging economic growth and national morale. Ultimately, the party's monopoly on power undermines the regime's legitimacy. China is trying to fight pervasive corruption through its Central Commission on Discipline Inspection, but many suspect it is used selectively to destroy political rivals. If they arrested all corrupt officials, none would be left to run China.

Methods

Tight Writing

Hemingway urged writers "to strip language clean, to lay it bare down to the bone." If you make your written work half as long, typically you make it twice as clear. Throw out unnecessary words. Ripest targets: adverbs, adjectives, and specialized jargon. Combine sentences that have the same subject. Ask yourself, "By making it shorter, have I really left anything out?" Use active voice rather than passive. Whenever possible, use verbs instead of nouns. Stanley Walker, city editor of the old *New York Herald Tribune*, told budding journalists "to avoid adjectives and to swear by the little verbs that bounce and leap and swim and cut."

Loose	**Tight**
Persistent governmental indifference and bureaucratic obstructionism over a long period of time tend to foster a political culture of apathy and nonparticipation.	Distant government and do-nothing bureaucrats turn people away from politics.

Uses Nouns	**Uses Verbs**
German elections show a marked tendency to the casting of ballots along confessional lines, with Catholic Länder favoring the Christian Democratic party and Protestant Länder favoring the Social Democratic party.	German Catholics tend to vote Christian Democrat, Protestants Social Democrat.
take a leadership role	lead
achieve success	succeed

Same Subject, Two Sentences	**Combined Sentence**
The Federal Election Commission figures showed Gore with a small (half a percent) lead in the popular vote nationwide. But the same commission showed that Bush had won in the electoral college by four votes.	The Federal Election Commission gave Gore a small lead in the popular vote but found that Bush had won in the electoral college.

Passive Voice	**Active Voice**
The popular vote was won by Gore.	Gore won the popular vote.

The above model of totalitarianism never matched reality. It was an *attempt* to impose total control, not the achievement of it. Starting in late 1989, as one country in Eastern Europe after another cast off its Communist system, we beheld how weak the system was. As to ideology, many citizens, even Party members, disdained communism. The single ruling parties collapsed and handed power over to non-Communists. Organized terror lost its punch. The official mass media, widely ignored for years, were simply discarded in favor of a free press. The controlled economies were turned, with much pain, into market economies. We now realize that these Communist regimes had never exercised total control.

Right-Wing Totalitarianism

We tend to focus on communism, but right-wing totalitarianism—Italian Fascism and German National Socialism—was somewhat different. It developed in industrialized nations plagued by economic depression, social upheaval, and political confusion and demoralization in which democracy was weak. Amid turmoil

whig democracy
Democracy for the few, typical of early stages of democracy.

demagogue
Politician who whips up masses with extreme and misleading issues.

Democracy

Why Democracies Fail

Democracy can actually come too soon in the political life of a nation. Stable democracy has historically taken root in countries with large, educated middle classes. As Barrington Moore observed in 1966, "No bourgeoisie, no democracy." People in poor countries care more about survival than democracy. In a 2004 UN survey of Latin America, a majority said they preferred a dictator who puts food on the table to an elected leader who does not. Middle classes bring with them moderation, tolerance, and the realization that not everything can be fixed at once. Without that, elections can undermine democracy, as seen in Iraq, Russia, and Zimbabwe.

The transition to democracy is delicate and happens best slowly and gradually, as it did in Britain with a series of Reform Acts during the nineteenth century. Typically, during the first decades of democracy, only the better-off can participate, a pattern called **whig democracy**. (In the United States, this ended with Jackson's election in 1828.) When the broad masses of citizens suddenly get the vote, the system can break down. Newly enfranchised and unsophisticated voters often fall for the extravagant or extremist promises of **demagogues**, who offer simple solutions to get the votes of the gullible. They vow to "share the wealth" but often wreck the economy with extravagant spending. Perón of Argentina, Vargas of Brazil, and Chávez of Venezuela are examples. Military coups sometimes throw out demagogues. If Saudi Arabia had free elections, many Saudis would vote for an Islamic fundamentalist. Attempting democracy too soon can lead to rule by demagogues, generals, or fanatics.

Several characteristics tend to block democracy:

1. Poverty
2. Major inequality
3. No middle class
4. Low education levels
5. Oil
6. Tribalism
7. Little civil society
8. Had been a colony
9. No earlier democratic experience
10. No democratic countries nearby

Actually, these items often come as a package. Democracy in a country with all or most of these characteristics rarely succeeds.

in 1922, Mussolini was named Italy's prime minister and soon turned himself into the first Fascist dictator. Germany after World War I suffered a punitive peace treaty (Versailles) and hyperinflation. When the Depression brought high unemployment and labor unrest, Communists and Nazis slugged it out in elections and street fighting. Hitler took over in 1933 with promises to restore order, to renounce the humiliating Versailles Treaty, and to protect private property from the Communist menace to the east. His program appealed to industrialists, militarists, and middle-class people, who typically support a fascist state.

Right-wing totalitarianism does not want revolution; rather, it aims to block leftist revolution by strengthening the existing social order and glorifying the state. It attempts to get rid of those deemed foreign or inferior, as Hitler strove to annihilate Jews and Gypsies. Citizens are also directed toward national glory and war. Private ownership is generally permitted, but obedient cartels and national trade associations carry out party directives.

Authoritarianism

5.4 **Distinguish authoritarianism from totalitarianism.**

authoritarian
Nondemocratic government but not necessarily totalitarian.

Authoritarianism and *totalitarianism* are often confused but are different. **Authoritarian** regimes are governed by a small group—usually a dictator or the army—that minimizes popular input. They do not attempt to control everything. Many economic, social, religious, cultural, and familial matters are left up to individuals. Most of the six points of totalitarianism discussed earlier are diluted or absent. Authoritarian regimes, for example, rarely have a firm ideology to sell. Some called the Saddam regime in Iraq totalitarian, but it was closer to authoritarian. The main types of authoritarianism are shown in Table 5.3.

Authoritarian regimes limit individual freedoms in favor of a hierarchical organization of command, obedience, and order. Citizens obey laws and pay taxes that they have no voice in establishing. Some trappings of democracy may exist for appearance's sake. Rigged elections confirm the rule of the dominant party; opponents have no chance, and some are arrested. Legislatures rubber stamp the dictator's laws, and puppet prime ministers and cabinets carry them out. The media and academia practice informal "self-censorship," avoiding critical

Table 5.3 Types of Authoritarianism

	Examples
Military	Mauritania, Niger
Personalistic	Uzbekistan, Venezuela
Traditional monarchy	Saudi Arabia, Kuwait
Dominant-party	Russia, Zimbabwe
Single-party	China, Cuba

comments in order to keep their jobs. Louis XIV of France showed an early form of authoritarianism with his famous phrase: *"L'état c'est moi"* (The state—that's me).

Spain under Franco (1939–1975) was "traditional authoritarian" rather than totalitarian, as the *caudillo* (leader) sought political passivity and obedience rather than enthusiastic participation and mobilization. Franco and his supporters had no single ideology to promote, and the economy and press were pluralistic within limits. Some observers now see a new model, the "authoritarian capitalist" regimes of China and Russia, which allow partially market economies but tightly retain political control. Their selling points are economic growth and rising living standards, and most citizens accept them and show little interest in democracy. But what happens when growth stops, as it has in Russia?

Political scientist Jeane J. Kirkpatrick (1926–2006), President Reagan's ambassador to the United Nations, argued that there is a difference between authoritarian and totalitarian regimes. The former (such as Argentina, Chile, and Brazil) can reform, but once a totalitarian system (such as communism) takes over, the system cannot reform itself. Argentina, Chile, and Brazil did return to democracy in the 1980s. Kirkpatrick's thesis was borne out in the fact that the Communist regimes of the Soviet bloc never did reform themselves; they collapsed while trying to reform. The big question of the twenty-first century: Is China's rapidly growing economy producing an educated middle class that starts demanding democracy? Or can the regime forever buy off its people with rising living standards plus Chinese nationalism? China is developing problems, and many Chinese thinkers call for reforms, usually privately.

Authoritarianism and the Developing Nations

In the decades after World War II, the European empires granted their colonies independence. All the new nations, proclaimed themselves "democratic," but it did not last long. The colonialists had never encouraged democracy. Democracy in the Western tradition grew out of individualism and a competitive market economy. The developing societies had preindustrial, traditional peasant economies that stressed families and tribes. Levels of education and income were low, and most people were absorbed in the struggle to survive. Postcolonial leaders had typically picked up socialist views while students in Britain and France and argued that political and economic survival and growth need centralized power and planning. The leaders claimed that they knew what the people needed and rigged elections.

In this way, much of the **Third World** fell into authoritarianism under single parties. Such systems are usually terrible. Government officials push wasteful, unrealistic projects, stifle individual initiative by regulations and taxes, and crush critical viewpoints. Corruption stunts economic growth. In this way, such countries as Tanzania and Myanmar (Burma) impoverished themselves, ending up with neither democracy nor economic growth. Zimbabwe, for example, started democratic in 1980, but some parties opposed the dominant party and its leader, Robert Mugabe, who cracked down harshly with soldiers of his

Third World
The developing areas: parts of Asia, Africa, and Latin America.

Case Studies

Democracy in Iraq?

Iraq was a new and artificial country the British put together in 1922 from three former Ottoman provinces. Its population groups do not like each other. Sixty percent of Iraqis are Shia Muslims, a repressed and suspect minority throughout the Arab world. Saddam Hussein had ruled through his Sunni Arabs (20 percent of the population) and murdered hundreds of thousands of Shias. Freed in 2003, Shias won subsequent elections and ignored Sunni demands to share power. Sunni extremists suicide-bombed Shias, who now controlled Iraq's police and army and retaliated by killing Sunnis. In the north of Iraq, Kurds (about 20 percent), who are Sunni but not Arab, rule themselves and are ready to declare independence. In 2014, Sunni militants from many countries proclaimed an Islamic State over much of Iraq and Syria. Funded by crime, they murdered all who did not share their faith.

Elections do not automatically produce democracy, which requires stable countries with much economic, educational, and political development. Most of Iraq's neighbors are dictatorships, some more authoritarian than others. Saddam was not an accident but a product of a rebellious country that was ready to fall apart—and still is.

In 2005, the United States launched a major promotion of democracy in the Middle East, but it made little headway. Free elections in Lebanon and Palestine increased the power, respectively, of the extremist Hezbollah and Hamas. As Jeane Kirkpatrick observed: "No idea holds greater sway in the mind of educated Americans than the belief that it is possible to democratize governments, anytime and anywhere, under any circumstances." Iraq was an expensive lesson that taught Americans a more realistic view. In 2011, Tunisia, Egypt, Libya, and Yemen overthrew their presidents for life, but this unleashed Islamists who had little interest in establishing democracy.

dominant tribe and created an authoritarian system, arguing that this was the only way to build unity and a socialist economy. Miscounted elections kept Mugabe in power as inflation topped 1,000,000 percent, most Zimbabweans were unemployed and hungry, and regime opponents were jailed or killed.

The Democratization of Authoritarian Regimes

5.5 Explain why new democracies often fail.

Since 1974, dozens of countries have abandoned authoritarian or totalitarian systems in favor of democratic systems, although recently some have slid backward. Still, around half the world's nations are at least a bit democratic. The expansion of democracy from the previous two dozen countries, mostly in Western Europe and North America, became a major scholarly topic. An excellent quarterly started in 1989, *Journal of Democracy*, explains why democracy appears and what policies encourage it.

Two types of regimes contributed to the latest wave of democracy: authoritarian regimes that enjoyed strong economic growth and collapsed Communist regimes whose economic growth lagged. The fast-growth systems—such as Chile, Brazil, South Korea, and Taiwan—were politically authoritarian but developed private market economies. It was as if the dictator said, "I'll take care of politics; you just work on your businesses." The pro-growth regimes set macroeconomic policy (sound currency, low inflation, plenty of capital for loans) and exported to the world market. After a time, the growing economy transformed the whole society into a democracy, a process that illustrates **modernization theory**: As countries improve from poor to middle income, they become ready for stable democracy. Democracy seldom lasts in poor countries—India is an exception, and Indonesia, after decades of dictators, is becoming democratic—but it works in most middle-income and richer countries.

modernization theory
Economic growth fosters a large, educated middle class that demands democracy.

Why should this happen? First, economic growth creates a large middle class, which has a stake in the system; they may wish to reform it but not overthrow it. Second, education levels rise; most people are high-school graduates, and many are college graduates. They are no longer ignorant and do not fall for demagogues, extremist ideas, or vote buying. Third, people increasingly recognize their interests and express them: pluralism. They voice business, professional, regional, and religious demands. They can spot cruel, corrupt, or inefficient governments and do not like being treated like children. Urban, educated Russians showed this attitude in 2012. Finally, the market itself teaches citizens about self-reliance, pluralism, tolerance, and not expecting too much, all attitudes that sustain democracy. Gradually, if everything works right, the regime eases up, permitting a critical press, the formation of political parties, and finally free elections. Taiwan carried out this transition from 1984 to 2000 and is now a vibrant democracy, one whose elections are followed with great interest by mainland Chinese.

This transition does not work with **petrostates**. Oil exports, because they concentrate wealth and power in the hands of a few, retard democracy. None of the twenty-three countries that get 60 percent or more of their export income from oil or natural gas is a democracy. And that includes petrostates with high per capita GDPs. The oil industry does not employ many workers. Citizens depend on the government for jobs and handouts and do not form an autonomous, pluralistic middle class. In other words, a high per capita GDP is not the same as a robust, educated middle class. Such countries, many around the Persian Gulf, are ripe for overthrow but not for democracy.

petrostate
Country based on oil exports, such as Saudi Arabia.

The collapse of Communist regimes shows the role of the economy in a negative sense. It was poor economic performance and slow growth, especially in comparison with the West and with the rapid-growth countries, that persuaded relatively liberal Communists, such as Mikhail Gorbachev (1931–), to attempt to reform their systems. They knew they were falling behind, especially in crucial high-tech sectors, and thought they could energize the system by bringing elements of the free market into an otherwise socialist economy. But communism, like other brands of totalitarianism, doesn't tolerate reform. By attempting to control everything, as in Friedrich's and Brzezinski's six points, they have created a brittle system that can break but not bend. Once they started admitting that the system needed to be fixed, they admitted that they had been wrong. The ideology was wrong, single-party control was wrong, the centralized economy was wrong, and so on. The reform attempt turned into system collapse.

Will the countries that emerge from the wreckage of dictatorship establish lasting democracies? So far, the ex-Communist lands of Poland and the Czech Republic have done so. Hungary, alas, has recently taken on authoritarian hues. Farther east and south, however, democracy is incomplete or in retreat. Market systems are strange and frightening to Russians, Uzbeks, and others, and indeed the transition from a controlled to a market economy inflicts terrible hardships. Some voters, never having known democracy, turn to authoritarian figures, who promise to restore stability and incomes. Vladimir Putin silenced or jailed opposition, and most Russians supported him. Russian political culture favors rule by one strong leader. The executive is extremely powerful and can rule by decree; the State Duma (parliament) is weak and obeys the executive. Putin brought the energy sector (oil and gas) back under state control, and most of the mass media obey him. A favored few get very rich. Some call this a **kleptocracy**, and it is found in much of the world.

kleptocracy
Rule by thieves, used in derision and jest.

Democracy is not easy. It is a complex, finely balanced system that depends on a political culture that grows best under a market economy with a large, educated middle class and a tradition of pluralism. Centuries of religious and philosophical evolution prepare democratic attitudes. Iraq lacked all of these. Eventually Iraq or any other country can turn democratic, but it may take decades. Most scholars look forward to it, as there is strong support for the theory of the **democratic peace**, that no two democracies have ever fought each other. If this is true, a more democratic world means a more peaceful world.

democratic peace
Theory that democracies do not fight each other.

Review Questions

1. Why does modern democracy mean representative democracy?
2. Which are the defining characteristics of democracy?
3. Which is more accurate, the elite or pluralist theory?
4. Why is totalitarianism a twentieth-century phenomenon?
5. What is the difference between totalitarian and authoritarian?
6. Are totalitarian systems bound to fail? Why?
7. Why have many countries turned democratic?
8. Why does democracy sometimes fail? Did it work in Iraq?
9. Should the United States try to export democracy?

Key Terms

authoritarian, p. 102
caste, p. 91
civil disobedience, p. 93
demagogue, p. 101
democratic peace, p. 106
democracy, p. 88
elites, p. 94
hierarchy, p. 98
illiberal democracy, p. 89

interest group, p. 96
kleptocracy, p. 106
mandate, p. 91
mass media, p. 94
modernization theory, p. 105

petrostate, p. 105
pluralism, p. 94
referendum, p. 89
representative
 democracy, p. 89

Third World, p. 103
totalitarian, p. 97
trustee, p. 91
whig democracy, p. 101

Further Reference

Ayittey, George B. N. *Defeating Dictators: Fighting Tyranny in Africa and Around the World*. New York: Palgrave, 2012.

Bartels, Larry M. *Unequal Democracy: The Political Economy of the New Gilded Age*. Princeton, NJ: Princeton University Press, 2008.

Coggan, Philip. *The Last Vote: The Threats to Western Democracy*. London: Allen Lane, 2013.

Collier, Paul. *Wars, Guns, and Votes: Democracy in Dangerous Places*. New York: Harper, 2010.

Diamond, Larry. *The Spirit of Democracy*. New York: Holt, 2009.

Dobson, William. *The Dictator's Learning Curve: Inside the Global Battle for Democracy*. New York: Doubleday, 2012.

Flathman, Richard E. *Pluralism and Liberal Democracy*. Baltimore, MD: Johns Hopkins University Press, 2005.

Halper, Stefan. *The Beijing Consensus: How China's Authoritarian Model Will Dominate the Twenty-First Century*. New York: Basic Books, 2010.

Jamal, Amaney. *Of Empires and Citizens: Pro-American Democracy or No Democracy at All?* Princeton, NJ: Princeton University Press, 2012.

Linz, Juan. *Totalitarian and Authoritarian Regimes*. Boulder, CO: Lynne Rienner, 2000.

McFaul, Michael. *Advancing Democracy Abroad: Why We Should and How We Can*. Lanham, MD: Rowman & Littlefield, 2010.

McWilliams, Wilson Carey. *Redeeming Democracy in America*. Lawrence, KS: University Press of Kansas, 2011.

Ross, Michael L. *The Oil Curse: How Petroleum Wealth Shapes the Development of Nations*. Princeton, NJ: Princeton University Press, 2012.

Rothkopf, David. *Power, Inc.: The Epic Rivalry Between Big Business and Government—and the Reckoning that Lies Ahead*. New York: Farrar, Straus & Giroux, 2012.

Ringen, Stein. *Nation of Devils: Democratic Leadership and the Problem of Obedience*. New Haven, CT: Yale University Press, 2012

Runciman, David. *The Confidence Trap: A History of Democracy in Crisis From World War I to the Present*. Princeton, NJ: Princeton University Press, 2013.

Stepan, Alfred., ed. *Democracies in Danger*. Baltimore, MD: Johns Hopkins University Press, 2009.

Teorell, Jan. *Determinants of Democratization: Explaining Regime Change in the World, 1972–2006*. New York: Cambridge University Press, 2010.

Tismaneanu, Vladimir. *The Devil in History: Communism, Fascism, and Some Lessons of the Twentieth Century*. Berkeley, CA: University of California Press, 2012.

Tilly, Charles. *Democracy*. New York: Cambridge University Press, 2007.

Wedel, Janine R. *Shadow Elite: How the World's New Power Brokers Undermine Democracy, Government and the Free Market*. New York: Basic Books, 2009.

Part II
Political Attitudes

Ch. 6 Political Culture Political culture searches for a given society's broad, general views on government and politics. A participatory and work-ethic culture sustains a free and prosperous society, but cynical culture can damage it. Political culture, once laid down, lasts a long time but under the pressure of events can decay. Any society shows elite-mass and subcultural differences. Political culture is learned chiefly from the family, sometimes bolstered by overt socialization in schools.

Ch. 7 Public Opinion Public opinion looks for specific views on leaders and problems; it is narrower and faster-changing than political culture. The opinions of individuals are shaped by social class, education, region, religion, age, gender, and ethnicity. Scientific polling can be accurate, provided the sample is random and the question is clear. U.S. presidents go through honeymoons and rally events but generally get less support over time. Polling is plagued by respondents' varying levels of interest and intensity, leading to great volatility.

Chapter 6
Political Culture

Learning Objectives

6.1 Distinguish political culture from public opinion.

6.2 Explain how a country's political culture can change over time.

6.3 Distinguish between elite and mass political subcultures.

6.4 Explain the effects of sharply distinct minority subcultures within a nation.

6.5 List with examples the main agents of political socialization.

The United States now has a partially split political culture, making the country hard to govern. While Americans still hold many values in common, for some years they have tended to form two camps. The liberal camp sees the need for government intervention in the economy, health insurance, and minority rights. The conservative camp bitterly opposes this in favor of smaller government that does not guarantee much of anything. The split goes deeper than rational policy debates; it goes to basic ways of looking at life and society. Same-sex marriage, abortion, racial equality, and gun laws are some of the gut issues that divide them. What liberals call fair, necessary measures to restore America's vitality, conservatives denounce as the erosion of personal responsibility that saps America's vitality. The two sides do not speak nicely to each other but try to block whatever the other side wants.

What Is Political Culture?

6.1 Distinguish political culture from public opinion.

Each society imparts its norms and values to its people, who pick up distinct notions about how the political system is supposed to work and about what the government may do to them and for them. These beliefs, symbols, and values about the political system are the political culture of a nation—and it varies considerably from one nation to another. (The business equivalent is "corporate culture," which can also be quite distinctive from one company to another.)

values
Deeply held views; key component of political culture.

The political culture of a nation is determined by its history, economy, religion, and folkways. Basic **values**, laid down long ago, may endure for centuries. Political culture is a sort of collective political memory. America was founded on the basis of "competitive individualism," a spirit of hustle and looking out for oneself, which is still very much alive. The millennia-old Hindu emphasis on caste persists in present-day India despite government efforts to abolish it. The French, after centuries of *étatisme*, still expect a big state to supervise the economy. Iraq, for centuries part of Arab and Turkish empires, has known only autocracy, for two decades under the brutal Saddam Hussein. Democracy has no roots in Iraq's political culture.

As defined by political scientist Sidney Verba, political culture is "the system of empirical beliefs, expressive symbols, and values, which defines the situation in which political action takes place." Much of this goes far back. Americans always liked minimal government. In Japan, where the vestiges of a traditional feudal class system still exist, those who bow first and lower indicate they are of inferior status. The Japanese still tend to submit to the authority of those in office, even when they dislike their corruption and incompetence. Americans, who traditionally do not defer to anyone, consider it their democratic birthright to criticize the way the country is governed, even if they know little about the issues. In political culture, Japan and the United States are vastly different.

Political Culture and Public Opinion

Political culture and public opinion overlap, for both look at attitudes toward politics. Political culture looks for basic, general values on politics and government. Public opinion, on the other hand, looks for views about specific leaders and policies. Political culture looks for the underpinnings of legitimacy, the gut attitudes that sustain a political system, whereas public opinion seeks responses to current questions.

The methodologies of political culture and public opinion may also overlap: Random samples of the population are asked questions, and the responses are correlated with subgroups in the population. The questions, however, are different. A political culture survey might ask how much you trust other people; a public opinion survey might ask if you think the president is doing a good job. A political culture study may ask the same questions in several countries to gain a comparative perspective. Both may keep track of responses over time to see, in the case of political culture, if legitimacy is gaining or declining or, in the case of public opinion, how a president's popular support changes.

Political culture studies often go beyond surveys, however. Some use the methods of anthropology and psychology in the close observation of daily life and in the deep questioning of individuals about their feelings. Public opinion studies rarely go beyond quantified data, whereas political culture studies can use history and literature to gain insights. For instance, the observations of nineteenth-century European visitors show continuity in American political and social values. Indeed, the brilliant observations of Frenchman Alexis de Tocqueville, who traveled through the United States in the early 1830s, still generally apply today. Tocqueville was one of the founders of the political-culture approach in political science.

It used to be assumed that political culture was nearly permanent or changed only slowly, whereas public opinion was fickle and changed quickly. Recent studies, however, have shown that political culture is rather changeable, too. Periods of stable, efficient government and economic growth solidify feelings of legitimacy; periods of indecisive, chaotic government and economic downturn are reflected in weakening legitimacy. Public opinion, if held long enough, eventually turns into political culture. In the 1960s, public opinion on Vietnam showed declining support for the war. Over precisely the same time, confidence in the U.S. government also declined. Public opinion on a given question was infecting the general political culture, making it more **cynical** about the political system.

To be sure, a country's political culture changes more slowly than its public opinions, and certain underlying elements of political culture persist for generations, even centuries. The basic values Tocqueville found in America are largely unchanged. The French still take to the streets of Paris to protest perceived injustice, just as their ancestors did. Italians continue their centuries-old cynicism toward anything governmental. Russians, who have never experienced free democracy, still tend to support strong leaders, although more now demand

cynical
Untrusting and suspicious, especially of government.

participatory
Interest or willingness to take part in politics.

political competence
Knowing how to accomplish something politically.

political efficacy
Feeling that one has at least a little political input (opposite: feeling powerless).

Classic Works

The Civic Culture

Gabriel Almond and Sidney Verba did the pioneering study of cross-national differences in political beliefs and values. Their researchers interviewed some 1,000 people each in five countries in 1959 and 1960 to measure underlying political views. From the data, Almond and Verba discerned three general political cultures: participant, subject, and parochial. Every country, they emphasized, is its own mixture of all three of these ideal types.

Participant

In a **participant** political culture, such as the United States and Britain, people understand that they are citizens and pay attention to politics. They are proud of their country's political system and are willing to discuss it. They believe they can influence politics and claim they would organize a group to protest something unfair. Accordingly, they show a high degree of **political competence** and **political efficacy**. They say they take pride in voting and believe people should participate in politics. They are active in their communities and often belong to voluntary organizations. They are likely to trust other people and to recall participating in family discussions as children. A participant political culture is the ideal soil to sustain a democracy.

Subject

Less democratic than the participant political culture is the **subject** political culture, predominant at that time in West Germany and Italy, in which people still understand that they are citizens and pay attention to politics, but they do so more passively. They follow political news but are not proud of their country's political system and feel little emotional commitment toward it. They are uncomfortable discussing politics and feel they can influence politics only to the extent of speaking with a local official. It does not ordinarily occur to them to organize a group. Their sense of political competence and efficacy is lower; some feel powerless. They say they vote, but many vote without enthusiasm. They are less likely to trust other people and to recall voicing their views as children. Democracy has more difficulty sinking roots in a culture where people are used to thinking of themselves as obedient subjects rather than as participants.

Parochial

Still less democratic is the **parochial** political culture, where many people do not much care that they are citizens of a nation, as in Mexico at the time of the survey. They identify with the immediate locality, hence the term *parochial* (of a parish). They take no pride in their country's political system and expect little of it. They pay no attention to politics, have little knowledge of it, and seldom speak about it. They have neither the desire nor the ability to participate in politics. They have no sense of political competence or efficacy and feel powerless in the face of existing institutions. Attempting to grow a democracy in a parochial political culture is very difficult, requiring not only new institutions but also a new sense of citizenship.

---

subject
Feeling among citizens that they should obey authority but not participate much in politics.

parochial
Narrow; having little or no interest in national politics.

democracy. Although not as firm as bedrock, political culture is an underlying layer that can support—or fail to support—the rest of the political system. This is one reason Russia's attempt at democracy faded.

Participation in America

Even in America, not all citizens actively participate in politics. How, then, could Almond and Verba offer the United States as their model of a "civic culture"? One of their key findings was that participation need only be "intermittent and potential." In effect, they offer a "sleeping dogs" theory of democratic political culture. Leaders in a democracy know that most of the time, most people pay little attention to politics. But they also know that if aroused—because of scandal, unemployment, inflation, or unpopular war—the public can vote them out of office at the next election. Accordingly, leaders usually work to keep the public passive and quiet. Following the **rule of anticipated reactions**, leaders in democracies constantly ask themselves how the public will likely react to their decisions. They are happy to have the public *not* react at all; they wish to let sleeping dogs lie.

rule of anticipated reactions
Politicians form policies based on how they think the public will react.

This theory helps explain an embarrassing fact about U.S. political life, namely, its low voter **turnout**, the lowest of all the industrialized democracies. Until recently, only about half of U.S. voters cast ballots in presidential elections, although it is now higher. Even fewer vote in state and local contests. In Europe, voter turnout has been about three-quarters of the electorate (but is declining there, too). How, then, can the United States boast of its democracy? Theorists reply that a democratic culture does not necessarily require heavy voter turnout. Rather, it requires an attitude that, if aroused, the people will participate—vote, contribute time and money, organize groups, and circulate petitions—and that elected officials know this. They fear a "Tea Party" developing that will vote them out. Democracy in this view is a psychological connection between leaders and followers that tends to restrain officials. It is the potential and not the actual participation that makes a democratic culture.

turnout
Percent of eligible voters who vote in a given election.

Democracy

Civil Society

The concept of "civil society" is closely related to political culture. Hobbes used the term to indicate humans after becoming civilized; Hegel used it to designate associations bigger than the family but smaller than the state—churches, clubs, businesses, and so on. Edmund Burke wrote that the "little platoons of society" form the basis of political life. They encourage cooperating with others, rule of law, restraint, and moderation—what Tocqueville called "habits of the heart." Without them, politics becomes a murderous grab for power.

With the fall of communism in Eastern Europe and the Soviet Union, the concept attracted new interest to explain the growth of democracy—or the lack of it. The Communist regimes had attempted to stomp out civil society and control nearly everything. When a totalitarian regime collapses, it leaves a vacuum where there should be a civil society. Nothing works right; lawlessness sweeps the land. Americans supposed that after communism Russia would quickly become like us, but Russia had no civil society and soon reverted to authoritarianism. Likewise, we supposed that, after Saddam Hussein, Iraq would become a stable democracy, but with little civil society Iraq degenerated into chaos.

A vibrant and developed civil society is the bedrock of democracy. Central Europe—especially Poland's strong Catholic Church, which always taught Poles to ignore communism—had some civil society and moved quickly to democracy. Without a civil society, democracy may not take root.

Another of Almond and Verba's key findings was the response to the question of what citizens of five countries would do to influence local government regarding an unjust ordinance. Far more Americans said that they would "try to enlist the aid of others." Americans seem to be natural "group formers" when faced with a political problem, an important foundation of U.S. democracy. In what Almond and Verba called "subject" cultures, this group-forming attitude was weaker.

Other studies show that Americans are prouder of their system and more satisfied with the way democracy works in their country compared with the citizens of other lands. A 1995 Gallup survey found that 64 percent of the Americans polled expressed some degree of satisfaction. Sixty-two percent of Canadians responded likewise, as did 55 percent of Germans, 43 percent of French, 40 percent of Britons, 35 percent of Japanese, and only 17 percent of Mexicans and Hungarians. Americans may complain about government, but their faith in democracy is still the strongest in the world.

Methods

Quotations

Do not quote everything. Quote only important statements from key figures, and only if the exact words and phrasing are important to your point. You might quote the secretary of state on a major foreign policy, but you should not normally quote a journalist or an academic. Their precise words are rarely that important. Instead, if you want to borrow their ideas, paraphrase them in your own words, but still cite them. For your paper, a short summary is better than a long quote.

Quote

"I have no problem with any of the substantive criticism of President Obama from the right or left," wrote columnist Thomas Friedman. "But something very dangerous is happening. Criticism from the far right has begun tipping over into delegitimation and creating the same kind of climate here that existed in Israel on the eve of the Rabin assassination" (Friedman 2009).

Paraphrase

Washington pundits grew alarmed at the partisan rage directed at President Obama.

Occasionally, a scholar says something so clear and provocative that it's worth quoting: "Islam has bloody borders" (Huntington 1993). Use partial quotes instead of long quotes. Pick out the interesting or operative phrase and quote it: Pentagon officials said they had "not anticipated" chaos in Iraq (Sinclair 2003). If you must include a long quote—more than three lines—make it an indented block quote. Use ellipses (...) to indicate you have omitted unnecessary words. Use brackets ([ ]) to indicate you have inserted a clarification of words not in the original.

> To slow down the tempo means to lag behind. And those who lag behind are beaten. The history of Old Russia shows...that because of her backwardness she was constantly defeated.... We [the Russians] are behind the leading countries by fifty to one hundred years. We must make up this distance in ten years. Either we do it or we go under. (Stalin 1931)

The Decay of Political Culture

6.2 **Explain how a country's political culture can change over time.**

The political cultures of most of the advanced democracies have recently grown more cynical, and voter turnout has declined. More citizens saw politicians as corrupt and government institutions as ineffective. The steepest drop was in Japan, where the economy was stagnant for two decades. In the 1960s and 1970s—the years of the Vietnam War, Watergate, and inflation—U.S. surveys showed a sharp decline in trust in government (see Figure 6.1). In the 1980s, under the "feel-good" presidency of Ronald Reagan, the trusting responses went up but never recovered the levels of the early 1960s. Trust fell in 2004 over the U.S. war in Iraq and in 2013 over unemployment and paralyzed government. The growth in cynicism made America harder to govern and is reflected in an electorate that seems to be permanently split and unhappy with Washington. American political culture is not as unified and legitimate as it used to be.

A related development is America's "culture wars," a nasty polarization between conservatives and liberals, who dislike and vote against each other. For two centuries, one spoke of the "Two Spains" because it was badly split by region and religiosity. Now America seems to be two countries. One is conservative, Christian, small-town, and living in the middle of the country; it votes Republican (the "red states" on news maps). The other is liberal, **secular**, urban, and living on

secular
Not connected to religion.

Figure 6.1 Americans' trust in government, 1964–2013.

SOURCES: 1965–1996, American National Election Studies of the University of Michigan; 1997–2013, Pew Research Center for People and the Press

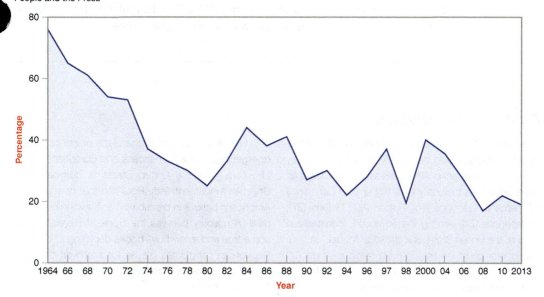

both coasts; it votes Democrat (the "blue states"). Conservatives dislike gay rights, big government, taxes, and Barack Obama and watch Fox News. Liberals dislike big corporations, the death penalty, guns, and George Bush and watch MSNBC.

Richard Nixon first exploited this split to win the 1968 election, and it has grown deeper ever since. The causes of this polarization are several and disputed. The 1960s was a time of upheaval in which younger Americans repudiated authority with "drugs, sex, and rock-and-roll." In reaction, what Nixon called the "silent majority" turned to conservative Christianity and the Republican Party, which espoused "family values." This left behind a big gap between religious and secular America (see box). Another possibility is that America never psychologically recovered from the Vietnam War, and the anger returned with the Iraq War. The big spending of healthcare reform and bank bailouts inflamed conservatives. Economically and demographically, the coasts of America grew more than much of the center (exception: Texas). If polarization keeps growing, some fear for U.S. political stability. Dialogue between the Two Americas fails, as their views are visceral, not rational.

One factor much discussed was the decline of the American tendency to form associations, anything from volunteer fire departments to labor unions. In the 1830s, Tocqueville noted, "Americans of all ages, all conditions, and all dispositions constantly form associations." He was impressed by this tendency, for it was (and still is) largely absent in France, and he held it was the basis of American democracy, a point supported much later by the *Civic Culture* study. Some observers claim that these grassroots associations are fading. Harvard political scientist Robert Putnam noted, for example, that the number of people bowling has increased, but league bowling has declined. His article, "Bowling Alone," caught much attention and controversy. Putnam argued the membership loss of many associations—unions, PTAs, Scouts, and fraternal orders—meant decline of our "social capital" and decay of civil society.

Case Studies

America the Religious

The United States is much more religious than other advanced industrialized nations. A 2009 Gallup survey found that 65 percent of Americans said religion plays an important part in their daily lives, higher than Canadians (42 percent), Germans (40), French (30), Britons (27), or Japanese (24). Among the advanced, industrialized nations, the United States is a statistical "outlier." In general, poorer countries are the most religious—India (90 percent), Nigeria (96), and Brazil (87)—along with Muslim lands—Indonesia (99) and Pakistan (92).

U.S. religiosity is also one of the points of cultural divergence between Americans and Europeans, many of whom think the United States is dominated by Christian fundamentalists. Polls find that nearly half of Americans believe in creationism and two-thirds in the devil. A majority believes the Book of Revelation will come true and avidly buys books depicting it. In 2016, Republican candidates played for and won the support of conservative Christians. This would not work in Europe or Japan.

Others argue that Americans volunteer and join as much as ever. Old associations, such as the Scouts and Elks, may be shrinking, but new ones, such as Habitat for Humanity and Meals on Wheels, may be growing. Forty percent of American college students volunteer to help the homeless, feed the needy, tutor, participate in religious life, clean up the environment, and participate in other altruistic activities. The sudden rise of the Tea Party movement shows Americans are still willing to form associations.

Those who see the decline of America's voluntary associations, however, fear political and economic repercussions. With individuals demanding their "rights" without a corresponding sense of "obligations," demands on government become impossible. Democracy becomes less a matter of concerned citizens meeting face to face to discuss a community problem than disgruntled citizens demanding "Gimme!" Furthermore, argued Francis Fukuyama (who earlier brought us the "end of history" theory), trust or "spontaneous sociability" underpins economic growth and stability. If you can trust others, you can do more and better business with them. Hence, "high trust" societies tend to be prosperous, low trust societies not.

Another school of thought sees the growth of distrust in government as natural and not necessarily bad. Politicians worldwide have for decades promised citizens more and more, promises they could not possibly deliver; there is simply not enough money. But citizens in the meantime have become more educated and aware of this gap and more willing to criticize. What some now call "critical citizens" protest massively against corrupt, out-of-touch governments in Turkey, Brazil, Egypt, Indonesia, and elsewhere—a warning to politicians and good sign for democracy.

Political culture changes. It is a combination of long-remembered and deeply held values plus reactions to current situations. These changes are responses to government performance, which almost always falls short of promises. Political cultures do not fall from heaven; they are created by government actions and inactions.

Elite and Mass Subcultures

6.3   **Distinguish between elite and mass political subcultures.**

The political culture of a country is not uniform and monolithic. One can usually find within it differences between the mainstream culture and **subcultures** and differences between elite and mass attitudes. Elites—used here more broadly than "governing elites" (a tiny fraction of 1 percent)—in political-culture studies means those with better education, higher income, and more influence (several percent). Elites are much more interested in politics and more participatory. They are more inclined to vote, to protest injustice, to form groups, and to run for office. One consistent finding of the *Civic Culture* study has been confirmed over and over: The more education people have, the more likely they are to participate in politics.

subculture
A minority culture within the *mainstream* culture.

Delegates to both Democratic and Republican conventions—who are clearly very interested in politics—illustrate the differences between elite and mass culture. Many of the delegates have some postgraduate education (often law school), far more than average voters. Most convention delegates have annual incomes much higher than average voters. Delegates are also more ideological than average voters, the Democrats more liberal and the Republicans more conservative. In other words, the people at conventions are not closely representative of typical voters. People with more education, money, and ideological convictions take the leading roles. There is nothing wrong with this; it is standard worldwide.

Why should this be so? Better-educated people show greater *political competence*; they know how to participate in political activity. They also show greater *political efficacy*, as in their self-confidence in writing to officials and the media, speaking at meetings, and organizing groups. They feel that what they do has at least some political impact. The uneducated and the poor lack the knowledge and confidence to do these kinds of things. Many of them feel powerless. "What I do doesn't matter, so why bother?" they think. Those at the bottom of the social ladder thus become apathetic.

The differences in participation in politics between elites and masses are one of the great ironies of democracy. In theory and in law, a democracy is open to all. In practice, some participate much more than others. Because the

Theories

Culture and Development

Asia's recent economic growth brought cultural explanations of why some countries stay poor while others get rich. Japan, South Korea, Taiwan, Hong Kong, and Singapore have no natural resources, but they do have disciplined people who work hard, save their money, and trust each other. (Most also turned into democracies.) Some point to their common Confucian heritage, which promotes such values. China, the origin of Confucianism, has enjoyed incredible economic growth recently. The Middle East, on the other hand, has rigidly Islamic people who do not trust each other. Its oil wealth has brought only superficial modernization, no democracy, and the world's highest unemployment.

A century ago, Max Weber argued that Protestantism laid down the cultural basis of capitalism. A "Protestant work ethic" pushed people to work hard and amass capital. The Protestant countries of northwest Europe were the first capitalist and democratic nations. Even today, these countries are rich and have high levels of trust, rule of law, and little corruption. Countries lacking this culture, such as Rwanda or Egypt, do not take quickly to economic growth or democracy.

According to the cultural theory of prosperity, countries will stay poor until they rid themselves of traditionalism, mistrust, and fatalism, all prominent in the Middle East. Without a shift of values, outside aid often disappears into corruption. Critics of the cultural theory point out that decades ago Confucianism was blamed for keeping East Asia *backward* and that values often change *after* economic growth has taken hold. No one has been able to predict which countries will grow rapidly based on their culture or anything else; it's always a surprise.

better-educated and better-off people (more education usually leads to higher income) participate in politics far more, they are in a much stronger position to look out for their interests. It is not surprising that the 2001 tax cut favored the wealthiest, who speak up and donate money; those lower on the socioeconomic ladder do not. There is no quick fix for this. The right to vote is a mere starting point for political participation; it does not guarantee equal access to decision making. A mass political culture of apathy and indifference toward politics effectively negates the potential of a mass vote. An elite political culture of competence and efficacy amplifies their influence.

Minority Subcultures

6.4   **Explain the effects of sharply distinct minority subcultures within a nation.**

The 2010 census showed that a third of U.S. residents are nonwhite. They might be black, Latino, Asian, Native American, or Pacific Islander. In California, Hawaii, New Mexico, and Texas, whites are a minority. Even among white Americans, there are differences among ethnic, religious, and regional groups. When the differentiating qualities are strong enough in a particular group, we say that the group forms a subculture. Defining subculture is tricky, as not every group is a subculture. The Norwegian Americans of "Lake Wobegon," Minnesota, do not form a subculture because their culture and politics are **mainstream**.

mainstream
Sharing the average or standard political culture.

But African Americans do form a political subculture. They are poorer and less educated than whites, much more liberal and Democratic in voting. The 2012 election split over race, with a majority of whites for Romney and most nonwhites for Obama. In attitudes toward the criminal justice system, African Americans sharply diverge from whites. African Americans tend to call the police killings of unarmed people of color racism; fewer whites do. A new movement, "Black Lives Matter," is convinced that the police are brutal and trigger-happy. Whites tend to see the police and courts as just and fair and believe that U.S. society has made great strides since the 1950s in **integrating** African Americans, but a great gap remains.

integration
Merging subcultures into the *mainstream* culture.

Subcultures may dislike being ruled by the dominant culture. Many of the French speakers of Quebec would like to withdraw from Canada and become a separate country. The Bengalis of East Pakistan, ethnically and linguistically distinct from the peoples of West Pakistan, did secede in 1971. The Basques of northern Spain and the Roman Catholics of Northern Ireland are sufficiently different to constitute political subcultures. The Scots and Welsh of Britain harbor the resentments of the "Celtic fringe" against the dominant English. Traditionally, they voted heavily Labour, whereas the English voted heavily Conservative. The Scots only narrowly voted to remain part of the United Kingdom in 2014, and in 2015 the Scot Nats trounced Labour in Scotland. Scots are a British subculture tending to separatism.

Case Studies

Quebec: "Maîtres Chez Nous"

The French arrived in North America about the same time the English did, but France was more interested in the lucrative fur trade than in colonization and sent few French settlers; as a result, the population of New France stayed tiny compared with that of the English colonies to the south. The two empires collided in the French and Indian War, which essentially ended when the British conquered Quebec City in 1759. After the historic battle on the Plains of Abraham—which was actually quite small with only a handful killed, including both commanders—the English let the French Canadians keep their language and Roman Catholic religion. It was a magnanimous gesture, but it meant that two centuries later Canada faced a Quebec separatist movement.

Culturally and politically, Quebec province fell asleep for two centuries, an island of tradition in an otherwise dynamic North America. Quebec missed the French Revolution and thus stayed far more conservative than France. Quebec has been called "France without the Revolution." English speakers led the economy, and Montreal became a mostly English-speaking city. Many **francophones** became **marginalized**, living as poor and isolated farmers in their own province. An unstated deal was struck: **Anglophones** would run the economy while francophones, a majority of Quebec's population, would obey local politicians and the Catholic Church.

In the 1960s, Quebec woke up in a "Quiet Revolution." Francophone attitudes shifted dramatically, away from traditional politicians and the priests. It was almost as if a new generation of Québécois said: "You have held us down and backward long enough. We want to be modern, rich, and *maîtres chez nous* (masters in our own house)." Out of this massive shift of values emerged the Parti Québécois (PQ) with its demand to separate Quebec from Canada. The PQ argued that Quebec really is a different culture and was tired of being under the thumb of English-speaking Canada.

The PQ and related Bloc Québécois became the province's largest parties. A 1980 referendum on separation failed 60–40 percent, but a 1995 referendum failed only by a whisker. Since then, Quebec separatism has subsided, and the PQ's vote has declined. Quebeckers simply got tired of the issue. For Americans, Quebec served as an example of what goes wrong with bilingualism and multiculturalism: They can lead to national fragmentation.

francophone
A French speaker.

marginalized
Pushed to the edge of society and the economy, often said of the poor and of subcultures.

anglophone
An English speaker.

Where subcultures are very distinct, the country itself may be threatened. The Soviet Union and Yugoslavia fell apart because citizens were more loyal to their ethnic groups than to the nation. Ethnic Albanians in Kosovo, by religion (Muslim) and language very distinct from their Serbian rulers, fought for and gained their independence. In India, some Sikhs seek independence for the Punjab, their home province, and resort to arms. Prime Minister Indira Gandhi's Sikh bodyguards assassinated her in 1985. Such countries as Lebanon and Nigeria are culturally fragmented, a dangerous condition that repeatedly erupts into violence.

Should a nation attempt to integrate its subcultures into the mainstream? Such efforts are bound to be difficult, but if left undone the subculture in later years may seek independence, as did the Tamils of Sri Lanka. The Spaniards in Peru who conquered the Incas let them retain their language and culture. But now the Spanish-speaking Peruvians of the cities know little of the Quechua-speaking Peruvians of the mountains. Any nonintegrated subculture poses at least a problem and at worst a threat to the national political system.

Starting in the 1870s, France deliberately pursued national integration through its centralized school system. Many regions were backwaters and spoke strange dialects. The French education ministry sent schoolteachers into the villages almost like missionaries. The teachers followed an absolutely standard curriculum that was heavy on rote learning and on the glory and unity of France. Gradually, in the phrase of historian Eugen Weber, they turned "peasants into Frenchmen." After some decades, a much more unified and integrated France emerged, an example of *overt political socialization* (see discussion following).

The United States used both schools and voluntary integration to create a mainstream culture in which most Americans feel at home. Immigrants know they have to learn English to get ahead. The achievement-oriented consumer society standardizes tastes and career patterns. The melting pot worked—and, with some one in eight U.S. residents foreign-born, is still working—but not perfectly. The 2013 Boston Marathon bombers never became psychologically American. Many Americans retain subculture distinctions in religion and cuisine, but these may not be politically important. Asian Americans integrated rapidly into the U.S. mainstream. Now some 5 percent of the total U.S. population, they hold several of the 535 elected seats on Capitol Hill.

Not all American groups have been so fortunate. African Americans and Hispanics are not fully integrated, but this too is changing. Now, with 13 percent of the population, African Americans hold about 10 percent of the seats of the House of Representatives. The election of Barack Obama, who had a mother from Kansas and a Kenyan father, helped psychologically integrate African Americans. His election marked a turning point in national integration that Catholics achieved only with John F. Kennedy in 1960.

Should integration be hastened? This has been one of the great questions of post–World War II U.S. politics. With the 1954 *Brown v. Board of Education of Topeka* decision, the Supreme Court began a major federal effort to integrate U.S. schools. It encountered massive resistance. In some instances, federal judges had to take control of local school systems to enforce integration by busing. The integrationist Kennedy and Johnson administrations argued that the United States, in its struggle against communism, could not field a good army or offer an example of freedom and justice to the rest of the world if some Americans were oppressed and poor. Integration was portrayed as a matter of national security.

By the same token, should language integration be forced? Should African Americans abandon black dialect in favor of standard English, and should Hispanics learn English? If they do not, they will be severely handicapped their whole lives, especially in employment. But some blacks, Hispanics, and Native Americans cling to their language as a statement of ethnic identity and pride. The U.S. Constitution does not specify any national language, nor does it outlaw languages other than English. In some areas of the United States, signs and official documents are in both English and Spanish. In 1986, California voters approved a measure making English the state's official language by a wide margin. People could, of course, continue to speak what they wished, but official documents

Democracy

The Three Israels

Where do political values come from? Israel offers a natural experiment. Israel was founded with a leftist tilt by Jews from Eastern Europe with the socialist values common there in the earlier part of the twentieth century. (Jews in Eastern Europe almost by definition could not be conservative, as the Catholic and nationalist East Europeans despised them.) Parts of the *kibbutz* (collective farm) movement were Marxist; the labor movement and Workers Party were social-democratic. Both, composed of European immigrants, resembled their European counterparts. Israel, from its founding in 1948 was ruled by a left coalition headed by Labor until it was ousted (over corruption) in the 1977 elections.

The massive influx of Middle Eastern Jews (from Yemen, Morocco, Algeria, Tunisia, Iran, and elsewhere) after 1948 brought in people without European leftist perspectives or the give and take of democracy. By the 1970s, Israel's Jewish population was about half European in origin and half Middle Eastern, and this showed up in voting patterns. Those of Middle Eastern origin (*Mizrahim*, from the Hebrew for "east") like strong leaders and tough, nationalist policies. They severely mistrust Arabs and vote for rightist parties such as Likud (now in power). Israeli left parties are a shadow of their former selves. Emblematic of the two Israeli cultures was the 1995 assassination of Labor Prime Minister Yitzhak Rabin, of East European origin, by Yigal Amir, of Yemini origin, who thought Rabin was too willing to concede peace measures to the Palestinians.

The influx of a million Jews from the ex-Soviet Union since the late 1980s brought Soviet attitudes of rigidity, intolerance, and black-and-white thinking: We are right, and all others are wrong and a threat. Absent are attitudes of fair play and minority rights. Israel is a Jewish state with little or no room for Arab Palestinians. The Russian Jews formed the Yisrael Beitenu ("Our Home Israel"), which in 2009 won 12 percent of the votes and 15 (out of 120) seats—the third-largest party in the Knesset. Its chief, Avigdor Lieberman, born in Soviet Moldova, became foreign minister but was so imperious that few foreign officials cared to meet with him. He was likened to a Russian Putin-era politician.

Israel demonstrates that democratic values come from one's culture of origin, something not easily changed. In Israel, immigrant political culture has formed roughly three layers, only one of them (the first) democratic. Democracy needs a democratic culture to support it, and this takes time to strike roots. Attempts to found a democracy in a country with no democratic culture is an uphill struggle, as we found out in Iraq.

and ballots would be in English only. In 1998, California voted to end bilingual education in order to speed the assimilation of subcultures. California is often an indicator of nationwide trends, and other states passed similar laws.

Political Socialization

6.5 List with examples the main agents of political socialization.

socialization
The learning of culture.

In the **socialization** process, children acquire manners, speech, and convictions that often last lifelong. Although some is formally taught, most is absorbed by imitating others. In the same way, political socialization teaches political values and specific usages. Learning to pledge allegiance to the flag, to sing the national anthem, and to obey authority figures from presidents to police officers is imparted by families, friends, teachers, and television. Children raised in

Classic Works

The Authoritarian Personality

One of the boldest attempts to link individual character traits with political attitudes was a 1950 book—*The Authoritarian Personality*, by Theodore Adorno and others, mostly refugees from Nazi Germany. Based heavily on the Freudian theory that personality is laid down in early childhood, Adorno and his colleagues devised a twenty-nine-item questionnaire that allegedly showed pre-fascist political views, hence its name, the F-Scale. Persons who scored high on it were conventional in lifestyle to the point of rigidity; were intolerant, prejudiced, and hostile toward outsiders and minorities; submitted to and liked power; and were superstitious and mystical.

The Adorno study attracted great interest but was criticized over its too-simplistic connection of personality and politics. Recent research has revived the approach, but based on genetics, not early childhood. Studies of identical twins suggest that individual inclinations to authoritarianism, religiosity, and conservatism—labeled "traditionalism" as a package—are partially inherited. Basic political values may be more genetic than learned or rational.

cultural ghettoes, such as minorities in America's inner cities, pick up subcultures that are sometimes at odds with mainstream culture. Political socialization is thus crucial to stable government.

The Agents of Socialization

THE FAMILY   What children encounter earliest—the family—usually outweighs all other factors. Attempts at **overt socialization** by government and schools generally fail if their values are at odds with family orientations. Communist regimes such as Poland's tried to inculcate socialist values in a child, but the family—in Poland, often strongly Catholic—taught the child to ignore these messages. Where family and government values are generally congruent, as in the United States, the two modes of socialization reinforce one another.

overt socialization
Deliberate government policy to teach culture.

Parents influence our political behavior for decades. Most people see politics and vote as their parents did. More basically, the family forms the psychological makeup of individuals, which in turn determines many of their political attitudes. It imparts norms, values, beliefs, and attitudes such as party attachment and trust or cynicism about government. The early years have the strongest effect, especially from ages three to thirteen. Children accept parental values unconsciously and uncritically and may retain them all their lives. People often give back to the world as adults what they got from it as children. One study found that people with authoritarian personalities had been treated roughly as children. Almond and Verba found that those who remembered having had a voice in family decisions as children had a greater adult sense of political efficacy.

THE SCHOOL   More deliberate socialization occurs in school. Most governments use history to inculcate children with pride and patriotism. Many African nations try to unify their tribes, usually with different languages and histories, by teaching in French or English about a mythical past when they were a great and united nation. It often does not work. Communist nations also used schools to inculcate support for the regime. As we saw in 1989, though, this effort failed; family and church overrode the attempts of schools to make East Europeans into believing Communists. U.S. schools did a brilliant job of turning immigrants from many lands into one nation, something critics of bilingual education say must be restored.

The amount of schooling also affects political attitudes. Uniformly, people with many years of education show a stronger sense of responsibility to their community and feel more able to influence public policy than do less-educated citizens. People with more schooling are more participatory. College graduates are more tolerant and open-minded, especially on questions of race, than high-school dropouts, who are often parochial in outlook. Education imparts more open-minded attitudes, and educated people generally enjoy higher incomes and status, which by themselves encourage interest and participation.

PEER GROUPS   Friends and playmates also form political values. The relative strength of peer-group influence appears to be growing. With both parents working, children may be socialized more by peers than by families. Upholders of "family values" see this as the underlying cause of youthful drug-taking and violence.

A different take suggests that in a mobile society, like the modern United States, parents often choose to live in a particular place near those similar to themselves. Conservatives lean toward suburbs and small towns near other conservatives seeking the same life. Liberals lean toward the same in big cities. Family socialization can then be reinforced by peer groups who see the world similarly. Empathy toward other perspectives, however, suffers—one explanation for the growth of polarized politics.

Case Studies

China Builds Unity

China, like France, is an example of overt political socialization through education, one that seems to be working. Chinese intellectuals have for centuries stressed that China is one country and must not be broken up. China's many languages, however, work against this. The Cantonese of the south, for example, do not understand the Mandarin of the north. A century ago, even under the tottering Empire, Beijing began a movement to make Mandarin the national language.

It made little headway until the Communists required Mandarin in all schools and use it on television. Now most educated mainland Chinese can speak it, although they may not use it much in daily life. For the first time in history, you can get by with one language in most of China (but not in Hong Kong or Macau, where Cantonese still reigns). The common language helps cement China together. (In precise parallels, India and Indonesia promoted, respectively, Hindi and Bahasa Indonesia as their national languages to unite their disparate peoples.)

Adding to this, Chinese are well aware and proud of their record-setting economic growth. The 2008 Beijing Olympics boosted Chinese pride. The spiffed-up capital, the extravaganza of the opening and closing ceremonies, and the gold medals won made Chinese (even Hong Kongers and Macanese) proud of their country and see it as a unified whole. The old ideal of one China may at last turn into a reality.

THE MASS MEDIA   Gaining in influence are the mass media, especially television. Many fear the influence is negative. Harvard political scientist Robert Putnam argues that heavy TV watching makes people passive and uninterested in community or group activities. American children watch thousands of hours of television (the "plug-in babysitter") a year, some of it violent, and play violent video games. Some, including the National Rifle Association, charge this tends to make them heartless and violent, but this has not been proven. TV reaches kids early; even 3-year-olds can recognize the president on television and understand that he is a sort of "boss" of the nation. Senators and members of Congress receive much less and less-respectful TV coverage, a view the children may hold the rest of their lives.

As with schools, the mass media may be unsuccessful if their messages are at odds with what family and religion teach. Even Soviet researchers found that families were much bigger influences on individuals' political views than the Soviet mass media. Iran's mass media, all controlled by the shah, tried to inculcate loyalty to him, but believing Muslims took the word of their local *mullahs* in the mosques and hated the shah. Now, ironically, with Iran's media controlled by Islamist conservatives, most Iranians believe the opposite of what the press feeds them. Mass media alone cannot do everything.

Mass media may also reinforce other forms of socialization. In a household with conservative parents and conservative neighbors, the kids may also be exposed to conservative messages on Fox News. Similarly, liberal parents driving their kids to school may expose their kids to relatively liberal messages on National Public Radio (NPR) news programs.

THE GOVERNMENT   The government itself is an agent of socialization, especially if it delivers rising living standards. Many government activities are intended to explain or display the government to the public, always designed to build support and loyalty. Great spectacles, such as the 2014 Sochi Winter Olympics, have a strengthening effect, as do parades with flags and soldiers and proclamations of top leaders. The power of government to control political attitudes is limited, however, because messages and experiences reach individuals through conversations with primary groups of kin or peers who put their own spin on messages. Alienated groups may socialize their children to dislike the government and ignore its messages.

Review Questions

1. What is political culture?
2. How does political culture differ from public opinion?
3. How do Russia and Iraq exhibit problems of political culture?
4. What three types of political culture did Almond and Verba find?
5. If Americans are participatory, why do they vote so little?

6. What happened to U.S. attitudes starting in the 1960s?

7. How do elite and mass political cultures differ?

8. Why do some cultures lead to economic growth?

9. How can you tell if a group forms a distinct subculture?

10. What are the most potent agents of political socialization?

Key Terms

anglophone, p. 120
cynical, p. 111
francophone, p. 120
integration, p. 119
mainstream, p. 119
marginalized, p. 120
overt socialization, p. 123

parochial, p. 112
participatory, p. 112
political competence, p. 112
political efficacy, p. 112
rule of anticipated
    reactions, p. 113

secular, p. 115
socialization, p. 122
subculture, p. 117
subject, p. 112
turnout, p. 113
values, p. 110

Further Reference

Alexander, Jeffrey C. *The Civil Sphere.* New York: Oxford University Press, 2007.

Blondel, Jean, and Takashi Inoguchi. *Political Cultures in Asia and Europe: Citizens, States and Societal Values.* New York: Routledge, 2006.

Brewer, Mark D., and Jeffrey M. Stonecash. *Split: Class and Cultural Divides in American Politics.* Washington, DC: CQ Press, 2007.

Brogan, Hugh. *Alexis de Tocqueville: A Life.* New Haven, CT: Yale University Press, 2007.

Buruma, Ian. *Taming the Gods: Religion and Democracy on Three Continents.* Princeton, NJ: Princeton University Press, 2010.

Damrosch, Leo. *Tocqueville's Discovery of America.* New York: Farrar, Straus & Giroux, 2010.

Diamond, Larry, and Marc F. Plattner, eds. *How People View Democracy.* Baltimore, MD: Johns Hopkins University Press, 2008.

Fischer, David Hackett. *Fairness and Freedom: A History of Two Open Societies, New Zealand and the United States.* New York: Oxford University Press, 2012.

Huntington, Samuel P. *Who Are We?: The Challenge to America's National Identity.* New York: Simon & Schuster, 2004.

Lane, Jan-Erik, and Svante Ersson. *Culture and Politics: A Competitive Approach,* 2nd ed. Williston, VT: Ashgate, 2005.

Perlstein, Rick. *Nixonland: The Rise of a President and the Fracturing of America.* New York: Simon & Schuster, 2007.

Putnam, Robert D. *Bowling Alone: The Collapse and Revival of American Community.* New York: Simon & Schuster, 2001.

Riley-Smith, Tristram. *The Cracked Bell: America and the Afflictions of Liberty.* New York: Skyhorse, 2010.

Warren, Mark E., ed. *Democracy and Trust.* New York: Cambridge University Press, 1999.

Westen, Drew. *The Political Brain: The Role of Emotion in Deciding the Fate of the Nation.* New York: PublicAffairs, 2008.

Chapter 7
Public Opinion

⌄ Learning Objectives

7.1 Distinguish between anecdotal and survey evidence.

7.2 List the main factors that produce public-opinion views.

7.3 Explain what can go wrong with polling.

7.4 Explain the intensity factor in structuring public opinion.

In the wake of the 2001 terror attacks, known as "9/11," Americans were determined to block terrorist depredations by any means, anywhere. This was no time to be overly solicitous about civil rights, many calculated. Get tough, was the message, and Congress heard it loud and clear. All people getting onto a jetliner should be thoroughly searched, even their shoes sniffed for explosives. Gradually, however, Americans got fed up by the intrusions into their personal lives, especially when they learned in 2013 that their phone calls and e-mails were under secret surveillance by a federal agency. Concern over terrorism shrank, and concern over privacy grew. The shift illustrated volatility in public opinion—a normal and standard occurrence.

What Public Opinion Is and Isn't

7.1 Distinguish between anecdotal and survey evidence.

public opinion
Citizens' reactions to current, specific issues and events.

Political culture and **public opinion** are linked but are not the same. Political culture focuses on long-standing values, attitudes, and ideas that people learn deeply. Most Americans firmly believe that government power is potentially tyrannical and must be controlled and that democracy is the only just form of government. Public opinion concerns people's reactions to specific and immediate policies and problems, such as sending troops overseas or voting intentions.

Public opinion is not the same as individual opinion. A woman's opinion of her neighbor's religion would not be part of public opinion, but her feeling on prayer in public schools would. Public opinion refers to political and social issues, not private matters.

anecdotal
Recounting the views of a few respondents.

As we will see, measuring public opinion is complex. **Anecdotal** evidence is a poor indication of public opinion, as we have no way of knowing if it is representative. Beware of the journalistic "one-person cross-section" of opinion. Similarly, a poorly designed survey can be misleading.

Public opinion does not necessarily imply that citizens have strong, clear, or united convictions; such unity is rare. So-called public opinion often involves several small, conflicting groups, plus many who are undecided, plus an even larger number with no interest or opinion on the matter. On most subjects, public opinion is an array of diverse attitudes that can change quickly.

Public opinion often shows widespread ignorance. A solid majority told a 1991 poll that they supported the policy of Bush senior on Lithuania, but few knew where Lithuania was. A 2006 Harris Poll found, after three years of news reports to the contrary, that half of Americans still thought Iraq had weapons of mass destruction in the 2003 war. And 64 percent said Saddam Hussein had "strong links" with al Qaeda (he did not).

So, should survey numbers make policy? Most Americans are opposed to raising taxes on gasoline. Does that mean government should never do it? Should elected leaders always bow to public opinion? President Truman shrugged off public opinion and was vilified for it. Decades later, many celebrated him as a leader who did the right thing without fear of disapproval. Some say current politicians pay too much attention to public opinion. If you are always following, how can you lead?

Public opinion is important in a democracy. Elections provide only a crude expression of the public's will. They may indicate what voters generally think of a candidate overall but rarely focus on specific issues. Public-opinion surveys may fill in the details so officials know what people think about specific problems, such as health care or a war. Public opinion can thus be seen as a backup and detailing device for inputting mass views into politics, a way to fine-tune elections.

But public opinion is often ignorant, fickle, and untrustworthy. Knowing this, public officials often try to create the public opinion they desire. British socialist Beatrice Webb long ago said: "There is no such thing as spontaneous public opinion. It all has to be manufactured from a center of conviction and energy." This sometimes works but sometimes backfires. A positive example came in 1971 when President Nixon announced that he would be the first president to visit China, and Americans supported the move. On the other hand, before the 2003 U.S. invasion of Iraq, the Bush 43 (so-called because he was the forty-third president; his father was 41) administration claimed that Iraq had weapons of mass destruction (WMD) that could threaten the United States. Most Americans believed it but turned against the war when no WMD were found and the war stretched on for years.

Public opinion can be led or manipulated by interest groups. Bringing grievances to public attention, especially when the media watch, can generate widespread sympathy. The televised brutality of sheriffs' deputies in Selma, Alabama, toward African Americans demanding the right to vote turned public opinion in favor of the Voting Rights Act of 1965.

Any government is vulnerable to public opinion. Mahatma Gandhi, by simple dramas of nonviolent protest, used public opinion to win independence for India. A gaunt, bespectacled old man in a loincloth, he led protests, wove his own cloth, and threatened to starve himself to death if the British did not quit India. His large Indian National Congress made the country ungovernable until the British gave India independence in 1947. Even Communist China backs down in the face of massive citizen protests against toxic-spewing factories and unbreathable air.

Because of its volatility, public opinion should be just one of many factors governments use to determine public policy. You have to carefully weigh whether polls reflect true public opinion, whether public opinion is best for the country, and the consequences of doing something different from what the public wants. In a democracy, crossing public opinion could lead to losing the next election. Public opinion can even matter to an undemocratic regime, where leaders ignoring it can be overthrown. In 2013, massive street protests in Kiev persuaded a corrupt Ukrainian chief to flee to Russia.

Democracy

A Short History of Polling

In 1824, the *Harrisburg Pennsylvanian* asked passersby whether they would vote for John Quincy Adams or Andrew Jackson. They called the very unscientific poll "straws in the wind." Other newspapers, using both careful and haphazard methods, conducted "straw polls" in elections thereafter. The popular magazine *Literary Digest* developed a prestigious survey that predicted the 1924, 1928, and 1932 presidential elections. The *Literary Digest*, using a huge sample on the theory that it was more reliable, mailed questionnaires to nearly 10 million of its subscribers, car owners, and people in phone books. In 1936, the magazine predicted Republican Alfred M. Landon would win with 59.1 percent of the vote. Roosevelt's landslide—with more than 60 percent of the vote—signaled the demise of both casual methods of sampling and of *Literary Digest* itself.

But 1936 was also the first year of the newly developed "scientific polling," a branch of another new field: market research. George H. Gallup's survey results, syndicated in newspapers, forecast Roosevelt's victory. Gallup predicted that the *Digest* poll was far off because its sample was drawn heavily from higher-income people, many of whom were angered by Roosevelt's social and economic policies. The new technique used by Gallup was to select a *sample* as *representative*, rather than as large, as possible.

This scientific sampling method has dominated the field since then, with a generally successful record. But even it failed in the 1948 election, when almost every poll predicted that Thomas E. Dewey would defeat Harry S. Truman by a landslide. Truman won with 49 percent in a four-way contest. The error was in assuming that respondents who said they were undecided would wind up voting in the same ratio as those who had already decided. In fact, the undecideds went much more heavily for Truman—close to 75 percent.

The major polls have further refined their methods since that time and today make special efforts to detect late swings. They do not claim to be able to predict divisions within closer than 2 to 3 percentage points. The margin of victory in several presidential elections has been less than 1 percent, so polls cannot confidently predict close elections. Elections such as those of 2000 are called "too close to call." One standing problem is in estimating who are "likely voters" when not all respondents cast ballots.

Aggregating surveys made polling more accurate in 2012. A young statistician, Nate Silver, who honed his skills on baseball statistics, used close studies of swing states to project trends and predict an Obama victory when many traditional pundits could not. Silver was one of several "aggregators" who averaged several polls, eliminating ones with bad track records and weighting the others by sample size. Aggregation smoothes out the statistical variations among polls. For example, a survey with a margin of error of plus or minus 3 percent statistically means there is a 95 percent chance that the margin is not *greater* than plus or minus 3 percent. But that means one survey in 20 will fail to capture public opinion within that range.

Government by sheer violence and coercion cannot last long. Even Stalin's Soviet Union, with all its brutal apparatus for suppressing dissent, depended first on the dream of a classless utopia and on Russian patriotism to repel the Nazi invader, and only secondly on the security police. After Stalin died in 1953, the regime turned to incentives and propaganda to keep up a veneer of legitimacy, which collapsed quickly in 1989 in Eastern Europe and then in the Soviet Union itself in late 1991. Ultimately, lack of public support ended these regimes.

The Shape of Public Opinion

7.2 **List the main factors that produce public-opinion views.**

Social scientists can uncover roughly who thinks what about politics. No social category, of course, is ever 100 percent for or against something. Indeed, 60 or 70 percent is quite high. We look for differences among social categories, the significance of which can be tested by the rules of statistics. We seek lighter and darker shades of gray—not black and white. Once we have found significant differences, we may be able to say something about **salience**, the degree to which social categories and particular issues divide public opinion of a country. In Scandinavia, for example, social class is salient in structuring party preferences: The working class tends to vote Social Democratic, and the middle class votes for more conservative parties. In Catholic Europe, social class is weakly salient, with the working class scattering its vote among parties of the left, right, and center. In Catholic Europe, religion and region are typically most salient. In the United States, race, religion, and urban–rural differences are salient.

salience
Literally, that which jumps out; the importance of given issues in public opinion or the characteristics of the public holding various opinions.

Social Class

Karl Marx saw **social class** as massively salient. Workers, he predicted, would become socialists. Actually, only some of them did, but social class does matter, even in the relatively classless United States. Over the decades, the American manual worker had tended to vote Democratic, the better-off person Republican. But these are only tendencies and often muddied by other factors. Poor people can be conservative on religious and social issues, and affluent people can be liberal or even radical. White working-class Americans, motivated by noneconomic issues such as race, gun control, morality (abortion, gay rights), or leadership in war, moved to the Republicans in the past few elections while more educated people trended toward the Democrats.

social class
A broad layer of society, usually based on income and often labeled lower, middle, and upper.

Social class can be hard to measure. There are two general ways: the objective and the subjective. An objective determination asks people their annual income or judges the quality of the neighborhood. The subjective determination simply asks respondents what their social class is, which sometimes diverges from objective criteria. A majority of Americans call themselves middle class even if they are not. Many are "working class," a category that most polls have dropped. Sometimes even wealthy people, thinking of their modest origins, call themselves middle class. The way a person earns a living may matter more than the amount he or she makes. Typically, American farmers are mostly conservative, and teachers and lawyers are not. Different political attitudes grow up around different jobs.

Sometimes social class works in precisely the opposite way envisioned by Marx. Highly educated professionals make some affluent U.S. suburbs quite liberal compared with the conservatism of poorer country dwellers. Spanish researchers found an *inverse* relationship between social class and preferring the left; that is, better off persons were more leftist than poorer Spaniards. In the Spanish study, education was most salient.

Class matters, especially in combination with other factors, such as region or religion. In Britain, class plus region structures much of the vote; in France, it is class plus region plus religiosity (practicing Catholic versus nonpracticing); in Germany, it is class plus region plus denomination (Catholic or Protestant). As Yale's Joseph LaPalombara put it, the question is "Class plus what?"

America after World War II had a relatively equitable division of income that made most citizens middle class. Starting in the 1970s, however, incomes grew more unequal. The income gap doubled between those with a bachelor's degree or higher and those with a high school diploma or less. The share of income of the top 1 percent soared while factory workers had their jobs "off-shored." America's famous **social mobility** fell behind that of West Europe's and Canada's. Americans lost some of their belief that coming generations would always be better off. Critics feared the hollowing out of the American middle class. Social class is taking on renewed salience, but its political impact is unclear. Many of the white working and middle classes, slipping down the socioeconomic ladder, accepted the conservative Republican argument that this was all the fault of big government, its taxes, and its debts. Many upper-middle-class citizens, on the other hand, saw the need for government to correct imbalances and voted Democrat.

social mobility
The rise and fall of people into another social class.

Education

Educational level is related to social class, and this contributes to polarization. Those with college degrees win the big bucks in fields like information technology and finance; those without have to scramble. The better off give their children more and better education, locking in their class position. Rising education costs prevent others from joining the educated classes, slowing the social mobility that allowed many Americans to rise during the postwar years.

Education in the United States often has a split political impact, meaning that educated people are more liberal on **noneconomic issues** but more conservative on **economic issues**. Survey data show that college-educated people are more tolerant, favor civil rights, and understand different viewpoints. But on economic issues, many of them are skeptical of efforts to redistribute income by higher taxes on the upper brackets—which happen to be them—and welfare measures. There are, to be sure, some educated people who are consistently liberal on both economic and noneconomic questions. The same is often true of the American working class: Its members want higher wages but can be intolerant in the areas of race, lifestyle, and patriotism. Middle-class college youths protesting the Vietnam War ran into the snarls and fists of unionized construction workers, an illustration of the split between economic and noneconomic liberalism.

noneconomic issues
Questions relating to patriotism, religion, race, sexuality, and personal choice.

economic issues
Questions relating to jobs, income, taxes, and welfare benefits.

Classic Works

Almond's Three Publics

In his 1950 *The American People and Foreign Policy*, political scientist Gabriel Almond proposed that there were three American public opinions, not just one:

1. A *general public* of a majority that does not know or care about much beyond their immediate concerns. For example, they show little interest in foreign policy unless the country is in a war or international crisis.

2. An *attentive public* of a minority who are among the better educated and who follow more abstract political concerns, such as foreign policy. They are the audience the elite plays to; in turn, this attentive public passes on views that mobilize the general public.

3. A *policy and opinion elite* of a few highly influential people who are involved in politics, often professionally. These members of Congress, appointed officials, and top journalists devise foreign and domestic policies and articulate them to the attentive and general publics.

Especially regarding foreign affairs, Almond makes a strong case. The number of Americans who follow the news is decreasing, and surveys show ignorance of world affairs. Attentive and elite opinion—such as business, media, and religious leaders and academics—favored NAFTA, trade expansion, and U.S. missions in the Balkans far more than did the general public.

Region

Every country has a south, goes an old saw, and this is true in politics. It is uncertain, however, whether a country's south is more conservative or more liberal than its north. France south of the Loire River and Spain south of the Tagus have for generations gone left. The south of Italy, though, is conservative, as is Bavaria in Germany's south. In Great Britain, England is heavily conservative, whereas Scotland goes for the Scottish Nationalists and Wales for Labour. The U.S. South was famous for decades as the "solid South," which went automatically Democratic but now is strongly Republican; it has, however, always been conservative.

A country's outlying **regions** usually harbor resentment against the capital, creating what are called *center–periphery tensions*. Often an outlying region was brought into the nation by force and has never been happy about it. Regional memories can last for centuries. This is true of Quebec and Scotland and the former Confederate states. Some regions feel economically disadvantaged by the central area and may have a different language, as in Spain's Catalonia and Basque country, Wallonia in Belgium (the French-speaking south), Quebec, Slovenia in ex-Yugoslavia, and several parts of India and China.

regions
Portions of a country with a sense of self and sometimes cultural differences.

Once a region gets set in its politics, it stays that way for a long time. Region plays a big role in the politics of Britain, France, Germany, and the United States. Most "sunbelt" states in the U.S. South and Rocky Mountains are conservative on both economic and noneconomic issues and jealous of states' rights. The "frostbelt" of northern and eastern states, where industry has declined, tends to be liberal, especially on questions of government spending programs. In recent years, the U.S. South's conservativism has aligned it with the Republican Party and the Northeast's liberalism has moved it toward the Democratic Party.

Religion

Religion is often the most explosive issue in politics and contributes a great deal to the structuring of opinion. Religion can mean either denomination or religiosity. In Germany, Catholics tend to vote Christian Democrat, Protestants Social Democrat. Here it is a question of denomination. In France, where most citizens are baptized Catholic, it is a question of **religiosity**, as most French are indifferent to religion. The more often a French person goes to Mass, the more likely he or she is to vote for a conservative party. Few Communist voters are practicing Catholics. In Poland, the Roman Catholic Church encouraged Poles to oust the Communist regime and support pro-Church parties. One of the biggest divisions in Catholic countries is between clericalists and **anticlericalists**. France, Italy, and Spain have long been split over this issue, with the conservative parties pro-Church and the parties of the left hostile to church influence.

Religion plays a major role in the United States, where Protestants, at least among whites, tend to vote Republican. Religion overlaps with ethnicity. U.S. Catholics, especially Polish Catholics, were once among the most loyal Democrats. In the great immigrations of a century ago, big-city Democratic machines welcomed and helped immigrants from Catholic countries, and their descendants stayed mostly Democratic, but this eroded as the Democratic Party endorsed "pro-choice" positions. For a long time, it was believed that no Catholic could be elected president; John F. Kennedy in 1960 put that view to rest. In 2004, however, Catholic John F. Kerry lost many Catholic votes when the clergy denounced him for being pro-choice. Catholics and fundamentalist Protestants now have a common cause in fighting abortion. The 2000 vice-presidential candidacy of Connecticut Senator Joseph Lieberman, an observant Jew, aroused little attention or public opposition, a measure of the increased tolerance of Americans.

The rise of the "religious right" in the 1980s brought a "God gap" into U.S. politics. Roughly one American in seven can be counted as religious right, and fundamentalist groups became highly political. Televangelists mobilized their flocks against pornography, abortion, and gay rights—and for Republicans. Christian conservatives became a major force inside the Republican Party. Bush 43, himself an evangelical, won with fundamentalist votes, most of whom stayed Republican. In the 2012 Republican primaries, Catholic Rick Santorum won more evangelical than Catholic votes, indicating that the old Protestant suspicion of Catholics had faded.

The old religious divide has been replaced with a religiosity divide. In 2012, two-thirds of weekly churchgoers voted for Mitt Romney; nearly two-thirds of those who never attend religious services voted for Obama. The religiosity divide spills over into opinions on issues ranging from abortion to support for

religiosity
Degree of commitment to one's religion; often affects political beliefs.

anticlericalism
Movement in Catholic countries to get Church out of politics.

Israel. Highly religious Protestants and Catholics now vote similarly and have very similar opinions on public policy issues.

Age

There are two theories on how age affects political opinions: the **life cycle** and generation theories. The first, widely accepted, holds that people change as they age. Thus, young people are naturally radical and older people moderate or even conservative. With few responsibilities, young people can be idealistic and rebellious, but with the burdens of home, job, taxes, and children of their own, people tend to become conservative. Young voters went strongly to Obama.

This life cycle theory does not always work because sometimes whole generations are marked for life by the great events of their young adulthood. Survivors of wars and depressions remember them for decades, and they color their views on war, economics, and politics. Sociologist Karl Mannheim (1893–1947) called this phenomenon **political generations**. Many who lived through the Vietnam War were instinctively critical of the U.S. war in Iraq. Those who personally experienced the Depression of the 1930s were more supportive of federal welfare measures than younger people who had been raised in postwar prosperity.

life cycle
Theory that opinions change as people age.

political generations
Theory that great events of young adulthood permanently color political views.

Gender

Even before the women's movement, gender made a difference in politics. Traditionally, and especially in Catholic countries, women were more conservative, more concerned with home, family, and morality. But as a society modernizes, men's and women's views change. Women work outside the home and develop their own perspectives on social and economic problems often at variance with male political views. In the United States, a **gender gap** appeared in the 1980s as women became several percentage points more liberal and Democratic than men. Women liked federal programs for home and family and disliked the Republican emphasis on war and disdain for women's rights. In most recent elections, women were several percentage points more likely to vote Democrat for president than were men. That gap, though, is much smaller once marital status and race are figured in.

gender gap
Tendency of American women to vote more Democratic than do men.

Race and Ethnicity

Race and ethnicity are related to region and religion but sometimes plays a distinct role, especially in the multiethnic United States, where some ethnic groups form political subcultures. America was long touted as a "melting pot" of immigrant groups, but ethnic consciousness lasts many generations. American politics is often described in ethnic terms, with WASPs (white Anglo-Saxon Protestants) and other northern Europeans generally conservative and Republican and people of southern and eastern European origin, African Americans, Hispanics, and Asians more liberal and Democratic. This oversimplifies the complexity of individuals and of politics but still worked in 2012.

Racial and ethnic politics changes over the decades. After the Civil War, most African Americans were Republican, the party of Lincoln. With Franklin D. Roosevelt and the New Deal, most African Americans became Democrats and stayed that way. In the nineteenth century, American Jews were mostly Republican, for the Republicans criticized the anti-Semitic repression of tsarist Russia. The Jewish immigrants of the turn of the twentieth century, introduced to U.S. politics by Democratic machines such as New York's Tammany Hall, went Democratic. More recently, some Jews, influenced by *neoconservatism*, swung to the Republicans. Republican support for tough laws against illegal immigrants alienated Hispanic voters.

Elite and Mass Opinion

There is often a gap between *elite* and *mass* opinion. The mass public does not understand much about complicated issues but can react after decisions have been made. Elites, educated and influential people, usually have more complex and sophisticated perspectives. The masses often misunderstand and resent decisions. They know what hits them in the pocket book or infringes on their basic values and may lash out at perceived unfairness.

For example, when the 2008 financial meltdown threatened to unleash a major recession, economists, bankers, congresspersons, and a Republican president and Fed chief agreed on the need for federal programs to urgently lend billions to giant firms. But this was an elite consensus, and at first the public did not know how to react; it was far beyond most Americans' expertise. By 2010, however, a majority opposed the *bailouts*—even though they had staved off a depression and were being repaid. They threatened electoral punishment against those who had voted for them, including Republicans. Particularly irksome were the massive bonuses financial chiefs gave themselves.

In a European parallel, most elites understood that weaker members of the "eurozone" (the nineteen countries that use the euro currency) needed emergency financial support. Without it, they could collapse and endanger the whole European Union. Said German Chancellor Angela Merkel: "If the euro fails, Europe fails." But average Europeans—especially Germans, who bore most of the financial burdens—were furious. They worked hard and lived within their means, so why should they bail out countries that had mindlessly run up huge debts? Notice the similarity between U.S. and European attitudes here.

Good public opinion studies, especially of complicated or specialized questions—such as foreign policy and finances—should always distinguish between elite and mass opinions. Mass public opinion can be poorly informed and angry, a poor basis for sound policy. The issue is a very old question of who should govern: experts who understand such complex matters or average citizens. Most political scientists are cautious about letting public opinion lead in decision making.

skewed
A distribution with its peak well to one side.

unimodal
A single, center-peaked distribution; a bell-shaped curve.

bimodal
A distribution with two large clusters at the extremes and a small center.

polarize
To drive opinion into a *bimodal* distribution.

Democracy

Opinion Curves

The ways people feel about issues are summarized statistically in curves that show the distribution of opinions on a range from one extreme position to the other. A matter on which there are few doubters shows opinions **skewed** to one side, a "J-curve." Few Americans, for example, did not wish to destroy Islamist terrorists after September 11 (see chart at top of right column).

On many issues, public opinion forms the familiar "bell-shaped curve," or **unimodal** distribution, which shows few people at the extremes and most in the moderate center. All industrialized democracies show ideological distributions with few extreme leftists or rightists and a big bulge in the center (see chart at middle of right column).

A third characteristic pattern is a **bimodal** distribution, or "U-curve," where the extremes are bigger than the center (see chart at bottom of right column). Most Democrats support a pro-choice position on abortion whereas most Republicans are pro-life, with few in the center. Abortion is a **polarizing** issue in U.S. politics.

Bell-shaped opinion curves are the basis of democracy. If many citizens take extreme positions and form a U-curve, the political system can break down. This can lead to extremist takeovers as in Germany in 1933, to civil war as in Spain in 1936, or to a military coup as in Chile in 1973. Almost all democratic countries have unimodal distributions of opinion on basic issues; that is, people cluster in the center. Democracy is a centrist thing.

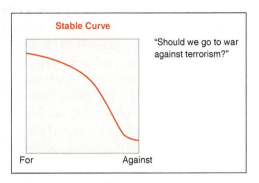

Stable Curve

"Should we go to war against terrorism?"

For   Against

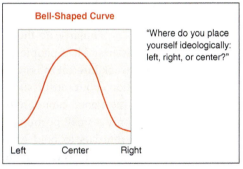

Bell-Shaped Curve

"Where do you place yourself ideologically: left, right, or center?"

Left   Center   Right

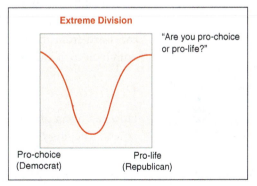

Extreme Division

"Are you pro-choice or pro-life?"

Pro-choice   Pro-life
(Democrat)   (Republican)

Public-Opinion Polls

7.3   **Explain what can go wrong with polling.**

Many ways exist to measure the public's opinion. Members of Congress measure public opinion daily based on the phone calls they receive. More recently, they count the "tweets" of social media to gauge mass (especially youthful) response. You could hang out at the local coffee shop to hear what people are talking about. But all of those methods leave out the possibility that people calling, tweeting, or talking about their opinions are nothing like the people who are not.

survey
A public-opinion poll.

Public opinion polls or **surveys** are designed to measure opinions so that we can say the results are reflective of a broader population. Published surveys, particularly in election years, are carefully watched. Almost daily we see statistics and percentages on what Americans think of war, unemployment, health care, and candidates. This is useful for policymakers and candidates.

But debate has developed over some of their political side effects. For example, do the polls give undue attention and influence to uncertain opinions? Do journalists create self-fulfilling prophecies by treating the polls as authoritative verdicts? Should public-opinion surveys be treated as a fair and democratic method of deciding public policies? Are polls reliable enough to determine policy? Who uses surveys, what purpose do they serve, and can we trust them?

Similarly, do the opinions people express really reflect how they feel about issues? Most people pay little attention to politics most of the time. They have weak interest in issues that do not directly touch them and acquire no information about most issues. Surveys, for example, find that nearly half of Americans questioned cannot name their representative in Congress. Thus, on most issues, only a small portion of the total public is attentive enough to news reports and editorials to hold a clear opinion. With all of the uncertainties, can surveys reflect an accurate picture of what people are thinking?

So while a well-designed public-opinion poll is the best way to measure the public's opinion, do not blindly follow poll data. There are limits to what you can learn from them. Policymakers must balance what they learn from polls with their own knowledge about the issues.

Polling Techniques

likely voters
Population of adults likely to vote in an upcoming election based on their voting history or intention.

How can a sample of 1,000 people depict the opinions of 200 million potential voters? The answer is complex, but it revolves around a technique that can be summarized as follows:

population
All people a poll is meant to represent.

SAMPLING FROM A POPULATION   A pollster first has to decide whose opinions they want the survey to represent. Generally, polls are only interested in the opinions of adults, not kids. But not all adults' opinions are of equal importance. Often, pollsters are only interested in the adults likely to vote in an upcoming election. Then they would be interested in the opinions of registered voters, or an even more select group: **likely voters**. The people the poll results represent is the **population**.

sample
Persons selected to be surveyed, usually representative of the whole.

inference
Accepting the opinions of a sample as reflecting those of a whole population.

There are too many people in most survey populations to talk to all of them for a survey. Pollsters take a **sample** of the population and use the sample's answers to the questions to **infer** the opinions of the whole population. As long as the sample is representative, inference is possible. For a sample to be representative, every member of the population has to have an equal chance of being selected for the sample. Then, statistics can show that a sample of 500, 1,000 or 1,500 people can represent the opinions of an entire population with a little wiggle room known as the **margin of error**, which goes down as the sample size gets larger.

margin of error
Range around sample's results within which the population's opinions likely fall; usually written "+/− 3%"

The most basic way to create a representative sample is through a **simple random sample**. Imagine drawing names out of a hat with everyone in the population's name in it. Pollsters often do somewhat more complex versions of random sampling like "cluster sampling," which saves travel costs for in-person interviews, or "stratified sampling," which ensures groups within the overall population are represented appropriately. Whatever sampling method is used, they must all meet the standard that each member of the target population has an equal chance of being selected for the poll to be valid.

simple random sample
Subset of population chosen by random chance.

REACHING THE SAMPLE The next step is to get the people in the sample, known as respondents, to answer the pollster's questions. Surveying respondents in person is very expensive because of travel costs and is rarely used anymore in the United States. In developing countries where phones and computers are rare, in-person surveys may be the only possible way to do a survey. Surveying respondents by mail is also expensive and relies on them returning the survey, limiting how many will respond. Surveying respondents online or by email is becoming more common, but not everyone has a computer and there are no comprehensive lists of email addresses.

The most common polling method in the United States is the telephone survey. Pollsters either use Random Digit Dialing (RDD), which randomly selects phone numbers in a targeted area code, or Registration Based Sampling (RBS), which uses samples of names from voter registration files. Each have their advantages and drawbacks. Telephone surveys are more affordable than in-person interviews, but the growing reluctance of people to answer their phone or pollsters' questions (more on this below) threatens their reliability.

ASKING THE QUESTIONS The unbiased wording of questions to avoid slanting responses is also important. In 1999, for example, a *Washington Post*/ABC poll asked half its sample whether President Clinton should resign if impeached or "fight the charges in the Senate." Fifty-nine percent said resign rather than fight. The other half was asked essentially the same question but worded with the alternative of resign or "remain in office and face trial in the Senate." To this, only 43 percent said resign. A slight difference in wording—"fight" sounds nastier than "face trial"—greatly shifted responses. In 1992, answers to a badly worded question (it had a double negative) suggested that one in five Americans doubted the Nazi Holocaust had really happened. When the question was worded clearly in 1994, only 2 percent denied the Holocaust had happened. The pollster must also avoid tones of voice or sympathetic looks that might encourage one response over another and skew the results.

How Reliable Are the Polls?

Public-opinion surveys are generally reliable, provided we recognize their limits. Overall, the U.S. opinion-research business takes in several billion dollars a year, and candidates commission thousands of quick "tracking polls" in primary and general elections. They use these polls to predict the election outcome and to understand the issues voters care about. Being able to know who will vote is important for a pre-election poll. Many respondents who say they intend to vote actually do not. These voters and the undecideds are likely not to divide the same way as those who do vote and those already decided. This underlays the mistaken predictions of Truman's defeat in 1948. A heavy turnout may shift election results. Pollsters must adjust raw findings for this factor, but no one can be certain of how high turnout will be or the effects of events such as weather or terrorist strikes.

volatility
Tendency of public opinion to change quickly.

Public opinion is **volatile**, able to change quickly under the impact of events. In 1965, as Lyndon Johnson escalated the war in Vietnam, an aide told him that "we have overwhelming public opinion on our side." Johnson, a crafty political pro who closely followed the polls, replied, "Yes, but for a very underwhelming period of time." He was right; two-thirds support for the war in 1965 turned into two-thirds opposition in 1968. Roughly the same happened with the war in Iraq: two-thirds for it in 2003 but two-thirds against it by 2006. Americans do not like long, inconclusive wars.

Volatility can also result if pollsters ask questions that respondents know nothing about. People want to seem knowledgeable and will give an opinion to a question, even if they haven't thought about the issue before. Pollsters must avoid accidently measuring these nonattitudes. New or complex issues are the most likely to result in nonattitudes. That's one reason why public opinion can seem so volatile on those kinds of issues. The public isn't necessarily changing its mind—it's just that respondents forget what they answered the last time they were asked about an issue they knew nothing about.

Another threat to the reliability of telephone surveys are increasing "no response" rates. Americans, harassed by telemarketers, decline or just hang up on callers asking anything. They use caller-ID to screen out any calls not coming from known numbers. With falling response rates, the survey is likely not random or representative. Surveys over the Internet have the same problem because respondents are "self-selected" and of above-average income and education. Any survey that records only those who want to participate is invalid.

The growth of cell phone usage causes a similar problem. Until recently, pollsters called only land lines. More people today have only cell phones and no home phone. Because young people were the most likely to only have cell phones, pollsters were not capturing their opinions. Recently, pollsters have adapted by including cell phones in their samples and by statistically adjusting for missing segments in their samples.

Pollsters have to continually update their methods as technology and public habits change. They make money by providing useful information to candidates,

Methods

Variables

A variable is a factor that varies; it shows some change. In this chapter, age, religiosity, education, and income are variables that structure public opinion. If you can, you quantify these factors. Variables come in two basic types: **independent** and **dependent**. The former is what you think influences or perhaps causes the change, but you cannot always be sure. You might hypothesize, for example, that increases in a country's per capita GDP lead it to democracy. The "per cap" is your independent variable, and democracy is your dependent variable—the one that depends on the impact of the other variable.

You might switch the two and make democracy your independent variable to see how it affects wealth. Causality is hard to prove, and the causal flow can go both ways. Some argue that democracy promotes prosperity. In some cases, of course, causality can flow only one way. We can posit "white Protestant male" as the independent variable related to a Republican vote, but we cannot say that voting Republican will turn people into white Protestant males.

If you have two variables with reliable numbers to measure them, you can follow them over time and put two lines on the same graph to show positive **covariance**—as one changes, so does the other—which may go a long way to supporting your thesis. Sometimes you see negative or inverse covariance—as one goes up, the other goes down—but this may still prove your thesis. If there is little or no covariance—if the two lines on a graph wobble around with no relation to each other—you should go back and change your thesis. Sometimes covariance happens with a time lag, giving you a more interesting thesis. For example, the president makes foreign-policy decisions, but public opinion reacts to them about six months later.

---

to the media, and to the public. If their methods are unreliable, they will lose business to their more reliable competitors. In 2012, Gallup's final poll showed Mitt Romney leading Barack Obama. Gallup was wrong because errors were made in some of the areas mentioned above, resulting in loss of future business.

American Opinion

7.4   **Explain the intensity factor in structuring public opinion.**

Presidential Ratings

One of the oldest and most important items in U.S. public-opinion polls asks how the president is handling the job—which is not necessarily how much people "like" the president. In practice, however, the respondent who likes the president will approve of the president's job performance, so the term "popularity" is often used for this poll. The correct terms are "support" or "approval."

Typically, presidents start with high support and then decline. During their first few months to a year in office, they enjoy a **honeymoon** with the press and the public. High public approval makes it easier for presidents to get their agenda

independent variable
The factor you think influences or causes something to happen.

dependent variable
The factor that changes under the impact of the *independent variable.*

covariance
How much two factors change together, indicating how strongly they are related.

honeymoon
High support for presidents early in their terms.

passed through Congress. Ironically, this early high public approval comes when the president's team is the least experienced and less able to take advantage to achieve the president's goals. After some years, however, problems accumulate— the economy sours or foreign policies fail. This brings an approval low point. Presidents seldom leave office as popular as they were during their first year.

When presidents come under intense pressure or take a major action, their support enjoys a temporary upturn or "spike." Americans rally to a president who faces a difficult decision and makes decisive responses. Political scientist John Mueller called these **rally events**. President Carter gained thirteen points over the seizure of American hostages in Iran in 1979, but he was soon blamed for helplessness and lost reelection the next year. Bush 41 enjoyed an eighteen-point gain when he began the Gulf War in 1991, but he lost reelection a year and a half later, the casualty of a lingering recession. Bush 43 gained a massive 35 percentage points after 9/11, support that continued through the U.S. conquest of Iraq in 2003 but declined as Iraq dragged on. President Obama's support briefly jumped 11 percentage points with the killing of Osama bin Laden in 2011.

rally event

Occurrence that temporarily boosts presidents' support.

Some suspect that presidents, especially later in their terms of office, deliberately try to appear decisive in a dramatic way to boost their sagging popularity. Foreign policy provides for dramatic moves and the best television coverage. A meeting with foreign leaders, a bold strike against terrorists, or the rescue of American hostages lifts support for a president. The highest support ratings of Presidents Truman, Kennedy, Nixon, Carter, Reagan, and both Bushes came with a dramatic foreign-policy event. Even a failure, the 1961 Bay of Pigs invasion to overthrow Castro, rallied Americans around President Kennedy. When a humiliating situation lasts a long time, however, presidential popularity sinks, as Carter and Reagan both found in dealing with Iran. Similarly, a long war destroys popularity; Truman experienced this in Korea, Johnson in Vietnam, and Bush 43 in Iraq. Economic recession is also bad for popularity; five Republican presidents (Eisenhower, Ford, Reagan, and both Bushes) were rated low during economic downturns. A good economy is great for presidents; Clinton's approval stayed high in the prosperous late 1990s, even during his impeachment. Obama's dropped as the economy refused to grow. As the economy improved, so did Obama's support.

Presidential approval based on one situation tends to spill over into other areas of presidential activity. As might be expected, President Reagan's support jumped several points in the wake of the successful 1983 U.S. takeover of Communist Grenada and the rescue of American students there. At that same time, approval of Reagan's economic policies also climbed, although little in the economy had actually changed.

Liberals and Conservatives

Is public opinion in the United State polarized? Political scientists debate whether the divide between liberals and conservatives is just a flap among elites or whether the American public has lost its unimodal distribution and become bimodal on ideology. Some surveys show that many people still call themselves moderate and have liberal opinions on some issues and conservative opinions on other issues. Some scholars caution that we should focus on those who pay attention to politics, not the uninformed. The politically engaged, to use political scientist Alan Abramowitz's term, have polarized. Liberals and conservatives agree on less and less. A large majority of liberals prefer a bigger government that provides more service whereas equal numbers of conservatives prefer a smaller government providing fewer services.

We must again note the difference between *economic* and *noneconomic* liberalism. Americans are not very clear about what they mean by "liberal" or "conservative." Retired people, for example, support Social Security and Medicare—the programs of economic liberals—but many call themselves conservatives because they have traditional values. They use "conservative" in the noneconomic sense. On economic issues, however, such as federal aid for prescription drugs, they (often unwittingly) assume ultra-liberal positions. The problem is self-identification, which often diverges from people's views on specific issues. People who say they are conservative—because where they live it is fashionable to do so—may actually be economic liberals when it comes to getting more federal dollars for themselves. Being "moderate" is also popular, but moderate can mean many things. Three people could variously be moderate on all issues, conservative on economic issues, and liberal on noneconomic issues or the reverse and all call themselves moderate. The term "liberal" by comparison has not been popular in recent years. Many liberals prefer to call themselves "progressives" or moderates.

Who Pays Attention?

Public opinion is fragmented; groups are interested in different questions. Farmers are concerned about crop prices, wealthy people about taxes, steel and auto workers about imports, and women and minorities about equality. A time when some groups are satisfied may be a time when others are dissatisfied. A growing economy may please the better off but leave many people behind.

The **attentive public** (see previous Classic Works box), although relatively few in number, has great political impact because those who pay attention have ideas and articulate them, demonstrating political competence. Sometimes they can rouse the general public. Opposition to the Vietnam and Iraq wars and to South Africa's apartheid started with a few critics who wrote and spoke in churches, newspapers, and colleges. While few people were paying attention, some of the attentive public raised concern over atrocities in the Middle East and Africa. The attentive public can act as "spark plugs" for the apathetic and slow-reacting general public.

attentive public
Those citizens who follow politics, especially national and international affairs.

This is why all regimes treat intellectuals with caution and sometimes with suspicion. Communist regimes expend great effort to ferret out a handful of dissident intellectuals. In Washington, administration officials devote much time and energy to win over the attentive public to minimize criticism that might influence the general public and the next election. Relations between the White House and the news media are a cat-and-mouse game. Political elites, aware of the ignorance and low interest of the general public, may convince themselves not to pay much attention to public opinion. A 1998 Pew study found that members of Congress, presidential appointees, and senior civil servants believed most Americans do not know enough to form sound opinions on vital issues of the day. Elites, in other words, believe elites must decide questions because they are the only ones following them. Unfortunately for democracy, they may be right.

intensity
The firmness and enthusiasm with which an opinion is held.

The general public's indifference and fragmentation mean that their views are often hard to discern and may have little impact on decision making. Elected leaders are apt to pay attention to the group with the most intensely held views. Polls show that most Americans would permit abortion, but few strongly support it. The "pro-life" foes of abortion, although a minority nationwide, feel such great **intensity** about the subject that they often drown out the greater numbers who are not passionately concerned. Jews are fewer than 2 percent of the U.S. population, but among them are such intense supporters of Israel that most elected officials take a pro-Israel stance. Most Americans favor some form of gun control, but they are mostly lukewarm about the issue. The opponents to gun control are red hot and thus quite influential. Intensely held views of a few often override large numbers of indifferent people.

The disproportionate influence of the attentive public and passionate opinion holders underscores one of the problems of public opinion. Often there is little "public" opinion—just the opinions of scattered and small groups who pay attention to issues and care intensely about them. Should their views be excluded as unrepresentative, or should they take on added weight as the only people who really care? Which is the more democratic approach? Most people would say democracy means going with the greatest numbers, even if their views are lukewarm. When it comes to a question that deeply concerns them, however, many people do not want a simple head count, arguing that the majority view is ignorant or mistaken and should not be heeded.

Is Polling Fair?

Polls do not merely monitor public opinion; they also help make it. Critics charge that published or broadcast poll results can distort an election. For example, the news media may highlight polls showing one candidate leading another. Such publicity, claim underdog candidates, devastates their campaigns by making supporters and contributors lose interest. Poor poll showings, especially early in the campaign, are a self-fulfilling prophecy of defeat for some candidates. Those who lead in the early polls get more contributions, more news coverage, and thus more supporters.

One current controversy is the effect of "exit polls," in which voters are questioned just as they leave the balloting place. With the three-hour time difference between the East and West Coasts, exit polls enable television to predict winners in the East while westerners still have hours in which to cast a ballot. Does the early prediction in the East persuade westerners not to bother to vote? Even if the early prediction of the presidential election is accurate, a falloff in voters could hurt state and local candidates who may have won if more people had voted. Some urge a delay in broadcasting the results of exit polls. France prohibits publishing polls for two days before and during election day; they can be published only after balloting ends at 8 p.m. No evidence has been found that exit polls influence the U.S. presidential vote, but they might influence other contests for the House, Senate, or state legislatures. Polls, especially when broadcast so quickly, are not neutral in their impact, but no constitutionally legal way has been found to control them.

Should the United States Be Governed by Polls?

Considering the preceding discussion, it would seem in most cases that the United States should not be governed by polls. First, public attention varies widely. On many issues, the general public has no knowledge or opinion, which lets the intensity of a minority dominate poll results. Leaders, especially with modern means of communication, influence public opinion in their direction and encourage them to create the kind of feedback they want to hear.

The wording of the questions and the selection of the sample can seriously skew results. The survey must be done by trained professionals using standardized questions and random samples. Polls designed to sway you—the obnoxious "push polls"—are not worthy of response; hang up on them. The low rate of response to telephone surveys undermines their reliability. Equally serious are the problem of volatility and nonattitudes. What the public likes one year it may dislike the next. Decisions made on the basis of a survey may turn sour when the consequences sink in. Bush advisor Karl Rove thought that war with Iraq would play well with voters. It did, for a while. Top officials who "go with the polls" may be trapping themselves. Polls, if done well, are useful snapshots of public opinion at a given moment but are no substitute for careful analyses and prudent anticipation.

Review Questions

1. Does government follow or create public opinion?
2. How important is religion in forming U.S. opinion?
3. What is the theory of political generations?
4. What are the three classic opinion curves?
5. Why did the *Literary Digest* miscall the 1936 election?
6. Why did polls miscall the 1948 election?
7. Why does it matter to know the population being sampled?
8. What is a random sample?
9. What does presidential "popularity" really measure?
10. What is intensity and volatility?

Key Terms

anecdotal, p. 128
anticlericalism, p. 134
attentive public, p. 143
bimodal, p. 136
covariance, p. 141
dependent variable, p. 141
economic issues, p. 132
gender gap, p. 135
honeymoon, p. 141
independent variable, p. 141
inference, p. 138

intensity, p. 144
life cycle, p. 135
likely voters, p. 138
margin of error, p. 139
noneconomic issues, p. 132
polarize, p. 136
political generations, p. 135
population, p. 138
public opinion, p. 128
rally event, p. 142
regions, p. 133

religiosity, p. 134
salience, p. 131
sample, p. 138
simple random sample, p. 139
skewed, p. 136
social class, p. 131
social mobility, p. 132
survey, p. 138
unimodal, p. 136
volatility, p. 140

Further Reference

Abramowitz, Alan. I. *The Disappearing Center: Engaged Citizens, Polarization and American Democracy.* New Haven, CT: Yale University Press, 2010.

Alvarez, R. Michael, and John Brehm. *Hard Choices, Easy Answers: Values, Information, and American Public Opinion.* Princeton, NJ: Princeton University Press, 2002.

Aronowitz, Stanley. *How Class Works: Power and Social Movement.* New Haven, CT: Yale University Press, 2003.

Asher, Herbert. *Polling and the Public: What Every Citizen Should Know*, 8th ed. Washington, DC: CQ Press, 2010.

Berinsky, Adam J. *In Time of War: Understanding American Public Opinion from World War II to Iraq.* Chicago: University of Chicago Press, 2009.

Dalton, Russell J. *Citizen Politics: Public Opinion and Political Parties in Advanced Industrial Democracies*, 5th ed. Washington, DC: CQ Press, 2008.

Druckman, James N., and Lawrence R. Jacobs. *Who Governs? Presidents, Public Opinion, and Manipulation.* Chicago, IL: University of Chicago Press, 2015.

Lardner, James, and David A. Smith, eds. *Inequality Matters: The Growing Economic Divide in America and Its Poisonous Consequences.* New York: New Press, 2005.

Mueller, John. *War, Presidents and Public Opinion.* New York: Wiley, 1973.

———. *Overblown: How Politicians and the Terrorism Industry Inflate National Security Threats and Why We Believe Them.* New York: Simon & Schuster, 2006.

Murray, Charles. *Coming Apart: The State of White America, 1960–2010.* New York: Crown, 2012.

Silver, Nate. *The Signal and the Noise: Why So Many Predictions Fail—But Some Don't.* New York: Penguin, 2012.

Stonecash, Jeffrey M. *Class and Party in American Politics.* Boulder, CO: Westview, 2000.

Traugott, Michael W., and Paul J. Lavrakas. *The Voter's Guide to Election Polls*, 4th ed. Lanham, MD: Rowman & Littlefield, 2008.

Wald, Kenneth D., and Allison Calhoun-Brown. *Religion and Politics in the United States*, 6th ed. Lanham, MD: Rowman & Littlefield, 2011.

Weisberg, Herbert F. *The Total Survey Error Approach: A Guide to the New Science of Survey Research.* Chicago: The University of Chicago Press, 2005.

Weissberg, Robert. *Polling, Policy, and Public Opinion: The Case Against Heeding the "Voice of the People."* New York: Palgrave, 2002.

Part III
Political Interactions

Ch. 8 Political Communication Modern politics revolves around the media, which electronics are rapidly changing. Especially important are the elite media. Newspapers are in decline, and television is now the most influential, although the Internet is gaining. TV news coverage, however, is spotty and leaves viewers poorly informed. U.S. government and media are frequently at odds, especially after the media finds they have been deceived.

Ch. 9 Interest Groups Interest groups are a bedrock of pluralism and thus important to democracy. Interest groups, however, can be created by government programs. Big money has led to undue interest-group influence and repeated scandals. Higher socioeconomic status gives interest groups greater access with which to influence legislatures, executives, court decisions, and public appeals. In some systems, strong interest groups work against democracy.

Ch. 10 Parties Parties are the great organizing device of government, especially in democracies. Parties may be classified in several ways, from degree of centralization and organization through ideology. Most modern democratic parties are now "catchalls," combinations of many groups and viewpoints. Party systems, logically distinct from parties, determine how the parties interact. They include one-party, dominant-party, two-party, and multiparty systems. The electoral system influences the party system, which under certain circumstances can break down.

Ch. 11 Elections First, we consider who is most likely to vote and find that turnout is uneven among groups. Next, we ask who votes how and find that the key variables are party identification, social class, region, religion, age, and urban–rural splits. The theory of electoral realignment, which claims that every few decades many voters switch their party ID to favor one party, has been called into question. The U.S. electorate has shown strong partisan polarization recently. Obviously, personality helps win elections, but some voters take a retrospective overview of incumbent performance. A candidate who modifies positions is merely responding rationally to mass demands.

Chapter 8
Political Communication

∨ Learning Objectives

8.1 List the modern mass media and show which are most influential.

8.2 Demonstrate the political impact of social media.

8.3 Argue that television has or has not ruined political discourse.

8.4 Define and explain "structural bias" in the mass media.

8.5 Show how adversarial media are necessary for democracy.

The Internet and social media have brought a communications revolution and a younger generation that embraces fast communications outside of regime control. The political impact of these changes is, however, uncertain. Some compare the rise of the Internet with the invention of printing in the fifteenth century—a widening of human horizons with the freedom to learn and think for oneself—but some are cautious. **Blogs** and websites are skewed by ideology and partisanship and further fragment and polarize politics as liberals read liberal blogs and conservatives read conservative blogs, never meeting for dialogue. The electronic media are eating into the mainstream media—both print and broadcast—replacing factual reports with opinionated blogs.

blog
Regularly updated web site, often linked to other sites and partisan.

Many peg the awakening of the Arab world to the satellite television of Al Jazeera, which began broadcasting in 1996 and quickly became the Arab world's most popular news source. Observers credit the Internet, Facebook, and Twitter in the hands of youthful activists as the catalysts of the 2010-2013 Arab Spring. Political unrest may appear a few years after the arrival of a new medium. One can see a triple confluence: (1) The social media arrive worldwide just as (2) corruption (related to economic growth) increases on top of (3) a demographic bulge. Communications studies, however, always stumbled over causality— proving that communications are causes rather than consequences of change elsewhere in the economy and society.

The Mass Media and Politics

8.1   **List the modern mass media and show which are most influential.**

The *mass media* strongly influence politics. In the 1780s, the *Federalist Papers* were published in newspapers throughout the thirteen U.S. states to win support for the new constitution. Andrew Jackson's victory in 1828 over John Quincy Adams was one of the dirtiest "media campaigns" ever; some papers accused Jackson and his wife of immorality. In 1904, Teddy Roosevelt was a "media candidate" with a rough-and-ready image that won press coverage and the election. And Franklin D. Roosevelt's "fireside chats" on the radio, along with hundreds of press conferences, won support for his policies. Today, the mass media are a recognized component of politics worldwide, and modern campaigns depend on television so much that critics complain that candidates no longer run for office on issues; instead, professional marketing consultants package and sell them like products.

Scholars have long recognized the dependence of politics on communication. Political scientist Karl W. Deutsch (1912–1992) showed how modernization and nationalism can be measured by the increase of mail, telephone calls, and newspapers. The more communication, the more modernization (which does not prove which causes which). The political system and the communication system parallel one another; it is doubtful that one could exist without the other.

Classic Works

The Two-Step Flow of Mass Communications

How do the mass media influence political opinions? Indirectly, said Paul Lazarsfeld and Elihu Katz, whose research in the 1940s and 1950s found a "two-step flow" in this process. The first step is the media messages, but the crucial second step is respected local **opinion leaders**—what Almond called the "attentive public." These people get political ideas from the mass media and pass them on to their less attentive friends in face-to-face contact. Mass-media persuasion depends on these opinion leaders.

opinion leaders
Locally respected people who influence the views of others.

face-to-face
Communication by personal contact.

stump
To campaign by personally speaking to voters.

All political action is a reaction to communication. There are different levels and types of communication. **Face-to-face** communication is the most basic and effective for altering or reinforcing political opinions because it allows for dialogue whereas mass media cannot. Until the early 1930s, face-to-face communication was the main method of political campaigning. Candidates **stumped** (in the old days, many spoke from tree stumps) their districts and addressed small groups of voters, appealing for their support with the help of ward bosses, precinct captains, and political organizers. The rise of television has largely bypassed grassroots stumping, except as a means of getting free media coverage or for local office where a candidate can reach a relatively large share of the electorate in person.

The mass media reach an infinitely larger audience and therefore yield a greater voter or public-opinion return than face-to-face communication. A speech at even the largest rally is heard by only a few thousand, but the mass media are one-way communication. Viewers cannot immediately tell the president they disagree with his or her TV message. Mass media generally reinforce existing political opinions but rarely convert anyone. Radio and television do have stronger persuasive power than the printed word because they mimic face-to-face communication, but their impact still depends partly on chats with friends afterward.

Television may have eroded the role of *opinion leaders* as television newscasters and commentators become opinion leaders on a grand scale. Television not only transmits direct political messages but also indirectly changes society by bringing news and ideas into the homes of all. Most observers agree that the 1960s civil-rights movement would not have succeeded without television. Racial discrimination in the South was largely unnoticed in the print media and radio. But television news showing fire hoses and police dogs attacking peaceful marchers turned most white Americans in favor of equal rights for African Americans. Some believe that television coverage of the Vietnam War—the world's first television war—turned many against the war and against President Johnson. Photos of U.S. soldiers mistreating Iraqi prisoners had a similar impact in 2004.

Fewer Americans now are interested in news than they were one and two generations ago. Only about a third watch television news or read newspapers. And news is shifting from politics and world affairs to human interest and "news you can use" about health, business, and lifestyles. This shift parallels the decline in Americans' interest in politics in general, confirming the close connection between communications and politics. The causes of this decline are debated. Some see a shift in values, especially among a new and **introspective** generation addicted to entertainment. Only terrorist attacks, involvement in war, or a financial meltdown can jolt them into paying attention to the real world.

introspective
Looking within oneself.

The various modern media appeal to different audiences distinguished by education, income, and age. The more educated individuals are, the more media they consume. College graduates and better-off people tend to read newspapers, magazines, and books as well as follow radio and television. Those with less education mostly use television, and largely for entertainment; few are regular magazine and book readers.

Age also affects mass-media usage. Older people pay far more attention to the editorial and news content of newspapers and magazines than do teenagers and young adults, who tend to use newspapers to follow sports, rock stars, and feature articles rather than hard news. Young people also love social media. The college student who keeps up on the news and editorial opinion is rare.

Modern Mass Media

NEWSPAPERS In 1910, the United States had more than 2,600 daily newspapers, and most American cities had two or more competing papers. Today, only about half that number remain, and few U.S. cities have two papers. Many major newspapers, long money losers, have drastically cut their staffs and Washington and overseas bureaus. Some have folded. As news on the Internet grows, many citizens prefer it but often do not get a variety of political and editorial opinion. Big corporations, seeking profits and not controversy, own some 75 percent of U.S. newspapers, giving them a **status-quo** orientation. Few newspapers present the news in an obviously partisan manner, for both practical and idealistic reasons. Most newspaper revenue comes from advertising, and ad rates depend on the papers' circulation, which usually leads to a middle-of-the-road news policy that does not antagonize but makes news coverage bland.

status quo
Keeping the present situation.

Journalism has a long tradition of objectivity in news reporting (not so on the editorial page). The profession's own standards influence newspeople to present the news fairly and honestly. Further, much news in U.S. newspapers is derived from a service, The Associated Press, which prides itself on objectivity and refrains from editorializing. Some question whether the choice of what to cover is influenced by the personal opinions of journalists, if not the coverage itself. Regardless, blogs share no tradition of neutrality and are often wildly partisan, more activism than journalism. Some fear the demise of objective reporting.

How much political impact do U.S. newspapers have? Not as much as they used to. In the 1960s, some 80 percent of Americans read a daily paper; now fewer than 30 percent do. Newspapers come in third, behind television and the Internet, as people's main source of news. Young people have largely abandoned newspapers in favor of the Internet and social media. Americans raised on television do not read much. The content of newspapers is mostly advertisements (one important reason people read them) and wire-service copy. The editorials of most newspapers carry little weight. The exceptions are the "elite" media.

RADIO Like newspapers, radio too has declined. Now three companies own half of America's radio stations. Clear Channel Communications alone controls more than 1,200 stations. It is programmed from its headquarters with homogenized news and no local content, not even tornado warnings. Between the two world wars, however, radio was popular, and its news, comments, and political addresses—such as Franklin D. Roosevelt's famous "fireside chats," which served as models for both Jimmy Carter and Ronald Reagan—were quite influential. Since the rise of television in the 1950s, radio became less important, with two exceptions. Popular "talk radio" shows, often hosted by angry right-wingers, reinforce conservative views. Reinforcing liberal views, the radio magazine "All Things Considered" on National Public Radio offers world events, economics, politics, and critical opinions.

THE NEWS SERVICES Most hard news in newspapers and on radio, and even a good deal of television's news, is not produced in-house but comes from a printer hooked up to the New York offices of The Associated Press (AP), hence the old-fashioned name **wire service**. The elite newspapers disdain wire-service copy, as it is a matter of pride to have their own reporters cover the story. But many papers in the United States are little more than local outlets for the AP, which provides them with photos, sports coverage, even recipes, as well as news.

wire service
News agency that sells to all media.

The AP is a publishers' cooperative, with members paying thousands of dollars a week in assessments based on their circulation. They also contribute local stories to the AP, which may rewrite them for national and even world transmission. The AP is one of the few news services not owned, subsidized, controlled, or supervised by a government. It is free of government influence and proud of it, but it too is in financial difficulty. Why buy information when you can get it free online? Britain's Reuters, France's AFP, and Germany's DPA have discreet government supervision, and China's Xin Hua is Beijing's spokesman. United Press International (UPI) used to compete with AP, but now Rev. Sun Myung Moon's Unification Church owns UPI, which is a faint shadow of its former self.

No government controls the AP, but other problems limit its quality and influence. First, it moves fast; every minute is a deadline. This means it does little digging; its stories are often superficial. Second, until recently the wire services' definition of news has been something from an official **source**. Most of its stories are carefully attributed to police, the White House, the State Department or Pentagon, and so on. The unstated motto was: If it's not official, it's not news, and if it is official, it must be true. This caused the wire services to miss many explosive situations in the world because they did not report on opposition people, average citizens on the street, or merchants in the bazaar, who might have a completely different—and sometimes more accurate—perspective than official spokespersons. The news media failed to notice the coming of the Iranian revolution for

source
Whom or where a news reporter gets information from.

this reason. Often the best news stories are not about a key event or statement but about what people are saying and thinking, which is a strong point of the blogs. Belatedly, newspapers and wire services now include synthesis and interpretation.

THE ELITE MEDIA *The New York Times, The Washington Post, The Wall Street Journal,* and *Financial Times* are read by a small fraction of the U.S. population, but they carry by far the most clout. Decision makers in Washington read them and take both their news stories and editorials seriously. Leading thinkers fight battles on their "op-ed" pages (opposite the editorial page). That is why these papers have influence out of all proportion to their circulation. They are the **elite media** because the people who read them are generally wealthier and better educated and have much more influence than readers of hometown papers. Many are *opinion leaders,* who transmit their views to other citizens.

The elite press pursues "investigative reporting," looking for government and partisan wrongdoing, something the average paper shuns for fear of lawsuits. *The New York Times* jolted the nation when it published the *Pentagon Papers* on the Vietnam War in 1971. The dogged pursuit of the 1972 Watergate burglary by *The Washington Post* brought down the Nixon administration in 1974. The editorials of *The Wall Street Journal* influence economic decisions in Washington. London's lively and brainy *Financial Times,* now distributed across the United States, has eaten into the readership of the NYT and WSJ. Some count the FT as the elite of the elite newspapers.

elite media
Highly influential newspapers and magazines read by elites and the attentive public.

oligopoly
A few big firms dominate a market.

Democracy

The Tendency to Media Oligopoly

If many competing media voices are good, America has some concerns, for media ownership has moved toward **oligopoly**. Some twenty corporations control most of what Americans read, hear, and view, as they own newspapers and radio and television stations. The five biggest:

- News Corp—owned by Australian-born press baron Rupert Murdoch, owns Fox TV, HarperCollins (books), the *Weekly Standard* (influential neocon magazine), *The Wall Street Journal, New York Post, London Times,* and DirecTV.
- General Electric—owns NBC and Universal-Vivendi, itself a major conglomerate.
- Time-Warner—was the merger of a big magazine publisher and major studio that now includes CNN and AOL.

- Disney—owns ABC and ESPN.
- Comcast, the biggest cable company, has tried to take over Disney.
- Clear Channel—owns a large fraction of U.S. radio stations and programs them centrally, eliminating local content.

What happens to democracy without free speech and multiple sources of information? Media critics worry that we receive bland uniformity and unquestioning acceptance of White House pronouncements. Some feel there is still adequate diversity and criticism, now bolstered by blogs and the social media, with their innumerable sources and viewpoints. The Federal Communications Commission is supposed to guard against oligopoly but in recent years has seen no problem with bigness and fewness.

Some small-circulation magazines of opinion are also influential. The conservative *National Review,* the liberal *American Prospect,* the leftist *Nation,* and the neoconservative *Weekly Standard* have considerable impact on opinion leaders. Students often ignore the elite press, but they provide critical overviews the bigger media miss.

Social Media

8.2   **Demonstrate the political impact of social media.**

The political impact of the Internet and social media is growing. You can look up whatever you want—such as a candidate's proposals—but that is often "preaching to the converted," to people who already like the candidate. Fewer Americans follow news on TV and in newspapers, but news online gains, especially among young people. It is free. You can read it any time and focus only on what interests you. Most prefer sports and finance to political news. Howard Dean's 2004 bid for the Democratic presidential nomination featured online fund-raising for the first time. It was quite successful and was copied by later presidential candidates; according to one estimate, Obama's 2012 campaign raised nearly $700 million online.

The Internet may catch stories the conventional media overlook. Beholden to no one, blogs uncovered dubious political contributions, torture, warrantless surveillance, and the financial crisis earlier and deeper than newspapers or television. *Talking Points Memo* first noticed in 2007 how the Bush administration was firing U.S. attorneys it deemed liberal. The online magazine *Salon* broke the story of Rev. Moon's 2004 coronation in the U.S. Capitol as the messiah. Such discoveries jolt the conventional media into covering what they previously neglected. In comparison to the Internet, mainstream media can be remarkably incurious.

A generation raised on social media, however, supposes that they bring everything to light. They do not; someone—preferably an experienced reporter—still has to go out and dig up news that many prefer to keep quiet. Without the original input of news, social media are largely gossip. Conventional media—especially print media—point out that only they practice "quality journalism" by professionals who know their areas and check their facts. They cover the basic news of government, courts, wars, and natural disasters. This is expensive, and the Internet simply puts out the stories as news digests without paying for them, under the slogan, "Information wants to be free." Blogs, operating on a shoestring, send no reporters into the field and base their stories on e-mails from unpaid volunteers (the good blogs sift submissions carefully). Newspapers and television boast of their "balance" (covering two sides of everything), something that does not interest blogs and tweets.

Will electronic media overall make well-informed citizens? Many doubt it. The Internet has drastically lowered the cost of entering the media world (just as digitized music has drastically lowered the cost of entering the music world).

Thousands now put out their own online magazines, most of them highly partisan. One study found that 85 percent of blog links were to those of the same political viewpoint. Thoughtful synthesis is not the Internet's strong point. You can get all manner of detailed information online, but you have to *want* to do it. You can read Japan's top daily at www.asahi.com/english, but how many will? Most newspapers and magazines now have parallel online publications as their print circulation declines. Millions now read *The New York Times* on their computer for $20 a month. One of the big media questions today is whether news organizations should charge an online subscription fee.

Case Studies

The Media and War

The 2003 Iraq War had strong media support going into it and during it. 9/11 was a huge *rally event* that produced emotional and uncritical support for President Bush, including from the press. The media accepted administration claims that Iraq was building weapons of mass destruction (WMD). After the war, however, no WMD were found, and efforts to implant a stable democracy amid deadly chaos were futile. As if in revenge for having been misled, much of the media turned critical, and the administration again fumed that the press was misinforming the public and undermining morale.

Were the media to blame for declining public support for the war? Political scientist John Mueller demonstrated that during Korea (1950–1953), Vietnam (1965–1973), and Iraq (2003–2011), two-thirds of the public initially supported the wars, but within three years one-third or fewer did. And the Korean War was essentially pre-television, so we cannot blame TV for this decline. Time and mounting casualties seem to cause the decline, not television. Americans simply do not like long wars. Opinion on Iraq declined more quickly, probably because no WMD were found.

The U.S. military still blames the media and keeps them under close control. In 2003, journalists could cover the Iraq War "embedded" into combat units. This generally brought positive coverage, as the newspeople quickly bonded with the soldiers. But it was narrow-angle coverage (the view from one Humvee) that did not explain what was happening overall. And it did not extend into the looting and violence that soon erupted. Public support for the occupation declined, but was it due to news coverage or to reality? E-mailed photos of U.S. guards sexually humiliating Iraqi prisoners in 2004 produced a major moral shift comparable to the impact of the 1968 Mylai massacre in Vietnam. In both cases, the photos were not taken by the media but by U.S. soldiers.

In unusual apologies, *The New York Times* and *The Washington Post* in 2004 regretted having believed administration claims that led to the 2003 war. They had not been sufficiently skeptical, editors said, and should have asked more questions. Later, both the Bush and Obama administrations threatened prosecution under the 1917 Espionage Act for news reports on secret U.S. antiterrorism programs. Journalists claimed a public right to know under the First Amendment; the government claimed it hurt antiterrorism efforts. If it came to trial, most bet the media would win.

Within a few years of the 2003 invasion, columnists of all sorts—including conservative Republicans—were denouncing the botched job in Iraq. Neither the White House nor the Pentagon can suppress bad news for long. There is no sure way to "manage" news coverage; reality eventually emerges, often angrily. The media seem to follow a "bounce-back" pattern: Initially they accept administration claims and frames but then, discovering that they have been misled, turn angry and negative.

Digital media can undermine undemocratic regimes. Iranians mobilized by computer and cell phones against rigged 2009 elections. Young Tunisians, Egyptians, and Syrians used their cell phones to mobilize against dictatorial regimes. Millions of Chinese social media users comment on the scandals and ousters of major political figures, much to the chagrin of a regime that muzzles such news. For the sake of economic growth, most countries allow social media, but with the economic and technical come the political and critical, cracking the regime's information monopoly. China employs tens of thousands of social media watchers and arrests critical bloggers, but Chinese take pride in their freeware that jumps over the "Great Firewall."

Digital media's unique feature that can support democratic participation is that it involves a two-way flow of ideas. Newspapers (except for letters to the editor), television, and even many websites convey information in one direction—from journalists to the public. Social media are more like conversations. The public can post comments to a news story, like a Facebook post or retweet an idea. The conversation about the original story can itself become the story if it "goes viral." Does this deliver more meaningful democratic debate? Maybe, but sometimes they simply rehash media elites' talking points.

The Giant: Television

8.3 Argue that television has or has not ruined political discourse.

When most people say "the media," they mean television, for television still has the greatest impact. Some two-thirds of Americans still get their news from television—down from 90 percent a few decades earlier—and most accord it higher credibility than newspapers. Young people, however, now get more of their news from the Internet and social media than from television.

Post World War II, television touched and changed almost everything in politics. Election campaigns now revolve around the acquisition of television time; winners are usually those who raise the most money to hire the best media consultants. Television became a suspect in the decline of both U.S. election turnout and political parties. Some observers claim television, which focuses on "sound bites" of a few seconds, trivializes politics. Penetrating analysis is out; the catchy phrase is in.

Television News

Television, by definition, favors the visual. "Talking heads" provide no more news than radio, although they do provide a sense of personality and hence credibility, an imitation face-to-face communication. News producers pay more attention to a news story with "good visuals" than without. Abstract, deeper topics go by with little coverage, but dramatic action—if there was a camera crew on hand to catch it—gets played up. Television, like most of the rest of the

U.S. news media, ignored the hatred that was brewing against Egyptian dictator Hosni Mubarak for years but caught the Cairo crowds chanting for his ouster in 2011. Television never did explain what the Vietnam War was about, but a brief film clip of a Saigon general shooting a Vietcong assassin in 1968 helped sicken Americans and turn them against the war. Television news is hooked on the eye-catching. Television is inherently a more emotional medium than the others; its coverage can go straight to the heart, bypassing the brain, as communications theorist Marshall McLuhan (1911–1980) observed.

Television camera crews are expensive to maintain in the field, especially overseas, so they usually arrive where the action is only *after* having read it on the AP wire or online. Television needs to know in advance what's going to happen; then it can schedule a camera crew. This makes television news lopsided with press conferences, speeches, committee hearings, and official statements. Some critics call these **media events**, things that would not have occurred without television coverage. Moving into the coverage vacuum are amateur videos taken on cell phones, posted on YouTube, and picked up by television. Although the images are poor, they convey a sense of "being there," an authenticity professional media cannot match. People worldwide watched protests in Turkey and Egypt and beheadings in Syria shortly after they happened.

media event
News incident planned to get media coverage.

Analysis is also not television's strong point. An average news story runs one minute; a four-minute story is an in-depth report. Walter Cronkite, long the dean of television anchors, emphasized that television news was just a "headline service," meaning that if viewers wanted detail and depth they should look elsewhere. Most Americans look no deeper and are left with the tardy, the eye-catching, and the media event as their daily diet of information. Thus, it is not surprising when polls repeatedly discover that Americans are poorly informed.

Television and Politics

Television changed politics in several ways. Incumbency, especially in the White House, has always brought recognition, and television has enhanced this, but not always to the advantage of the **incumbent**. Television news is heavily focused on the president. Congress gets much less coverage, the courts even less. This deepens a long-term American tendency to president-worship. The president—especially with the way television socializes small children—is seen as an omnipotent parental figure, a person who can fix all problems. That should make a president happy. But then the president fails to fix the problems, and ultracritical media imply he is making them worse. The flip side of being treated as all-powerful is catching all the blame. The media, especially television, whip up president-worship and then whip up mass dissatisfaction with the president's performance. Expectations, heightened by the media, are too high, and disappointments are correspondingly bitter. Some critics charge that the media wreck the political system with that kind of coverage, making the country unstable and ungovernable.

incumbent
Official who already occupies the office.

NOMINATION BY TELEVISION   Television does much to nominate presidential candidates. With all eyes focused on the early presidential primaries, commentators grandly proclaim who is the "real winner" and who has "momentum." The candidate thus designated as front-runner goes into the remaining primaries and the national convention with a **bandwagon** effect, enhanced recognition, and even more television coverage. In the nominating process, television has become a king-maker, so candidates arrange their schedules and strategies to capture as much television exposure as possible.

bandwagon
Tendency of frontrunners to gain additional supporters.

Television coverage of candidates focuses more on personalities rather than issues. Television, with its sharp close-ups and seeming spontaneity, gives viewers what they think is a true glimpse of the candidate's character. Actually, this may not be so; some candidates play the medium like professionals (Ronald Reagan), and others tense up and hide their normal personalities (Bob Dole). How candidates perform on television is a poor indicator of how they will perform in office, but it is the one most voters use.

While television is playing this major role in nominating and electing candidates, political parties are bypassed. Increasingly, candidates raise funds through their own team and use television to speak directly to voters. Because the leading contenders have already picked up their "momentum" going into the convention, they do not need party professionals to broker a nominating deal. Politics has come out of the proverbial smoke-filled back room and into the glare of television lights, not always for the better. Party chiefs used to know a thing or two about politics and were often capable of putting forward effective candidates. With television, a candidate can come out of nearly

Methods

Defining Variables

You must define the variables you use so clearly that neither you nor the reader can mistake them for anything else. This means deliberate narrowing. For example, it is difficult to use the term "democracy" in all its complexity. There are just too many things to keep track of. You would find that many countries have some democratic characteristics but not all. A good definition allows you to easily put items into categories. You might define a flat or falling economy in presidential election years as "bad times" and see if incumbents lose.

Even something like "voting" needs to be narrowed. Do we mean voting in primary, local, presidential, or congressional elections? We cannot compare turnout in the 2016 presidential election with turnout in the congressional 2014 elections; presidential elections bring higher turnout. We must compare like elections, such as the presidential elections every four years.

Especially difficult are broad and unclear terms that carry emotional baggage, such as "isolationism." How would you demonstrate that senators of certain regions or parties are more isolationist? If you ask them, all will deny being isolationists, as the term connotes ignorance. You might come up with a narrower term, such as "noninterventionist," and define it as unwillingness to send U.S. troops overseas. Then, by surveying senators' voting records, you might discern patterns of noninterventionism.

nowhere and win the top national office with little political experience, such as Obama did.

We must be careful, though, in blaming television for the weakening of parties. American parties, with the exception of a few urban machines, were never as strongly organized as most European parties (which are also declining). American parties began declining long ago, not just with the advent of televivision. Other factors—special-interest groups, political action committees, and direct-mail and online solicitation—have also undermined party strength. Television is not the sole culprit.

TELEVISION AND APATHY   Observers have long suspected that television induces passivity and apathy. Harvard political scientist Robert D. Putnam, reviewing the decline of "civic engagement" in the United States, found that people born before World War II, are more trusting and more inclined to join groups and participate in politics. His reason: They were raised before the television age began in the 1950s. Younger people, raised on television, lack these qualities. Says Putnam: "Each hour spent viewing television is associated with less social trust and less group membership, while each hour reading a newspaper is associated with more." Solitary screen time (now including computers, tablets, and smartphones) prevents the social interaction that builds trust in neighbors.

A related charge is that television has lowered Election Day turnouts. There is a close coincidence in time; U.S. turnout dropped 13 percentage points from 1960, when television first established itself as the top means of campaigning, to 1988; then it stayed at the same low level until recent upticks. Television saturates viewers so far in advance that they lose interest. The top two candidates sometimes sound so similar that many voters see little difference. Negative ads disgust many voters, who stop paying attention. Charges and countercharges—especially from the limitless funding of super-PACs—come so thick and fast that the voter is **cross-pressured** into indecision and apathy. In Western Europe, where paid-for political television spots are generally prohibited and campaigns are much shorter—usually about a month instead of more than a year in the United States—voter turnout is higher. Only the United States does not regulate TV political ads.

cross-pressured
Pushed by opposing political forces; said to produce apathy.

U.S. television campaigning costs have grown into the billions. Depending on the time of day and locale, a one-minute spot can go for $100,000 or more. The cost factor has transformed American politics. Some members of Congress need little television advertising, but virtually all senatorial and presidential candidates need it. Most presidential campaign spending—most of it in 2016 by super-PACS—now goes for television. Political consulting—the right themes, slogans, and speeches presented in scripted television spots—has become a big business. In most contests (but not 2012), the winner is the side that spent the most money, most of it on television. This heightens the importance of special-interest groups and political action committees, which in turn weakens the role of the parties and perhaps deepens feelings of powerlessness among average citizens. Many voters ignore party labels—a trend that some political scientists call voter "dealignment," citizens *not* lining up with a party. Some fear that these voters, lacking party identification, are persuaded by television. The 2012 presidential race put a question mark by this, as massive TV spending, mostly by Republicans, did not lead to a win. Negative ads may have cancelled each other out; voters simply tuned them all out and paid them no mind.

framing
A news story's basic direction and interpretation.

Theories

The Framing of News

Developed by sociologist Erving Goffman, **framing** is used by many social scientists but has special relevance in communication studies to mean the basic line of a news story. Akin to oversimplifying and stereotyping, framing means setting up a frame of reference, which for a while dominates news stories on a given topic. Newspersons call it the "lead," sometimes deliberately misspelled "led" or "lede," the crucial first paragraph, which sets the story's direction.

Framing does not necessarily mean conscious slanting; rather, it is a necessary narrowing that allows reporters, editors, and readers to make sense of the news. You cannot lead with, "Gee, this 'fiscal cliff' thing sure is complicated." Instead, newspeople must pick one frame at any given time. As usual, in late 2012 they accepted the official Washington frame—shared by some economists and business chiefs—that the U.S. economy would suffer a terrible recession in 2013. It didn't. The media ignored analyses that the fiscal cliff would not happen or not be so bad. (In 1999, the media framed "Y2K" as a catastrophe that would crash all computers.) Mainstream media stories tend to have the same leads; almost all accept the prevailing frame and shy away from complicated or skeptical frames.

Politically, framing gives great power. Whoever frames a problem guides public discourse. The Bush administration framed the Iraq War in terms of weapons of mass destruction and terrorism and won the media's initial support. Later, when the media learned they had been misled, they reframed the Iraq story as

one of civil war and chaos. The White House hated that. The Iraq War was a high-stakes framing contest between the White House and the media.

Elites have the upper hand in framing news stories. Media are the sheep; political elites are the border collies. The White House blames the media, but usually the media at first accept the frames provided by the White House and other elites. They must; they have no other sources. When huge U.S. financial firms threatened to collapse in 2008, newspeople had to interview financiers, who favored a bailout plan. Later, some newspeople developed different and critical frames from academic and think-tank economists, but for months, the media did not question the White House frame that we were on the verge of another Great Crash. Most news stories led with "Economic collapse threatens if we don't accept the Paulson plan, and fast!" No lede suggested that the Paulson plan might not work or that there were better alternatives.

What can you do to protect yourself from sometimes misleading frames? First, use multiple news sources; blogs may be among the first to question the standard frame. Second, be aware that several sides are trying to frame stories for their own political or financial ends to guide policy, win elections, or promote the flow of money. Third, note the sources used in news stories: Do they have a stake in the issue? If so, expect a self-serving frame. Finally, treat all news stories with skepticism and patience; be prepared to wait a week or two to gain a balanced perspective. Panic works against sound judgment.

TELEVISION OWNERSHIP AND CONTROL   The U.S. government exercises the least control of communications of any industrialized country. Since the invention of the telegraph, Washington has stood back and let private industry operate communications for profit. In Europe, in contrast, telegraphy was soon taken over by the postal service, as were telephones. The U.S. government—partly because of First Amendment guarantees of free speech and partly because of the U.S. ethos of free enterprise—simply does not like to butt in. For European nations, with traditions of centralized power and government paternalism, national control of electronic communications is as normal as state ownership of the railroads. Now European TV is partly state-run and partly private, and both of them face continual charges of politically partisan coverage.

The U.S. attitude of **nonpaternalism** has led to the freest airwaves in the world, but it has also brought some problems. With the rapid growth of radio in the 1920s, the **electromagnetic spectrum** was soon jammed with stations trying to drown each other out. To bring some order, the Radio Act of 1927 designated the airwaves public property that should serve "the public interest, convenience and necessity." The Federal Communications Commission (FCC), which licenses broadcasters, does not supervise the content of programs. "Equal time" requirements once tried to ensure fairness, but they have been dropped.

nonpaternalism
Not taking a supervisory or guiding role.

electromagnetic spectrum
The airwaves over which signals are broadcast.

Are We Poorly Served?

8.4   Define and explain "structural bias" in the mass media.

The U.S. mass media do not serve Americans very well. First, news coverage is highly selective, overconcentrating on some areas while ignoring others. This is called "structural bias." The presidency, which occupies more than half the news time given to the federal government, is inherently more dramatic and eyecatching than the other branches. Editors and producers are afraid that full coverage of Congress and the courts will bore readers and viewers. The president gets in and out of helicopters, greets foreign leaders, travels overseas, and gets involved in scandals; all provide good television footage. Congress may get some attention when its committees face tense, controversial, or hostile witnesses. Then the committee members hurl accusatory questions, the witness stammers back denials, and sometimes shouting erupts. That's good drama; the rest of Congress is pretty dull. And the courts face the biggest obstacle of all: No cameras are allowed in most courtrooms. Accordingly, Americans grow up with the notion that the White House does most of the work and has most of the power, whereas Congress and the courts matter far less.

Especially undercovered are the civil service and state governments. Myriad departments, agencies, and bureaus govern any country, but bureaucrats give boring interviews, and regulations are unintelligible. Still, many of next year's news stories lurk in the federal bureaucracy. What agency using what criteria allowed a nuclear power plant to operate? The media pay no attention until a Three Mile Island occurs. What department gave millions in contracts to presidential-campaign contributors? The wrongdoings of the financial industry went on for years unnoticed by regulators and the media. What federal agencies warn of hurricanes, and who listens? (Post-Katrina, more listen.) The news media usually wait until something goes wrong and then evince shocked surprise. The very stuff of politics is in the federal agencies, but few pay attention.

Coverage of state governments may be even worse. Much of the problem here is that there are national media—the big networks and elite newspapers—and there are local media—your town's stations and paper. But there are no state media, partly because states are not "market areas" (population centers) that advertisers try to reach. Accordingly, outside of state capitals, there is little news about state politics, even important items. To some degree, digital media coverage of state politics has filled that gap, but only for those that seek it out.

On the world scene, the news media wait for something to blow up before they cover it. Except for the elite media, there is little background coverage of likely trouble spots. Thus, when terror hits the United States or a distant land erupts in violence, most Americans are surprised. They shouldn't be; even moderate news coverage of these problems over the years would have kept Americans informed about the increasing problems. But the U.S. media send few reporters overseas. Latin America, with all its implications for the United States, is largely uncovered. We live in a tumultuous world, but the U.S. media pay little attention until the shooting starts. Providers of "good visuals" rather than analysis and early warning is the way they define their role, and this sets up Americans to become startled and confused.

The biggest problem with the U.S. media is that they do not give a coherent, comprehensive picture of what is happening in the world. Operating under tight deadlines, flashing the best action footage, and basing reports heavily on official sources, the media bombard us with many little stories but seldom weave them together into a big story. They give us only pieces of a jigsaw puzzle. Part of this problem is the nature of any news medium that comes out daily: Newspapers and television take events one day at a time. Such news is usually incomplete and often misleading. We see people shooting, but we do not know why. The media world is, in Shakespeare's phrase, "full of sound and fury, signifying nothing."

What Can Be Done?

The mass media—except for the elite media—do not provide *meaning*. Few reporters are equipped to explain historical background or long-term consequences. Reporters are expected to be generalists, to be able to cover anything. All you have to do is write down what the official source says. It is for this reason that editorials and columns of opinion often contain more "news" than the straight news stories, for the former set the news into a meaningful

Case Studies

The Media and Watergate

In 1972, a news story triggered the fall of the Nixon administration and, for at least portions of the media, a new self-image as guardians of public morality. Persons connected to the White House were caught burglarizing and planting telephone "bugs" in the Democratic campaign headquarters in the Watergate office and apartment complex. Dogged investigation by two young *Washington Post* reporters, who later wrote the book *All the President's Men,* revealed a massive cover-up led by the Oval Office. The more Nixon promised to come clean, the guiltier he looked. Nixon was never impeached. A House special committee voted to recommend impeachment; then Nixon resigned in 1974. The House certainly would have voted impeachment, and the Senate probably would have convicted.

Would the same have happened without media coverage? Ultimately, the legal moves came through the courts and Congress, but the media made sure these branches of government would not ignore or delay their duties. Did the media bring Nixon down? The Nixon people thought so, but they always loathed the press. Others have argued that the same would have happened without the investigative reporting but more slowly and with less drama. The point is that media and government are intertwined and part of the same process.

Since Watergate, some branches of the media, namely the elite press and the national television networks, have adopted generally adversarial stances toward the executive branch. Criticism of later presidencies of both parties was immoderate and sometimes unreasonable. Typically, all presidents now claim the press is out to get them. Presidential policies are almost automatically doubted and criticized. The media see scandal everywhere in Washington and then descend in a "feeding frenzy" that leaves no reputation untarnished.

context, while the latter just give scattered bits and pieces. Unfortunately, most Americans make do with the bits and pieces as they make decisions on candidates, economic matters, and sending troops abroad.

Can anything be done? Professional newspeople generally agree that the public is ill-informed and that their coverage could be wider and deeper. But the limiting factor, they emphasize, is the public itself. A handful of business journalists warned of trouble in the financial system, but most people—even bankers and investors—were totally surprised at the 2008 meltdown. How do you get people to pay attention? Afghanistan, which cost more than $1 trillion and 2,000 American lives, went essentially unmentioned in the 2012 election, but the love life of an American general in Kabul fascinated the public. Few want to be well-informed, especially about things distant or complicated. Audience surveys find that people care least about foreign news and most about local news. Newspapers can go broke pushing world news; sports and local human interest are what works. Most people are not intellectuals, and most dislike complicated, in-depth analyses. They notice the shooting but do not care about the reasons behind it.

Do the media have any responsibility in educating the mass public so that citizens can comprehend our complicated world? Some idealists in the media do feel a responsibility, but these idealists are offset by hardheaded business types, who have the last word. After a while, the idealists become cynical. We cannot expect any major improvements any time soon. For you, however, the student of political science who is already among the more attentive, the answer is the elite media. Use the mass media for sports coverage.

The Adversaries: Media and Government

8.5 **Show how adversarial media are necessary for democracy.**

The role of the press as critic in a democracy has long been recognized. Thomas Jefferson wrote in 1787: "Were it left to me to decide [between government without] newspapers and newspapers without government, I should not hesitate a moment to prefer the latter." In Russia and Mexico, journalists who investigate crime, corruption, and abuse of power are routinely killed, and few suspects are caught. Many news organizations there now practice "self-censorship" to stay open and alive.

adversarial
Inclined to criticize and oppose, to treat with enmity.

Over the centuries, the press has criticized government. In the late 1960s and early 1970s, however, a new **adversarial** relationship between media and government emerged that is still with us. To be sure, not all the media entered into the fray; most newspapers with their wire-service stories continued to quote official sources. But the elite media and television often adopted hostile stances toward the executive branch.

The causes are not hard to see: Vietnam and Watergate. In both episodes, the executive branch lied to the media to soothe public opinion. Many media people resented being used and struck back with sharp questioning in press conferences and investigative reporting. Nixon's presidency made things worse; he had long feared and hated the press. On losing the governor's race in California in 1962, he slouched off muttering that the press "won't have Nixon to kick around anymore." Before presidential press conferences, Nixon used to calm his nerves by relaxing in a darkened room. He liked to operate in secrecy and then spring his decisions on the public in direct telecasts without any newspeople getting in the way. In turn, the press resented him all the more.

In Saigon, the U.S. military held afternoon press briefings, dubbed the "five o'clock follies," in which upbeat spokesmen portrayed progress in the war. Journalists soon tired of the repetitive, misleading briefings and snooped around for themselves. They found a corrupt, inept Saigon regime that was not winning the hearts and minds of its people, a Vietcong able to roam and strike at will, and tactics and morale inadequate to stop them. One young *New York Times* reporter was so critical of the Diem regime that his stories undermined American confidence in Diem and paved the way for Diem's 1963 ouster and murder by his own generals. Such is the influence of the elite media.

Vietnam is described as the first television war: bloody bodies of young GIs in full color. We should be careful of the widely accepted charge that television coverage turned Americans against the Vietnam War. The Korean War (1950–1953) had essentially no television coverage, but U.S. public opinion turned against it precisely the same way: As U.S. casualties mounted, support dropped. It was combat deaths, not television coverage, that changed Americans' minds. Vietnam also brought the *Pentagon Papers* in *The New York Times* and *The Washington Post* (see box). The Nixon administration was outraged—although the *Papers* made the Johnson officials the chief culprits—and ordered their publication halted, the first time the U.S. government ever censored newspapers. The Supreme Court immediately threw out the government's case. By this time, there was open warfare between government and the media.

Does the press go too far? Some people are fed up at the high-handedness with which the media impugn all authority. The media seem to think they are always right, the government always wrong. Republicans charge that the media are strongly liberal. Radicals, on the other hand, charge that the media defer to the president and big corporations. There is some truth to both charges, but one should note that eventually most institutions come under media scrutiny. The press washed President Clinton's dirty laundry in prime time. It is as if the media are "out to get" all politicians. Facilitated by the Internet, some now practice "accountability journalism" that is willing to uncover everything—including classified material on torture and drone strikes—in order to let the public judge. Classified documents leaked by Edward Snowden and posted by organizations like WikiLeaks provide the media avenues to practice this form of journalism, but some say at a cost to national security.

Studies show that news reporters and writers indeed tend to be liberals and Democrats, and this sometimes shows up in their coverage. Owners of stations and newspapers, though, tend to be conservative and Republican, and they curb the liberal impulses of their employees. Radio talk shows tend to the angry right, documentary films and blogs to the radically liberal. Charges of media bias are hard to prove because you can usually show that the media mistreat all politicians, Republican and Democrat. The White House tries to keep a tight rein on information, which the media resent.

What is the proper role of the media in a democracy? That they can and should criticize is clear; this keeps government on its toes. But how much should they criticize? Should they presume wrongdoing and cover-up everywhere? Should many reporters model themselves after Woodward and Bernstein of Watergate fame and try to ferret out scandals at every level of government? The press is largely protected from charges of libel, for under the Supreme Court's **Sullivan** rule, "public" persons are presumed to be open to media scrutiny. This has left some public figures feeling helpless and bitter at the hands of an all-powerful press and has increased cynical attitudes about politics in general. Public opinion has grown critical of the too-critical media. Perhaps the United States can find some happy middle ground.

Sullivan
Short for *New York Times v. Sullivan*, 1964 Supreme Court decision protecting media against public officials' libel suits.

Review Questions

1. How do mass media and face-to-face communication have different impacts?

2. What journals constitute the elite media?

3. How has the Internet changed political communication?

4. What are the weaknesses of television news coverage?

5. Can money buy television time and hence buy elections?

6. Has television created political apathy?

7. Which country has the freest mass media?

8. Are the media to blame for declining support for the Afghanistan War?

9. How can you stay well informed?

10. Is it good that media and government are adversaries?

Key Terms

adversarial, p. 164
bandwagon, p. 158
blog, p. 149
cross-pressured, p. 159
electromagnetic spectrum, p. 161
elite media, p. 153
face-to-face, p. 150

framing, p. 160
incumbent, p. 157
introspective, p. 151
media event, p. 157
nonpaternalism, p. 161
oligopoly, p. 153

opinion leaders, p. 150
source, p. 152
status quo, p. 151
stump, p. 150
Sullivan, p. 165
wire service, p. 152

Further Reference

Bennett, W. Lance, Regina G. Lawrence, and Steven Livingston. *When the Press Fails: Political Power and the News Media from Iraq to Katrina.* Chicago: University of Chicago Press, 2008.

Boehlert, Eric. *Bloggers on the Bus: How the Internet Changes Politics and the Press.* New York: Simon & Schuster, 2010.

Buell, Emmett H. Jr., and Lee Sigelman. *Attack Politics: Negativity in Presidential Campaigns since 1960.* Lawrence, KS: University Press of Kansas, 2008.

Cohen, Jeffrey E. *The Presidency in the Era of 24-Hour News.* Princeton, NJ: Princeton University Press, 2008.

Gant, Scott. *We're All Journalists Now: The Transformation of the Press and Reshaping of the Law in the Internet Age.* New York: Simon & Schuster, 2007.

Ghonim, Wael. *Revolution 2.0: The Power of the People Is Greater Than the People in Power: A Memoir.* New York: Houghton Mifflin Harcourt, 2012.

Goodwin, Doris Kearns. *The Bully Pulpit: Theodore Roosevelt, William Howard Taft, and the Golden Age of Journalism.* New York: Simon & Schuster, 2013.

Graber, Doris A. *On Media: Making Sense of Politics.* Boulder, CO: Paradigm, 2012.

Hall, Kermit L., and Melvin Urofsky. *New York Times v. Sullivan: Civil Rights, Libel Law, and the Free Press.* Lawrence, KS: University of Kansas Press, 2011.

Jones, Alex S. *Losing the News: The Future of the News that Feeds Democracy.* New York: Oxford University Press, 2009.

Kumar, Martha Joynt. *Managing the President's Message: The White House Communications Operation.* Baltimore, MD: Johns Hopkins University Press, 2009.

Levy, David A. L., and Rasmus Kleis Nielsen. *The Changing Business of Journalism and Its Implications for Democracy.* New York: Peter Lang, 2010.

Mindich, David T. Z. *Tuned Out: Why Americans Under 40 Don't Follow the News.* New York: Oxford University Press, 2004.

Morozov, Evgeny. *The Net Delusion: The Dark Side of Internet Freedom.* New York: PublicAffairs, 2011.

Perlmutter, David D. *Blogwars.* New York: Oxford University Press, 2008.

Prior, Markus. *Post-Broadcast Democracy: How Media Choice Increases Inequality in Political Involvement and Polarizes Elections.* New York: Cambridge, 2007.

Wasik, Bill. *And Then There's This: How Stories Live and Die in Viral Culture.* New York: Penguin, 2010.

West, Darrell M. *Air Wars: Television Advertising in Election Campaigns, 1952–2008,* 6th ed. Washington, DC: CQ Press, 2013.

Wu, Tim. *The Master Switch: The Rise and Fall of Information Empires.* New York: Knopf, 2011.

Chapter 9
Interest Groups

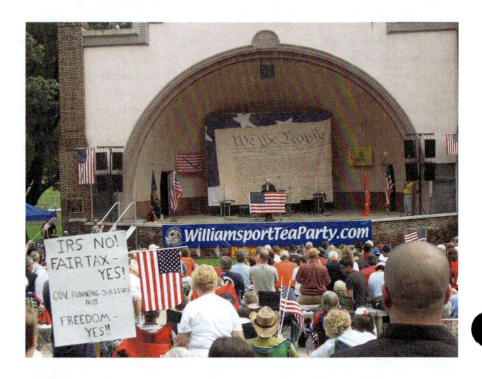

Learning Objectives

9.1 Define interest groups and distinguish them from parties.

9.2 Explain the relationship between interest groups and democracy.

9.3 List, with examples, the factors that make interest groups effective.

9.4 Explain the several strategies interest groups use.

9.5 Explain and give examples of how interest groups may become too strong.

A series of U.S. Supreme Court decisions boosted interest groups to new—some said dangerous—heights. Dubbed "super-PACs," the new groups allowed super rich anonymous donors to pour unlimited funds into political campaigns. Billionaires contributed millions to candidates and groups that supported their financial and ideological interests through these super-PACs. Campaign contributions and spending soared, but the overall net effect on election outcomes was unclear.

Republicans celebrated the decisions—made by the Court's Republican majority—figuring they would gain a spending advantage, but the first victims of the decision were the 2012 Republican presidential hopefuls, whose super-PAC-funded primary contests denounced and caricatured each other, tarnishing the overall image of the party. Ironically, conservative intellectuals had originated the phrase "unforeseen consequences." On election day, the super-PACs' massive spending seem to have little impact, partly because Democrats also raise prodigious sums, and oversaturated voters may ignore the shrill exaggerations and accusations.

The Ubiquity of Interest Groups

9.1   **Define interest groups and distinguish them from parties.**

The super-PACs are just the latest iteration of well-funded interest groups influencing politics. Critics complain about the political dominance of the very wealthy, but in a democracy, there is nothing to stop it. To curb such influence would require limiting group inputs—including their freedom of speech—to the political process. Who would decide which groups should have how much influence? Anyone making that decision could seriously skew democracy.

The theory behind interest groups argues that, on your own, even in the finest democracy, you can do little. The solution: Form a group of like-minded individuals. After hard work organizing, fund-raising, and lobbying, you can start having an impact. In this view—a *pluralist* view—the crux of politics is groups. It is a somewhat naive view, as it pays no attention to the very unequal resources of various groups. U.S. lobbying now runs at some $9 billion a year. Rich individuals and corporations have major influence, average citizens little or none. Interest-group activity is especially strong in the pluralistic United States but is found everywhere, even in dictatorships, where groups quietly try to win the favor of the dictator.

The term *interest group* covers just about any collection of people trying to influence government. Some interest groups are transient, others permanent. Some focus on influencing a particular policy, others on broad changes. Some work through the executive or administrative agencies, others through the judicial or legislative sectors, and still others through public opinion. But all are non–publicly accountable organizations that attempt to promote shared private interests by influencing public-policy outcomes.

Interest Groups and Political Parties

Interest groups are a bit like political parties. Both try to influence public policy, but interest groups do it outside the electoral process and are not responsible to the public. A party must win elections. Interest groups may influence the nomination of candidates who are sympathetic to their cause, but the candidates run under the party banner—not the interest group banner.

GOALS   Parties seek power though elections. Interest groups usually focus on specific programs and issues and are rarely represented in the formal structure of government. Instead, they try to influence legislators and executives. They often seek the favor of all political parties. Economic groups want the support of both Republicans and Democrats. Some interest groups favor one party. The National Rifle Association, for example, strongly tilts to Republican candidates.

NATURE OF MEMBERSHIPS   Political parties seek broad support to win elections and draw many interests into their ranks. Even the Republican Party includes people in all income brackets. The Democratic Party, billing itself as the party of the common person, has many wealthy supporters, including those from big finance. Interest groups have a narrower membership. Labor unionists share similar living and working conditions and goals. Idealistic interest groups draw those aiming at religious, environmental, or gender goals. Some groups link disparate groups, as when Roman Catholics and fundamentalist Protestants unite to oppose abortion.

For several reasons, including the length of a ballot, there are rarely more than a dozen or so political parties. But there is no limit on interest groups, and some countries, such as the United States, foster their growth. As Tocqueville observed in the 1830s, "In no country of the world has the principle of association been more successfully used or applied to a greater multitude of objects than in America." Tocqueville is still accurate. Open a Washington, D.C. phone book to "National…" and count the hundreds of national associations, federations, and committees. Washington's prosperity is based on its attraction as a headquarters for more than 20,000 interest groups.

Who Belongs to Interest Groups?

Every advanced society is pluralistic, with many industrial, cultural, economic, educational, ethnic, and religious groups. Divergent interests lead almost automatically to group formation. In a pluralist democracy, a multiplicity of interest groups push their own claims and viewpoints, creating a balance of opposing interests that, in theory, prevents any one group from dominating the political system. In this optimistic view, government policy is the outcome of competition among many groups, which represent the varied interests of the people.

Interest groups, however, over-represent the better-off and businesses. Because some groups are rich and well-connected, the democratic playing field is not level. Critics argue that if group theory really operated, the poor would

Theories

Countervailing Power

One of the theories of pluralists is that no interest group can monopolize power because there are always one or more groups working against it. The theory of countervailing power argues that business associations are offset by labor unions, the Jewish lobby by the Muslim lobby, industries fearful of imports by industries eager to export, and drug companies by retiree associations. Such balances keep us free and democratic, argue pluralists.

But do things always balance? As in most of the world, U.S. unions have declined in membership and are now much weaker than business associations.

Producers of electric power and gasoline form powerful lobbies that face no countervailing lobby of 320 million consumers. The battle over health-care reform was fought by giant insurers, hospital and physician organizations, employers, and drug companies, spending $1.4 million a *day* in lobbying. The 2010 bill contained no provision for public insurance options—only private—because the insurance industry blocked them. Consumers of health care, on the other hand, are essentially unrepresented. Only in a few areas does countervailing power actually exist.

organize groups to get a bigger piece of the economic pie. But the poor, who have less education, are slow in forming groups to promote their interests. Better-off and better-educated people are more likely to participate in politics, and this includes organizing and running interest groups and super-PACs.

With few organizations to represent their interests, the lower classes may act explosively rather than working within the political system. Their grievances can burst out, as in the storming of the Bastille to start the French Revolution. In recent U.S. history, inner-city riots reflected the anger of race-related issues among many African Americans. The ghetto riots, while publicizing grievances, did little to challenge the power of business, labor unions, or other groups that keep things as they are. Not all sectors of society can effectively form and use interest groups.

Interest Groups and Government

9.2   **Explain the relationship between interest groups and democracy.**

Interest groups try to influence government. But what if there is little government, as in Afghanistan, where government writ does not extend much beyond the capital, Kabul? There are plenty of groups: tribes, clans, warlords, opium growers, and Taliban fighters, but we would not call their interactions "pluralistic." In Mexico, drug-related crime is a major economic activity and leads to armed interest groups called "cartels." Weak states are characterized by the interpenetration of crime and politics. Not all "interest group" activity is good or peaceful; it depends on the groups' willingness to operate within the law, which in turn requires strong states.

Once government is funding something, the groups that benefit develop constituencies with a strong interest in continuing the programs. As government has become bigger and sponsored more programs, interest groups have proliferated. By now, virtually every branch and subdivision of the U.S. government has one or more interest groups watching over its shoulder and demanding more grants, a change in regulations, or their own agency. The Departments of Education and Energy were created under these circumstances, and Ronald Reagan vowed to abolish them. He was unable to do so: The interests associated with them—in part created by them—were too powerful.

Sometimes interest groups participate in government legislation and implementation. In Britain, "interested members" of Parliament are those who openly acknowledge that they represent industries or labor unions. This is not frowned on and is considered quite normal. (Quietly selling government influence to British interest groups, however, is considered "sleaze" and has produced scandals.) In Sweden, interest groups are especially large and powerful. Swedish "royal commissions," which initiate most new legislation, are composed of legislators, government officials, and interest-group representatives. After a proposal has been drafted, it is circulated for comments to all relevant interest groups. Some Swedish benefits for farmers and workers are administered by their respective farm organizations and labor unions. Some call this **corporatism**, meaning interest groups taking on government functions. Top representatives of business, labor, and the cabinet meet regularly in Sweden to decide much public policy. Critics charge that this too-cozy relationship bypasses parliamentary democracy altogether.

corporatism
The direct participation of interest groups in government.

Government-Created Interest Groups

Government calls many interest groups into life, for they are associated with government programs. There are farm lobbies because there are farm programs, education lobbies because there are education programs, and veterans' lobbies because the government goes to war.

In 1938, as part of FDR's program to get out of the Depression, Congress created the Federal National Mortgage Association—soon known as "Fannie Mae"—to underwrite home loans and encourage home purchases and construction. In 1968, Congress made Fannie Mae private, turning it into a regular corporation that makes money by buying banks' mortgages, repackaging them, and selling them like bonds. To ensure competition in this important "secondary mortgage market," Congress in 1970 created the Federal Home Loan Mortgage Corporation ("Freddie Mac"), which is also private and does the same things as Fannie Mae.

Platoons of Fannie and Freddie lobbyists made sure Congress kept supporting the two mortgage giants. Critics described Fannie and Freddie as basically lobbying operations with mortgage side businesses. When the U.S. housing market turned sour in 2008, Congress quickly authorized unlimited taxpayer dollars to back up Fannie and Freddie, which were deemed "too big to fail." Many criticized the bail-out that let Fannie and Freddie keep profits private but passed risks on to taxpayers.

This circular flow is common: Congress creates a program, the program creates an interest group, and then the interest group works on Congress to keep supporting it. U.S. farm subsidies, originally to help struggling farmers during the Depression, now cost billions a year, much of it to "agri-business," and few try to curb them. Programs, once set up, are hard to terminate due to interest-group influence.

Bureaucrats as an Interest Group

Government and interest groups are related in another important but sometimes overlooked way: Bureaucracies have become big and powerful interest groups. Civil servants are not merely passive implementers of laws; they also have input in the making and application of those laws. Much legislation originates in specialized agencies. Many of the data and witnesses before legislative committees are from the executive departments and agencies. In Japan, the powerful bureaucrats of the finance and trade **(METI)** ministries routinely tell the **Diet** what to legislate.

METI
Japan's Ministry of Economy, Trade, and Industry; formerly MITI, Ministry of International Trade and Industry.

Bureaucracies develop interests of their own. They see their tasks as terribly important and demand bigger budgets and more employees every year. When was the last time a civil servant recommended abolishing his or her agency or bureau? It was earlier proposed that interest groups are offshoots of society and

Diet
Japan's national legislature.

Case Studies

French Antipluralism

The United States and Britain are highly pluralistic, for interest group activity is acceptable and desirable, and lobbying is normal for a healthy democracy. In France, on the other hand, interest-group activity exists but is frowned on and considered dirty. France is heir to centuries of centralized and paternalistic government. The French are used to Paris ministries setting national goals and supervising much of the economy.

Philosopher Jean-Jacques Rousseau still has a hold on the French mind. He argued that there must be no "particular wills" to muddy and distort the "general will," that which the whole community wants. Rousseau presumed there was such a thing as a general will, something pluralists deny. Accordingly, interest groups are seen as trying to pervert the good of the whole community. French bureaucratic elites pay little attention to interest groups, considering them "unobjective." French interest groups operate in a more constrained atmosphere than their American or British counterparts.

By comparison, American's pluralistic heritage traces back to the *Federalist Papers*, where James Madison argued that a large diverse republic with many interests (which he called factions) was the best way to limit the power of the majority to use the government to tyrannize political minorities.

the economy, but they are also offshoots of government. Government and interest groups were born twins. The more government, the more interest groups.

To say that every political system has interest groups says little, for interest groups in different systems operate quite differently. One key determinant in the way interest groups operate is the government. Pluralism is determined not by the mere existence of groups, each trying to influence government, but by the degree to which government permits or encourages the open interplay of groups. Pluralism has a normative component, an "ought" or a "should."

Effective Interest Groups

9.3   **List, with examples, the factors that make interest groups effective.**

Political Culture

Interest groups flourish in pluralistic societies that have traditions of local self-governance and of forming associations. Where this is weak (see box on France), interest groups have tough going. Americans, Britons, and Swedes are more likely to participate in voluntary associations than French, Italians, and Mexicans. The more-educated and males (but that is changing) are more likely to belong to an interest group. Not all groups are political, but even nonpolitical groups, by discussion among members, have some political influence. Members of a bicycle club become involved in politics when they support rails-to-trails bicycle paths. In societies where many join groups, people have a greater sense of political competence and **efficacy**. Some worry that the U.S. tendency to form groups has declined.

efficacy
The feeling that what one does can make a difference.

The Rise of Big Money

Money is probably the single most important factor in interest group success. With enough money, interests hardly need a group. Money is especially important for elections, and groups help candidates who favor their causes. Most democracies have recognized the danger in too close a connection between interests and candidates, the danger that we will have the "best politicians money can buy." In 2010, the U.S. Supreme Court lifted limits on giving to super-PACs, and some fear that this will lead to influence buying and *corruption*. U.S. oil and agricultural interests give generously and get federal subsidies. The healthcare and financial industries are the biggest campaign contributors—to both parties—and receive ample consideration. Said California political boss Jesse Unruh: "Money is the mother's milk of politics."

Many countries have tried reforms. Japanese reformers tried to break "money politics," the extreme dependence of politicians on interest groups—business conglomerates, banks, farmers, even gangsters—but have not yet succeeded. Germany and Sweden provide for almost complete **public financing** of the major parties in national elections. Spain, which rejoined the democracies only in 1977, subsidizes parties after the election according to how many votes they received and parliamentary seats they won. Some countries—Britain, France, and Germany, among others—try to limit campaign spending.

The United States has been reluctant to go to public financing of campaigns or campaign spending limits for several reasons. First, there is the strong emphasis on freedom. The U.S. Supreme Court has interpreted the First Amendment to include dollars as a form of free speech. When a person gives money to a candidate or a candidate spends it, those are political statements that must not be curbed. Second, U.S. campaigns are much longer and more expensive than in other democracies, the result of our weak, decentralized parties and nominating system. In Western Europe, elections can be short and cheap because the parties are already in place with their candidates and platforms. And third, given these two previous conditions, American legislators have not been able to find a formula for public financing that really works in the manner intended. Some efforts turn out to have negative **unforeseen consequences**.

Some individuals and **political action committees (PACs)** contribute to parties and interest groups not directly working for a candidate's election campaign. This **soft money** funds groups that produce "issue ads" aimed *against* the other side without mentioning their own candidate's name. Soft money thus contributes to the trend toward negative advertising in political campaigns. In 2004, for example, a special "Swift-boat committee" that was clearly Republican ran TV ads accusing John Kerry of exaggerating his war heroism. In 2012, billionaires, most of whose income was taxed at a low 15 percent, contributed millions, mostly to Republicans, to keep the tax law that way. (This rate went up to 20 percent, still low.)

In 2002, after a hard struggle, the McCain-Feingold Campaign Reform Act passed, and the Supreme Court ruled it constitutional. Many cheered, but by 2004 it was irrelevant, skirted in three ways. First, limits are not very limiting; individuals may give up to $2,600 directly to a presidential candidate, $31,000 to a national party, and much more to state and local parties and candidates. Second, many presidential hopefuls, including Barack Obama, simply walked away from public campaign financing, which imposed spending ceilings, in favor of funds they raised on their own (now often gathered online), which have no limit. Third, well-funded groups with no formal ties to candidates—called super-PACs under innocuous names such as "Committee to Save America"—spent prodigiously on "issues" that denounced opposing candidates.

It is now apparent that parties and candidates will work around whatever reforms or laws attempt to curb big money in politics. In 1907, Teddy Roosevelt, reacting to the big-money politics of his predecessor McKinley, supported the first reform, the Tillman Act, prohibiting corporations from giving funds. It looked good but was ineffective and has now in effect been ruled unconstitutional. If the Supreme Court's decisions stand intact, any statutory limits on campaign contributions will now likely be ruled as restrictions on free speech.

public financing
Using tax dollars to fund something, such as election-campaign expenses.

unforeseen consequence
Bad or counter-productive result when laws or policies do not work as expected

political action committee (PAC)
U.S. interest group set up specifically to contribute money to election campaigns.

soft money
Campaign contributions to parties and issue groups so as to skirt federal limits on contributions to candidates.

Critics fear that money politics is out of control. Defenders say this is just the workings of pluralist democracy and the amounts are peanuts compared with the overall U.S. economy. Can or should anything be done about interest groups and money? Some suggest we go to a European-type system in which parties are better organized and campaigns are short and relatively cheap. But that is simply not the U.S. nominating and electoral system, which is complex and long. And Europe's interest groups still give plenty (sometimes under the table) to their favored candidates.

Public financing of all candidates—presidential nominees who gain at least 5 percent of the national vote are already entitled to federal financing—would be terribly expensive. Many U.S. taxpayers do not check off the option on their tax returns to contribute a few dollars to presidential campaigns, even though it costs them nothing. For the foreseeable future, it will not be possible to break the tie between big money and candidates in the United States.

Another alternative is to make it easier to know who is donating what to whom. Currently, campaigns must report where their donations come from, but the reports are not easily available in time for a candidate's opponent or the media to share with the public. If reporting requirements were changed so that records for donations were made available online to the public immediately, then watchdogs could spread the word if a candidate received large donations from politically questionable sources. You are who your friends are. If you don't want to be associated with a rich interest group's ideas, don't take their money. Similar reporting *transparency* could be created for super-PACs.

The Rise of Single-Issue Groups

single-issue group
Interest association devoted to one cause only.

AFL-CIO
American Federation of Labor-Congress of Industrial Organizations, the largest U.S. union federation.

NAM
National Association of Manufacturers, a major federation of U.S. industrial executives.

Perhaps the second greatest factor in the influence of interest groups (after money) is the intensity of the issue involved. The right issue can mobilize millions, give the group cohesion and commitment, and boost donations. Or, as with the super-PACS in 2012, it can persuade one wealthy individual to donate $100 million. There have always been American interest groups pursuing one or another idealistic objective, but since the 1970s the rise of **single-issue groups** has changed U.S. politics. Typically, interest groups have several things to say about issues, for their interests encompass several programs and departments. Organized labor tries to persuade government on questions of Social Security, medical insurance, education, imports and tariffs, and the way unemployment statistics are calculated. The **AFL-CIO** has a long-term, across-the-board interest in Washington. The same can be said for many business groups, such as the **NAM**.

But to the single-issue groups, only one issue matters, and it matters intensely. Typically, their issues are moral—and therefore hard to compromise—rather than material. The most prominent of them is the right to life, or anti-abortion, movement. In 1973, the Supreme Court ruled that states could not arbitrarily restrict a woman's right to an abortion. Many Roman Catholics

Case Studies

How Powerful Are U.S. Unions?

Labor unions in the United States are not very powerful, especially in comparative perspective. Since the 1950s, the percentage of American workers in labor unions has dropped by more than two-thirds. The percentages of unionized workforces are shown in the right column, and most of them are in the public rather than the private sector. U.S. schoolteachers, police, firefighters, and civil servants—many of them prohibited from striking—are more unionized than factory workers. U.S. unions seem powerful because they attract much attention when they strike at major firms, but business has far more clout than unions.

Sweden	78%
Britain	28
Germany	20
Japan	19
United States	12
France	8

and Protestant fundamentalists were shocked, for they believe that human life begins at the moment of conception and that aborting a fetus is murder. "Pro-life" people would like to amend the Constitution to outlaw abortion. Opposing them are "pro-choice" forces, many linked to the women's movement. Feminists and others argue that abortion is a matter for the individual woman to decide and no one else; the right to choose gives women control over their lives and is part of their liberation from second-class status.

The antiabortionists make life miserable for many legislators. They care about nothing else—where officials stand on taxes, jobs, defense, and so on. They want to know where they stand on abortion, and a compromise middle ground—the refuge of many politicians faced with controversial issues—is not good enough. Some elections turn on the abortion issue. Meanwhile, the pro-choice forces organize and grow militant to offset the pro-life forces. The 2005 Terri Schiavo case—whether to pull the plug on a comatose woman—also rallied pro-lifers.

Other single-issue causes appear, such as prayer in public school and same-sex marriage. Taken together, these two and the abortion question are sometimes referred to as the "morality issue." Gun control grew into a major issue, fanned by the assassinations of John and Robert Kennedy and Martin Luther King Jr. The powerful National Rifle Association (NRA) opposes such groups as Handgun Control. None of these issues makes elected representatives any happier. They like to be judged on a wide range of positions they have taken, not on one narrow issue on which it is hard to compromise.

Size and Membership

Their size and the intensity of their members give groups clout. The biggest and fastest-growing U.S. interest group is AARP (formerly the American Association of Retired Persons), with some thirty-seven million members (one American in eight), many of them educated, forceful, and strongly committed to preserving and enhancing Social Security and Medicare. Both parties proclaim that they want to safeguard the two vast programs. When AARP speaks, Congress trembles.

Size alone, however, is not necessarily the most important element in interest-group strength. Money and intensity often offset size. The well-funded American-Israel Public Affairs Committee (AIPAC), supported not only by Jews but by many evangelical Christians, keeps Congress pro-Israel. The NRA fights gun-control laws, mostly successfully. These three—AARP, AIPAC, and the NRA—are reckoned as Washington's most influential lobbies. All things being equal, a large group has more clout than a small one—but things are never equal.

socioeconomic status

Combination of income and prestige criteria in the ranking of groups.

The **socioeconomic status** of members gives groups clout. Better-off, well-educated people with influence in their professions and communities can form groups that get more respect. The socioeconomic status of doctors, organized as the American Medical Association (AMA), helps them prevail in Washington. As Japanese Americans climbed educationally and professionally, their Japanese American Citizens' League (JACL) started having an impact and won apologies for the unconstitutional internment in World War II; JACL then worked

Methods

Tables

The table shows a list of the things you are studying—counties, countries, years, voters, legislators, interest groups—with numerical measures attached to each. Later, you may use some of these as *variables*. Measures are whatever is relevant to the case you wish to make—dollars, population, or how many listings in a phone book. You list these things in some order—the biggest, most, or latest. Alphabetical order is often useless. In this chapter, we might list which PACs gave the most money, with the biggest givers first.

To take another example, the relative wealth of countries can be measured in several ways. The most basic is gross domestic product (GDP), the first column, here corrected for cost of living (purchasing-power parity, PPP). Dividing that by population (the second column) gives per capita GDP (GDPpc) at PPP, the third column, the best comparison of relative wealth. Figures are 2014 estimates. Note how the table goes from richest to poorest.

Country	GDP ($ Billion)	Population (Million)	Per Capita GDP at PPP
United States	$17,420	314	$54,600
France	2,581	63	40,400
Russia	3,565	142	24,800
Mexico	2,141	115	17,900
Colombia	640	45	13,400
China	17,620	1,343	12,900
Indonesia	2,676	255	10,600
India	7,376	1,250	5,900

SOURCE: *CIA World Factbook*

on getting compensation. The National Association for the Advancement of Colored People (NAACP), on the other hand, speaks for millions but has relatively little influence. Disadvantaged groups with the biggest grievances are among the least likely to be listened to.

Access

Money, issue, and size may not count for much unless people in government are willing to listen. The careful cultivation of members of Congress and civil servants over the years makes sure doors are open. When a group has established a stable and receptive relationship with a branch of government, it is said to enjoy, in the words of Yale's Joseph LaPalombara, **structured access**. Greek American members of Congress are, quite naturally, receptive to Greek arguments on questions concerning Turkey, Cyprus, and Greece's debt. Michigan legislators likewise heed the complaints of the automobile industry. Arab Americans complain bitterly that Jews enjoy too much access on Capitol Hill and organize their own groups to gain access. There is nothing wrong with access as such; it is part and parcel of a working democracy.

structured access
Long-term friendly connection of interest group to officials.

But what happens when groups are shut out and have no access? Pluralists think this cannot happen in a democracy, but it does. African American and Native American militants argued that no one was listening to them or taking their demands seriously. Only violence in urban ghettos and on Indian reservations got Washington to listen. When the wealthy and powerful have a great deal of access, the poor and unorganized may have none. The consequences sometimes lead to violence.

Interest Group Strategies

9.4   **Explain the several strategies interest groups use.**

Approaching Lawmakers

Lobbying receives the most attention. The campaign contributions and favors to legislators given by corporations convince many that lobbyists buy Congress. Indeed, any major interest threatened by new laws spares no expense to make sure the laws are not passed, and they are usually successful. Senator John McCain (R-Ariz.), a critic of big money, said sadly, "Money buys access." He referred to a 2003 energy bill as "no lobbyist left behind." Big tobacco, which is especially generous to incumbent Republican candidates, routinely blocks or dilutes antismoking legislation. Favors big companies provide cooperative congresspersons include trips in the corporate jet and corporate boxes at sports events. The average lobbying group, however, has little money to give, so most see themselves as providers of information.

lobbying
Interest-group efforts to sway legislation.

Recently, many Washington influence peddlers, to avoid having to register as lobbyists, call themselves "strategic consultants." They do what lobbyists do, but they do not disclose their clients or their fees. By some estimates, there are as many of these unregistered consultants as there are regular lobbyists.

Approaching the Administration

Depending on the issue, the executive branch may be a better interest-group target. The interest group may not need or want a new law, merely favorable interpretation of existing rules and regulations. For this, it turns to administrators. Antipollution groups, for instance, seek tighter definitions of clean air; industry groups seek looser definitions. Interest groups concentrate on the department that specializes in their area. Farm groups deal with the Department of Agriculture, public service companies with the Federal Power Commission, and so forth. As a rule, each department pays heed to the demands and arguments of groups in its area. Indeed, many government bureaucracies are "captured" or "colonized" by the groups they deal with. The flow goes the other way, too. Some 200 former senators and congressmen along with many former top administration officials stay in Washington—with offices on famous K Street—as lobbyists billing clients $500 or more an hour.

Interest groups employ many of the same tactics on executive departments that they use on legislators, including personal contacts, research, and public relations. Some provide money; in most of the world, corruption of public officials is the norm. The U.S. federal bureaucracy is one of the least corrupt in the world—state and local are something else. Federal officials caught on the take are usually political appointees and not career civil servants. Interest groups really make their influence felt in nominations to top-level government posts, including cabinet secretaries, to get officials who serve their interests.

Approaching the Judiciary

Interest groups may also use the courts, especially in the United States, for the U.S. judicial system has far more power than most judiciaries, which are merely part of the executive branch. In countries where rule of law is strong, the courts become an arena of interest-group contention, as in Germany, where groups have taken cases on abortion and worker rights before the Federal Constitutional Court.

Every year, U.S. state and federal courts hear cases filed or supported by such interest groups as the American Civil Liberties Union and Sierra Club. In recent years, the U.S. Supreme Court has dealt with several social issues brought to it by interest groups, including women's rights, the death penalty, guns, and same-sex marriage. Interest groups use two judicial methods. First, they may initiate suits directly on behalf of a group or class of people whose interests they represent (such suits are commonly referred to as **class actions**). The second is for the interest group to file a "friend of the court" brief (**amicus curiae**) in support of a person whose cause they share.

Aware of the importance of the U.S. judicial system, especially of the Supreme Court, the National Association for the Advancement of Colored People (NAACP) focused much of its fight against racial segregation on the courts. It paid off. The legal staff of the NAACP, whose chief attorney was Thurgood Marshall (later a U.S. Supreme Court justice), successfully challenged the constitutionality of all state laws requiring racial segregation in public schools in the famous *Brown* decision of 1954. Then the NAACP challenged the legality of state laws on segregation in public transportation, restaurants, lodging, and other areas. The vast changes in U.S. civil rights happened first in the courts, not through legislation, because Congress would not tackle the issue—Southerners blocked it—until the mid-1960s. The Supreme Court led; Congress followed.

class action
Lawsuit on behalf of many persons acting together.

amicus curiae
Statement to a court by persons not party to a case.

Appeals to the Public

Organized interests often take their case to the public with peaceful—or not so peaceful—appeals. Even powerful interest groups realize the importance of their public image, and many invest in public relations campaigns to explain how they contribute to the general welfare and why their interests are good for the country. For example, railroads used television to explain their case for "fair" government policies so they could stay alive and compete with trucking. The gasoline lobby explained why environmental restrictions work against building new refineries.

Some interest groups maintain a low profile by promoting their objectives without advertising themselves. Such groups may plant news stories that promote their cause and quietly work against the publication of stories detrimental to them. The Tobacco Institute, for example, discreetly funds research that casts doubt on findings that smoking is bad for health. The American Petroleum Institute seeks no news coverage but has its officers quoted as unbiased experts above the political fray.

Demonstrations

Certain organizations, such as the American Cancer Society and the Heart Fund, may get free advertising space and time, but most interest groups do not, and many cannot afford to purchase such publicity. Such a disadvantaged group may hold demonstrations to publicize its cause. Mahatma Gandhi used this tactic to get the British to leave India. Gandhi learned about nonviolent protest from an influential essay on "civil disobedience" by American Henry David Thoreau, who protested the war with Mexico in 1846–1848. Thoreau's idea was also adopted by the Rev. Martin Luther King Jr. to push for African American civil rights in the 1950s and 1960s.

Classic Works

Olson's Theory of Interest Groups

American economist Mancur Olson (1932–1998) is best known for his 1965 *Logic of Collective Action*. He noted that small and well-organized groups, especially with money, often override the broader public interest. The reason: The former have much to gain from favorable but narrow laws and rulings, so they lobby intensely. The latter see nothing to gain, are not organized or intense, and lobby little. The public does not care if the price of shoelaces jumps up, but shoelace manufacturers do. The few trump the many.

Related to this is Olson's "free rider syndrome": Why buy a ticket when you can ride for free? People will not invest their time and money in a cause when they get the same results anyway. Why pay union dues when you are already under a union contract? Why should Europeans contribute much to NATO when the Americans provide them with free security?

Olson warned in his 1982 *The Rise and Decline of Nations* against what happens when interest groups

become too strong: They choke off change and growth, leading to national stagnation. Politicians, responding to one or more powerful interests, do not consider the wider public good. A prime example is Britain, which, with highly organized interests and politicians listening closely to those interests, went into economic decline until Margaret Thatcher blasted policy loose from both unions and owners.

Japan, its organized interests destroyed in World War II, was free for spectacular growth in the decades after the war. By the late twentieth century, however, Japan was so gunked up with industry and farming associations that its growth stagnated. Japan has an "iron triangle" of economic interest groups, politicians, and bureaucrats that defies reform. Some followers of Olson fear that such "sclerosis" is the fate of all countries. Has the United States fallen victim to overstrong interests, or has it been able to periodically shake loose from them?

Some critics of Wall Street, totally outclassed by the financial and political resources of investment banks, felt that direct protest was their only option. At first the news media paid little attention to Occupy Wall Street in 2011, but the social media brought them supporters, contributors, and eventually news coverage. A placard carried by one Occupier—"We are the 99 percent"—went viral and influenced political debate nationwide.

Violent Protest

A group that loses faith in conventional political channels may see violent protest as its only alternative. The United States is no stranger to violent protests, which require a psychological buildup nurtured by poverty, discrimination, frustration, and a sense of personal or social injustice. An incident may spark pent-up anger, and mob behavior can escalate. Shootings and arrests of African Americans still spark riots in U.S. cities. Defenders of the rioters claim they are simply *opposing* the violence they suffer daily at the hands of police, all levels of government, and an economy that keeps them underpaid or unemployed.

Does violent protest work? Perhaps it was no coincidence that the Great Society was passed during a period of U.S. urban riots. The British got out of India and Palestine when violence made the areas impossible to govern. The white government of South Africa started offering reforms only when blacks turned to guerrilla warfare. In certain circumstances, violence works. As African American radical H. "Rap" Brown put it, "Violence is as American as cherry pie." (He is now in prison for murder.)

Interest Groups: An Evaluation

9.5   **Explain and give examples of how interest groups may become too strong.**

Interest groups are at the core of every democracy, but how well do they serve the needs of citizens? Interest groups help represent a wider range of interests in the legislative process, a good thing. Many smaller organizations, however, have neither the members nor the money to have any input. Unless they are able to form coalitions, they cannot defend their interests from larger, more powerful groups. The mere fact that interest groups articulate demands does not mean the demands will be heeded. Resources are highly unequal among interest groups. Some are rich and powerful and have a lot of influence. Others are ignored.

There is a further problem: What about individuals who are not organized into groups? Who speaks for them? Many citizens are not members or beneficiaries of interest groups. They vote for elected leaders, but the leaders pay more attention to group demands than to ordinary voters. If legislators and executives are attuned to interest groups, who is considering the interests of the whole country? At times, it seems as if no one is. Then we may begin to appreciate Rousseau's emphasis on the "general will" over and above the "particular wills" that make up society.

For this reason, the "citizens' lobby" Common Cause was formed in 1970. Supported by donations, it won public funding of presidential campaigns, an end to the congressional seniority system, and disclosure of lobbying activities. In a similar vein, Ralph Nader set up several public-interest lobbies on law, nuclear energy, tax reform, and medical care. Although groups such as these have done much good work, they raise an interesting question: Can a society as big and complex as America's possibly be represented as a whole, or is it inherently a mosaic of groups with no common voice?

Another problem is whether interest groups really speak for all their members or for a small, militant minority. Most interest groups are dominated by a few leaders who have stronger views than the people they claim to speak for. Jewish organizations are stronger supporters of Israel than are most American Jews. The Roman Catholic hierarchy takes positions on contraception and abortion that many ordinary Catholics do not. AARP received pushback from its members when they learned that the organizations had lobbied for the Affordable Care Act (called "Obamacare" by its critics), which many members opposed. Do not confuse the statements of interest groups with the views of all they claim to represent.

Skewing Policy

Interest-group input may skew policy. The finance industry, for example, is a major interest group that contributes heavily to both parties and lobbies intensively. (Barack Obama got millions from Wall Street groups for his campaigns. McCain got less from them in 2008, but Romney got more in 2012.) Since Reagan, Congress has generally delivered whatever the finance industry specified, and regulations and safeguards were rolled back so much of U.S. finance was little supervised. It was supposed to be "self-policing." One result was the 2006 "**subprime** crisis" that turned into a world-shaking financial crisis in 2008. Lenders had pushed unqualified borrowers to take out home mortgages they could not afford. The dubious loans were packaged and sold off in pieces, like bonds. They were presumed to be safe, but then home foreclosures shot up, and billions of dollars were lost. Frantically, Washington pumped taxpayer money into banks and into Fannie Mae and Freddie Mac, as their collapse would bring a new Depression.

subprime
Risky mortgage made to unqualified borrower.

The subsequent bailout of major financial institutions created a **scandal**, but it was nothing new; indeed, there is about one every decade. In the 1980s, savings and loans got Congress to roll back restrictions so they could make foolish and sometimes crooked loans. Then the whole thing collapsed, and the federal government had to step in. In 2001, the mighty Enron, which manipulated electricity prices, collapsed amid massive, hidden debts. Enron executives walked away with more than $1 billion while employees and investors lost everything. Enron also had given $5.9 million in political contributions, mostly to Republicans, to Bush 43, to seventy-one senators, and to nineteen of the twenty-three members of the House energy committee. Several Enron executives were convicted, and the blue-chip accounting firm of Arthur Andersen (also a major Bush contributor) was found to have rigged audits and forced to close. Congress, by deregulating reasonable safeguards, bears much responsibility. Such scandals are found worldwide; most trace back to laws that interest groups set up to favor themselves.

scandal
Corruption made public.

Stalemating Political Power

Interest groups compete with one another and in so doing limit the influence that any group can have on the legislature or a government agency. Interest groups may stalemate government action. Certain issues are "hot potatoes" because government action either way angers one group or another. Typically, such issues are ardently supported and vehemently opposed by competing groups with enough voting power and influence to drive politicians to equivocation. Government may get stuck, trapped between powerful interests and unable to move on important problems. Italy has been called a "stalemate society" for this reason, and the United States may not be far behind.

Both Republican and Democratic members of Congress agree that the U.S. federal tax code is outrageous—thousands of pages long and so complex that no one understands all of it. Attempts to simplify it and make it fairer, however, are immediately blocked by more interest groups that have a stake in its provisions. Result: a perfect stalemate. As Mancur Olson observed (see above box), the few can trump the many. Some despair that the monstrous code is unreformable. Piecemeal reforms only make it longer and more complex, chuckle tax accountants and tax lawyers, giving them even more business.

In two-party systems, especially, issues tend to be muted by political candidates who try to appeal to as broad a segment of the voting public as possible. The result is a gap between the narrow interest of the individual voter and the general promises of an electoral campaign—a gap that interest groups attempt to fill by pressing for firm political actions on certain issues. But how well do interest groups serve the needs of the average citizen? The small businessperson, the poorly informed citizen, and minority groups with little money tend to get lost in the push and pull of larger interests and government. The successful interest groups, too, tend to be dominated by a vocal minority of political activists. In some cases, interest groups have become so effective that they overshadow parties and paralyze policymaking with their conflicting demands. The precise balance between the good of all and the good of particular groups has not yet been found.

Review Questions

1. Can democracy exist without interest groups?

2. Are all citizens equal in organizing interest groups?

3. How does government create interest groups?

4. Are interest groups and their money too powerful?

5. What are PACs and "soft money"?

6. Why are the French antipluralist?

7. Which is more effective: lobbying legislators or lobbying executives?

8. Can interest groups bypass democracy?

Key Terms

AFL-CIO, p. 176
amicus curiae, p. 181
class action, p. 181
corporatism, p. 172
Diet, p. 173
efficacy, p. 174
lobbying, p. 179

METI, p. 173
NAM, p. 176
political action committee (PAC), p. 175
public financing, p. 175
scandal, p. 184
single-issue group, p. 176

socioeconomic status, p. 178
soft money, p. 175
structured access, p. 179
subprime, p. 184
unforeseen consequence, p. 175

Further Reference

Abramoff, Jack. *Capitol Punishment: The Hard Truth About Washington Corruption from America's Most Notorious Lobbyist.* Washington, DC: WND Books, 2011.

Biersack, Robert, Paul S. Herrnson, and Clyde Wilcox, eds. *After the Revolution: PACs, Lobbies, and the Republican Congress.* Needham Heights, MA: Allyn & Bacon, 1999.

Browne, William P. *Groups, Interests, and U.S. Public Policy.* Washington, DC: Georgetown University Press, 1998.

Cigler, Allan J., Burdett A. Loomis, and Anthony J. Nownes, eds. *Interest Group Politics*, 9th ed. Washington, DC: CQ Press, 2016.

Graziano, Luigi. *Lobbying, Pluralism and Democracy.* New York: Palgrave, 2001.

Grossman, Gene M., and Elhanan Helpman. *Special Interest Politics.* Cambridge, MA: MIT Press, 2002.

Johnson, Haynes, and David S. Broder. *The System: The American Way of Politics at the Breaking Point.* Boston: Little, Brown, 1996.

Kaiser, Robert G. *So Damn Much Money: The Triumph of Lobbying and the Corrosion of American Government.* New York: Knopf, 2009.

Leibovich, Mark. *This Town: Two Parties and a Funeral—Plus Plenty of Valet Parking!—in America's Gilded Capital.* New York: Penguin, 2013.

Lessig, Lawrence. *Republic, Lost: How Money Corrupts Congress—and a Plan to Stop It.* New York: Twelve, 2011.

Lindsay, D. Michael. *Faith in the Halls of Power: How Evangelicals Joined the American Elite.* New York: Oxford University Press, 2007.

Rauch, Jonathan. *Government's End: Why Washington Stopped Working.* New York: PublicAffairs, 1999.

Smith, Bradley A. *Unfree Speech: The Folly of Campaign Finance Reform.* Princeton, NJ: Princeton University Press, 2001.

Thomas, Clive S., ed. *Political Parties and Interest Groups: Shaping Democratic Governance.* Boulder, CO: Lynne Rienner, 2001.

Tilly, Charles, and Sidney Tarrow. *Contentious Politics.* Boulder, CO: Paradigm, 2006.

Wilcox, Clyde, and Carin Larson. *Onward Christian Soldiers? The Religious Right in American Politics.* Boulder, CO: Westview, 2006.

Chapter 10
Parties

Learning Objectives

10.1 Explain the function of political parties as *inputting devices*.

10.2 Contrast U.S. with European parties.

10.3 Explain the ideological spectrum for classifying parties.

10.4 Enumerate the several *party systems*, and give examples.

10.5 Explain how parties are like product brands.

political party
Group seeking to elect office-holders under a given label.

For much of the twentieth century, U.S. **political parties** tended to move to the center, where they figured the most votes were. Starting with Reagan in 1980 (some say with Goldwater in 1964), U.S. politics and parties *polarized* into two increasingly hostile camps. Voting in the House and Senate became narrowly partisan with few crossovers. Ideology took on a bigger role, eliminating most liberal Republicans and some conservative Democrats. Many political scientists deplored the disappearance of the center. Ironically, in 1950 the American Political Science Association had deplored U.S. parties being so much alike they offered voters no meaningful choice. U.S. voters now have a choice, but within a nasty and possibly dangerous context. Be careful what you wish for.

Methods

Cross-Tabulations

A cross-tabulation ("cross-tab") is a table that shows two variables, arrayed so the reader can see a relationship between the two. When one is high, for example, is the other also high or is it low? Consider Table 10.1 below. It presents two variables, per capita GDP and Freedom House's ranking of countries on a scale from 1 to 7, with 1 being the most free and democratic and 7 the least. It is hard to see a clear relationship or pattern.

If we put the same information into a cross-tab, Table 10.2, readers quickly see that rich countries are democracies, but poorer countries generally are not. A cross-tab is not your whole paper; it is just a starting point and may raise questions. Here, for example, two countries, India and Russia, do not fit. Why is poor India a democracy and high-income (but declining) Russia not? We might study the long development of India's Congress Party and how it set India on the course (sometimes unsteady) to democracy. Russia, whose experience with parties was approximately the opposite, sank down in the FH ratings even as its oil income climbed. Mexico declined from the lowest rung of free to partly free. Indonesia for a long time was not free but recently held reasonably free and fair elections. This cross-tab shows that economic level is only part of the story; you must also get into each country's history, institutions, and culture.

Table 10.1

Country	2014 Per Capita GDP at PPP	Freedom House	2012 Ranking
United States	$54,600	1	free
France	40,400	1	free
Russia	24,800	6	not free
Mexico	17,900	3	partly free
Colombia	13,400	3.5	partly free
China	12,900	6.5	not free
Indonesia	10,600	3	partly free
India	5,900	2.5	free

SOURCE: *CIA World Factbook* and Freedom House

Table 10.2

Freedom House 2015 Ranking	2014 Per Capita GDP	
	Less than $25,000	Greater than $25,000
not Free	2	
partly Free	3	
free	1	2

Some political scientists still think that beneath the hullabaloo the two major U.S. parties' basic values and proposals and most voters are still centrist, especially in comparison to parties in many other countries. Extremists may do well in exciting their party's base for primaries but come up short in the general election, where candidate personality, grass-roots organizing, and fund-raising is usually more important than party.

Highly partisan politics is not new. The United States was the first country to develop mass political parties, which appeared with the presidential election of 1800, decades before parties developed in Europe. Europeans, however, may have developed political parties more fully. Americans have tended to forget that parties are the great tools of democracy. As E. E. Schattschneider (1892–1971) put it, "The rise of political parties is indubitably one of the principal distinguishing marks of modern government. Political parties created democracy; modern democracy is unthinkable save in terms of parties."

Almost all present-day societies, democratic or not, have parties that link citizens to government. Military dictators in Spain, Chile, and Brazil tried to dispense with parties, blaming them for the country's political problems. But even these dictators set up obedient parties to bolster their rule, and after the dictators departed, free parties appeared almost immediately. Whether they love political parties or hate them, countries seem to be unable to do without them.

Functions of Parties

10.1   **Explain the function of political parties as *inputting devices*.**

In both democracies and authoritarian systems, parties perform several important functions that help hold the political system together and keep it working.

A Bridge Between People and Government

To use a systems phrase, political parties are major "inputting" devices, allowing citizens to get their needs and wishes heard by government. Without parties, individuals would stand alone and be ignored by government. By working in or voting for a party, citizens can have some impact on political decisions. At a minimum, parties give people the feeling that they are not utterly powerless, and this belief helps maintain government legitimacy, one reason even dictatorships have a party.

Aggregation of Interests

If interest groups were the highest form of political organization, government would be chaotic and unstable. One interest group would slug it out with another, trying to sway government officials. There would be few overarching values, goals, or ideologies that could command nationwide support. (Some worry that the United States is already moving in this direction.) Parties help tame and calm interest group conflicts by **interest aggregation**—pulling together their separate interests into a larger organization. The interest groups then find that they must moderate their demands, cooperate, and work for the good of the party. In return, they achieve at least some of their goals. Parties, especially large parties, can be analyzed as coalitions of interest groups.

interest aggregation
Melding separate interests into general party platforms.

A classic example of a party as interest aggregator was the Democratic Party that Franklin D. Roosevelt built in the 1930s—a coalition that got Democratic presidents elected five times in a row. It consisted of workers, farmers, Catholics, Jews, and African Americans. Labor unions, for example, working with the Democrats, got labor legislation they could never have won on their own. As long as this coalition held together, the Democrats were unbeatable; since then the coalition has fallen apart. In the 1980s, Ronald Reagan aggregated economic and noneconomic conservative groups into the Republican Party. In 2008 and 2012, Obama aggregated young people, women, African Americans, Hispanics, and Asian Americans into winning coalitions. The key is that each interest can accomplish its separate goals only in cooperation with others' interests who need the favor returned under the umbrella of the party.

Integration into the Political System

Parties also pull into the political system groups that had previously been left out. Parties usually welcome new groups into their ranks, giving them a say or input into the formation of party platforms. This gives the groups both a pragmatic and a psychological stake in supporting the overall political system. Members of the group feel represented and develop a sense of efficacy and loyalty to the system. The British Labour Party and the U.S. Democratic Party, for example, enrolled workers by demanding union rights, fair labor practices, welfare benefits, and educational opportunities. A potentially radical labor movement turned moderate and soon supported the system. Now, ironically, British and American workers are so successfully integrated that many vote Conservative or Republican. In the United States, parties also integrate successive waves of immigrants and minorities—currently Hispanics—into American political life. In countries where parties were unable to integrate workers into the political system, labor movements turned radical and sometimes revolutionary.

Political Socialization

Parties also teach their members how to play the political game. Parties introduce citizens to candidates or elected officials and show members how to speak in public, to conduct meetings, and to compromise, thus deepening their *political competence* and building among them legitimacy for the system as a whole. Parties are also the training grounds for leaders. Historically, some European parties attempted to set up distinct subcultures—with party youth groups, soccer leagues, newspapers, women's sections, and so on. The effort was self-defeating, however, for as these parties socialized their members to participate in politics, they emerged from their subcultures. The fading remnants of this effort can still be found in Italy both in the renamed Christian Democrats, now the Popular Party, and the renamed Communists, now the Democratic Party of the Left. Some American parties provided social services. New York's Tammany Hall welcomed European immigrants, helping them find jobs and housing, while enrolling them as Democrats.

Political scientists note how this often produces **partisan identification** or **party ID**. Party ID is not the same as party registration but rather an often enduring psychological attachment a person feels to a political party. It can become part of their identity, like their religion. Once formed, it can be hard, but not impossible, to change. The socialization to identify with a political party often begins early in childhood through the influence of parents, who pass along all sorts of values, including political ones, to their children. Without party ID, every candidate or interest would need to win new supporters. When that candidate or issue faded, those supporters would have no natural place to shift their support. Party ID gives continuity; when a Reagan or a Clinton leaves office, most supporters shift to the next Republican (Bush) or the next Democrat (Obama).

partisan identification (party ID) Enduring psychological attachment to a party, often from childhood socialization

Mobilization of Voters

Parties get out the vote. In campaigning for their candidates, parties are **mobilizing** voters—whipping up interest and boosting turnout, as in the 2008 and 2012 U.S. elections. Without party advertising, many citizens would ignore elections. Most political scientists believe there is a causal connection between weak U.S. political parties and low voter turnout. In Sweden, strong and well-organized parties have produced voter turnouts of 90 percent (recently lower). Some critics object that party electoral propaganda trivializes politics. This is true, but simplifying and clarifying issues is a worthwhile function that enables

mobilization Rousing people to participate in politics.

voters to choose among complex alternatives. Indeed, for those otherwise unin-terested in keeping up with politics, they can just vote based on a candidate's party affiliation. Is it better for a citizen to vote on such limited information or to not vote at all?

neo-institutional theory
Institutions take on lives of their own, sometimes disconnected from electorates.

Organization of Government

The winning party gets government jobs and power and shifts policy its way. The party with the most seats in the U.S. House of Representatives or Senate appoints the chamber's leaders and committee chairpersons. A new president

Democracy

Parties That Ignore Voters

Can a political party in a democracy ignore voters? According to democratic theory, no, for it will soon lose elections and have to change its tune. But according to **neo-institutional theory**, parties can be so self-absorbed that they rumble on with little regard to what voters want. An old, established party with strong traditions and leadership patterns may be so focused on struggles *inside* the party that members neglect voter opinion *outside* the party. The party as institution can take on a life of its own apart from try-ing to win elections. The British Labour Party, talking mostly to itself and assuming positions too far left for most voters, lost four elections in a row. Finally getting sensible and centrist, it won in 1997, 2001, and 2005. Again losing direction and coherence, it lost in 2010 and 2015.

The Canadian Progressive Conservatives (PC) in 1983, under Brian Mulroney, won a majority of the House of Commons's 295 seats. Mulroney and the PC adopted Thatcherite free-market policies and stayed with them even though unemployment climbed and their popularity declined. The PC and Mulroney cam-paigned on the new free trade agreement (NAFTA) and won again in 1988 but with a reduced majority. A worsening economy, the Quebec question, and favoritism to certain firms brought the PC into public disrepute. Why didn't the PC change? Why didn't Mulroney resign? Eventually he did, but not until late in his second five-year term; he passed power to Kim Campbell, Canada's first woman prime minister, a

short-lived sacrificial lamb. In the 1993 elections, the PC almost disappeared, winning only two (2!) seats. The Liberals took over Ottawa, and the PC disap-peared, replaced by a new Conservative Party, which won Canada's 2006 and 2011 elections. In a parallel in 2011, the Canadian Liberals suffered leadership prob-lems and dropped into a distant third place behind the center-left New Democrats.

Japan's Liberal Democratic Party (LDP), which governed Japan for decades, also ignored voters. In 1990, Japan entered a long economic slump. Inept LDP leaders talked about financial reforms but deliv-ered little. Factions inside the LDP blocked each other. LDP chiefs figured they would always be reelected because Japanese voters dislike change, but they grew fed up with the LDP and in a series of elections brought it down to less than half of the Diet seats. Many LDP politicians left the party to start new par-ties. Voters finally booted out the LDP in favor of the DPJ in 2009, which in turn was booted out in late 2012, replaced by a renewed LDP, which also failed to deliver economic reforms.

When a party loses, it is time to reassess. Often the debate is between ideological purists who claim the message was not clear and moderates who claim the purists scare independent voters away. The winner of this battle for control of the party then controls the candidates and message in the next election. In some circumstances, the loser of the fight leaves to form another party, which happened in Canada and Japan.

can appoint some 3,000 people to executive departments and agencies, allowing the party to steer policy for at least four years. Party control of government in Britain is tighter than in the United States because Britain's parliamentary system gives simultaneous control of both the legislative and executive branches to the winning party. What a prime minister wants, he or she usually gets—and with minimal delay because party discipline is much stronger. In no system, however, does a party completely control government, for bureaucrats are also quite powerful. Parties *attempt* to control government; they do not always succeed.

Parties in Democracies

10.2 **Contrast U.S. with European parties.**

In democracies, three points of party organization are important: the degree of **centralization**, the extent to which a party participates in policy, and how parties finance themselves.

centralization
Control exercised by national headquarters.

Centralization

The amount of control party leadership exerts on its elected people varies widely. Israel has highly centralized candidate selection; each party draws up a *party list* of 120 nominees to the Knesset (parliament), and voters pick one list. Under proportional representation, only those listed at the top can expect to win seats. Party chiefs place tried and trusted people higher on the list and newcomers lower. This ensures centralized party discipline.

Britain is a little less centralized. British parties select candidates by bargaining between national headquarters and local constituency organizations. The national headquarters may suggest a candidate who is not from that district—often the case in Britain—and the local party will look the person over to approve or disapprove the candidate. The local party may also run its own candidate after clearing the nomination with national headquarters.

Germany, like Israel, uses party lists but is divided into sixteen states, thus partly decentralizing national party control. The varying degrees of centralization of these systems gives their parties **coherence**, discipline, and ideological consistency. When you vote for a party in Israel, Britain, or Germany, you know what it stands for and what it will try to implement if elected. Once elected, members of these parliaments do not go their separate ways but vote according to party decisions.

coherence
Sticking together to make a rational whole.

Party discipline in the United States, where parties have historically been decentralized, is weaker. Most candidates rely on themselves to raise funds and campaign. Candidates for the House and the Senate, in effect, create a new local or state party organization every time they run. Between elections, U.S. parties lie dormant. The Republican and Democratic National Committees may not have many resources to distribute to candidates. Candidates appeal directly to voters through television and other media. Increasingly, TV spots do not even mention the candidate's party affiliation. Candidates are thus in a position to tell their national parties, "I owe you little. I didn't get much party help to win, and I won't necessarily obey you now that I'm in office." This makes U.S. parties decentralized and often incoherent. Elected officials answer to their conscience, to their constituents, and to their PACs, not to their political parties. After the parties realigned to become more ideologically coherent in the 1980s and 1990s, the parties' leadership used their power to recruit candidates and distribute dollars to create more coherence and discipline. By 2012, the self-proclaimed **Tea Party** split the GOP into pragmatists willing to compromise and militants unwilling to bend, once again splitting the Republicans. While most parties contain factions and are threatened by potential splits, the election system in the United States creates more room for such factions to weaken party cohesion when governing.

Tea Party
Very conservative Republicans.

Setting Government Policy

To what extent can the winning party enact its legislative program? Here the U.S. party system faces its severest criticism. In parliamentary systems, the ruling party must resign when it can no longer muster the votes in parliament to carry on its program. The U.S. problem is often identifying where the majority lies. "Blue Dog Democrats"—typically, those elected from conservative districts—vote with Republicans on some issues, though their numbers have declined considerably. Some change parties, as did Senators Jim Jeffords of Vermont and Arlen Specter of Pennsylvania. The platform the president won on is not binding on congressional members of the party. Often, the president's party is not the majority party in one or both houses. And the party's legislative program is usually the product of inputs by the president, the speaker of the House, and the Senate majority leader. In recent years, however, young Tea Party affiliated, Republican members of the House prevented Speaker John Boehner from exercising power when he sought compromises with Obama and the Democrats. In 2014, Majority Leader Eric Cantor even lost his seat in the primary to an unknown Tea Party challenger.

The U.S. president may present a legislative program, but it must be acted on by 535 individual senators and representatives, all ultimately responsible for their own vote, as they are for their own reelection. Is the president, then, to be blamed for failing to fulfill campaign promises, or does the fault lie with too-loose party discipline? Schattschneider argued that, because U.S. national parties are so decentralized, they cannot agree on a strong national platform, making Washington "a punching bag for every special and local interest in the nation." Most Americans, however, prefer senators and representatives to vote their consciences rather than the dictates of party leadership as is the case in Europe.

Party Participation in Government

A European type of parliamentary system is more conducive to what Schattschneider regarded as **responsible party government**. The U.S. system, with its checks and balances, makes it difficult for parties to bridge the separation of powers to enact platforms. Occasionally, when a powerful president controls both the White House and Congress, party platforms turn into law, as when Lyndon Johnson got his **Great Society** program through the Democratic Congress of 1965–1966. When party control is divided or when party discipline is weak, voters don't know whom to boot out of office when things go bad. If party discipline is high but control of the presidency, the House, or the Senate is divided, little gets done, as happened under Obama.

In European parliamentary systems, the winning party is the government, or, more precisely, the party's leadership team becomes the cabinet. This system allows for more clear-cut accountability and voter choice than in the decentralized American party system. In both systems, parties participate in government by providing jobs for party activists in departments and agencies. In Britain,

responsible party government
Voters electorally reward or punish governing party for its policies.

Great Society
President Johnson's ambitious program of social reforms.

Theories

What Is a "Relevant" Party?

Columbia University political scientist Giovanni Sartori asks just what counts as a party. Is there some minimum size—such as winning a certain percentage of votes or a seat in parliament—that makes a small group a party? We should count as relevant, Sartori argues, parties that the main parties have to take into account either in campaigning for votes or in forming coalitions. If a party is so small that no major party needs to worry about trying to win over its adherents, it is irrelevant. Likewise, if it is unnecessary in forming a governing coalition, it is irrelevant. Thus, British Trotskyists and Irish Communists are ignored by all and do not count as parties, but Sweden's Liberals and Israel's small religious parties, each with only a few percent of the vote, may be necessary coalition partners and thus count as relevant parties.

Using Sartori's definition of relevant parties, would we include various American third-party efforts? Although the Democrats in 1948 denied the importance of the States' Rights Party (Dixiecrats) and in 1968 the importance of George Wallace's forces, in

both elections they took them into account. In 1968, Democratic nominee Hubert Humphrey visited the South and emphasized that the Democratic Party was a "very big house" that could accommodate many viewpoints, a lame attempt to make white Southern voters forget the civil rights reforms of the Johnson administration.

In 1980, the independent candidacy of John Anderson probably forced President Carter to emphasize foreign and ecological policies he might otherwise have minimized. In 1992, Ross Perot forced Bush 41 and Clinton to pay more attention to the federal budget deficit. In 2004, John Kerry paid attention to Ralph Nader's effort, for it had cost the Democrats the 2000 election. In these cases, we could say the United States had relevant third parties. The tiny Communist, Socialist Worker, and Socialist Labor parties no one has to take into account, so under Sartori's definition, we should not consider them relevant. If the Republicans start worrying that Libertarian candidates are taking some of their vote, the Libertarians will become a relevant party.

about 100 members of the winning party's parliamentary faction take on cabinet and subcabinet positions, compared with the 3,000 Americans who can receive **political appointments** when a new president takes office.

political appointment
Government job given to non–civil servant, often as reward for support.

transparency
Political money and transactions open to public scrutiny.

Financing the Party

Parties must finance their activities, and these are increasingly expensive, deepening the parties' dependence on rich donors. There is little **transparency** in these relationships. We could learn a great deal if we just knew how parties funded themselves, but they seldom tell the whole truth. Japan's Liberal Democrats were notorious for the sums they received from businesses, banks, farmer federations, and even *yakuza* gangsters. The traditional European style of small membership dues does not provide nearly enough, and parties have become desperate to raise money. Some do it crookedly. Almost every democratic country suffers scandals related to party fund-raising: the United States, Britain, France, Germany, and Japan. The problem may be incurable, related to the political competition that is the crux of democracy. In 1976, an estimated $500 million was spent on U.S. political campaigns. In 2012, $6.5 billion was spent for presidential, senatorial, and congressional campaigns, not counting the "pools of dark money" from groups doing "social policy." In contrast, total spending in the 2010 British general elections was only $150 million, but it too is growing rapidly.

mass party
One that attempts to gain committed adherents; usually has formal membership.

cadre party
One run by a few political professionals and only intermittently active.

devotee party
One based on a single personality.

Many democracies have laws to restrict or regulate political contributions. Germany, Spain, Sweden, and Finland use government funds to subsidize political parties in proportion to each party's electoral strength. This obviously discriminates against new parties. The U.S. Congress in 1974 passed a similar plan (the Presidential Campaign Fund), which allowed taxpayers to authorize the Internal Revenue Service to designate $3 of their income tax payment for the fund, which subsidized presidential nominees in proportion to the votes they received,

Classic Works

Duverger's Three Types of Parties

One of the first typologies of political parties was devised by French political scientist Maurice Duverger (1917–2014), who developed three categories: mass, cadre, and devotee. The **mass parties** are well organized and strive for a large and ideologically committed membership, such as West European Socialist parties. They fund themselves with members' dues. In contrast, **cadre parties**, such as the U.S. Democratic and Republican Parties, are weakly organized and based on a politically active elite. **Devotee parties** are those such as the Nazis under Hitler, where the party is built around one person. Akin to that are the *personalistic* parties of Latin American strongmen, such as Perón of Argentina and Vargas of Brazil. One example was Saddam Hussein's Ba'ath (Arab Renaissance) Party in Iraq. Personalistic parties, however, seldom outlive their founders.

provided they got a minimum of 5 percent nationwide. But only one taxpayer in four pays into the Presidential Campaign Fund, far too few to cover campaign expenses. Presidential candidates in the last few elections have decided to not bother to take the money, which comes with restrictions on how much you can spend. PACs and super-PACs have filled the vacuum with a vengeance.

Classifying Political Parties

10.3 **Explain the ideological spectrum for classifying parties.**

One basic way to classify parties is on a left-to-right spectrum, according to party ideology. Left-wing parties, such as Communists, propose leveling of class differences by **nationalizing** major industries. Center-left parties, such as the Social Democratic parties of Western Europe, favor welfare states but not nationalized industries. Centrist parties, such as the Swedish and Italian Liberals, are generally liberal on social questions but conservative (that is, free market) on economics. Center-right parties, such as the German Christian Democrats, want to rein in (but not dismantle) the welfare state in favor of free enterprise. Right-wing parties, such as the British Conservatives under Thatcher, want to dismantle the welfare state, break the power of unions, and promote vigorous capitalist growth. Now almost every European country also has anti-immigrant, anti-EU parties that some classify as far-right. Sweden has a rather complete political spectrum (see Figure 10.1).

nationalization
Putting major industries under government ownership.

Communist Parties

Communist systems—that is, countries ruled by Communist parties—have become rare. In Eastern Europe and the Soviet Union, Communist parties were voted out of power. China, Vietnam, North Korea, and Cuba try to preserve the party-controlled state, but they too appear ripe for change.

Figure 10.1 The parties in Sweden's unicameral Riksdag (parliament) show a left-right ideological spectrum. Sweden uses proportional representation. Lacking a majority of Riksdag seats, the Social Democrats formed a minority coalition with the Greens and occasional support from smaller centrist parties.

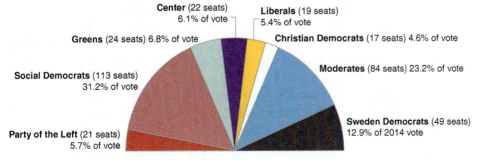

Center (22 seats) 6.1% of vote
Liberals (19 seats) 5.4% of vote
Greens (24 seats) 6.8% of vote
Christian Democrats (17 seats) 4.6% of vote
Social Democrats (113 seats) 31.2% of vote
Moderates (84 seats) 23.2% of vote
Sweden Democrats (49 seats) 12.9% of 2014 vote
Party of the Left (21 seats) 5.7% of vote

The "classic" Communist system founded by Lenin and developed by Stalin in the Soviet Union featured the interlocking of a single party with government and the economy. The Communist Party did not rule directly; instead, it supervised, monitored, and controlled the personnel of the state and economic structures. Members—about 10 percent of the adult population—were hand-picked from among the most reliable, energetic, and enthusiastic.

Most Soviet officials wore two hats: one as government functionary and another as Communist Party member. Every level of government, from local to national, had a corresponding party body that nominated its candidates and set its general lines of policy. At the top of the state structure, for example, was the legislature, the Supreme Soviet. Corresponding to it in the party system, the Central Committee oversaw the nomination of candidates to the Supreme Soviet, set its agenda, and guided its legislative outcomes. Supervising the Central Committee, the **Politburo** of a dozen or so top party leaders was the real heart of Soviet governance. Guiding the Politburo was the party's general secretary, who could appoint loyal followers to high positions and thus amass great power. China continues the Soviet pattern but with the addition of a higher layer, the powerful seven-member **Standing Committee** of the Politburo, which includes China's president and prime minister.

Why did Soviet President Mikhail Gorbachev (1985–1991) deliberately undermine the Soviet party structure? A single party that attempts to control everything important develops severe problems over the years. Because it gives members the best jobs, housing, and consumer goods, the party fills up with **opportunists**, many of them corrupt. The party **apparatchiks** also become highly conservative. The system favors them, and they have no desire to reform it. With such people supervising it, the Soviet economy ran down and fell further behind the American, West European, and Japanese economies. A Communist Party that was to lead the Soviet Union into a radiant future came to be seen as leading the country backward. Gorbachev concluded that to save his country, he had to break the party's monopoly on power. He failed to understand (as did many Western political scientists) how brittle the system was. Unable to reform, it collapsed.

The Soviet experience suggests that single parties that monopolize power are not workable over the long term. Without the invigorating elements of debate, competition, and accountability, Communist-type parties become corrupt, inflexible, and unable to handle the new, complex tasks of a modern world. The Chinese Communist Party (CCP) has tried to avoid this by letting most of the economy revert to private hands while retaining major enterprises (including banks) and political control. The CCP now also admits businesspersons as members. It is not clear that this will work in the long run, as China's rapid economic growth is creating a large, educated middle class, which grows increasingly critical over corruption.

Politburo
Russian for "political bureau"; the ruling committee of a Communist party.

Standing Committee
Top governing body of Chinese Communist Party.

opportunists
Persons out for themselves.

apparatchik
Russian for "person of the apparatus"; full-time Communist party functionary.

Classic Works

Kirchheimer's "Catchall" Party

Accompanying the tendency of most democracies to *two-plus* party systems has been the growth of big, sprawling parties that attempt to appeal to all manner of voters. Before World War II, many European parties were ideologically narrow and tried to win over only certain sectors of the population. Socialist parties were still partly Marxist and aimed their messages largely at the working class. Centrist and conservative parties aimed at the middle and upper classes, agrarian parties at farmers, Catholic parties at Catholics, and so on. These were called **Weltanschauung** parties because they tried not merely to win votes but also to promote their view of the world.

With prosperity growing after World War II, people began to reject the old ideological narrowness. In most of Western Europe, big, ideologically loose parties that welcomed all voters either absorbed or drove out the *Weltanschauung* parties. German political scientist Otto Kirchheimer coined the term **catchall** to describe this new type of party. His model was the German

Christian Democratic Union, a party that sought to speak for all Germans: businesspersons, workers, farmers, Catholics, Protestants, women, you name it. The term now describes virtually all ruling parties in democratic lands; almost axiomatically, they must be catchalls to win. The British Conservatives, Spanish and French Socialists, and Japanese Liberal Democrats are catchall parties. And, of course, the biggest and oldest catchall parties of all are the U.S. Republicans and Democrats.

Most political scientists welcome this move away from narrowness and rigidity, but with it comes another problem. Because catchall parties contain many viewpoints, they are plagued by factional quarrels. Struggles within parties replace struggles between parties. Scholars counted many factions in the Italian Christian Democrats and Japanese Liberal Democrats, parties that resembled each other in their near-feudal division of power among the parties' leading personalities. Much of American politics also takes place within rather than between the major parties.

Party Systems

10.4 Enumerate the several *party systems*, and give examples.

"Party systems" are not the same as "parties." Parties are organizations aimed at winning elections. **Party systems** are the interactions of several parties with each other. With parties, we look at the trees; with party systems, we look at the forest. Much of the health of a political system depends on the party system, whether it is stable or unstable, whether it has too many parties, and whether the parties compete in a *center-seeking* or *center-fleeing* manner. An unstable party system can wreck an otherwise good constitution. Stable, moderate party systems made democracy possible in West Germany after Hitler and in Spain after Franco.

Britain's party system led to a "hung parliament" and shaky government following the 2010 elections. The Tories lacked a majority of seats, so the small Lib Dems became their coalition partners, even though the two parties did not agree on much. Britain held a referendum in 2011 to reform the electoral system to give the Lib Dems a fairer slice of seats, but it failed. In the 2015 elections,

Weltanschauung
German for "worldview"; parties that attempt to sell a particular ideology.

catchall
Large, ideologically loose party that welcomes all.

party system
How parties interact with each other.

Democracy

Multiparty Systems Are More Fun

In a multiparty system, you get to choose from a bigger menu. With several relevant parties, as in Sweden, you can find a party that matches your preferences much better than just the two big U.S. parties. In most of Europe, people concerned about the environment can vote for a Green Party. Serious Christians can vote for a Christian Democratic Party. Leftists can vote for a Socialist Party and conservatives for a Conservative Party.

True, U.S. ballots (depending on the state) may list more than a dozen parties, ranging from Green to Libertarian to Socialist Workers, but if you vote for them, you feel you are throwing your vote away. Such is the impact of our winner-take-all electoral system, so a vote for a third party in the United States is simply a protest vote. Voters in much of Europe and in Israel know they are not throwing their votes away; if their party gets some minimum threshold (5 percent in Germany, 4 percent in Sweden), the party wins some seats in parliament. The interesting choices on European ballots help explain Europe's higher voter turnout. In the United States, voting in a major-party primary substitutes for the range of choices of a multiparty system. Republicans, for example, get to choose between business conservatives, religious conservatives, Tea Party conservatives, and isolationists and interventionists.

the Tories won an outright majority and had no need of the Lib Dems, who slumped way lower. Party system, in part related to electoral system, really matters in politics.

Classifying Party Systems

The simplest way to classify party systems is to count the number of parties in them: one, two, and multiparty. In between one and two, we put "dominant-party system." In between two and multiparty, we put "two-plus party system." Theoretically, there can be a no-party system, but, as we discussed, even dictators like obedient parties to support them. And some systems may be so messy we call them fluid or **inchoate** party systems.

inchoate
Not yet formed.

ONE-PARTY SYSTEMS Associated with totalitarian or authoritarian regimes, this is a twentieth-century phenomenon that lingers into the twenty-first. The Soviet Union, China, and many of the emerging nations of Africa and Asia are or were one-party states. These have a single party that controls every level of government and is the only legal party. The leaders of such parties rationalize that they are still democratic because they represent what the people really want and need. No fair election or public-opinion poll can substantiate this claim. When allowed, as in Eastern Europe in 1989, citizens repudiate one-party systems. Some developing lands, especially in Africa, argue that having several parties spells chaos and violence, for they form along tribal lines.

DOMINANT-PARTY SYSTEMS   In contrast to one-party systems, opposition parties in dominant-party systems contest elections, but the deck is stacked against them. The dominant party is well-organized and offers many inducements—such as jobs and payoffs—to supporters. Most importantly, it controls television. Competing parties are kept deliberately weak and do not have a chance. Some currently democratic nations had dominant-party systems but grew out of them as voters got fed up with the dominant party's corruption and ineptitude. India was long governed by the Congress Party, Japan by the Liberal Democrats, and Mexico by the Party of Institutional Revolution (PRI). In 2000, Mexico's conservative National Action Party (PAN) overcame PRI's lock on the presidency with the election of Vicente Fox, thus moving Mexico from a dominant-party to a multiparty system (with the Revolutionary Democratic Party on the left). The Democratic Party of Japan finally ousted the Liberal Democrats in 2009 (but they returned in 2012). Russia now has a dominant-party system under Putin's United Russia Party, but many Russians would like to see genuine competition. Many U.S. congressional districts are in effect dominant-party systems where the weaker party has no chance.

TWO-PARTY SYSTEMS   Most familiar to us is the two-party system of the United States and Britain. Here, two major parties have some chance of winning. Although third parties such as the U.S. Libertarians and Britain's Liberal Democrats seldom win, they serve to remind the two big parties of voter discontent. Often, one or both of the two main parties then offer policies calculated to win over the discontented. In this way, even small third parties can have an impact. Some observers argue that new political ideas come mostly from third parties as the big parties are too stuck in their ways.

MULTIPARTY SYSTEMS   These have several competing parties. The Swedish party system has eight parties arrayed on a left-to-right spectrum. Each receives seats in parliament in proportion to its share of the vote. This system is often criticized as being unstable, but that is not always the case. Israel, the Netherlands, Sweden, and Norway generally construct stable multiparty coalitions that govern effectively. The number of parties is not the only reason for cabinet **instability**. Much depends on the political culture, the degree of agreement on basic issues, and the rules for forming and dissolving a cabinet. Scholars have long debated which is better: two-party or multiparty systems. It's hard to say, for both have fallen prey to paralysis and **immobilism**. In the meantime, there has been a drift in both systems toward a middle ground, "two-plus" party systems.

instability
Frequent changes of cabinet.

immobilism
Getting stuck over a major political issue.

TWO-PLUS PARTY SYSTEMS   Many democratic countries now have two large parties with one or more relevant smaller parties. Germany has large Christian Democratic and Social Democratic parties, but the Liberal, Green, and Left parties win enough votes to make them politically important. Austria was long dominated by two big parties but now has a third party: the nationalistic and anti-immigrant Freedom Party. Britain is usually referred to as a two-party system, but it has long had third parties of some importance. In 2015, the Scottish Nationalists effectively booted out Labour, long Scotland's dominant party. Spain, which has a history of multiparty fragmentation, now has a **two-plus party system**: a large Socialist Party, a large center-right Popular Party, and several smaller parties. Looked at more closely, the U.S. system is at times two-plus, for it too has long had temporarily relevant third parties. While the Tea Party movement is not an organized party, other third parties like the Reform Party of the 1990s or the Green Party in 2000 arguably impacted U.S. elections and subsequent major party platforms.

two-plus party system
Country having two big and one or more small parties.

FLUID PARTY SYSTEMS   New and unstable democracies often have party systems so fluid and inchoate they change before your eyes and fit none of the previous categories. "Mess" is the only way to describe them. In such countries, parties rise and fall quickly—often just **personalistic** vehicles to get leaders elected but otherwise stand for no program or ideology. Poorly organized, many of them soon fall apart. Charismatic Latin American politicians often invent new parties, but they rarely last. In Poland, Czechoslovakia, and Hungary, broad catchalls ousted the Communists in 1989, won free elections, but soon fragmented. The Russian party system was fluid; President Putin founded his own Unity Party just before the 1999 election and by 2004 turned it into Russia's largest, but it is personalistic, just a tool for Putin to govern with. The Japanese system broke down from a dominant-party system to an inchoate one in the 1990s. After some years, these systems may settle down into two-plus or multiparty systems. Parties in Iraq and Afghanistan in the years following U.S. military involvement in each country have been very fluid.

personalistic
Based on personality of a strong ruler.

As long as there are at least two parties, we call the system a "competitive party system," the essence of which is to impede corruption. A single party that locks itself in power, whatever its ideology, inevitably becomes corrupt. Corruption can be kept in check—but never fully cured—by an "out" party hammering away at alleged corruption in the administration of the "in" party. The utility of a competitive party system is on display in Russia and China, where the friends and families of leaders stash millions of often ill-gotten gains in foreign banks, investments, and properties. When such transfers are uncovered in competitive-party systems, the "ins" are soon out.

The Party System and the Electoral System

How a nation gets its party system is complex and rooted in historical developments. When and under what circumstances was the electoral franchise expanded? Some very different countries have similar party systems: Culturally segmented India produced a dominant party system (under the Congress

Theories

Sartori's Party Competition

Giovanni Sartori, among others, is not satisfied with simply counting the number of parties to classify party systems. Also important is the degree and manner in which the parties *compete*. The term *multiparty system* does not differentiate between those systems that are stable and those that are unstable. Sartori does; he delineates party systems of "moderate pluralism" from those of **polarized pluralism**.

In the former, there are usually five parties or fewer, and they compete in a **center-seeking** or centripetal manner; that is, their platforms and promises appeal to middle-of-the-road voters. Left-wing parties curb their radicalism and right-wing parties dampen their conservatism, for both know that the bulk of the voting public is in the center. Thus, political life in moderate pluralism tends to be calm and stable, with ideological considerations toned down.

When the number of parties is greater than five or six, Sartori finds, there is the danger of polarized pluralism. Here the parties compete in a **center-fleeing** or centrifugal manner, becoming ideologically extreme and engaging in a "politics of outbidding" with their rivals. Some parties offer more and more radical solutions, either radical left or radical right. Some are "antisystem" or revolutionary. Parties that stick to the center find themselves attacked from both sides. Such a situation causes political instability and can lead to civil war, as in Spain in the 1930s, or to military takeover, as in Chile in 1973.

Party), as did culturally homogeneous Japan (under the Liberal Democrats). Both India and Japan, however, have recently seen their party systems fragment. Single-factor explanations do not suffice, but political scientists generally agree on the importance of the **electoral system**.

One of the most important institutional choices a country can make is between an electoral system based on single-member districts or on proportional representation. Single-member election districts, such as U.S. congressional districts, where a simple plurality wins, tend to produce two-party or two-plus systems. The reason is clear: Small third parties are underrepresented in such systems and often give up trying. Such is the case in the United States and Britain, based on the original English model. The British call this "first past the post" (FPTP), as it resembles a horse race: Even a nose better wins. There is a big premium in single-member districts on combining political forces to form the party with a majority or at least a plurality. If one party splits, it may throw the election to the party that hangs together. Wilson won in 1912 only because Teddy Roosevelt split the Republican Party. The factions within a party may not love each other, but they know they must stay together to have any political future. This factor helps explain why the two big American parties remain intact despite considerable internal differences.

Proportional representation (PR) allows and perhaps even encourages parties to split. PR systems use multimember districts and assign parliamentary seats in proportion to the percentage of votes in that district. Accordingly, there is not such a big premium on holding parties together; a splinter group may decide that it can

polarized pluralism
System in which parties become more extremist.

center-seeking
Parties become moderate to win the many votes in center of political spectrum.

center-fleeing
Parties become extremist, ignoring voters in center.

electoral system
Laws for running elections; two general types: single-member district and proportional.

get a few people elected without having to compromise with other viewpoints. Israel's PR system elects ten parties to the Knesset. Sweden's PR system elects eight parties to the Riksdag. Modification of electoral laws can change a country's party system, pushing a country from a multiparty to a two-plus system, as in Germany; from a multiparty system to a "two-bloc" system, as in France; or from an exceedingly fragmented multiparty system to a moderate one, as in Poland.

The Future of Parties

10.5 Explain how parties are like product brands.

Scholars are divided about the future of political parties. On the one hand, in most democracies party membership is down, and voters are less loyal. The big ideological clashes of the twentieth century are over; most major parties are centrist and similar. The mass media and interest groups have taken over some of the functions of parties. New policy ideas often come from specialists in think tanks. If campaigns are run by rich donors or if interest groups circumvent parties—and even candidates—to get their preferred candidates into office, then what use are political parties?

Similarly, most local offices and even many states are consistently won by members of one party. An area's minority party has little incentive to work hard if they never win. The dominant party organization also goes flabby because they never have to try hard to hold on to their offices. So while party organizations at the national level are made irrelevant by the media or interest groups, at the local level they can be irrelevant based on their consistent failure or success.

On the other hand, some see political parties as more relevant now than they have been in generations. In the United States, clearer ideological differences exist. Democrats in Congress are more clearly liberal, and Republicans are more clearly conservative. Few cross over to vote with members of the other party any more. Party identifiers in the public, especially those particularly interested and engaged in the political process, are increasingly distinct in their ideology and share fewer political values with members of the opposite party. As a result, party cohesion has increased, not because the incentives to cooperate with other party members have increased, but because people in the party tend to agree more.

Could it be that parties are getting more relevant and less relevant at the same time? Party organizations could be less important in terms of providing money and manpower to help shape elections, while the cohesion of parties within government and the relevance of parties to political socialization and aggregating the public's interest remains. Maybe parties of the future will be just brands. If so, we can think about voters in the United States choosing between Republican and Democratic brands, much like they choose between Coke and Pepsi. The brands themselves are the result of fights by activists, candidates, and officeholders seeking to shape the direction of their chosen brand.

Review Questions

1. Can democracy exist without competing parties?

2. What is *interest aggregation*, and how do parties do it?

3. How do individuals become socialized to identify with a political party?

4. What good is party centralization, as in Britain?

5. How can a party seemingly commit electoral suicide?

6. How did Communist parties differ from democratic parties?

7. How do you classify parties on an ideological spectrum?

8. What is a "catchall" party?

9. What are the several types of *party systems*?

10. How do competitive party systems handle corruption?

Key Terms

apparatchik, p. 198
cadre party, p. 196
catchall, p. 199
center-fleeing, p. 203
center-seeking, p. 203
centralization, p. 193
coherence, p. 193
devotee party, p. 196
electoral system, p. 203
Great Society, p. 195
immobilism, p. 201

inchoate, p. 200
instability, p. 201
interest aggregation, p. 190
mass party, p. 196
mobilization, p. 191
nationalization, p. 197
neo-institutional theory, p. 192
opportunists, p. 198
partisan identification, p. 191
party system, p. 199
personalistic, p. 202

polarized pluralism, p. 203
Politburo, p. 198
political appointment, p. 196
political party, p. 188
responsible party government, p. 195
Standing Committee, p. 198
Tea Party, p. 194
transparency, p. 196
two-plus party system, p. 202
Weltanschauung, p. 199

Further Reference

Black, Earl, and Merle Black. *Divided America: The Ferocious Power Struggle in American Politics.* New York: Simon & Schuster, 2007.

Dalton, Russell J., and Martin P. Wattenberg, eds. *Parties without Partisans: Political Change in Advanced Industrial Democracies.* New York: Oxford University Press, 2001.

Edwards, Mickey. *The Parties versus the People: How to Turn Republicans and Democrats into Americans.* New Haven, CT: Yale University Press, 2012.

Eldersveld, Samuel J., and Hanes Walton Jr. *Political Parties in American Society,* 2nd ed. New York: Palgrave, 2000.

Fiorina, Morris P., Samuel J. Abrams, and Jeremy C. Pope. *Culture War? The Myth of a Polarized America,* 3rd ed. New York: Pearson, 2010.

Hershey, Marjorie Randon. *Party Politics in America,* 16th ed. Upper Saddle River, NJ: Pearson, 2014.

Hetherington, Marc J., and Thomas J. Rudolph. *Why Washington Won't Work: Polarization, Political Trust, and the Governing Crisis.* Chicago, IL: University of Chicago Press, 2015.

Kabaservice, Geoffrey. *Rule and Ruin: The Downfall of Moderation and the Destruction of the Republican Party: From Eisenhower to the Tea Party.* New York: Oxford University Press, 2012.

Karvonen, Lauri, and Stein Kuhnle, eds. *Party Systems and Voter Alignments Revisited.* New York: Routledge, 2001.

Lawson, Kay, and Peter H. Merkl, eds. *When Parties Prosper: The Uses of Electoral Success.* Boulder, CO: Lynne Rienner, 2007.

Luther, Kurt, and Ferdinand Müller-Rommel, eds. *Political Parties in the New Europe: Political and Analytical Challenges.* New York: Oxford University Press, 2005.

McCarty, Nolan, Keith T. Poole, and Howard Rosenthal. *Polarized America: The Dance of Ideology and Unequal Riches.* Cambridge, MA: MIT Press, 2008.

Mayhew, David R. *Partisan Balance: Why Political Parties Don't Kill the U.S. Constitutional System.* Princeton, NJ: Princeton University Press, 2011.

Rosenblum, Nancy. *On the Side of the Angels: An Appreciation of Parties and Partisanship.* Princeton, NJ: Princeton University Press, 2008.

Skocpol, Theda, and Vanessa Williamson. *The Tea Party and the Remaking of Republican Conservatism.* New York: Oxford University Press, 2011.

Ware, Alan. *Political Parties and Party Systems.* New York: Oxford University Press, 1996.

Chapter 11
Elections

Learning Objectives

11.1 Explain the low turnout in U.S. elections.

11.2 Review the variables that predict who is most likely to vote and why.

11.3 Review the variables that predict who votes how.

11.4 Criticize the theory of *electoral realignment*.

11.5 Explain the strategies of winning elections.

In this chapter, we ask three general questions about elections, each followed by a more specific question about U.S. elections. First, we ask why people vote. This leads us to the puzzle of why voting *turnout* in the United States is low. Second, we ask how people vote. This brings us to the question of whether party loyalties in the United States are shifting. Finally, we ask what wins elections. This takes us to some of the strategies used in U.S. elections.

Why Do People Vote?

11.1 **Explain the low turnout in U.S. elections.**

The 2012 U.S. election largely turned on turnout. The Democrats understood that boosting the participation rates of their typical voters—young people, women, African Americans, Hispanics, historically people who voted less—would bring victory. Accordingly, the Democrats concentrated much money and effort on local organizing to get favorably disposed people to register and vote. The Republicans, having lost in 2008 and 2012, started taking more interest in grass-roots work instead of TV advertising. Some Republicans accused the Democrats of unfairly boosting the turnout of their voters, but that is exactly what an effective campaign is supposed to do.

In 2012, 59 percent of those eligible voted, lower than the 63 percent in 2008 but better than in several earlier elections. Historically, voter *turnout* in the United States was never high; its previous peak in 1960 was 63 percent. Turnout in Sweden, Germany, and Italy often tops 80 percent. Black South Africans in 1994, allowed to vote for the first time, produced a turnout of 86 percent, a measure of how much they appreciated the right to cast a ballot.

In nonpresidential elections, U.S. turnout seldom reaches 40 percent. Why do Americans vote so little? Typically, more than half of U.S. nonvoters say they are uninterested in or dissatisfied with candidates. Many feel their vote makes no difference or that none of the candidates is really good. Another reason is the U.S. party system, in which the two large parties may not offer an interesting or clear-cut choice; the out-party starts off fiery but usually returns to centrist positions by election day. In most presidential elections, both candidates denounce each other but toward the end sound somewhat alike as they promise jobs, health care, and a strong America. Television saturates voters so long in advance—increasingly with primitive, dirty political spots that disgust many with both parties by election day. Fewer than one in 20 American adults is involved enough in politics to attend a political meeting, contribute money, or canvass a neighborhood; however, such forms of participation are more frequent in the United States than in most other democracies.

Two out of five Americans never vote. U.S. nonvoting has brought major debate among political scientists. One school argues that low electoral participation means that many Americans are turning away from the political system, which loses legitimacy. Another school is unworried, arguing that low turnout means that many Americans are basically satisfied with the system or not sufficiently dissatisfied to register and vote. Countries with very high voter turnouts may have a sort of political fever in which partisan politics has become too intense. The United States experienced some of this intensity in 2012, when very distinct personalities and a divided electorate brought out more voters. Some thinkers propose mandatory U.S. voting (several countries do), but Americans resent impositions on their freedom.

Why the difference between European and American turnout? One obvious reason is that in Europe registration is automatic; upon reaching 18, local authorities register you. Americans must register personally, sometimes months before the election and before campaign excitement mounts. U.S. elections are held on Tuesdays; in much of Europe, they're held on Sundays. (Starting in 2008, many states began to allow early voting, which boosts turnout.) The United States' long ballot with many local, state, and national candidates plus referendums baffles voters. European ballots are simple, usually just a choice of party, and most countries control and limit television political advertising; some allow none.

Who Votes?

11.2 **Review the variables that predict who is most likely to vote and why.**

Voters in most democracies tend to be middle aged and better educated with white-collar jobs, more urban and suburban than rural. They are also more likely to identify with a political party. Nonvoters show the reverse of these

Theories

Downs's Theory of Voting

Contributing to rational-choice theory, Anthony Downs's landmark 1957 work, *An Economic Theory of Democracy*, argued that people vote if the returns outweigh the costs, especially once they factor in the low chance of being the deciding vote in the election. In other words, if the stakes seem important, citizens will go to the trouble of voting. Property owners fearing tax hikes are more likely to vote than renters not immediately hurt by the tax. The cost of political information, both financial and personal, also determines whether a person will vote. Not all have the energy or interest to follow political news or attend political meetings. Accordingly, the poor and uneducated in most societies are the least likely to vote. (India may be an exception.)

Downs' theory encourages us to ask why most people vote at all. If the costs to vote outweigh the benefits and the chances of casting the deciding vote are low, one would expect few people to vote, but in fact many people do vote. Why? The answers include civic duty, the personal satisfaction created in participating in the democratic process, and uncertainty about being the deciding vote. This gives a more complete understanding of voting than by asking only why people don't vote.

characteristics: young, lacking education, and with blue-collar or no jobs. Income and education, race, age, gender, and area of residence are key factors in who votes.

Income and Education

High-income people vote more than the less affluent, the well-educated more than high-school dropouts. These two characteristics often come together (good education leads to good incomes) and reinforce each other. High income gives people a stake in election outcomes, and education raises levels of interest and sophistication.

Factory workers in small towns may see little difference between candidates. They pay taxes, follow rules, try to make a living, and see little change from one administration to another. In contrast, executives and professionals feel involved and see a direct relationship between who wins and their personal fortune. Blue-collar workers are also affected by a change in administration, but they are less likely to know it.

The difference between voters and nonvoters is a sense of *efficacy*, the feeling that one has at least a little power, which tends to be low for workers and high for professionals. Better-off and better-educated people have seen interest groups succeed in changing policy. Ordinary workers often see political life as a "silent majority." Friends, neighbors, and family rarely had much wealth and rarely organized to pressure the government.

Well-educated people have broader interests in elections beyond personal economic stakes. The college-educated person—wealthy or not—is more interested, better informed, and more likely to participate in elections. Education lifts the sense of participation and abstract intellectual curiosity, which makes people more likely to follow political news and feel involved. Much research shows that education is the strongest determinant of who votes, but this leads to a puzzle, as U.S. turnout declined precisely as U.S. educational levels *climbed*. Americans, with many college-educated citizens, should be very participatory and eager to vote.

Several explanations, none definitive, have been advanced. Education may not mean what it used to. The sheer numbers of U.S. college graduates have diluted its former elite status. A bachelor's degree, in terms of getting a job nowadays, is more like a high-school diploma before World War II. Many majors are vocational or career-related and do not awaken curiosity or knowledge of the nation and world. And voting may not mean what it used to. Even well-educated citizens may not see value in voting for parties and candidates, none of which they like. Potential voters may be turned off by negative campaigning and conclude that all politicians are dirty. Some blame television for a decline in political participation.

postmaterialism
Theory that modern culture has moved beyond getting and spending.

Postmaterialism offers another explanation. According to this cultural theory, in all industrialized nations the economy has moved away from manufacturing and into knowledge and information industries. With this has come a shift of values, away from society and toward self. Only personal things matter in the New Age: relationships, correct diet, outdoor activities, and music. Social and political questions no longer interest many. If the post-materialism theory is accurate, education will not necessarily make citizens more participatory.

Race

Despite federal laws and black organizations, African American voting rates until recently have been lower than white voting rates, a gap that closed as African American income and education levels rose and when Barack Obama ran for president. Several surveys found that African American turnout actually edged white turnout in 2012. The 1965 Voting Rights Act overcame some of the barriers placed in the way of African American registration, chiefly in the South. Many African Americans have gone through political consciousness-raising and learned the value of participation and voting, a trend accelerated by Obama's candidacies. Some previously racist white politicians got the message and became respectful toward their African American constituents. Latinos now have the weakest turnout but recently have also participated more. Race is a diminishing factor in U.S. election turnout.

multicausal
Several factors making something happen.

if-then statement
Says that two variables are linked: Where X happens, so does Y.

tendency
Finding that two variables are linked but not perfectly.

Methods

Tendency Statements

It is hard to show that one thing causes another, especially in the social sciences. Often, the best we can do is show how one thing correlates to or covaries with another. For example, we have noted how rich countries are democracies and poor not, but this is only approximately true. There are many exceptions, so instead of saying "is," we say "tends to." Further, which causes which? Does being rich make countries democratic? Or does being democratic make countries rich?

Most social scientists are cautious about making causal statements—X causes Y—and say that causality is indirect and complex. X might give rise to Q, which in turn might influence Z to move in the direction of Y. In our example, wealth creates a large middle class, which places a high value on education and articulates its interests, which in turn undermines authoritarian rule. Simple it ain't.

Much of what we study is **multicausal**: P, Q, and R working together lead to Z. Which matters most—per capita GDP, education, or interest-group formation—to the founding of democracy? They all matter and are hard to disentangle. They tend to come as a package. Instead of making causal statements, we learn to make **if-then statements**: If we find X, then we also find Y. We also learn that this connection is rarely one to one: Where we find X, two-thirds of the time we find Y. This is called a **tendency** statement, the standard fare of the social sciences. For example: "Poor countries tend not to be democracies, but several are." And, remember, individuals often defy the tendency of their group: "African Americans tend strongly to vote Democratic, but some vote Republican." Most causal relationships are established through theory, which explains why one thing should cause another and then be supported by evidence of their correlation. In other words, data cannot stand alone to explain relationships; it must be supported with logical explanations—theories.

Age

Young people—those under 25—feel less politically involved and vote less. About half of U.S. citizens ages 18 to 25 are not registered to vote. Young people, with little income and property, feel economically uninvolved with election outcomes. When they start paying taxes, their interest grows. Focused on the concerns of youth, few have time for or interest in political questions, which seem abstract and distant.

In 1971, the Twenty-Sixth Amendment lowered the U.S. voting age from 21 to 18 at almost the same time that most other democracies did. The results were similar: With their new **franchise**, young people did not vote as much as their elders did. Middle-aged and older people are more likely to vote than the young, probably because the middle-aged person is at peak earning power and the old person is concerned about Social Security and Medicare. In recent U.S. elections, those over 70 showed the highest turnout.

franchise
The right to vote.

Gender

Traditionally, men were more likely to vote than women in almost every society. Women had only comparatively recently won the right to vote. (Switzerland enfranchised women only in 1971.) Since 1920, when female **suffrage** was granted in the United States, the gap between men's and women's voter turnout narrowed and then reversed; in recent U.S. elections, women have voted more than men, a reflection of women's higher education levels.

suffrage
The right to vote.

Place of Residence

In most of the world, cities have higher turnouts than rural areas, partly because urbanites on average have higher education levels. Polling stations are nearer in cities. People who have long lived in the same place are more likely to vote than are transients or newcomers; longtime residents feel more involved in local affairs and are more likely to participate in groups and activities in the community.

Voter turnout in the U.S. South is somewhat lighter than in the North and West, a reflection of lower living standards and a lack of party competition. But the South and its politics have changed, and now turnout in the South is approaching that of other regions. Other nations are also characterized by regional differences in voter participation. In France, the areas south of the Loire River have a lower voter turnout than the northern areas of the country.

Who Votes How?

11.3 Review the variables that predict who votes how.

The reasons that people vote as they do are many and complex. Factors can be divided into *long-term* and *short-term* variables. Loyalty to a political party is a long-term influence that can affect a person's votes for a lifetime. Short-term variables may cause a person to vote one way for one election but another way a few years later. Margaret Thatcher shrewdly called British elections in 1983 to catch the glow of military victory in the Falklands and again in 1987 during an economic upswing and disarray in Labour's ranks. Her Conservatives won both times. Similarly, in 1976 in the United States, Jimmy Carter benefited from a "morality factor" brought by the Watergate scandal. Economic conditions matter, especially economic growth in the months leading up to the election. The 2008 downturn hurt the Republicans, but the slow climb out of it in 2012 aided the Democrats. Such short-term variables, however, rarely mean a permanent shift in party loyalty.

Partisan Identification

Partisan identification—party ID, for short—is an attachment many feel toward one party for a long time, sometimes all their lives. Strong party identifiers habitually vote for that party; weak identifiers can be swayed to vote for another party. People with no party ID are up for grabs and may shift their votes every election. Remember, party ID is something that people carry in their heads; there is no sign-up. In the United States, in some states people indicate a preferred party when they register to vote; this is called party registration.

Party ID is heavily influenced by parents early in life. Some children proclaim they are Democrats or Republicans and may never change, like the early acceptance of a religion. It is also easier to vote along party lines, especially important with complicated U.S. ballots. Party ID is a "standing decision" on how to vote. Strong identifiers feel good about their party's candidates and view other candidates with suspicion. You can think of it as a shortcut to reduce the costs of voting associated with becoming informed on the candidates and the issues (See the box "Down's Theory on Voting").

Party ID is important to electoral stability. People who stick largely to one party allow politicians to anticipate what people want and to try to deliver it. Weak party ID produces great volatility in voting, as citizens shift their votes too easily, often in response to clever TV ads. Some political scientists worry that declining party ID in the United States bodes ill for democracy, but others argue that it makes democracy livelier. Party ID declined in the United States in the 1970s and 1980s but has seen some resurgence in recent years.

Party ID in much of Europe (but not in France) and Japan used to be stronger than in the United States, but the differences may be fading. Britain, Germany, Sweden, Japan, and other countries were long characterized by consistent splits between their two biggest parties. Typically, the **swing** from one major party to another ranged from only about 1 percent to 5 percent, as strong party ID anchored voters to parties. With the decline in **class voting** and rise of *postmaterialism*, party ID has been fading and volatility increasing, sometimes to U.S. levels. French voters are less likely than Americans to have a party ID, partly the result of

swing
Percentage of voters switching parties from one election to the next.

class voting
Tendency of a given social class to vote for a party that promotes its economic interests.

the splitting, merging, and renaming that French parties engage in. Such changes do not give party IDs time to take root and leave French voters mobile.

Political scientists can describe what kinds of people tend to identify with the various parties. No social category votes 100 percent for a given party; some people disregard group norms. If more than half of a given social category votes for one party, there is probably a significant relationship between the category and the party. If three-quarters votes for a party, there is a strong relationship. We are making statements here that indicate a tendency, not an absolute relationship. (See the box on tendency statements in this chapter.)

voting bloc
Group with a marked tendency.

Practicing politicians and political scientists call a group with a tendency to identify with a certain party a **voting bloc**. The candidates' strategy is then to secure enough blocs to deliver a plurality of the electorate, and they tailor their campaign to win over the blocs most likely to vote for them. The concept of voting blocs is an oversimplification; there is no such thing as a solid bloc.

Class Voting

Social class is one determinant of party identification and voting behavior. Even in the United States, where class distinctions are blurred, wage workers tend to register and vote Democratic, especially in families in which breadwinners are union members. In 2012, a majority of voters from families earning under $50,000 a year voted for Obama; however, many well-off professional people went for Obama as well, suggesting he enjoyed bimodal support. In most European countries, class voting is stronger for unions are often connected to social-democratic or labor parties. The big Swedish and German unions, respectively the LO and DGB, persuade most of their members to vote Social Democrat. Better-off Britons, French, Germans, and Swedes are likely to support their respective conservative parties.

Two things muddy class voting. Some working-class people—because they consider themselves middle class, have a family tradition, or have individual convictions on non-economic issues—vote for conservative parties. Sometimes a majority of the U.S. and British working class vote, respectively, Republican and Conservative. Conversely, some middle- and even upper-class people—because they are of working-class origins, have a family tradition, or picked up liberal views in college—vote for parties on the left. Such people are especially important in providing working-class parties with educated leadership. This two-way crossover—working class going conservative and middle class going left—dilutes class voting. Class voting has receded everywhere; it just happened first in the United States.

Regional Voting

Some regions identify strongly with certain parties. Often these are areas that were conquered and subjugated centuries ago, and the inhabitants still harbor resentments. In the Middle Ages, Paris kings extended their reach, often by the sword, south of the Loire River, where people still tend to vote Socialist. Scotland and Wales, England's "celtic fringe," vote more Labour than England. Scots still remember losing the Battle of Culloden in 1746 and in 2015 gave almost all their seats to the Scot Nats. The Civil War made the southern United States solidly Democratic—because the damn Yankees were Republicans—but since the 1980s the South has been the strongest Republican region, and the Northeast—which following the Civil War had been a Republican bastion—is now the strongest region for the Democrats (see the section that follows on realignment).

Outlying regions may harbor economic and cultural resentments at rule by a distant capital, *center-periphery tensions*. Scotland and Alberta do not like sharing their oil revenues, respectively, with London and Ottawa. The south of Italy resents the north, and vice versa; they vote differently. Germany's *Ossis* (easterners) resent rule by *Wessis* (westerners) and vote that way. India's many languages are reflected in voting patterns: Hooray for our local language!

Race and Ethnicity

Race and ethnicity are strong determinants for voting in the United States, especially for minority groups. African Americans vote heavily Democratic; in 2012, Obama received 93 percent of their vote. Hispanics, categorized as an ethnicity—they can be racially white or black—also vote predominantly for Democrats, especially because of recent Republican stances on immigration policy; in 2012, Obama received 71 percent of their votes. Whites lean toward Republicans; 59 percent supported Romney in 2012. Because the white vote is more divided, political scientists often look carefully for voting blocs within the white vote, such as gender, religion, or marital status.

Nonwhites are a growing electoral force. A Pew study found that racial minorities formed 28 percent of the electorate in 2012, up from 26 percent in 2008. So far, this demographic shift works against the Republicans. In 2012, African Americans made up 13 percent of the electorate and Hispanics made up 10 percent. Both groups are growing faster than the white population. The U.S. Census estimates that by 2043, no racial or ethnic group will form a majority in the population; African Americans, Hispanics, and whites will all be minorities. If Republicans cannot find a way to win African American or Hispanic votes, Democrats will dominate elections. Parties are good at adapting, though, at least over time.

Religious Blocs

After race, the divide between the religious and the secular is the single strongest predictor in U.S. voting. In 2012, Romney won most white Protestant evangelicals; Obama won most "seculars" (nonreligious), Catholics, and Jews. Mainstream Protestants were more evenly divided. In France, devout Catholics vote mostly conservative; secular people vote mostly left. In Italy, the Popular Party was founded by and is still linked to the Roman Catholic Church. Catholic areas of Germany vote more for the center-right Christian Democrats than do Protestant areas, which tend to the Social Democrats.

Age Groups

Younger people are not necessarily more radical than their elders. Rather, they tend to catch the tide that is flowing in their youth and stay with it. Young people socialized to politics during the Depression tended to vote Democratic all their lives. The enthusiasm for Reagan among young voters in the 1980s gave some of them a permanent identification with the Republican Party. Age groups react in part to the economic situation. In 2008 and 2012, most 18-to-29-year-old voters went for Obama, partly because they were less concerned about race but more worried about jobs during the financial crisis. Older voters were less open on race but disliked government in the economy.

Gender Gap

It used to be assumed that women were more traditional and conservative than men, but that has reversed in the United States and several other countries. Women now vote Democrat by several percentage points more than men. Women tend to like the Democrats' support for welfare measures and for contraception and abortion rights and dislike the Republicans' opposition to such views and Republican vows to increase defense spending.

Marriage Gap

Starting in 2000, observers noticed a "marriage gap." (It had probably existed earlier but had not been included among survey questions.) Unmarried people are several percentage points more Democrat than married couples. The responsibilities of raising a family make voters conservative, and Republicans stress "family values." Romney won among marrieds, Obama among singles. In fact, the gender gap largely disappears when you only compare married men and married women. A problem for Republicans is that only half of adult Americans are married.

Gay Gap

Electoral College
U.S. system of weighting popular presidential vote to favor smaller states.

In 2012, for the first time, exit polls asked voters their sexual orientation. Five percent identified as gay, and of them three-fourths voted for Obama. Ironically, Obama had shied away from the issue of same-sex marriage until Vice President Biden pushed him into supporting it. Minus the gay vote, voting strength was about even, so Obama's narrow margin of victory may have come from gay voters.

Case Studies

Is the U.S. Electoral System Defective?

No electoral system can guarantee translating the public's will into governance in a way that is both fair and simple. All have problems. If the system is fair (say, proportional representation), it is likely not simple. If the system is simple (say, single-member districts with plurality win), it is likely not fair. In 2012 congressional races, Democrats outpolled Republicans by 1.4 million votes nationwide, but Republicans won 33 more seats, the result of gerrymandering.

The 2000 U.S. presidential election was a double disaster, and both were waiting to happen: (1) An anachronistic **Electoral College** was eventually going to deny victory to the popular-vote winner, and (2) a defective balloting mechanism was eventually going to really matter. Al Gore, with a nontrivial half-a-million more votes (0.51 percent), lost in electoral votes to George W. Bush, 271–266. Similar situations happened three times in the nineteenth century.

States and counties use whatever balloting system they wish, including defective ones. Some still use paper ballots, some hand-lever voting machines designed in 1892, and some light-scanned ballots. Counties are slow to upgrade to electronic and touch-screen systems because of cost. The worst system was in Palm Beach County, Florida, which used a common and cheap 40-year-old technology: Voters

The Canadian ballot—paper marked with pencil—is clear, simple, standard, bilingual, and hand-counted in four hours nationwide. Any hints for the United States?

(continued)

put an IBM-type card into a frame and punched out a rectangle by their choice. Some of the little "chads"—as high as 6 percent—were not completely punched out, so counting machines read them as "no vote." The system was long known to be defective and had spawned court cases in several states; Massachusetts had outlawed it.

Making things worse in Palm Beach was a two-page "butterfly ballot" that confused voters, many of whom accidentally voted for right-wing populist Pat Buchanan instead of the intended Al Gore. Those who tried to fix the error by making another punch invalidated their ballot. This strongly Democratic county lost some 20,000 votes for Gore, several times more than were needed to win Florida and thus win the electoral vote.

The Electoral College was designed to overrepresent states with fewer voters. Each state gets as many electors as its senators and representatives, so even very small states get three electors, who vote as a unit for whomever got a plurality of votes within a state, even if just a fraction of a percent more. A vote for president in a thinly populated state has several times the power of a vote for president in a populous state. A vote in Wyoming is worth almost four times that of a vote in California. And small states, a huge swath of the middle of America, tend to go Republican. States with big cities, clustered in the Northeast and on the Great Lakes and West Coast, tend to go Democrat. Winning a state by a large margin gives the winner no advantage over winning by just a few votes.

The Electoral College is widely thought to be an undemocratic **anachronism**. It breaks the connection between popular will and electoral result but can't be seriously reformed because seventeen small states with five or fewer representatives like being overrepresented. These states can block constitutional change, which requires two-thirds of each house plus three-fourths of the state legislatures.

Defenders of the Electoral College system argue that moving to a system that relies purely on the popular vote would not necessarily be preferable. If a third-party candidate were to get several percent, as happened in 1992, when Ross Perot received 19 percent, the winner could win with a minority of the vote. Bill Clinton only won 43 percent of the popular vote but a solid 69 percent in the Electoral College.

The United States is not alone in its problems with electoral systems. The 2010 British elections produced a "hung Parliament," one where no party held a majority of seats. The United States, with its separation of powers, could shrug off such a situation; the president still governs. But in Britain, where a majority of Commons selects the prime minister, the Conservatives had to form a coalition with the Liberal Democrats.

anachronism
Something out of the past.

Urban Voting

Big cities worldwide tend strongly to vote liberal or left. The working-class vote is concentrated in cities. Cities are also centers of education and sophistication, places where intellectuals are often liberal and leftist. Country and suburban dwellers tend to embrace conservative values and vote for conservative parties. England votes overwhelmingly Tory, but the city of London does not. Germany's Bavaria is a conservative stronghold, but not Munich. Italy was long dominated by Christian Democrats, but not Italy's cities, most of which had leftist mayors.

A map of U.S. elections shows a major urban-rural split. Cities went strongly for Obama in 2012 as did many highly educated "monied burbs." Romney, tieless and in blue jeans, spoke to country values—religion, anti-abortion, anti–gun control, anti-tax, and pro-defense—that won small towns and rural areas.

Electoral Realignment

11.4 **Criticize the theory of** *electoral realignment.*

Political scientists have long debated a theory of **realignment**. Two forms of realignment have been identified. Typically, people retain their party identification for decades, but according to one version of the realignment theory, several watershed presidential elections have resulted in the party loyalties of many voters shifting. These **critical elections** do not determine how every subsequent election will go, but they establish new voting blocs and the main topics for future debate. They give one party an advantage but not absolute control. The critical or realigning elections in U.S. history are usually seen as the following:

> 1800: emergence of Jeffersonian Democratic Republicans
> 1828: emergence of Jacksonian populist Democrats
> 1860: emergence of Lincoln Republicans
> 1896: emergence of business Republicanism
> 1932: emergence of Roosevelt's New Deal Democrats

Between these critical elections, party IDs are stable and most people vote according to them. This is called the "normal vote" or "maintaining elections." Occasionally, enough voters disregard their party identification to elect the weaker party: Democrat Grover Cleveland in 1884 and 1892, Democrat Woodrow Wilson in 1912 and 1916, and Republican Dwight Eisenhower in 1952 and 1956. These are called "deviating elections" because the party shift was only temporary; afterward, voters went back to their long-term party ID.

An alternative theory contends that critical elections like 1932 that signify a sudden and enduring shift in party ID are exceptions and that most such shifts are **secular realignments**, happening gradually over the course of several elections. Voters change how they vote in response to new issues without immediately changing their party ID. It may take years or even decades for secular realignments to occur or to become apparent. Instead of national realignment, some researchers see *regional* realignment.

For example, the shift to the Republicans in the South started around 1948, coinciding with Democratic President Truman's desegregation of the military, continued with Goldwater's conservatism after passage of the Civil Rights Act of 1964, and culminated with the Reagan sweeps of 1980 and 1984 and the Republican takeover of Congress in 1994. Even though Southerners, mainly whites, voted for Republican candidates for president and eventually other offices, it wasn't until the 1990s that the majority identified with the Republican Party.

A New Realignment?

In 2008 and 2012, Democrats' argued that the U.S. electorate had realigned in their favor. The winning coalition of young people, women, and minorities indicated the emergence of a new, liberal bloc, many pundits said. But some political

realignment
Major, long-term shift in party ID.

critical election
A single election which proves to result in a realignment.

secular realignment
A slow, gradual shift in party ID.

Democracy

Partisan Polarization

Political scientists note growing **polarization** in the U.S. electorate and worry that it could harm democracy. Party identifiers have become more militant, as have dislikes and slurs against the other party. Although the trend was under way for some time, by the 1990s Republicans despised Clinton even when the economy boomed. In recent elections, Republicans and Democrats snarl at each other. Reason and consistency are not in command. Several factors contribute to the polarization tendency:

1. Under Reagan (1981–1989), the Republicans became more consistently conservative, until there were few moderate Republicans in Congress. To a lesser extent, the Democrats tended to become more consistently liberal.

2. Elites articulated more strongly ideological agendas than previously. New think tanks, periodicals, and websites, especially on the conservative side, took positions that the big parties, always seeking the centrist vote, had usually avoided.

3. The Supreme Court's 1972 "one person, one vote" rule requires states to make their congressional districts equal in population. Now many states redistrict after every census. Computers gerrymander with great accuracy, so that congressional districts now contain like-minded voters who consistently return incumbents to office. These incumbents, knowing they cannot lose, turn more ideologically partisan and less concerned about votes in the center.

4. Mobile Americans move to areas that culturally suit them, making whole regions of the country purer ideologically, the South conservative and the Northeast liberal. What the media designated as "red" (Republican states) and "blue" (Democratic states) did not speak nicely to each other. Researchers—some political, some marketing—can tell you the tastes of each ZIP code.

5. The trend reflects America's "culture wars," which are based heavily on **religiosity**. Religious Americans rallied to the "moral values" espoused by Republicans. Less-religious Americans focused on equality for women and minorities, tax fairness, and health care and rallied to the Democrats. The two cultures, interested in different issues, disdain and vote against each other.

Some historians and political scientists say U.S. politics has always been like this; regional and cultural politics have always loomed large in U.S. elections. Polarization is not all bad. In 2008 and 2012, it markedly boosted voter turnout.

polarization
Opinion fleeing the center to form two hostile camps.

religiosity
Degree of commitment to one's religion; often affects political beliefs.

scientists argue that there was neither a Republican nor a Democratic realignment, just voters reacting to current questions. It takes several elections to tell if there has been a realignment, that is, a durable shift in voting patterns. Most are betting against it.

And if there has been realignment, it may be difficult to spot the precise election in which it occurred. After Nixon's 1968 election, Kevin Phillips concluded that a Republican majority was emerging. But which was the critical election, Nixon's in 1968 or Reagan's in 1980? Or neither? If it was 1968, it would mark Carter's election in 1976 as a "deviating election," and, indeed, Carter's victory was largely the result of the Watergate scandal. The Nixon administration, however, lacked the ideological conservatism that came with Reagan. Perhaps the ingredients for a Republican realignment came with the 1968 election but did not coalesce until 1980 and was confirmed and deepened in 2004, thus a "secular realignment." Instead of a single "critical" election, it occurred over many years.

There are problems with realignment theory. Some political scientists would throw the whole package out. Many argue that it applies only to voting for president, which is often out of sync with voting for Congress. Americans sometimes vote for "divided government"—legislative and executive under different parties—to deadlock them and limit the damage they can do. (French voters do the same.) The Clinton victories in 1992 and 1996 and the Obama victory of 2008, all based on the economy, undermine the theory of electoral realignment. If voters react mostly to current situations and candidates' personalities, the basic supposition of party identification will have to be reconsidered. Perhaps party ID is not as important as it once was.

Instead of realignment, some suggest we are going through **dealignment**. Since the mid-1960s, the number of voters committed to neither major U.S. party increased. In 1948, fewer than a fifth of U.S. voters called themselves independents, but this has grown to about a third. Independents now determine presidential elections. They tend to be young, college-educated, and skeptical. Many came of age in turbulent times and heard a few lies. In 1964, Lyndon Johnson promised not to send Americans to fight in Vietnam. In 1974, they saw Nixon resign in shame. After the 2003 war, they learned that Iraq had no weapons of mass destruction. Their faith in conventional party politics was shaken; both major parties appeared to be dishonest. Some would go for a third party if a plausible one presented itself.

dealignment
Major, long-term
decline in party ID.

Some political scientists noted that dealignment—which proceeded during both bad and good economic times—coincided with three trends: (1) declining voter turnout, (2) declining party ID, and (3) declining trust in Washington. Do the three items hang together? Which causes which? Declining trust is probably the underlying cause. The higher turnouts of 2008 and 2012, however, suggested that American voters had not entirely despaired of politics. Indeed, levels of partisanship have recently stabilized and even increased.

Some researchers doubt there is much dealignment and independent voting. Many voters who call themselves "independent" actually lean to one party or the other, so that only 15 percent are genuine neutrals, and this amounts to only 11 percent who actually cast ballots (because true independents tend to vote less). By the time you count the weak identifiers, these researchers say, party ID in the United States is largely unchanged.

What Wins Elections?

11.5 **Explain the strategies of winning elections.**

In theory, elections enable citizens to choose and guide their government. In modern elections, however, the element of rational choice is heavily manipulated by the twin factors of personality and the mass media. People vote without clearly realizing what they are voting for or why, and this could become a threat to democracy.

Modern parties showcase their leaders' personalities. Especially in the advanced industrialized world, ideology is seldom emphasized. Ads and TV spots feature the leaders' images, sometimes without even mentioning their parties. The leader is presented as **charismatic** and decisive but calm and caring. Ronald Reagan and Barack Obama were excellent examples of winning political personalities, and leaders in other countries have adopted similar approaches. British Prime Minister Tony Blair won in part by copying the style of Bill Clinton. French presidential candidates often project an image of a caring, parental figure above the political fray, almost nonpartisan. German candidates for chancellor project a tried-and-true, reliable, and upbeat image but also say little about what policies they will pursue. The pattern worldwide: Keep it general, keep it happy, don't mention parties, and smile a lot.

charismatic
Having strong personal drawing power.

U.S. presidential candidates who present the most upbeat image of America almost always win. Pessimistic candidates, who worry about things going wrong, tend to lose. In 2008, Obama was more optimistic than McCain. The leaders' personalities are sold through the mass media, especially through television, where the candidate's image is controlled; even physical appearance can be altered. "Photo opportunities" instead of question-and-answer sessions avoid embarrassing probes by journalists. The photo op shows seemingly spontaneous candidate activity; words explaining the activity can be added later. The photo op is wordless; the candidates' professional "handlers" worry that their candidate could say something foolish and ruin a carefully built-up image. Journalists must be kept distant.

And this is happening worldwide. One British observer argued that "television very largely *is* the campaign." In 2010, for the first time the chiefs of the top three British parties debated each other live on TV. (The United States had held TV debates since 1960.) The three debates riveted Britons' attention and may have boosted turnout. In France, journalists complain about the *hypermédiatisation* of French politics. On television, everything is professionally controlled: set, lighting, music, makeup, narration—a mini-drama more perfect (and often more expensive) than many regular programs. The television spot, developed in America, now blankets Europe. The French call it *le clip politique*. French political scientist Jean-Paul Gourevitch saw three types: (1) the "jingle clip," a simple attention-getting device; (2) the "ideological clip," which sets an idea in images; and (3) the "allegorical clip," which portrays the hero-candidate in an epic. Increasingly, elections are won by the candidate with the sunniest personality and best ads. This generally means the candidate with the most money, for television is terribly expensive. Candidates, desperate for money, sell themselves to interest groups. Parties become little more than fund-raising organizations. This is not just an American problem; it started in the United States but has since spread to Europe.

While the televised upbeat, issueless image works to appeal to moderate, swing voters, campaigns often use fear to motivate their most loyal supporters—but out of the general public's view. In mailings, talk radio, and social media, which target the base of voters with strong party loyalty and ideological views on the issues, campaigns paint dire pictures of what will happen if the other side wins. These scare tactics are designed to motivate reliable supporters to turn out to vote. In 2012, Obama's team accused Romney of wanting to cut Medicare benefits for senior citizens to motivate older Democrats to vote. Republicans often look to motivate gun owners by telling them that Democrats want to take away their guns.

Retrospective Voting

Few voters carefully evaluate issues in a presidential election, but they do form an overall evaluation of the performance of an incumbent president. They feel the president has done a good job or a poor one, especially on the economy. Morris P. Fiorina called the accumulated or package views of voters toward incumbent presidents **retrospective voting** because it views in retrospect a whole four years of performance in office. When voters think the government in general is doing a good job, they reward the incumbent's party: Johnson in 1964, Nixon in 1972, Reagan in 1984, and Clinton in 1996. When they think the government in general is doing a poor job, they punish the incumbent's party: Humphrey in 1968, Ford in 1976, Carter in 1980, Bush 41 in 1992, and McCain in 2008. The Index of Consumer Confidence—a measure of how economically secure Americans feel—predicts most presidential elections. When they feel good about the economy, they generally vote for the incumbent's party. The financial meltdown of 2008 turned the election decisively to Obama.

retrospective voting Voters choosing based on overall incumbent performance.

Retrospective voting is colored, naturally, by party identification, issues, and the candidate's personality. For weak party identifiers plus independents, the perception of overall performance determines much of their vote. A strong positive retrospective view could even turn into party identification. Voting behavior is complex. When people say they "like" candidates, it could mean that they like the candidates' party, their stands on issues, their personal images, or the performance of the economy. Unraveling such puzzles is the crux of campaign strategy.

Candidate Strategies and Voter Groups

Campaign strategies try to keep "one foot on home base" by not alienating the normal party supporters while trying to win crucial votes from independents and undecideds. This is why, toward the end of the campaign, most U.S. presidential candidates sound centrist. Above all, campaigns try to boost turnout among those who favor them but often do not vote. The Democrats' emphasis on "microtargeting" likely supporters and neighborhood turnout operations gave them their 2012 victory.

Presidential candidates focus on states with more electoral votes and close to 50–50 voting, concentrating on such "battleground" states as Florida, Ohio, and Colorado. States lopsided for one party—such as California (Democrat) and Texas (Republican)—get little time and money. This rational strategy reached a high point in 2012, when presidential candidates campaigned in only ten "swing" states, ignoring the other 40, where party IDs were well understood in advance.

constituency
The people or district that elects an official.

Most campaigns are designed to fit the opinions and needs of the candidate's **constituency**, often determined by public-opinion polls. Candidates must be aware of pockets of party strength and resistance, what various groups are thinking about, what districts have the lowest turnouts (and therefore merit less candidate time), and which issues anger constituents. Aware of the direction and intensity of voter opinion, candidates then typically try to assemble enough "voting blocs" to win.

Coalitions of several smaller blocs of voters often win. On a national scale, the Democrats used to represent a coalition of labor, African Americans, Catholics, Jews, and urban voters; the Republicans received their support from a coalition of rural and farm voters, Protestants, and nonunion workers. By the 1960s, though, these traditional blocs had begun to break up, but both parties attempt to construct new blocs. The breakup of the blocs, it should be noted, coincides with the declining voter turnout and party loyalty discussed earlier.

Many Americans do not fit neatly into demographic, ethnic, or religious pigeonholes. Instead, attitudes on religion, free enterprise, welfare, patriotism, civil rights, and other issues cut across the old voting blocs, and a person's group identities may have contradictory political leanings. "Liberal" and "conservative" are tricky categories because people are often liberal on some things and conservative on others. Campaigns have become increasingly sophisticated at identifying likely supporters and motivating them to vote based on their unique interests rather than on general appeals to their group identities, party ID, or ideological leanings.

Each party maintains massive databases on every voter—in 2012, the Democrats' database was better—cataloging everything from the issues they care about to their buying habits and how often they vote. The files are used to pinpoint voter concerns in the swing states. They then set up local offices to contact, persuade, and boost turnout among party identifiers and undecideds. The Democrats' success in 2012 surprised both Republicans and mainstream pundits.

Democracy

Changing Positions

Candidates are endlessly opportunistic and modify their positions on issues to win the most votes. Many call this "slippery" or "unprincipled," but it is really just democracy in action. Elected officials who support discredited or unpopular policies get voted out. Those who urge politicians to stand by their principles and "do the right thing" meet the hard-nosed reply: "But if I'm not elected, all

the good and just things I'm trying to accomplish will be thrown away. So I've got to bend on this issue."

The 1994 Republican "Contract with America" included a ten-year phaseout of farm subsidies, something the GOP had long championed. By 2002, Republicans were shoveling more money into farm subsidies than ever. To do otherwise, said President

Bush, would be "political suicide" for his 2004 reelection. Democrats, seeking those same farm-state votes, also supported the subsidies.

The 2008 election cycle began with the candidates far apart on Iraq. McCain mentioned he would be willing to keep U.S. forces in Iraq "a hundred years." Obama said he would bring them home "immediately." During the campaign, both modified their positions toward the middle. McCain (and indeed President Bush) said "as soon as possible," when Iraq stabilized, possibly in a couple of years. Obama said withdrawal should not be precipitate, possibly in 16 months. By the fall of 2008, they were not far apart, as both played for the big vote in the center. (Actually, the troop withdrawal stretched out three years, to the end of 2011.)

This dynamic means that issues seldom dominate U.S. political campaigns: By election day, both candidates have adjusted their positions toward the center.

Can it be otherwise in a democracy? Politicians who uphold "consistency" or "principle," as Rick Santorum did in the 2012 Republican primaries, lose. Others, who change their views, are held up to ridicule by the media and their opponents, as Mitt Romney was, but they are really adjusting to new realities on a continuous basis. Asked what drove his policies, British Prime Minister Harold Macmillan (1957–1963) replied, "Events, dear boy, events." Much of political life is the opportunistic reaction to events. It is a delicate balance for a politician to have a backbone—and to respond to the will of the people.

Review Questions

1. Why has U.S. voting turnout risen recently?
2. What went wrong with the U.S. electoral system in 2000?
3. Should we view U.S. nonvoting with alarm?
4. How does party ID help decide elections?
5. Why is there a "gender gap" in U.S. voting?
6. Does income predict how a person votes?
7. Are we seeing a critical election, a secular realignment, a dealignment, or none of these?
8. How does the economy influence elections?

Key Terms

anachronism, p. 218
charismatic, p. 222
class voting, p. 213
constituency, p. 224
critical election, p. 219
dealignment, p. 221
Electoral College, p. 216
franchise, p. 212
if-then statement, p. 211
multicausal, p. 211
polarization, p. 220
postmaterialism, p. 210
realignment, p. 219
religiosity, p. 220
retrospective voting, p. 223
secular realignment, p. 219
suffrage, p. 212
swing, p. 213
tendency, p. 211
voting bloc, p. 214

Further Reference

Abramowitz, Alan I. *The Polarized Public? Why American Government Is So Dysfunctional.* Upper Saddle River, NJ: Pearson, 2013.

Bishop, Bill, and Robert G. Cushing. *The Big Sort: Why the Clustering of Like-Minded America Is Tearing Us Apart.* Boston: Houghton Mifflin, 2008.

Cahn, Naomi, and June Carbone. *Red Families v. Blue Families: Legal Polarization and the Creation of Culture.* New York: Oxford University Press, 2010.

Caplan, Bryan. *The Myth of the Rational Voter.* Princeton, NJ: Princeton University Press, 2007.

Claggett, William J. M., and Byron E. Shafer. *The American Public Mind: The Issues Structure of Mass Politics in the Postwar United States.* New York: Cambridge University Press, 2010.

Edsall, Thomas Byrne. *The Age of Austerity: How Scarcity Will Remake American Politics.* New York: Doubleday, 2012.

Flanigan, William H., Nancy H. Zingale, Elizabeth a. Theiss-Morse, and Michael W. Wagner. *Political Behavior of the American Electorate*, 13th ed. Washington, DC: CQ Press, 2015.

Gerken, Heather K. *The Democracy Index: Why Our Election System Is Failing and How to Fix It.* Princeton, NJ: Princeton University Press, 2009.

Halperin, Mark, and John Heilemann. *Double Down: Game Change 2012.* New York: Penguin, 2013.

Issenberg, Sasha. *The Victory Lab: The Secret Science of Winning Campaigns.* New York: Crown Publishers, 2012.

Johnson, Dennis W. *No Place for Amateurs: How Political Consultants Are Reshaping America.* New York: Routledge, 2007.

Kennedy, Randall. *The Persistence of the Color Line: Racial Politics and the Obama Presidency.* New York: Pantheon, 2011.

King, Desmond S., and Rogers M. Smith. *Still a House Divided: Race and Politics in Obama's America.* Princeton, NJ: Princeton University Press, 2011.

Nelson, Michael, ed. *The Elections of 2012.* Washington DC: CQ Press, 2014.

Paulson, Arthur. *Electoral Realignment and the Outlook for American Democracy.* Boston, MA: Northeastern University Press, 2006.

Polsby, Nelson W., Steven E. Schier, and David A. Hopkins. *Presidential Elections: Strategies and Structures of American Politics,* 13th ed. Lanham, MD: Rowman & Littlefield, 2011.

Reiter, Howard L. & Jeffrey M. Stonecash. *Counter Realignment: Political Change in the Northeastern United States.* New York: Cambridge University Press, 2011.

Sabato, Larry, ed. *Pendulum Swing.* New York: Longman, 2011.

Winters, Jeffrey A. *Oligarchy.* New York: Oxford University Press, 2011.

Wuthnow, Robert. *Red State Religion: Faith and Politics in America's Heartland.* Princeton, NJ: Princeton University Press, 2011.

Part IV
Political Institutions

Ch. 12 Legislatures Presidential systems, like the one in the United States, have a powerful chief executive who is elected separately from the legislature and cannot be easily ousted, a "separation of powers." Parliamentary systems, like the British, on the other hand, have the national legislature elect a prime minister from its own ranks, a "fusion of powers." Parliaments can recall prime ministers with a "vote of no confidence," which usually happens when the governing coalition has fallen apart. Federal systems need an upper house, like the U.S. Senate, but unitary systems can be unicameral, although many are still bicameral. In theory, legislatures formulate laws, but in practice they take their cues from the executive and deliver "pork" to their constituencies. Supervision and criticism of the executive are now their most useful functions. Legislatures have, perhaps unfortunately, declined in importance as executives have grown.

Ch. 13 Executives and Bureaucracies The U.S. presidential system frequently suffers from "deadlock," and parliamentary systems suffer from "immobilism." These issues are normal for democracies; only authoritarian systems eliminate executive-legislative difficulties, as Putin has done in Russia. Prime ministers have tended to "presidentialize" themselves by gathering more power. Some American scholars fear an overstrong president, one who prevails by projecting a friendly personality. Within the executive branch, power has been flowing to bureaucrats because they are the only ones who understand complex situations and policies. Japan's bureaucrats virtually rule the country. No political system has succeeded in controlling its bureaucracy.

Ch. 14 Judiciaries Law plays an especially strong role in the U.S. system, which makes the judiciary an equal branch, not the case in most countries. Common law systems, like that of the United States, feature "judge-made law" that changes over time. Code law systems, like those of Europe, feature relatively fixed formulas, some of them tracing back to ancient Rome. Likewise the Anglo-American accusatory and adversarial system is quite different from European inquisitorial systems. Few other countries have a Supreme Court as important or interesting as the American one, which decides issues related to the constitution, a power it gave itself with *Marbury v. Madison*. The political impact of the Warren Court was especially strong and controversial; it changed civil rights, criminal procedure, and legislative districts.

Chapter 12
Legislatures

12.1 Trace the origin of parliaments.

12.2 Contrast parliamentary and presidential systems.

12.3 Explain the purpose of a bicameral legislature.

12.4 Argue that lawmaking is no longer a legislature's primary function.

12.5 Explain the weaknesses of legislative compared to executive authority.

The world has been horrified recently at a U.S. Congress so polarized and paralyzed that it can barely pass a budget. This is the greatest democracy, many wondered, that is going to lead the rest of the world? U.S. public respect for Congress reached record lows. A major financial-rating agency downgraded U.S. government bonds, not for economic reasons but in fear that Congress lacked the political will to take necessary if painful steps. English philosopher John Locke posited the "legislative" as the most important branch of government. The U.S. Congress seemed determined to prove him wrong.

The Origins of Parliaments

12.1 Trace the origin of parliaments.

Political institutions, it is theorized, become more specialized, complex, and differentiated as they become more modern. Primitive clans mostly had a single leader to govern them. Tribes added councils to debate major problems and adjudicate disputes. City-states such as Athens had assemblies that combined legislative, executive, and judicial functions. The Roman senate combined several roles, and its powers declined as Rome went from republic to empire. In the Middle Ages, the prevailing feudal system was a balance among a monarch, nobles, and leading churchmen, and it is in **feudalism** that we first glimpse the "balance of power."

feudalism
System of political power dispersed among layers.

Countries with limits on government have usually had feudal pasts, which teach that dispersion of power is good and concentration of power is bad. Countries with absolutist traditions, such as China, have trouble founding democracies. An example of this balancing of power is the oath the nobles of medieval Aragon (in northeast Spain) pledged to a new king: "We, who are as good as you, swear to you, who are no better than we, to accept you as our king and sovereign lord provided you observe all our statutes and laws; and if not, no."

Ambitious monarchs, who were often at war, desperately needed revenues. Some of them started calling assemblies of notables to levy taxes. In return for their "power of the purse," these assemblies got a modest input into royal policies. Such were the beginnings of the British **Parliament**, which had two houses (Lords for peers and church leaders and Commons for knights and burghers), and the Swedish **Riksdag**, which originally had four chambers (for nobles, clerics, burghers, and farmers). The French **Estates General**, with three houses (for nobles, clerics, and commoners), got off to a weak start and was soon forgotten as French monarchs gathered more and more personal power in what became known as **absolutism**.

parliament
National legislature; when capitalized, British Parliament, specifically House of Commons.

Riksdag
Sweden's parliament.

Estates General
Old, unused French parliament.

absolutism
Post-feudal concentration of power in monarch.

In Britain, Sweden, and some other European countries, though, legislatures slowly grew in power and were able to resist monarchs' absolutist demands. In sixteenth-century Britain, Henry VIII, who broke with Rome over a divorce, developed a partnership with Parliament because he needed its support in passing laws to break England away from the Roman Catholic Church. By the seventeenth century, Parliament considered itself coequal with the monarch and even supreme in the area of taxes. The English Civil War was a quarrel between royalists and parliamentarians over who had top power. In 1649, Parliament decided the issue by trying and beheading Charles I.

John Locke, the English philosopher who lived through this momentous period, extolled the power of the "legislative" as the most basic and important. During the Age of Enlightenment in the eighteenth century, French philosopher Montesquieu declared that liberty could be secured only if government were divided into two distinct branches, the legislative and the executive, with the ability to check and balance each other. Modern governments still have these two branches, but only in the United States do they check and balance each other. Theoretically, at least, the legislature enacts laws that allocate values for society, and the executive branch enforces the statutes passed by the legislature. (A coequal judicial branch is rare; it is a U.S. invention found in few other systems.) But these responsibilities often overlap, and the separation of powers is rarely clear-cut.

presidential systems
Those with separate election of executive (as opposed to symbolic) president.

president
In U.S.-type systems, the chief political official; in many other systems, a symbolic official.

parliamentary systems
Those with election of parliament only, which in turn elects the prime minister.

prime minister
Chief political official in parliamentary systems.

coalition
Multiparty alliance to form a government.

fall
In parliamentary system, a cabinet is voted out or resigns.

Presidential and Parliamentary Systems

12.2 Contrast parliamentary and presidential systems.

Presidential systems most clearly show the separation of power between the executive and legislative branches. These systems, a minority of the world's governments, have a **president** who combines the offices of head of state with chief of government. He or she is elected more or less directly by the people (in the United States, the quaint Electoral College mediates between the people and the actual election), is invested with considerable powers, and cannot be easily ousted by the legislature. In **parliamentary systems**, the head of state (figurehead monarch or weak president) is an office distinct from the chief of government (**prime minister**, premier, or chancellor). In this system, the prime minister is the important figure.

Notice that in parliamentary systems, voters elect only a legislature (see Figure 12.1); they cannot split their tickets between the legislature and executive. The legislature then elects an executive from its own ranks. If the electoral system is based on *proportional representation*, there will likely be several parties in parliament. If no one party has a majority of seats, two or more parties must form a **coalition**. Whether one party or several, a majority of parliament must support the cabinet; if not, it "**falls**." Usually a monarch (as in Britain and Spain) or weak president (as in Germany or Israel) "asks"—there's no real choice in the matter—the head of the largest party to become prime minister and "form a government."

Figure 12.1 Parliamentary versus presidential systems.

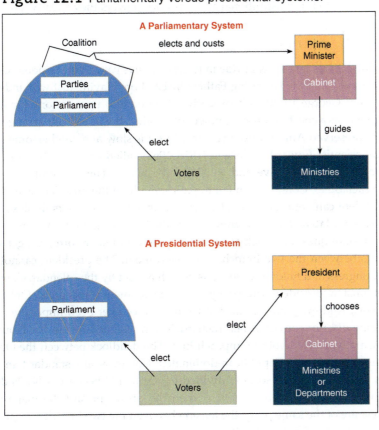

Cabinet and government, terms used interchangeably, are what Americans call an **administration**. One used to say the Cameron government but the Obama administration. Recently, however, some other countries have begun using the term "administration." The prime minister, after consulting with the parties likely to support him or her, names a team of ministers for the cabinet who are members of the parliament. These ministers then guide the various ministries or departments of government that form the executive branch. The prime minister and cabinet are "responsible" (in the original sense of the word, "answerable") to the parliament. (Prior to democratization in the nineteenth century, ministers were responsible only to the monarch.)

Presidents in presidential systems are not responsible to legislatures. The close connection between the legislative and executive branches is broken. Presidents are elected on their own and choose cabinet ministers or department secretaries mostly from outside the legislature. In the United States, of course, top executive and judicial officers must be confirmed by the Senate. The two branches of government cannot control, dissolve, or oust the other, as happens in parliamentary systems. This gives presidential systems great

cabinet
Top executives who head major ministries or departments.

government
In Europe, a given cabinet, equivalent to U.S. "administration."

administration
Executives appointed by U.S. president, equivalent to European "government."

stability. Presidents may be unpopular and face a hostile Congress, but they can still govern with the constitutional and statutory powers they already have.

Separation and Fusion of Powers

The United States takes great pride in its *separation of powers*, the famous "checks and balances" that the Founding Fathers insisted on. Having just won independence from George III and his executive dictatorship, they set one branch of government as a check against the power of another. It was a clever arrangement and has preserved America from tyranny. But it is slow and cumbersome, what political scientist Edward S. Corwin (1878–1963) called an "invitation to struggle" between the executive and legislative branches. The two branches often stymie each other. Congress can fail to pass something the president wants, and the president can veto something Congress wants. Some scholars think such an executive-legislative *deadlock* is common for the U.S. presidential system.

Important questions, such as economic policy and tax reform, can get stuck for years between the two branches of government. The president cannot dissolve Congress and hold new elections, which are set by the calendar. Congress cannot oust a president except by the impeachment procedure. Only two presidents, Andrew Johnson and Bill Clinton, have ever been impeached, and the Senate did not convict either. Richard Nixon resigned before the House of Representatives could vote to impeach him. The deadlock between the Obama administration and a Republican-dominated Congress are standard in U.S. history. Some prefer this sort of "divided government" because it holds down spending and foolish policies. Even when the president and the majority of Congress are of the same party, the tension between the two branches exists and can prevent either from getting its way.

Classic Works

Where Did the U.S. System Originate?

The U.S. system of checks and balances originated with a French nobleman, the Baron de Montesquieu (1689–1755), who traveled all over Europe to gather material for one of the classics of political science, *The Spirit of the Laws*. In trouble with the king of France, Montesquieu spent some years in England and admired its liberties, which he thought came from the mutual balancing of the king (the executive) and Parliament (the legislative). The French parliament, the Estates General, was unused for generations; French kings ran everything on an absolutist basis.

By the time Montesquieu wrote about English checks and balances, they had been overturned, and Parliament was supreme over king. Montesquieu was describing an idealized version of the English "mixed monarchy" that had slid into the past. The U.S. Founding Fathers, however, read Montesquieu literally and attempted to construct his theory of checks and balances. Few other countries have done this.

West Europeans consider the American system inefficient and unintelligible, and they have more modern systems that evolved after the U.S. Constitution was devised. Their parliamentary systems have a **fusion of power** that does not set the branches against each other. In fact, it's hard to distinguish between legislative and executive branches for the top executives are themselves members of parliament. In the British, German, Japanese, and Dutch systems, prime ministers must be elected to parliament, just like ordinary legislators, before they can become chief of government. As leaders of the biggest parties, they are formally called on (by the monarch or figurehead president) to form a government. The individuals forming this government or cabinet have both their seats in parliament and offices in the executive departments. They report back often to parliament. At any time, about a hundred British **MPs** (members of Parliament) also serve in the executive ministries and departments. Legislators are also executives. The cabinet, in effect, is a committee of parliament sent over to supervise the administration of the executive ministries.

fusion of power
Executive as an offshoot of the legislature.

MP
British member of Parliament, namely, the House of Commons.

When Britain's parliament is in session, the cabinet members show up to answer questions from their fellow MPs. Britain's House of Commons holds a Question Hour most afternoons. The members of the two main parties sit facing each other across an aisle on, respectively, the "government benches" and **"opposition** benches." The front bench of the former is reserved for cabinet ministers, the front bench of the latter for the opposition's "shadow cabinet," the MPs who would become ministers if their party were to win the next election. MPs with no executive responsibilities sit behind the cabinets and are called **backbenchers**. Most questions to the prime minister and his or her cabinet come from the opposition benches—first written questions and then oral follow-ups. The answers are criticized, and the opposition tries to embarrass the government with an eye to winning the next election. Most parliamentary systems operate in a similar fashion.

opposition
Those parties in parliament not supporting the government.

backbencher
Ordinary member of parliament with no leadership or executive responsibilities.

In the U.S. system, with its separation of powers, committees of the Senate or House can summon cabinet members and other officials of the executive branch to committee hearings. But appearing before a committee is not the same as a grilling before the entire legislative body. The president, as equal to and separate from Congress, cannot be called to testify.

Advantages of Parliamentary Systems

There are several advantages to a parliamentary system. The executive-legislative deadlock (now usually called *gridlock*), frequent in the American system, cannot occur because both the executive and legislative branches are governed by the same party. If the British Conservative Party wins a majority of the seats in the House of Commons, the leaders of the party are automatically the country's executives. When the Conservative cabinet drafts a new law, it is sent to the House of Commons to be passed, which is rarely difficult or delayed because the Conservative MPs, a majority, obey the party's leaders.

If members of the governing party disagree with their own leaders in the cabinet, they can withdraw their support and vote "no confidence" in the government. This is rare. The government then falls and must be replaced by a new leadership team that commands the support of a majority of the House of Commons. If a new election gives the opposition party the numerical edge in parliament, the cabinet resigns and is replaced by the leaders of the newly victorious party. Either way, there cannot be a long disagreement between executive and legislative branches; they are fused into one.

The prime minister and cabinet can be speedily ousted in parliamentary systems. Any important vote in parliament can be designated a **vote of confidence**. If the prime minister loses—a "vote of no confidence"—the cabinet falls. There is no agony of impending impeachment of the sort that paralyzed Washington under Presidents Nixon and Clinton. A new prime minister and cabinet are voted in immediately. If the government makes a major policy blunder, parliament can get rid of the cabinet without waiting for its term to expire. When Americans become unhappy with presidents' policies, there is little the system can do to remove them from the White House early. Parliamentary systems do not get stuck for long with unpopular prime ministers.

Parliamentary systems have other difficulties, however. First, because members of parliament—supervised by their parties' **whips**—obey their party leaders, votes in parliament can be closely predicted. The parties supporting the government vote for almost any bill the cabinet has drafted. Parties opposing the government vote against it. Floor speeches and corridor persuasion have no impact; the legislators vote the way their party instructs. MPs in such systems have lost their independence, and their parliaments have become little more than rubber stamps for the cabinet. The passage of legislation is more rational, speedy, and efficient, but parliament cannot "talk back" to the executive or make independent inputs. This makes European parliaments rather dull and less important than **Capitol Hill** in Washington, where legislators often oppose the president, even of their own party. Many European legislators are jealous of the independence and separate resources that American representatives and senators enjoy.

Second, depending on the party system and electoral system, parliamentary democracies often have many parties, with no single party controlling a majority of seats in parliament. This means the largest party must form a coalition with smaller parties to command more than half the seats. In Britain's 2015 elections, Conservatives won a majority (with 330 out of 650 seats) and so could govern with no help from the smaller Liberal Democratic Party, their coalition junior partner from 2010 to 2015.

Occasionally, parliamentary systems form a **minority government** that depends on the support of smaller parties but does not form a coalition with them (current example: Sweden). When a minority government fails to get support from some small parties on an important bill—say, the budget—they would lose a vote of no confidence and hold new elections. This happened in Britain

vote of confidence
Vote in parliament to support or oust government.

whip
Legislator who instructs other party members when and how to vote.

Capitol Hill
Home of U.S. Congress (note the spelling: -ol).

minority government
Cabinet lacking firm majority in parliament.

in the 1970s, when a minority Labour government depended on the support of small parties. In 1979, however, they stopped supporting the cabinet, which was ousted on a vote of no confidence. Notice how Britain's legendary governing stability evaporates when no party commands a majority of parliamentary seats. Party system determines much of governing stability.

In coalitions, the head of the largest party becomes prime minister, and the head of the second largest party usually becomes foreign minister. Other cabinet positions, or **portfolios**, are assigned by bargaining. Italy is an example of coalition governments, and it illustrates what can go wrong: The coalition partners quarrel over policy, and one or more parties withdraw from the coalition, bringing it below the required majority in parliament. The government then falls for lack of parliamentary support, with or without a formal vote of no confidence. This leads to instability, frequent cabinet changes, and loss of executive authority. Italy has had some sixty governments since World War II.

This is not as bad as it sounds—remember, the "government" simply means "cabinet"—and the cabinets are often put back together again after bargaining among the same coalition partners. The trouble is that prime ministers must concentrate on not letting the coalition fall apart, and thus they hesitate to launch new policies that might alienate one of the member parties. The problem here is not one of too much change but of too little: the same parties in the same coalitions getting stuck over the same issues. *Immobilism*, the inability to decide major questions, is the danger of multiparty parliamentary systems. Notice how this parallels the problem of *deadlock* in presidential systems.

Not all parliamentary systems, to be sure, suffer from immobilism. In Britain, the largest party usually has a majority of seats and can govern alone. Some coalition cabinets, as in Sweden, are cohesive and effective because their parties are in general agreement. German and British governments have fallen on votes of no confidence only once each since World War II. In general, the more parties in a coalition, the less stable it is.

portfolio
Minister's assigned ministry.

Bicameral or Unicameral?

12.3 Explain the purpose of a bicameral legislature.

Some two-thirds of parliaments in the world have two chambers, an upper house (the U.S. Senate, British House of Lords, French Sénat, German Bundesrat) plus a lower house (the U.S. House of Representatives, British House of Commons, French **National Assembly**, or German **Bundestag**). These are called **bicameral** (two chambers) legislatures. Despite its name, the upper house usually has much less power than the lower house. Typically, if the upper house objects to something passed by the lower house, the lower house can override the upper house's objections, often by a simple majority. Only the two houses of the U.S. Congress are coequal and must pass identically worded versions of a bill.

National Assembly
Lower, more important chamber of French parliament.

Bundestag
Lower, more important chamber of German parliament.

bicameral
Parliament having two chambers: upper and lower.

unicameral
Parliament with one chamber.

Bundesrat
Upper, weaker chamber of German parliament.

Lords
Upper, weaker chamber of British parliament.

life peer
Distinguished Briton named to House of Lords for his or her life, not hereditary.

A smaller number of parliaments are **unicameral** (one chamber), such as China's National Peoples Congress, Sweden's Riksdag, and Israel's Knesset. Yugoslavia once experimented with a five-chambered parliament. South Africa had a curious and short-lived three-chambered parliament with one house each for whites, mixed-race peoples, and East Indians. The majority black population was unrepresented. (Since 1994, South Africa has had a bicameral parliament with a black majority.)

The reason for two chambers is clear in federal systems. The upper house represents the component parts, and the lower house represents districts based on population. This was the great compromise incorporated in the U.S. Constitution: The Senate represented the states and the House the people. A federal system requires an upper chamber. Germany's **Bundesrat**, for example, represents the sixteen *Länder* and is coequal to the lower house on constitutional questions. On other issues, it can be overridden by the Bundestag.

The utility of an upper house in unitary systems is unclear. Britain's House of **Lords**—reformed in 1999 by keeping **life peers** and excluding most hereditary peers—is still mostly an elderly debating society that sometimes catches errors in laws passed too quickly and obediently by Commons. Otherwise, the Commons overrides any objection from the House of Lords with a simple majority vote. This is also true of the French Sénat, an indirectly elected body that largely expresses farming interests. New Zealanders, Danes, and Swedes—all with unitary systems—concluded that their upper houses served no purpose and abolished them in recent decades.

What Legislatures Do

12.4 Argue that lawmaking is no longer a legislature's primary function.

Consider the old high-school civics question: How does a bill become law? They may have told you that individual members introduce proposals, but they usually cover small matters, such as getting a tax break for a constituent. Most important bills originate in the government or administration. Typically, an executive agency develops an idea, the administration drafts a proposal, and members of the president's party introduce it to the legislature, which then debates and modifies it.

The Committee System

Much power in modern legislatures resides in their committees, which can make or break proposals. Democratic parliaments often hold public hearings to get input from experts and interest groups. If the bill is reported favorably out of committee, it goes to "the floor," the full chamber, where it needs a majority vote to pass.

Methods

Longitudinal Studies

One good way to study something is to see how it changes over time, a **longitudinal** study. For example, suppose you want to see if interest groups headquartered in Washington have grown in number. You could find a reliable secondary source (perhaps Common Cause) that keeps track of these things. You might also count the numbers of "National" and "Associations" in D.C. phone books over several years or decades. Then you would list the numbers (these are just for illustration), probably with most recent first, looking something like this:

2015	1,937
2010	1,879
2000	1,754
1990	1,628
1980	1,607
1970	1,592

For a longer-range study, you might take every fifth or tenth year over many decades or a century. Other longitudinal studies might take a closer look at the behavior of one or several interest groups, campaign spending, laws initiated by Congress, or presidential votes by states. You may be able to display such numbers graphically, which helps readability.

Not all longitudinal studies need to be quantified. Some do not lend themselves to numbers. A longitudinal study of Senator J. William Fulbright, for example, might use quotes and paraphrases from his speeches and writings to show how he changed over time, from supporting the administration on foreign affairs to opposing it over the Vietnam War.

Virtually every legislature has a number of standing or permanent committees and may from time to time create special ad hoc committees to study urgent matters. The British House of Commons has five standing committees plus several specialized committees. These committees are less important than their U.S. counterparts, for the fusion of powers of the British system means that Parliament is not supposed to criticize or reject bills the cabinet has submitted. It may, however, modify them. With separation of powers, the committees of the U.S. Congress are most fully developed. The House of Representatives has twenty-one standing committees—the Senate, twenty—and they often make the news. Assignment to the more prestigious of these committees, such as the House Ways and Means Committee or Armed Services Committee, can help careers, for they give members media exposure.

U.S. congressional committees and subcommittees screen the thousands of bills that are introduced at every session and pick out the few that merit serious consideration. A government bill in a parliamentary system is automatically important; "private members' bills" may be quickly weeded out in committee. Legislatures are so large that bills cannot be drafted by the entire membership; to work out an agreement on the precise wording and scope of legislation, proposals must be referred to committees. The bulk of legislative work is not performed on the floor but in committee rooms.

longitudinal
Studying how something changes over time.

Standing committees in the U.S. Congress are balanced to represent both political parties and the states or geographic regions with the greatest interest in the committee's work. A Nebraskan is often on the Agricultural Committee and a New Yorker on the Education and Labor Committee. Each standing committee is bipartisan, made up of Democrats and Republicans in proportion to each party's seats. Party committees in each house make committee assignments and usually try to take members' interests and expertise into account. Political considerations also factor in. Rarely will leaders put new members who haven't proven their ability to get reelected on important committees that require substantive expertise (although Speaker of the House Newt Gingrich did in the 1990s to help the new Republicans raise interest group contributions and get reelected.) Party leaders sometimes reward loyal members with plum assignments.

Changes in the 1970s weakened the sometimes tyrannical powers of committee chairpersons. Committee chairs were generally assigned on the basis of seniority. Now, when the parties caucus at the beginning of a session in each house, members vote for committee chairpersons by secret ballot, effectively breaking the seniority system. A discharge petition can force committees to report out bills against the chair's will. Subcommittees are more easily established and have the right to name their own staffs.

Committee chairs are weaker than they used to be, but power doesn't disappear—it shifts. Some worry that subcommittees have decentralized and fragmented power too much. Others worry that reduced committee power results in power becoming too concentrated in the party leaders' hands. This is not a problem, however. Leaders in Congress are only empowered when their party is united—in other words, when a strong leader is least necessary.

A Closer Look at Legislatures

The main purpose of legislative bodies, in theory, is to formulate laws. This, however, varies among political systems and is generally in decline. Ideally, legislatures initiate laws, propose constitutional amendments, ratify treaties, control tax revenues, and scrutinize government activities. In authoritarian systems, however, legislatures are for show.

LAWMAKING   Although legislatures *pass* laws, few of them *originate* laws—which is why we must take their "rule-initiation function" with a grain of salt. As we noted, much legislation originates in government departments and agencies. In parliamentary systems, especially where one party has a majority of seats, the cabinet gets what it wants. Party discipline makes sure that members of the ruling parties will automatically vote the way party leaders instruct. Votes in such legislatures are highly predictable along party lines; some observers say such parliaments have become rubber stamps for the executive.

In the U.S. Congress, where party discipline is more lax, usually several members buck their own party. But even here much of the legislative agenda is set by the White House: economic initiatives, wars, mass surveillance, and expanding or cutting programs. Even the budget, the original "power of the purse" that gave legislatures their importance, is now an annual congressional reaction to the budget produced by the White House budget office. Typically, Congress takes the president's budget, adds its own spending, and passes it. Accordingly, "lawmaking" is not the only, or perhaps even the most important, thing that legislatures do.

CONSTITUENCY WORK   Legislators spend much time helping constituents. Most have staffs to answer letters, make sure people get their government checks, and generally show that the elected representatives really care. Often "lawmakers" are so busy with **constituency casework** that they pay little attention to making laws. In effect, elected representatives have partly transformed themselves into **ombudsmen**, specialists who intervene with government on behalf of people with complaints. (Standard complaint: "Where's my check?") Is there anything wrong with this? Is it not a perfectly valid and necessary role for legislators to play? It is, but something gets lost: the wider view that a representative should have in looking out for the good of the whole country. A legislator immersed in constituency casework has no time for or interest in bigger questions, so the initiative goes more and more to the executive branch, and democracy grows a little weaker.

constituency casework
Attention legislators pay to complaints of people who elect them.

ombudsman
Swedish for "agent"; lawyer employed by parliament to help citizens wronged by government.

Constituency service is mainly how representatives keep getting reelected. They are in a position to do favors. They frequently visit their home districts to listen to local problems and arrange for government help, something an out-of-office challenger cannot do. Thus, legislators in systems as different as the United States and Japan can lock themselves into power.

SUPERVISION AND CRITICISM OF GOVERNMENT   Potentially the most important role of modern legislatures is keeping a sharp and critical eye on the executive branch. Even if they originate little legislation, parliaments can powerfully affect the work of government by monitoring government activity to make sure it is in the nation's interest, incorrupt, and effective.

In Britain, the **Question Hour** allows members of Parliament to grill ministers, sometimes with devastating results. Even if the British cabinet knows it is almost immune to a vote of no confidence—because it controls the majority of Commons—its members must answer questions carefully. A bad, unconvincing answer or lie can hurt the ruling party in the next election.

Question Hour
Time reserved in Commons for opposition to challenge cabinet.

Virtually every U.S. administration must modify its policies because Congress raises difficult and sometimes embarrassing questions, even though it may pass little legislation on these matters. Members of both parties on Capitol Hill criticized the Obama administration for spending too much, for bailing out financial institutions, and for a complex healthcare reform. The Obama administration had to change some of its policies because of congressional criticism. Keeping the government on its toes is one of the best things a legislature can do, even if it passes few laws.

EDUCATION   Legislatures also inform and instruct the citizenry on the affairs of government; they create mass demands by calling public attention to problems. In the mid-1960s, Senator J. William Fulbright (D-Ark.), chair of the Senate Foreign Relations Committee, educated Americans about the Vietnam War by televising his committee's hearings. Democratic control of Congress later allowed Congress to hold critical hearings on the Iraq War. All democratic countries carry extensive press reports on parliamentary debate, and many now televise them.

REPRESENTATION   The most elemental function of a legislature is to represent people, or at least make them feel they are represented. Although legislators are elites, most legislators in democracies consider the interests of their constituents; it gets them reelected. A large part of representation is psychological; people need to feel they are represented. When they do not, they resent government power, and the government loses legitimacy. "No taxation without representation," chanted American colonials. Tea Party supporters, feeling estranged from Washington, vow to "take back" the government. The **apartheid** laws of South Africa, passed by a whites-only legislature, evoked no support and much disobedience from the black majority. Because of this, the apartheid system cracked.

apartheid
System of strict racial segregation formerly practiced in South Africa.

The foregoing are some of the roles performed by legislatures. Notice that only one of them is lawmaking, and that is usually just a follow-up on ideas initiated by bureaucrats and executives. Still, if legislatures carry out the other functions mentioned, they are doing a lot.

The Decline of Legislatures

12.5 Explain the weaknesses of legislative compared to executive authority.

By the late nineteenth century, observers were noticing that parliaments were not working the way they were supposed to. Contrary to Locke's expectations, legislatures were losing power to the executive. Most political scientists would agree that the trend has continued and grown. Some, however, hold that the original Lockean expectations were too high and that parliaments provide useful checks on the executive even though they do not originate much legislation. Congress (but not your own Congressperson) consistently ranks at the bottom in public respect, often in the single digits.

Structural Disadvantages

In parliamentary systems, party discipline is strong and legislators obey party whips. In European parliaments, we can usually predict within a vote or two how the issue will be decided: in favor of the government because the government (that is, the cabinet) commands a majority of seats. In such systems, individual members do little, and there is no special excitement in the press and public about parliamentary affairs. Only when coalitions break up do things get unpredictable and therefore interesting. The European parliaments really are more rational and efficient than the U.S. Congress, but they are also less powerful and less interesting. Efficiency has led to atrophy.

The U.S. Capitol Hill has no such problem with efficiency. Its near-feudal dispersion of power with weaker party discipline and its tendency to deadlock with the executive have made it most inefficient. But this is why Congress is lively and important. In few other countries can the national legislature as a whole talk back to the executive and even override a presidential veto. On occasion, members change parties to show their displeasure. Nevertheless, even in the United States power has drifted to the executive. The president speaks with one voice, Congress with many. Congress is fragmented into committees and subcommittees—with chairpersons vying for media attention—and this delays and often prevents agreement. Congress expects and even demands presidential leadership and usually gives presidents most of what they want after some controversy and debate.

Another structural problem appeared when a sixty-vote minimum to pass anything important in the Senate became the norm. Senate rules allow a member

pork barrel
Government projects aimed at legislators' constituencies, also called earmarks.

log rolling
Legislators mutually supporting each other to get pork-barrel bills passed.

Democracy

Pork-Barrel Politics

Legislators everywhere ensure their reelection by looking after their districts. Projects that bring improvements to or spend money in their district are called **pork barrel**, after the gifts of plantation owners to their slaves of a barrel of pickled pork parts. Under the politer label "earmarks," these programs include highways, bridges, flood control, military contracts, and farm subsidies. The U.S. pork barrel always took second place to the Japanese, whose legislators are famous for delivering massive (and often unneeded) public-works projects to their districts and shielding farmers from competition.

Congress banned earmarks in 2010, and pork dropped by 98 percent. Some sneak by informally or as "softmarks" introduced by someone other than the district's Congressperson. Individual legislators support others' favorite projects so their projects will get support, a process called **log rolling**: "You help roll my log, and I'll help roll yours." Republicans long denounced Democratic pork but did not resist it when they controlled Congress. Legislators do whatever

gets them reelected, and that usually includes projects in their constituencies. If the United States and Japan wish to really end pork, they would have to break the close connection between elected representatives and home districts. But this connection is precisely what these democracies prize. Would you want a system in which congresspersons are distant and uncaring about their districts?

Without pork as a persuader, much good and important legislation does not pass, one explanation for the deadlocked Congress. Earmarks have been likened to little bribes to get legislators to support the White House budget and bills. Even Republicans used pork to get things done. Earmarks were only about 0.5 percent of the U.S. federal budget, so not much was saved by eliminating them. Do not get angry at a fact like earmarks; instead, analyze it. Why does it exist? What functions does it serve? You may find that it is built into the system and cannot be fixed. Some propose bringing pork back.

to declare a "filibuster" (without even speaking) to block legislation, which can be ended only with a vote of "cloture" (closure) by three-fifths of the Senate, now sixty members—hard to reach when the parties are so polarized. The average annual number of filibusters went from 3.2 in the 1950s to 16.5 from 1981 to 2004 to more than one hundred since. Anything forty-one Senators do not like, they can block. The Founding Fathers intended that a simple majority (now fifty-one, possibly fifty with the vice president voting) be needed to pass laws, but now sixty are usually needed. This seriously alters the Constitution, paralyzes Congress, and turns the United States into a "vetocracy" where the smaller party blocks majority rule. On the other hand, some argue that the filibuster protects minority rights and prevents rash decisions favored by the majority.

Overspending

The tendency of most legislatures to overspend is built into their situation. In the abstract, they are all for a balanced budget. When it comes to their pet interests—usually linked to getting reelected—they like spending increases. New bridges and highways, military hardware, and farm subsidies often directly benefit their constituents (see box on "Pork-Barrel Politics"). Paying for prescription drugs under Medicare shows they hear the cries of senior citizens. Rationally, individual self-interests drive the system as a whole to overspend, allegedly something nobody wants. What's good for the individual is not

aggregate
Thing or population considered as a whole.

necessarily good for the **aggregate**.

At various times, the U.S. Congress tries to restrain itself. In 1985, Congress attempted to hand the power to limit spending to an appointed congressional official. The Supreme Court threw it out as unconstitutional. Congress then attempted to hand the power to the White House with the 1996 "line-item" veto, a major shift in power from the legislative to the executive. The Supreme Court threw it out; the Constitution does not permit the veto of part of a bill. It was almost as if Congress said, "We give up; we're too divided. So here, Mr. President, you take over our constitutional duties." The astonishing thing about the U.S. Congress, the last Mohican of independent parliaments, is that it *wants* to surrender power to the executive.

The Republicans who took over both houses in 1994 were determined to end deficits by setting "spending caps." The caps were evaded almost immediately, but an economic boom provided unforeseen tax revenues and budget surpluses by the turn of the millennium. Quickly, the limits were forgotten as both Republicans and Democrats put forward their pet spending projects. With the end of the boom, the 2001 tax cut, two wars, and the mammoth financial bailouts of 2008 and 2009, revenues shrank and deficits soared. As the baby boom generation retires, spending will only go up. In control of both houses, Republicans swear they will cap spending, but they also demand major defense-spending increases.

Incomprehensible Legislation

Laws keep getting longer and harder to understand. The average U.S. law passed in 1948 was two and a half pages; now the average is twenty pages. The 2010 Affordable Care Act (termed "Obamacare" by some Republicans) took 2,400 pages, plus far more explanations and regulations. President Bush's 2001 No Child Left Behind education act tops 1,000 pages. No one, on Capitol Hill or the Internal Revenue Service, fully understands the tax code, which is several feet thick. Tax accountants laugh every time Congress "reforms" the tax code; they just make it worse and create more business for the tax accountants.

Few Congresspersons read the bills; they lack the time. Instead, they rely on brief, partisan reports to tell them how to vote. Many are later surprised at what they voted for. Citizens are even more baffled; many are disgusted with the whole legislative process, one reason Congress's repute is so low. And the U.S. Congress is not the only culprit; worldwide, many laws are overly complex.

Modern society, economy, and medical care are complex, so legislation cannot be short and simple. But too complex means practically no one can understand it. This happens chiefly because legislators and lobbyists get rewarded by slipping provisions, often unrelated, into bills on behalf of donors and clients. As German Chancellor Bismarck quipped in the nineteenth century, you don't want to know what goes into the making of laws and sausages.

Lack of Expertise

Few legislators are experts on technical, military, economic, or social problems. Of the 535 senators and representatives in both houses of Congress, typically more than half are lawyers. (Tocqueville in the 1830s first noted the tendency of U.S. politicians to be lawyers.) European parliaments have fewer lawyers and more schoolteachers, journalists, and full-time party officials. But hardly anywhere are technical experts elected to legislatures, and few legislators are professionally equipped to deal with such matters as intelligence estimates, medical care, reckless lending, and environmental pollution. Accordingly, legislators must rely chiefly on experts from the executive departments. Much legislation originates with these specialists, and they are often called as witnesses to committee hearings. The ensuing legislation usually grants these executive specialists considerable discretion in applying the law.

Most parliaments have little or nothing in the way of independent research support; their data come either from the government or from private interest groups. Only the U.S. Congress—again, based on the idea of separation of powers—can generate its own data. The Government Accountability Office (GAO, formerly the General Accounting Office), Congressional Research Service (CRS), and Congressional Budget Office (CBO) are all part of the legislative branch. They provide independent evaluations and data to lessen Congress's dependence on the executive. No other legislature in the world has a fraction of this research capability, which still cannot counterbalance the massive information advantage of the executive branch.

Psychological Disadvantages

Citizens everywhere are more impressed with presidents or prime ministers than with parliaments. There may be a deep human need to respond to a single chief. A president can have charisma, but a legislature cannot. American children are socialized to revere the president but to disdain members of Congress. Even in parliamentary systems, voters now respond to the personalities of the candidates for prime minister. Television, by giving much more air time to chief executives than to other political figures, heightens this tendency. People come to see their president or prime minister as a parental figure, calmly guiding the country toward safety while the silly parliamentarians squabble among themselves. This leads to what some political scientists fear is "president worship." By comparison, legislatures speak with a divided voice with one party pointing out the flaws of the other. With the parties denigrating one another, it is no wonder the public doesn't typically approve of the whole. Disagreements within the executive are not usually aired publicly.

The Absentee Problem

If you visit a legislature in session, you might be disappointed, for usually the chamber is nearly empty. Most of the time, most members need not be present, and they aren't. They have many other things to do: helping and visiting constituents, talking with interest groups, and sitting on committees. Why bother listening to speeches? They will not change anyone's vote, and everyone knows their content in advance. The speeches are for the mass media.

Absent most of the time, the member is really needed only to vote and sometimes not even then. British party whips can get a high turnout for an important vote. In Sweden, an electronic system summons members from all over the Riksdag after the speeches are over. They press their *ja* or *nej* button according to their parties' wishes, glance up at the electronic tabulation (which was never in doubt), and then leave. The Riksdag chamber has been full for fewer than 10 minutes (photo on p. 228).

Most systems have ways of recording members' votes without their presence. When the French National Assembly votes, a few members of each party move down the rows of absent fellow party members' desks and flick their voting switches to a *pour* or *contre* position, as the party has commanded. The press then reports that the measure passed by a vote of around 300 to 200, but that is deceptive, as often only three dozen members were present. Theoretically, the French system could function with just one member present from each party.

The U.S. House and Senate require members to be present to vote, but even if absent they can arrange to have their votes "paired against" that of another absent legislator with the opposite viewpoint. The yes vote cancels out the no vote, so the passage of the measure is unaffected, and the member can still claim to have voted for or against something.

What is the impact of legislative absenteeism? It may indicate that the legislator is busy doing other important things. It may also indicate just plain laziness. But it surely means that legislators no longer regard legislating as their chief function. By their absence they admit that they are not important, at least not in the way originally intended. Is there any way to fix the problem? Only by weakening party discipline and party-line voting so that no one could predict how a vote would go. If bills were up for grabs, some excitement and tension would return to floor debate, and members would have an interest and incentive to show up and participate. The trade-off would be that the passage of legislation would be more chaotic and unpredictable.

Lack of Turnover

In democratic parliaments, members tend to become career, lifetime legislators. Once elected, they usually get reelected as long as they wish to serve. This means little fresh, young blood enters parliament with new ideas, and on average parliamentarians are in their fifties. In U.S. House contests, more than 90 percent of incumbents seeking reelection win. Incumbency brings terrific advantages: gerrymandered districts, name recognition, favors done for constituents, media coverage, and plentiful campaign funds from corporations and interest groups. Unless representatives are tarred by scandal, they almost cannot lose. Challengers are so discouraged that several dozen House incumbents run unopposed. In many other contests, opposition is only token. Why waste time and money in a hopeless race?

What happens to democracy when elected representatives stay until retirement? It loses some of its ability to innovate and respond to new currents in public opinion. It gets stodgy. The Founding Fathers made the House term deliberately short, just two years, to let fresh views wash into the chamber. Alexander Hamilton described the frequent elections to the House in this way: "Here, sir, the people govern. Here they act by their immediate representatives." He could not imagine that turnover is actually higher in the Senate, a chamber designed to be insulated from mass passions. All this raised the question of limits on congressional terms, which some promised but few practiced. Once in power, they modestly discover that they are the only ones who can truly serve their constituents.

Parliamentary systems have similar problems. Few legislators are replaced by elections, and most consider their membership in parliament a career. In proportional representation systems, the more senior party people are higher up on the party list, ensuring their election. Young newcomers may be entered at the bottom of their party lists with scant chance of winning. However, PR systems do have the advantage of letting new, small parties into parliament with fresh faces and new ideas. In the 1980s, the Greens (ecology parties) entered several West European parliaments, forcing the big, established parties to pay attention to environmental problems.

The Dilemma of Parliaments

What Russia has gone through recently illustrates the dilemma of parliaments. In the 1990s, Russia experienced a deadlock between President Boris Yeltsin and the Russian legislature, the Duma. To get things done, power must be concentrated in the hands of a powerful executive. To keep things democratic, however, power must be dispersed, that is, divided between an executive and a legislature. Russia urgently needed vast reforms—the economy teetered on the brink of collapse—but the Duma, dominated by Communists and nationalists who opposed Yeltsin, disputed and blocked reforms. Putin solved the problem by founding his own party, which now controls two-thirds of the Duma's seats. Putin owns parliament, but Russia is no longer a democracy.

Even in the United States, Congress works as intended only when dominated by the party opposed to the president, what is called "divided government," something many voters prefer. Philosopher John Locke was right: Parliaments are the foundation of democracy. But worldwide their functions have atrophied and power is flowing to chief executives.

Review Questions

1. How did parliaments first come to be?

2. What is the difference between presidential and parliamentary systems?

3. Why does the U.S. Congress overspend?

4. What is executive-legislative "deadlock"?

5. What good is a bicameral legislature in a unitary system?

6. Do legislatures originate the laws they pass?

7. Is the "pork barrel" necessary for the system to work?

8. Have legislatures declined in importance? Why?

Key Terms

absolutism, p. 229
administration, p. 231
aggregate, p. 242

apartheid, p. 240
backbencher, p. 233
bicameral, p. 235

Bundesrat, p. 236
Bundestag, p. 235
cabinet, p. 231

Further Reference

Brady, W. David, and Craig Volden. *Revolving Gridlock: Politics and Policy from Jimmy Carter to George W. Bush,* 2nd ed. Boulder, CO: Westview, 2005.

Copeland, Gary W., and Samuel C. Patterson, eds. *Parliaments in the Modern World: Changing Institutions.* Ann Arbor, MI: University of Michigan Press, 1994.

Deering, Christopher J., and Steven S. Smith. *Committees in Congress,* 3rd ed. Washington, DC: CQ Press, 1997.

Dodd, Lawrence C., and Bruce I. Oppenheimer, eds. *Congress Reconsidered,* 10th ed. Washington, DC: CQ Press, 2012.

Draper, Robert. *Do Not Ask What Good We Do: Inside the U.S. House of Representatives.* New York: Free Press, 2012.

Hayes, Michael T., and Lou Frey Jr., eds. *Inside the House: Former Members Reveal How Congress Really Works.* Lanham, MD: University Press of America, 2001.

King, Anthony. *Running Scared: Why America's Politicians Campaign Too Much and Govern Too Little.* New York: Free Press, 1997.

Laver, Michael, and Norman Schofield. *Multiparty Government: The Politics of Coalition in Europe.* New York: Oxford University Press, 1990.

Lijphart, Arend, ed. *Parliamentary versus Presidential Government.* New York: Oxford University Press, 1992.

Mann, Thomas E., and Norman J. Orenstein. *It's Even Worse Than It Looks: How the American Constitutional System Collided with the New Politics of Extremism.* New York: Basic Books, 2012.

Mayhew, David R. *Congress: The Electoral Connection,* 2nd ed. New Haven, CT: Yale University Press, 2004.

Miller, Kristina C. *Constituency Representation in Congress: The View from Capitol Hill.* New York: Cambridge University Press, 2010.

Polsby, Nelson W. *How Congress Evolves: Social Bases of Institutional Change.* New York: Oxford University Press, 2005.

Rawls, W. Lee. *In Praise of Deadlock: How Partisan Struggle Makes Better Laws.* Baltimore, MD: Johns Hopkins University Press, 2009.

Shapiro, Ira. *The Last Great Senate: Courage and Statesmanship in Times of Crisis.* New York: PublicAffairs, 2012.

Wolfensberger, Donald R. *Congress and the People: Deliberative Democracy on Trial.* Baltimore, MD: Johns Hopkins University Press, 2000.

Chapter 13
Executives and Bureaucracies

 Learning Objectives

13.1 Compare and contrast presidents and prime ministers.

13.2 Evaluate the charge that the U.S. presidency has become too powerful.

13.3 Contrast cabinet ministers in parliamentary systems with departmental secretaries in the U.S. system.

13.4 Consider the thesis that bureaucratization is inevitable.

13.5 Explain with examples how bureaucracy can become pathological.

Blocked at every turn by congressional Republicans who hated him, President Obama turned to techniques developed by a long line of presidents of both parties—use existing laws and powers to bypass Congress. Republicans charged Obama with exceeding constitutional limits on presidential power, but Nixon, Reagan, and both Bushes had done the same with Republican approval. Constitutional challenges to it seldom work because hundreds of laws allow the president to issue "executive orders" to fill in the details, make exceptions, and go slow on enforcement.

It was an old problem—one at the heart of the 1776 American Revolution—how to keep executives from amassing so much power they could rule without legislatures. The Republicans were right to worry about a too-powerful presidency, but a major rollback is unlikely. Presidents, faced with economic and security threats, refuse to be paralyzed by what President Truman first called a "do-nothing Congress." Economic and technological change in a continent-sized republic mean we can no longer get by with the minimal governance the U.S. Founding Fathers had in mind for the thirteen largely rural original states. The Founders had an ingenious solution for the time: a legislative branch that would check and balance a potentially abusive executive. But, in an unstoppable trend, executives have become more powerful than legislatures. Furthermore, some political scientists see another trend: Within the executive branch, power is shifting from elected officials to bureaucrats. There is no simple cure for these two trends.

There have been executives a lot longer than there have been legislatures. Kings and emperors appeared with the dawn of civilization; only recently have they had legislatures to worry about. Indeed, the word *government* in most of the world means the executive branch. In Europe, *government* equals *cabinet*. The "Cameron government" is just another way of saying Prime Minister David Cameron's cabinet plus some additional subcabinet assistants. In the United States (and increasingly in some other countries), this configuration is called the *administration*. What Americans call "the government," meaning all of the bureaus and bureaucrats, is known in the rest of the world as the **state**.

state
In Europe, all branches of the national political system; what Americans call "the government."

Presidents and Prime Ministers

13.1 **Compare and contrast presidents and prime ministers.**

Two terms that sound almost alike often confuse students. A *head of state* is theoretically the top leader but often has only symbolic duties, such as the queen of England or king of Sweden. These monarchs represent their nations by receiving foreign ambassadors and giving restrained speeches on patriotic occasions. In republics, their analogues are presidents, some of whom are also little more than figureheads. The republics of Germany, Italy, and Israel, for example, have presidents as heads of state, but they do little in the way of practical politics. (They are also not well known. Can you name them?)

The *chief of government* is the real working executive, called prime minister, premier, or chancellor. They typically also head their parties, run election campaigns, and guide government. In Britain, this is Prime Minister David Cameron, in Germany Chancellor Angela Merkel. The United States combines the two offices—our president is both head of state and chief of government.

In parliamentary systems, a national legislature indirectly elects a chief executive from its own ranks, a prime (originally meaning "first") minister. Such parliaments serve as electoral colleges that stay in session to consider legislation. They can also oust a prime minister and cabinet by a vote of no confidence, although this is now rare. Still, prime ministers are responsible to parliament. If they represent a party with a majority of seats, they are secure in office and can get legislative programs passed quickly and with little backtalk. A British prime minister with a sizable and disciplined majority in the Commons wields powers that might make a U.S. president jealous.

If no party has a majority, however, a government is formed by a *coalition* of parties, each of whom gets one or more ministries to run. Sometimes the coalition partners quarrel over policy and threaten to split up. This weakens the hand of the prime minister, as he or she knows that any major policy shift could lead to new quarrels. It is not quite right to say that prime ministers are "weaker" than presidents in presidential systems; it depends on whether prime ministers have a stable majority in parliament.

A presidential system bypasses this problem by having a strong president who is not dependent on or responsible to a parliament but is elected on his or her own for a fixed term. The U.S. Congress may not like the president's policies and may vote them down, but it may not vote out the president. The U.S. president and Capitol Hill stand side by side, sometimes glaring at each other, knowing that there is nothing they can do to get rid of each other. It is sometimes said that presidents are "stronger" than prime ministers, and in terms of being able to run the executive branch for a fixed term, they are. But they may not be able to get vital new legislation or budgeting out of their legislatures. This "**deadlock** of democracy," the curse of the U.S. political system, parallels parliamentary *immobilism*. Neither system can guarantee cooperation between legislative and executive. Any system that could would be a dictatorship.

deadlock
In presidential systems, executive and legislative branches blocking each other (current term: *gridlock*).

"Forming a Government" in Britain

Great Britain is the classic of parliamentary systems, one in which we still see its historical roots. The monarch, currently Queen Elizabeth II, formally invites the leader of the largest party in the House of Commons—usually just after an election—to become prime minister and "form a government," meaning take office with a cabinet. The prime minister appoints two dozen **ministers** and a greater number of subcabinet officials. All are members of Parliament (MPs) and mostly from the prime minister's party, usually chosen to represent significant groups within the party. Theoretically, the prime minister is *primus inter pares*

minister
Head of ministry, equivalent to U.S. departmental secretary.

(first among equals) and guides the cabinet to consensus. But the prime minister is the chief and can dismiss ministers. Ministers who oppose government policy are expected not to go public but to resign and return to their seats in Commons. Recently, the British cabinet mostly concurs on decisions the prime minister has reached earlier with a few advisors, on the American pattern.

"Constructive No Confidence" in Germany

The **chancellor** of Germany is as strong as a British prime minister. The chancellor, too, is head of the largest party in the lower house (Bundestag). Once in the office, the chancellor can be ousted only if the Bundestag votes in a replacement cabinet. This is called "constructive no confidence," and it has contributed to the stability of Germany's governments. It is much harder to replace a cabinet than just oust one; as a result, constructive no confidence has succeeded only once, in 1982, when the small Free Democratic Party defected from the Social Democrat–led coalition to the opposition Christian Democrats. A prime minister with constructive no confidence is more powerful than one without it, as one might see in a comparison of the average tenures of Italian and German cabinets (several months as compared with several years).

chancellor
Germany's prime minister.

"Cohabitation" in France

President Charles de Gaulle of France (1958–1969) designed a semipresidential system that has both a working president and a prime minister (as have Russia and China). The president was elected directly for seven years (now reduced to five) and a parliament elected for five years. If both are of the same party, there is no problem. The president names a like-minded **premier**, who is the link between president and parliament. The 1993 Russian constitution incorporated a French-style system with both president and premier, and it produced executive-legislative deadlock, no longer the case under Putin, who controls both the executive and the Duma. In China, the head of the Communist Party is also the president; under him a prime minister carries out day-to-day operations.

premier
France's and Italy's prime ministers.

In 1986 and again in 1993, though, a French Socialist president, François Mitterrand, with two years left in his term, faced a newly elected parliament dominated by conservatives. The constitution gave no guidance in such a case. Mitterrand solved the problem by naming opposition Gaullists as premiers and letting them dismantle many Socialist measures. Mitterrand reserved for himself the high ground of foreign policy. The French called the arrangement "cohabitation," like an unmarried couple living together. In 1997, the reverse happened: Gaullist President Jacques Chirac called parliamentary elections early, lost them, and had to face a Socialist-dominated National Assembly. The solution was cohabitation again; Chirac named Socialist chief Lionel Jospin as premier. Cohabitation works, and the French accept it. France thus handled the problem of deadlock that is common in the United States.

Democracy

Israel's Directly Elected Prime Ministers

In 1996, Israelis, under a new law, elected a parliament and a prime minister *separately and directly*, something never before done in the world. Each Israeli voter had two votes: one for a party in the legislature and one for prime minister. By definition, parliamentary systems elect prime ministers indirectly, usually the head of the largest party in parliament, while presidential systems directly elect their chief executives. So, Israel turned from purely parliamentary to presidentialism, but not all the way. The **Knesset** could still vote out the prime minister on a motion of confidence, and coalition cabinets were as hard to form as ever.

Even worse, Israeli voters, figuring that selection of prime minister was taken care of by one ballot, used the other to scatter their votes among a dozen small parties, making the Knesset even more fractionated. After two unhappy tries of the unique hybrid system, the Knesset repealed it in 2001. The experiment showed that halfway borrowings from one system (presidential) into another (parliamentary) do not work. If you want stability, go all the way to presidentialism.

Knesset
Israel's 120-member unicameral parliament.

The "Presidentialization" of Prime Ministers

Parliamentary systems tend to "presidentialize" themselves. Prime ministers with stable majorities supporting them in parliament start acting like presidents, powerful chiefs only dimly accountable to legislators. They know they will not be ousted in a vote of no confidence, so the only thing they have to worry about is the next election, just like a president. This tendency is strong in Britain and Germany. (Japan, whose faction-ridden parties produce mostly weak and short-lived prime ministers, shows little such tendency.)

Increasingly, elections in parliamentary systems resemble presidential elections. Technically, there is no "candidate for prime minister" in parliamentary elections. Citizens vote for a party or a member of parliament, not for a prime minister. But everybody knows that the next prime minister will be the head of the largest party, so indirectly they are electing a prime minister. For these reasons, virtually all European elections feature posters and televised spots of party chiefs as if they were running for president. As in U.S. elections, personality increasingly matters more than policy, party, or ideology.

Executive Terms

Presidents have fixed terms, ranging from four years for U.S., Brazilian, and Nigerian presidents (they can be reelected once) to a single six-year term for Mexican presidents. French and many other presidents can be reelected without limit. Putin changed Russia's two four-year terms to two six-year terms, repeatable after an interval out of office. When presidents are in office a long time, even if "elected," they often become corrupt and dictatorial, as President Robert Mugabe did in three decades at Zimbabwe's helm, even as the country's economy collapsed.

Democracy

Putin's Authoritarianism

Vladimir Putin (president 2000–2008 and again in 2012, prime minister in between) used democratic-looking moves to consolidate authoritarian power. The 1993 Russian constitution, which set up a de Gaulle-type semipresidential system, tilted power to the presidency; Putin made it even stronger. He had been a **KGB** colonel and headed the post-Soviet equivalent, the Federal Security Service (FSB in Russian). Unstable President Yeltsin plucked Putin from obscurity and named him his fifth prime minister in seventeen months.

Some thought Putin would be another temporary, but he pulled what amounted to a KGB coup. He used his police sources—detailing who had robbed what—to keep and expand his power. With Russia in steep decline, the unpopular Yeltsin in late 1999 handed over the presidency to Putin, who was easily elected to it in 2000, 2004, and 2012. He set up his own United Russia Party, which won most of the Duma seats.

Putin pulled Russia out of a climate of despair and immediately became popular. Russians like a strong hand at the top, and Putin continually strengthened his. He brought the energy industry and television back under state control, waged war against Chechens, and cracked down on uncooperative regional governors and the "oligarchs"—people who had gotten rich fast through insider privatization deals.

Putin called his system "managed democracy," staffed with KGB comrades—the *siloviki*, the "strong men." He paid little attention to the Duma, where few opposed him. Some who criticized Putin were arrested or assassinated, but few Russians cared when the economy was good, thanks to oil and natural-gas revenues.

In 2008, Putin pulled a bold switch: He named an obedient protégé, Dmitri Medvedev, to be elected president and accepted, by prearrangement, the prime ministership. Putin "demoted" himself but stayed in charge and set things up to return to the presidency four years later. Playing to Russian nationalism, Putin made himself even more powerful and popular with his thinly disguised invasion of Ukraine in 2014.

In parliamentary systems, prime ministers have no limits on their tenure in office, provided their party wins elections. As noted, increasingly their winning depends on the personality of their leader, almost as if they were presidential candidates. Britain's Margaret Thatcher was elected for a third time in 1987, but by 1990 her mounting political problems persuaded her to resign after eleven years in office. German Chancellor Helmut Kohl won four elections in a row and served sixteen years (1982–1998). Most prime ministers can **dissolve** parliament when they wish, namely, when they believe they'll do best in elections. A good economy, sunny weather, and high ratings persuade prime ministers to call elections a year or two early. Powers such as these might make an American president jealous.

On the other hand, British prime ministers can get ousted quickly if they lose the support of a majority of parliament. When Labour Prime Minister James Callaghan, head of a *minority government*, lost the support of the eleven Scottish Nationalist MPs in 1979, he slipped below a majority in Commons and was replaced overnight by **Tory** chief Thatcher. Some Italian premiers have held office only briefly as their coalitions disintegrated. Japanese prime ministers, the playthings of powerful faction chiefs within the two large parties, have recently averaged only about a year in office. Theoretically, prime ministers can serve a

KGB
Soviet Committee on State Security, powerful intelligence and security agency.

dissolve
Send a parliament home for new elections.

Tory
Nickname for British Conservative.

Classic Works

Lasswell's Psychology of Power

Harold Lasswell of Yale introduced concepts from Freudian psychology into political science. In his 1936 classic *Politics: Who Gets What* and other works, Lasswell held that politicians start out mentally unbalanced and that they have unusual needs for power and dominance, which is why they go into politics. Normal people find politics uninteresting. If Lasswell is right, many executives should be removed from office, and only people who don't want the job should be elected. This is the kind of analysis that cannot be applied in practice; it is fascinating but useless.

It was Plato who first wrote that even sane people who become too powerful in high office go crazy. They've got to, as they can trust no one. They imagine, probably accurately, that they have many enemies, and they amass more and more power to crush these real and imaginary foes, thus creating even more enemies. It's an insightful description of Hitler and Stalin. According to Plato, tyrants must go insane in office; there's no such thing as a sane tyrant. The problem is not personal psychology but the nature of a political office that has grown too powerful. The solution, if Plato is right (and we think he is), is to limit power and have mechanisms to remove officeholders who abuse it. In the U.S. system, the threats of electoral defeat and impeachment tend to keep the presidency and its occupants healthy.

long time; in practice, their tenure depends on political conditions such as elections, coalition breakups, and scandals. Parliamentary systems practice a kind of easy-come, easy-go with their prime ministers, something an American president would dislike. Presidents in presidential systems are partially insulated from the ups and downs of politics. In his second term, for example, President Obama's popularity sagged, but there was no way to oust him until his term expired.

impeachment
President indicted by the House and tried by the Senate.

A U.S. president can face **impeachment**, but this is a lengthy and uncertain procedure that has been attempted only three times. Andrew Johnson was impeached by the House in 1868 but acquitted in the Senate by one vote. Richard Nixon was about to be impeached by the House but resigned just before the vote. Bill Clinton was impeached but not convicted. If a problem character becomes chief executive, parliamentary systems have a big advantage over the U.S. system—a simple vote of no confidence and the rascal is out. This helps explain why, even though there are many scandals in parliamentary systems, few have the opportunity to become as big and paralyzing as Watergate.

Executive Leadership

13.2 Evaluate the charge that the U.S. presidency has become too powerful.

Back to back, America saw two distinct leadership styles. President Carter (1977–1981) was a hands-on, detail person; he tried to supervise much of his administration. With intelligence and energy, he put in long hours and memorized much data. Critics, including management experts, say this is the wrong

Democracy

An Imperial Presidency?

"The accumulation of all powers, legislative, executive, and judiciary, in the same hands," James Madison wrote in *The Federalist* no. 47, "may justly be pronounced the very definition of tyranny." Checks and balances, John Adams declared, are like "setting a thief to catch a thief." In recent years, however, many fear that the modern presidency has amassed power and overturned the checks and balances of the constitution.

Congress and the presidency no longer balance (maybe they never did). Samuel Huntington noted that from 1882 to 1909, Congress initiated 55 percent of significant legislation; between 1910 and 1932, the figure dropped to 46 percent; and from 1933 to 1940, Congress initiated only 8 percent of all major laws. The legislative function, said Huntington, "has clearly shifted to the executive branch."

As the Vietnam War wound down and Watergate boiled up, historian Arthur Schlesinger Jr. captured the worried feeling of the time in his book *The Imperial Presidency.* Lyndon Johnson had taken the country to war without a declaration of war. Richard Nixon had expanded that war into Laos and Cambodia, again with no declaration. Nixon also "impounded" **appropriations** made by Congress; he simply refused to spend funds in certain areas, in effect exercising an illegal item veto. Was the president overstepping constitutional bounds? Was America becoming an imperial presidency, going the way of ancient Rome, from republic to rule by Caesars?

Congress attempted to reassert some of its authority, passing the War Powers Act in 1973 and moving toward impeachment of Nixon the following year. It looked like the beginning of a new era, with Congress and the president once again in balance.

But this failed to happen, for the U.S. system *needs* a strong president to function properly.

When Jimmy Carter took office in 1977, he attempted to deimperialize the presidency, but this led to an ineffective White House. As an outsider, Carter was ignorant of the ways of Washington and quickly alienated a Congress dominated by his own party. His legislation stalled on Capitol Hill and was diluted by amendments, especially his energy proposals. By the 1980 election, much of the American electorate and Congress wished for a more forceful and experienced chief executive.

Congress's reassertion of independent authority in the 1970s proved brief, for with the arrival of Ronald Reagan in the White House in 1981, the president once again commanded Capitol Hill. In 1986, it was revealed that officials of the president's National Security Council bypassed Congress in selling arms to Iran and using the money to fund the overthrow of the Nicaraguan government. Even Reagan's supporters in Congress turned angry and grilled his appointees in committee hearings. Once again, a Congress disappointed with executive misuse of power tried to check the executive branch it had repeatedly invested with enormous powers.

With the terrorist attacks of 2001, Congress gave even more powers to the executive branch. Bush 43 advisors argued a "unitary executive theory" that gives the president essentially unlimited power to safeguard the country, including warrantless wiretaps, imprisonment and trial outside of normal courts, and "aggressive interrogation techniques." As he signed new laws, Bush issued more than 800 "signing statements," telling Congress that he would enforce this law as he saw fit. Critics feared the unitary executive theory was a step toward one-man rule.

---

approach and that chief executives only scatter and exhaust themselves if they try to run everything.

President Reagan (1981–1989) was a hands-off president, preferring to set the broad course and leaving the details to trusted subordinates. He took afternoon naps and frequent vacations. Critics say Reagan paid no attention to crucial matters, letting things slide until they turned into serious problems. The

appropriation
Government funds voted by legislature.

Y axis
The vertical leg of a graph.

X axis
The horizontal leg of a graph.

line graph
Connection of data points showing change over time.

Iran-contra fiasco showed what happens when subordinates get only general directions and go off on their own. The National Security Council staff thought it was doing what the president wanted when it illegally sold arms to Iran and illegally transferred the profits to the Nicaraguan contras.

Can there be a happy middle ground between hands on and hands off? Some say President Eisenhower (1953–1961) achieved it by appearing to be a hands-off president with a relaxed style. Princeton political scientist Fred Greenstein, however, analyzed Eisenhower's schedule and calendar and concluded that he was a very active president who made important and complex decisions but did

Methods

Graphs

Thanks to computers, graphs are easy and colorful but sometimes misused. A bunch of numbers does not necessarily make a good graph. The numbers should display some pattern. If upward, you would show the growth of something; if up and down, you would show cycles. We could do a longitudinal study of the growth of Washington-based interest groups taking them over 30 years, from 1970 to 2010. Our hypothesis is that they grow over time.

We can either have the computer set up a graph or do it with paper and a ruler. First, draw a big "L." The upright leg is the **Y axis**, on which you draw a scale, usually from zero to a little more than the highest number we find, say 2,937, plus a little more to make it 3,000. Divide that scale into increments of whatever interval fits the study. It might be every 5 percent or every $5,000 per capita GDP or every hundred interest groups. A metric ruler can make drawing scales easier.

Now take the horizontal leg, the **X axis**, and mark off steps from 1970 to 2015. Measuring rightward from the Y axis, mark with a dot the number of interest groups above the year on the X axis. For easier readability, you may connect the dots (or have the computer do it), thus making a **line graph**.

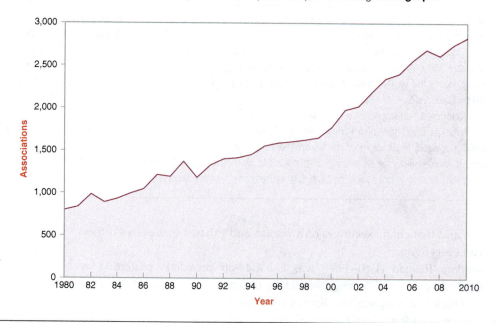

not show it, preferring to let others take the credit (and sometimes the blame). Greenstein called it the "hidden-hand presidency." In 1954, for example, faced with sending U.S. forces to help the French in Indochina, Eisenhower called top senators to the White House. He knew they would be cautious for we had just ended the unpopular Korean War. The senators opposed sending U.S. forces, and Eisenhower went along with their view. Actually, he never wanted to send troops, but he made it look as if the senators had decided the issue.

President Franklin D. Roosevelt (1933–1945) used a style that some call deliberate chaos. Setting up numerous agencies and advisers, some of them

bar graph
Stand-alone data points comparing categories.

If the line generally rises (and it will always have some ups and downs), you have demonstrated your thesis: Interest groups keep growing in Washington. If the line trends downward, alter your thesis, now stating a decline of D.C.-based interest groups (unlikely). And if the line is generally flat, neither trending up nor down, change your thesis to match your findings.

If you want to compare how two or more things change over time (covariance), you could use different-colored lines, say, blue for the percent Democratic vote in Altoona, PA, and red for size of the railroad workforce in Altoona, to show how both decline at about the same rate. (Unionized workers tend to vote

Democrat.) Pie charts are not very useful; use them to show popular preferences in pies.

Not every graph should be a line graph. The zigzags of line graphs show change over time but are meaningless for comparing categories at the same time. For that, use a **bar graph**. A line graph indicates that one data point sets the stage for the next; a bar graph does not. If you want to show change over time, say, percent voting Republican over several elections, use a line graph. If you want to show differences between items at the same time, say, voting differences among income levels in the 2016 election, use a bar graph.

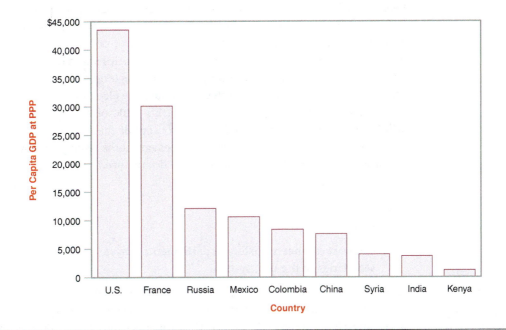

working at cross-purposes, Roosevelt would let them clash. The really difficult and important decisions would reach his desk; the others would be settled without him. This, too, was a kind of middle ground between hands on and hands off. The Clinton White House borrowed this spontaneous and creative approach, but Clinton participated personally in many policy deliberations in a more hands-on manner. Obama was noted for his keen intellect and balanced decisions but also for the long time he took to make decisions; a readiness to dilute and compromise; and loose, uncoordinated management.

The Danger of Expecting Too Much

In both presidential and parliamentary systems, attention focuses on the chief executive. Presidents or prime ministers are expected to deliver economic growth with low unemployment and low inflation. They are expected to keep taxes low but government benefits high. They are held responsible for anything that goes wrong but told to adopt a hands-off management approach and delegate matters to subordinates. The more problems and pressure, the more they have to delegate.

How can they do it all? How can they run the government, economy, subordinates, and policies? They cannot, and increasingly they do not. Instead, the clever ones project a mood of calm, progress, and good feeling to try to make most citizens happy. President Reagan was a master of this tactic. The precise details of governance matter little; they are in the hands of advisers and career civil servants, and few citizens care about them. What matters is getting reelected, and for this personality counts for more than policy, symbols more than performance.

Worldwide, power has been flowing to the executive, and legislatures have been in decline. The U.S. Congress has put up some good rear-guard actions, but it too has been in slow retreat. Some observers have argued that this cannot be helped and that several factors make this shift of power inevitable. If true, what can we do to safeguard democracy? Democracies still have a trump card, and some say it is enough: electoral punishment. As long as the chief executive, whether president or prime minister, has to face the electorate at periodic intervals, democracy will be preserved. Friedrich's "rule of anticipated reactions" will keep them on their toes. Perhaps the concept of checks and balances was a great idea of the eighteenth century that does not fit the twenty-first. Maybe we will just have to learn to live with executive dominance.

Cabinets

13.3 Contrast cabinet ministers in parliamentary systems with departmental secretaries in the U.S. system.

ministry
Major division of executive branch; equivalent to U.S. department.

Chief executives are assisted by cabinets. A cabinet member heads one of the major executive divisions of government called a *department* in the United States and a **ministry** in most of the world. The former is headed by a *secretary* and the latter by a *minister*. Cabinets range in size from a compact fifteen in the United States to twenty or more in Europe.

The United States enlarges its cabinet only slowly and with much discussion for it takes an act of Congress and the provision for the related department's budget. For most of its history, the United States had fewer than ten departments. Health and Human Services, Housing and Urban Development, Transportation, Energy, Education, Veterans Affairs, and Homeland Security were added only since the 1960s. In Europe, chief executives add, delete, combine, and rename ministries at will; their parliaments routinely support it. In the 1980s, for example, most West European governments added environmental ministries. The U.S. Environmental Protection Agency stayed at the sub-cabinet level, and environmental responsibilities were divided between it and several other departments.

What is the right size for a cabinet? That depends on how the system is set up and what citizens expect of it. The United States has been dedicated to keeping government small and letting the marketplace make decisions. When this led to imbalances—for example, bankrupt farmers, unemployed workers, and collapsed businesses—the U.S. system added the Departments of Agriculture, Labor, and Commerce. The Department of Energy was added after the "energy shocks" of the 1970s. Slowly, U.S. cabinets have been creeping up to European size.

Who Serves in a Cabinet?

In parliamentary systems like those of Britain and Germany, ministers are drawn from parliament and keep their parliamentary seats. They are both legislators and executives. Usually they have had years of political experience in winning elections and serving on parliamentary committees. The chair of Germany's Bundestag defense committee, for example, is a good choice to become defense minister. In a presidential system like that of the United States or Brazil, secretaries or ministers are generally not working politicians but businesspersons, lawyers, and academics. They may have some background in their department's subject area, but few have won elective office. President Bush 41 named four members of Congress to his cabinet; Presidents Clinton and Obama named three each. This made U.S. cabinets look a bit European, but the secretaries had to first resign their seats in Congress.

Which is better, a cabinet member who is a working politician or one from outside government? The elected members of European parliaments who become ministers have a great deal of both political and subject-area knowledge. They know the relevant members of parliament personally and have worked closely with them. Ministers and parliament do not view each other with suspicion, as enemies. The ministers are criticized in parliament but from the opposition benches; their own party generally supports them.

Outsiders appointed to the cabinet, the traditional U.S. style, may bring with them fresh perspectives, but they may also be politically naive, given

Classic Works

American Paranoia

In 1964, historian Richard Hofstadter wrote his celebrated essay "The Paranoid Style in American Politics" to explain the right-wing takeover of the Republicans and their nomination of hawkish Barry Goldwater. More generally, the work pointed to a persistent tendency in U.S. politics, the "sense of heated exaggeration, suspiciousness, and conspiratorial fantasy." With this comes a belief in evil empires out to get us, "a conflict between absolute good and absolute evil."

The paranoid then aims at "total triumph," whatever it may cost. This, wrote Hofstadter, leads to

impossible goals, but failure to reach them "heightens the paranoid's sense of frustration," and he redoubles his efforts. Only traitors and weaklings criticize; they must be denounced and ignored. The media are branded cowardly and defeatist. Some critics claimed the paranoid tendency appeared in the Bush 43 administration. Actually, paranoia is an ever-present danger in all regimes, especially those with no checks on power, such as Stalin's, Hitler's, and Saddam Hussein's.

to brash statements and unrealistic programs that get them in trouble with Congress, where members of their own party do not necessarily support them. Their lack of political experience in the nation's capital leads to another problem.

In the United States especially, the cabinet counts for less and less. A cabinet meeting serves little purpose and takes place rarely. Few Americans can name three or more cabinet members. Why has the cabinet fallen into such neglect? Part of the problem is that few cabinet secretaries are well-known political figures. And their jobs are rather routine: Get more money from Congress to spend on their department's programs. Cabinet secretaries are in charge of administering established programs with established budgets, "vice presidents in charge of spending," as Coolidge's Vice President Charles G. Dawes called them. Presidents generally rely on advisors on their staff for political and policy decisions rather than cabinet secretaries, who often become advocates of the bureaucratic agencies they head, lobbying the president and his staff. As such, they are not consulted on much. They are largely administrators, not generators of ideas.

Bureaucracies

13.4 Consider the thesis that bureaucratization is inevitable.

bureaucracy
The *career* civil service that staffs government executive agencies.

The term **bureaucracy** has negative connotations: the inefficiency and delays citizens face in dealing with government. The great German sociologist Max Weber, who studied bureaucracy, disliked it but saw no way to avoid it. A bureaucracy is any large organization of appointed officials who implement laws and policies. Ideally, it operates under rules and procedures with a chain of command or *hierarchy* of authority. It lets government operate with some rationality, uniformity, predictability, and supervision. As Stanford political scientist Francis Fukuyama argues, the early founding of effective bureaucracies builds strong, prosperous states. Corrupt bureaucracies permanently retard their nations' development.

Initially and for centuries, officials were simply relatives of the king and nobles. They treated their jobs as private property to enrich themselves. In much of the world, this is still true. Ancient China initiated the first nationwide merit-based bureaucracy, in which **mandarins** were selected by rigorous competitive exams based on Confucius and other classics. Like a modern civil service, mandarins were arrayed hierarchically in ranks, usually nine. Some argue that Confucius invented the very notion of good governance, one that strove for stability and prosperity, centuries before European thinkers.

mandarin
Official of imperial China, schooled in Confucianism.

Another definition of bureaucracy—or "civil service"—is that it is the *permanent* government. Much of what we have studied might be called the "temporary government" of elected officials who come and go. The **career** civil servants often spend their working life with one agency. They take orders from elected officials, but they also follow the law and do things "by the book." They usually know a lot more about their specialized areas than their new politically appointed boss, who wants to redo the system with bold, new ideas. The bureaucrats, who have seen bold, new ideas come and go, move with caution. A bureaucracy, once set up, is inherently conservative, and trying to move it is one of the hardest tasks of politicians.

career
Professional civil servant, not political appointee.

Bureaucracy comes automatically with any large organization, public or private. In the Middle Ages, when European states were weak balances of feudal powers, the Roman Catholic Church had a complex and effective administrative system. Through a hierarchy of trained people who spent their life in the

Classic Works

Weber's Definition of Bureaucracies

Max Weber (1864–1920) was the first scholar to analyze bureaucracy. His criteria for defining bureaucracy included the following:

1. Administrative offices are organized in a hierarchy.
2. Each office has its own area of competence.
3. Civil servants are appointed, not elected, on the basis of technical qualifications as determined by diplomas or examinations.
4. Civil servants receive fixed salaries according to rank.
5. The job is a career and the sole employment of the civil servant.

6. The official does not own his or her office.
7. The official is subject to control and discipline.
8. Promotion is based on superiors' judgment.

Weber felt he was studying a relatively new phenomenon. Some of the above characteristics could be found in classic China, but not all. Like the nation-state, bureaucracies started in Western Europe around the sixteenth century but were reaching their full powers, which Weber distrusted, only in the twentieth century.

Church, authority flowed from the pope down to the parish priest. Until they developed their own administrators in the Renaissance, kings depended on clerics, who were among the few who could read and write. Armies also have bureaucratic structures, based on the military chain of command and myriad regulations.

The United States

Fewer than 15 percent of American civil servants are federal. Of our 21.5 million civil servants, some fifteen million are employed by local governments, four million by state governments, and only 2.8 million (not counting military personnel) by the federal government. Remember, most government services—schools, police, and fire protection—are provided by local governments.

The United States was later than Europe in establishing a merit-based civil service. American politicians used patronage appointments to reward political supporters. Fukuyama argues that this is what happens when democracy starts earlier than the establishment of a rational, merit-based bureaucracy. Only the 1883 Pendelton Civil Service Reform Act required competitive examinations for federal jobs. State and local patronage jobs, the basis of political machines, lingered into the twentieth century.

The fifteen current U.S. cabinet departments (George Washington started with four) employ between 85 and 90 percent of all federal civil servants. They share a common anatomy. Each is funded by Congressional appropriations and headed by a secretary appointed by the president (with the consent of the Senate). The undersecretaries and assistant secretaries are also political appointees and, thus, in Weber's definition are not bureaucrats. This differs from most other systems, where officials up through the equivalent of our undersecretaries are permanent civil service.

Bureaucracies may be more important in innovating laws than the public or Congress. A prominent example was the fight to place health warnings on cigarette packages and in advertisements. Congress would never have moved by itself because the tobacco industry is generous to candidates. Change came via a branch of the bureaucracy—public-health specialists and statisticians equipped with computer models. In 1965, the Advisory Committee on Smoking and Health and the surgeon general (the nation's chief public health officer) presented solid data that cigarette smoking increased lung cancer and shortened lives. The report built public pressure on Congress, which in 1966 had cigarette manufacturers print warnings on all packs, and in 1969 the FCC banned cigarette advertising on radio and television.

The departments carry out legislative and executive policies whose details are often unclear. Most laws are general and let the department establish specific working policy, so experts can tune policy. Bureaucrats have a lot of knowledge, and knowledge is power. The Reagan administration said it would abolish the Department of Energy (DOE). One of the authors of this book asked a friend, an official of the department, why he wasn't worried. "They won't abolish us," he asserted knowingly. "They can't. DOE manufactures nuclear bombs, and the administration needs the DOE budget to disguise how big the nuclear-bomb budget is." Reagan did not abolish the DOE. The U.S. bureaucracy is relatively small and light compared with many other countries. Europe and Latin America, with their strong statist traditions, have more bureaucracy and regulation than the United States.

Communist Countries

The Soviet Union was one of the world's most bureaucratic nations, and that was one of the causes of its undoing. Tied to the Communist Party, the Soviet civil service was corrupt, inefficient, and unreformable. According to Marxist theory, a dictatorship of the proletariat had no need for Western-style bureaucracy, but immediately after the 1917 revolution the Soviets instituted strict bureaucratic management, and Stalin increased it with his **Five-Year Plans** in the 1930s.

Top Soviet bureaucrats, the **nomenklatura**, were a privileged elite, often the most energetic and effective. They got nice apartments, special shops, and country houses. At the top of each ministry was a minister, who was a member of the Council of Ministers (roughly equivalent to a Western cabinet), the highest executive authority that was made up of high-ranking party members, some of whom were also members of the party's Politburo. Trusted party members were placed in subordinate positions to carry out party policy. This made the Soviet bureaucracy conservative, an obstacle no Soviet president could overcome.

In China, too, all officials, called **cadres**, are party members and the backbone of the Communist system. The party is supposed to fight corruption, but China's administration is dangerously decentralized to the provincial and local levels, leaving officials free to collect bribes and fake "taxes" and to transfer land from peasants to developers. Major riots break out in China every year over such corruption, the system's Achilles heel. Since 2012, corruption among high officials—many stashed millions in overseas banks—has shaken the regime. The Communist Party's Central Commission for Discipline Inspection has broad powers to demote or expel party members or send cases to criminal courts, where some are sentenced to death. Party chief and President Xi Jinping swore to root out corruption and had the Discipline Inspection investigate higher cadres, even in Beijing. It is difficult to end all corruption in China, however, because the cadres are precisely the people the regime depends on to run the country.

France

In the seventeenth and eighteenth centuries, France set the pattern for most of Europe with its highly bureaucratized state. After the French Revolution destroyed the monarchy, Napoleon restored central control by the bureaucracy and made it more rational and effective. Napoleon, with the *intendants* of Richelieu as his model, created the *prefects* to carry out government policy in each **département**.

Five-Year Plans
Stalin's plans for rapid, centrally administered Soviet industrial growth.

nomenklatura
Lists of top Soviet positions and those eligible to fill them, the Soviet elite.

cadre
In Asian Communist systems, party members serving as officials.

département
Department; main French territorial subunit, now numbering 96.

Top French civil servants are now graduates of one of the "Great Schools," such as the Ecole Polytechnique, an engineering school, or, since World War II, the Ecole Nationale d'Administration, created to train government officials. The instability of the Third (1871–1940) and Fourth (1947–1958) Republics increased the bureaucracy's power because it had to run France with little legislative or executive guidance. France is still heavily bureaucratic, and centralization is often extreme.

Germany

Junker
(Pronounced: YOON-care) Prussian state nobility.

Prussia and its ruling class, the **Junkers**, put their stamp on German administration. Obedient, efficient, and hard-working, the aristocratic Junkers were a state nobility, dependent on Berlin and controlling all its higher civil service positions. Frederick the Great of Prussia, who ruled from 1740 to 1786, had a passion for effective administration and established universities to train administrators. Germany unified in 1871 under Prussia's leadership, which brought Prussian culture, namely loyalty to nation and emperor, to much of Germany. One of the reasons the short-lived Weimar Republic (1919–1933) failed was because the civil-servant class had only contempt for democracy. With the coming of the Third Reich, most flocked to Hitler.

The current German government has a strongly federal structure that puts most administration at the *Land* level. Today's German civil servants are committed to democracy. A section of Berlin's interior ministry, for example, in cooperation with *Land* agencies, does educational programs to fight political extremism. Generally trained in law—throughout Europe law is at the undergraduate level—German bureaucrats tend to bring with them the mentality of Roman law, that is, law neatly organized into fixed codes rather than the more flexible U.S. and British common law.

Britain

Britain, unlike France, has strong traditions of local self-government and dispersion of authority. This pattern of administration is an outgrowth of the Anglo-American emphasis on representative government, which encourages legislative control of administrative authorities. During the nineteenth century, the growth of British government at the local level also encouraged the dispersion of administrative authority; it was not until the twentieth century that the central government began to run local affairs. Until the 1854 Northcote-Trevelyan reforms, the bureaucracy was rife with corruption and nepotism. Positions in the bureaucracy (including military commissions) were openly bought and sold. By 1870, earlier than in the United States but later than in most of Europe, a **merit civil service** based on competitive examinations had been established.

merit civil service
One based on competitive exams rather than patronage.

British ministers are accountable to Parliament, but real bureaucratic power is in the hands of the career "permanent secretary" and the career deputy secretaries, undersecretaries, and assistant secretaries who serve at lower ranks. Thus, even though the British and American bureaucracies share the same tradition of decentralized authority, control over the bureaucracy is tighter in Britain than in America. British bureaucrats pride themselves on being **apolitical** and claim to faithfully carry out the ministry's policies, whichever government is in power.

apolitical
Not interested or participating in politics.

Japan

Japan is an extreme example of rule by bureaucrats. Modeled on the French civil service by the Meiji modernizers in the 1870s, Tokyo's ministries were always powerful. Before, during, and after World War II, the same bureaucrats were in charge, boosting economic growth by guided capitalism rather than the free market. Japan's bureaucrats view elected officials as clowns who should be ignored.

The key Tokyo ministries are finance; economy, trade, and industry; agriculture; and construction. They guide their respective sectors by arranging loans, subsidies, and government contracts. Top Japanese bureaucrats are often graduates of Tokyo University (nicknamed "Todai"), Japan's most selective. Many civil servants retire young to go into lush jobs in the industries they supervised, called "descent from heaven."

Tokyo's ministries are self-contained and do not cooperate with each other or seek the good of the whole, provoking some to say that in Japan "no one is in charge." The ministry supervises its specific economic sector, which mostly obeys the ministry. The minister is a political appointee, usually a member of the Diet, but the **vice minister**, who really runs things, is a career civil servant, much like a British "permanent secretary."

vice minister
Civil servant who directs a Japanese ministry.

The most famous ministry was **MITI**, the brains of Japan's export mania that set economic growth records after World War II and suggested Japanese guided capitalism as a model for others. Since the 1990s, however, the Japanese economy has been flat, and bureaucratic supervision was blamed for industrial overexpansion, money-losing investments, bankrupt banks, and the world's highest consumer prices. A new generation of Japanese politicians is now trying to reform their bureaucracies and bring them under democratic control.

MITI
Japan's Ministry of International Trade and Industry (now METI).

The Trouble with Bureaucracy

13.5 Explain with examples how bureaucracy can become pathological.

The world does not love bureaucracy. The very word is pejorative. In France and Italy, hatred of the official on the other side of the counter is part of the political culture. Americans like to hear candidates denounce "the bureaucrats"—allegedly meddlesome, overpaid (especially in pensions), and unfireable—but none ever solve the problem because at least some regulation is necessary, and someone has to run the day-to-day operations of government. Politicians don't have the incentives or the inclination to do so. Incoming U.S. administrations, particularly Republican, vow to bring business-type efficiency to public administration

Theories

Bureaucratic Politics

Some political scientists argue that struggles—often behind the scenes—among and within bureaucracies contribute to or even control policy decisions. Bureaucrats provide the information on which top officials depend. Whoever controls information controls decisions, goes the theory. America's many bureaucracies gather, analyze, and disseminate information in different ways, often quarreling among themselves.

Harvard's Graham Allison found that the 1962 Cuban missile crisis turned on when the photographic evidence of Soviet missiles in Cuba arrived at the White House. It had been delayed because the Air Force and Central Intelligence Agency quarreled over who should pilot the U2 spy plane. Competition among agencies and "standard procedures" created the informational world in which Kennedy and his advisors operated. With a widely read 1969 article, Allison founded the **bureaucratic politics** model, which political science briefly embraced.

Control of information became a hot issue with 9/11 and the 2003 U.S. invasion of Iraq. Before 9/11, the FBI and CIA did not share information, partly due to legal restrictions. The Department of Homeland Security, formed in 2002, combined 22 existing agencies but did not solve the problem, as the FBI and CIA are not part of it. Department of Defense (DoD) analysts claimed to have solid evidence that Iraq had weapons of mass destruction (WMD) and was sponsoring terrorism. State Department and CIA analysts were cautious, saying evidence was unclear. DoD prevailed, making war a certainty. No WMD were found after the war. Furthermore, State, claiming that it had the expertise, drew up plans for the occupation of Iraq after the war. DoD ignored State and its plans. The result was a chaotic occupation and great anger in the State Department.

The bureaucratic politics model is still not persuasive because the president really is in charge and often has strong personal preferences in advance and decides which agency to listen to. In 2003, President Bush had long hated Iraq, and DoD told him that Iraq was guilty. DoD even had a special staff to make the case for attacking Iraq; it excluded evidence to the contrary. By structuring bureaucracies, the White House created the informational world it preferred. Washington bureaucracies played a blame game for 9/11 and Iraq's WMD—several top CIA people resigned—but it was more a question of how these agencies were used. Bureaucrats mostly obey.

---

bureaucratic politics
Infighting among and within agencies to set policy.

productivity
The efficiency with which goods or services are produced.

by drastic deregulation of private industry and trimming the number of bureaucrats. One result was that no one said no to Wall Street's reckless loans and investments. Efficiency, profitability, and **productivity** are hard to apply in government programs. Bureaucracies have a momentum, making cuts to most programs like Social Security or Medicare impossible.

At its worst, bureaucracy can show signs of "Eichmannism," named after the Nazi official who organized the death trains for Europe's Jews and later told his Israeli judges that he was just doing his job. Nazi bureaucracy treated people like things, a problem not limited to Germany. On the humorous side, bureaucracy can resemble Parkinson's Law: Work expands to fill the staff time available. Parkinson never called himself a humorist, and many who have worked in featherbedded, purposeless, paper-shuffling agencies confirm Parkinson's Law.

Bureaucracy and corruption are intertwined. Wherever officials carry out rules, some are bent for friends and benefactors. The more regulations, the more bureaucrats, the more corruption. A few countries with a strong ethos of public service—Denmark and New Zealand, for example—have been able to maintain incorrupt public administration. Most countries are corrupt, some a little and some egregiously. Chile became the least corrupt Latin American country by cutting the amount of administration and number of bureaucrats. Under the argument that only specialists from private industry can monitor that industry, businesses often "capture" or "colonize" administrative agencies. Financiers were placed atop the U.S. Securities and Exchange Commission. They gutted its regulatory role and let it march to the 2008 financial meltdown. It should be noted, however, that political appointees, not career civil servants, made these dangerous decisions.

Early theorists of bureaucracy assumed that professional bureaucrats would never make public policy but merely carry out laws. Indeed, nonpartisan administration was the original motivation behind merit civil services, but most nations have administrators who make policy and are not publicly accountable. Japan shows this to an extreme. Making bureaucracies flexible, creative, and accountable is one of the great tasks of this century.

Review Questions

1. Is power shifting first to executives and then to bureaucrats?

2. Why have prime ministers become more like presidents?

3. Is the U.S. presidency too powerful?

4. What are the various styles of presidential leadership? What is the current president's style?

5. Explain Lasswell's psychology of political power.

6. Are cabinets as important as they used to be?

7. Must every large organization be bureaucratic?

8. How did Max Weber characterize bureaucracy?

9. Why is it hard for a government to control bureaucrats?

Key Terms

apolitical, p. 265
appropriation, p. 255
bar graph, p. 257
bureaucracy, p. 260
bureaucratic politics, p. 266
cadre, p. 263
career, p. 261
chancellor, p. 251
deadlock, p. 250
département, p. 263

dissolve, p. 253
Five-Year Plans, p. 263
impeachment, p. 254
Junker, p. 264
KGB, p. 253
Knesset, p. 252
line graph, p. 256
mandarin, p. 261
merit civil service, p. 264
minister, p. 250

ministry, p. 258
MITI, p. 265
nomenklatura, p. 263
premier, p. 251
productivity, p. 266
state, p. 249
Tory, p. 253
vice minister, p. 265
X axis, p. 256
Y axis, p. 256

Further Reference

Ackerman, Bruce. *The Failure of the Founding Fathers: Jefferson, Marshall, and the Rise of Presidential Democracy.* Cambridge, MA: Harvard University Press, 2005.

Baker, Peter. *Days of Fire: Bush and Cheney in the White House.* New York: Doubleday, 2013.

Burke, John P. *The Institutional Presidency: Organizing and Managing the White House from FDR to Clinton,* 2nd ed. Baltimore, MD: Johns Hopkins University Press, 2000.

Cheibub, José Antonio. *Presidentialism, Parliamentarianism, and Democracy.* New York: Cambridge University Press, 2007.

Ghaemi, Nassir. *A First-Rate Madness: Uncovering the Links Between Leadership and Mental Illness.* New York: Penguin, 2011

Greenstein, Fred. *Inventing the Job of President: Leadership Style from George Washington to Andrew Jackson.* Princeton, NJ: Princeton University Press, 2009.

Helms, Ludger. *Presidents, Prime Ministers and Chancellors: Executive Leadership in Western Democracies.* New York: Palgrave, 2005.

Jones, Charles O. *The American Presidency.* New York: Sterling, 2009.

Jreisat, Jamil E. *Comparative Public Administration and Policy.* Boulder, CO: Westview, 2002.

Kerwin, Cornelius M., and Scott R. Furlong. *Rulemaking: How Government Agencies Write Law and Make Policy,* 4th ed. Washington, DC: CQ Press, 2010.

Lindblom, Charles E. *The Policy-Making Process,* 3rd ed. Englewood Cliffs, NJ: Prentice Hall, 1992.

Maraniss, David. *Barack Obama: The Story.* New York: Simon & Schuster, 2012.

Maranto, Robert, Tom Lansford, and Jeremy Johnson, eds. *Judging Bush.* Stanford, CA: Stanford University Press, 2009.

Miklis, Sidney M., and Michael Nelson. *The American Presidency: Origins and Development,* 7th ed. Washington, DC: CQ Press, 2015.

Morris, Irwin L. *The American Presidency.* New York: Cambridge University Press, 2010.

Neustadt, Richard E. *Presidential Power and the Modern Presidents: The Politics of Leadership from Roosevelt to Reagan.* New York: Free Press, 1991.

Nye, Joseph. *Presidential Leadership and the Creation of the American Era.* Princeton, NJ: Princeton University Press, 2013.

Peters, Guy. *Politics of Bureaucracy: An Introduction to Comparative Public Administration,* 6th ed. New York: Routledge, 2009.

Pika, Joseph A., and John Anthony Maltese. *The Politics of the Presidency.* 8th ed. Washington, DC: CQ Press, 2013.

Poguntke, Thomas, and Paul Webb, eds. *The Presidentialization of Politics: A Comparative Study of Modern Democracies.* New York: Oxford University Press, 2005.

Rudalevige, Andrew. *The New Imperial Presidency.* Ann Arbor, MI: University of Michigan Press, 2005.

Savage, Charlie. *Takeover: The Return of the Imperial Presidency and the Subversion of American Democracy.* New York: Little, Brown, 2007.

Wills, Gary. *Bomb Power: The Modern Presidency and the National Security State.* New York: Penguin, 2010.

Wilson, James Q. *Bureaucracy: What Government Agencies Do and Why They Do It.* New York: Basic Books, 1990.

Chapter 14
Judiciaries

⌄ Learning Objectives

14.1 Distinguish among the several types of law.

14.2 Compare and contrast common law and code law.

14.3 Contrast the conduct of Anglo-American and European trials.

14.4 Explain judicial review and how it originated in the United States.

14.5 Review the changes brought about by the Warren Court.

When the United States gets stuck over a controversial issue—usually something a divided Congress cannot solve—it turns to the courts. In 2010, Congress passed the Affordable Care Act (ACA)—dubbed "Obamacare" by its critics. Republicans claimed it was unconstitutional because it required citizens to purchase health insurance. (Romney's 2006 Massachusetts healthcare law requires the same.) In 2012, the Supreme Court ruled 5–4 that requiring payment was constitutional (under the power to tax). Most Republicans were furious, but none suggested defying the Court's decision.

law
That which must be obeyed under penalties.

The United States prides itself on "rule of law." One indication of this is the number of American lawyers—281 for every 100,000 people, as compared with 94 in England, 33 in France, and only 7 in Japan. **Law** plays very different roles in these systems. America's legions of lawyers express the country's ethos of freedom and competitive individualism. In few other countries does the "little person" have our ability to sue the powerful. Many Americans complain that we have too many lawsuits, but few would accept a Japanese system where citizens are expected simply to obey government and corporations. Law without lawyers means law administered by bureaucrats. If you want freedom under law, you must have lots of lawyers.

Types of Law

14.1 **Distinguish among the several types of law.**

positive law
That which is written by humans and accepted over time—the opposite of natural law.

We focus on positive law, which is written and compiled by humans over the centuries. Unlike natural law (see box), **positive law** uses law books to reach decisions. Our complex society requires many types of law, of which there are five major branches.

Criminal Law

plaintiff
The person who complains in a law case.

With 2.3 million people (0.7 percent of all adults) in U.S. jails, the criminal law system is the one we hear most about. Modern criminal law is largely statutory and covers a specific category of wrongs that are considered social evils and threats to the community. Consequently, the state, rather than the victim, is the prosecutor, or **plaintiff**. Offenses are usually divided into three categories. Petty offenses, such as traffic violations, are normally punished by a fine. Serious but not major offenses such as gambling and prostitution are misdemeanors, punishable by larger fines or short jail sentences. Major crimes, felonies, such as rape, murder, robbery, and extortion, are punished by imprisonment. In the United States, some criminal offenses such as kidnapping and interstate car theft are federal; others, such as murder and robbery, are mainly state concerns; and a few, such as bank robbery and drug trafficking, are both.

Civil Law

Many statutes govern civil rather than criminal matters. In most English-speaking countries, **common law** supplements statutory law in civil cases. Marriage and divorce, inheritance, contracts, and bankruptcy are civil concerns. **Civil law** provides redress for private plaintiffs who can show they have been injured. The decisions are in dollars, not in jail time. Private individuals, not the state, conduct most civil litigation. Some cases can be pursued as both criminal and civil cases, as when the federal government accuses investment houses of wrongdoing and investors who lost money sue them.

common law
"Judge-made law," old decisions built up over the centuries.

civil law
Noncriminal disputes among individuals.

Constitutional Law

Written constitutions are usually general documents. Subsequent legislation and court interpretation must fill in the details. An important role of U.S. courts, under our system of judicial review, is to make sure that statutory laws and administrative usages do not violate the Constitution. Judicial review is America's great contribution to governance, and since World War II most democracies added some sort of judicial review.

In the United States, the ultimate responsibility of interpreting the Constitution rests with the U.S. Supreme Court, and this means that laws change over time: The Constitution is what the Supreme Court says it is. In 1896, for example, the Court ruled in *Plessy v. Ferguson* that state laws requiring racial segregation in public transportation did not necessarily violate the Fourteenth Amendment, which provides for equal protection under the laws, as long as the transportation facilities for whites and African Americans were physically equal. In *Brown v. Board of Education of Topeka* (1954), the court reversed itself and ruled that separate public schools for whites and African Americans are *inherently* unequal, even if physically alike. The Constitution had not changed, but society's conception of individual rights did. **Constitutional law** (indeed, law itself) is not static but a living, growing institution.

constitutional law
That which grows out of a country's basic documents.

Administrative Law

A relatively recent development, administrative law covers regulatory orders by government agencies. It develops when agencies interpret statutes, as they must. For example, federal statute prohibits "unfair or deceptive acts" in commerce. But what business practices are "unfair"? The Federal Trade Commission must decide. As the agencies interpret the meaning of Congress's laws, they begin to build up a body of regulations and case law that guides the commission in its future decisions. These rulings may be appealed to the federal courts. The federal government now codifies administrative regulations, and they fill many volumes.

International Law

International law (IL) consists of treaties and established customs recognized by most nations. It is different because it cannot be enforced in the same way as national law: It has some judges and courts, but compliance is largely voluntary. IL is generally observed because it is in the interests of most countries not to break it. IL's key mechanisms are **reciprocity** and **consistency**. Countries like being treated nicely, so they must extend the courtesy to others. They also do not like being accused of applying different standards to various countries, so they try to keep their dealings consistent. Some IL is enforced by national courts. The U.S. Supreme Court has ruled that U.S. states have to observe international treaties that the United States has ratified. A U.S. business harmed abroad can seek redress in U.S. courts against the assets of the foreign firm that did the damage. We mostly study international public law, but international private law is a rapidly growing field as more and more businesses operate globally.

Primitive legal systems are oral and consist of customs and beliefs. Modern legal systems are written and largely codified, that is, systematically arranged. Putting laws in writing makes them more precise and uniform. Codification began in ancient times and has been a major feature in the development of civilization. The Ten Commandments and the Code of Hammurabi were early law codes, but the great ancient code was Roman law. Its details, covering all aspects of social life and based on "right reason," were so universal, flexible, and logical that they are still in use in much of the world today. Roman law

reciprocity
Mutual application of legal standards.

consistency
Applying the same standards to all.

higher law
That which comes from God.

natural law
That which comes from nature, understood by reasoning.

Classic Works

The Roots of Law

Higher law is an old concept that grew out of the Christian melding of Greek philosophy with Judeo-Christian thought. Attributed to God or the Creator, it was thus higher than laws made by humans. It is behind the idea that people are "endowed by their Creator" with the rights to life, liberty, and the pursuit of happiness and the right to own property and enjoy the fruits of their labor—rights that no just government can take away. Many argue that higher law takes precedence over laws enacted by humans, and some justify their defiance of ordinary laws by citing it. Mahatma Gandhi in India and Martin Luther King Jr. in the United States claimed that their actions, which violated human-made laws, were moral because they conformed to higher law.

Natural law, developed by medieval Catholic theologians, argues that observing nature reveals God's will. God created life, so ending it is manifestly wrong. You need no law books to tell you that mass murder is evil; just observe nature. Israel's attorney general, in prosecuting Nazi official Adolph Eichmann in 1961, argued from natural law that Eichmann had to know that mass murder is wrong and no amount of Nazi rhetoric could make it right. Rick Santorum, running for the Republican nomination in 2012, showed his Catholic background by arguing from natural law that marriage is for producing children and that abortion is unnatural and therefore ought to be illegal.

was incorporated by the Catholic Church in its canon law and in the East by the Byzantine Emperor Justinian, whose celebrated Code of Justinian (*Corpus Juris Civilis*) of A.D. 533 is the foundation of most of Europe's modern legal systems. Modern European law is based on an amalgamation of Roman, feudal, and church law.

The Courts, the Bench, and the Bar

14.2 Compare and contrast common law and code law.

As legal systems developed, so did judicial systems, for they handle day-to-day administration of the law. Judicial systems are always hierarchical with different courts having specific jurisdictions; that is, they hear different kinds of cases or have authority in specific geographical areas.

The U.S. Court System

The U.S. court system is unique, consisting of fifty-one judicial structures: the national system, comprising the federal courts, and fifty state systems. The federal system overlaps that of the states. The federal courts hear many cases in which the issue is one of state laws but the parties are residents of different states, the so-called "diversity jurisdiction." Also, of course, they hear cases concerning federal laws. Conversely, issues of federal law (constitutional or statutory) may first arise in state courts. The Supreme Court of the United States can review the state court's judgment on a federal question.

THE NATIONAL COURT STRUCTURE   The ninety-four federal district courts form the base of the U.S. national court system. They employ 677 judges and serve as trial courts in civil suits arising under federal law, criminal cases involving federal infractions, and the diversity jurisdiction. Most criminal cases, however, even those involving federal law, are tried in state courts.

Federal district court decisions can be appealed to a U.S. court of appeals. The thirteen courts of appeals, presided over by 179 judges, may also review the rulings of administrative tribunals and commissions, such as the Federal Trade Commission, the Federal Aviation Administration, and the Food and Drug Administration. Each court of appeals consists of three or more judges, depending on need. Panels of three judges hear arguments but rarely question the facts of the case; they consider only whether the law has been misinterpreted or misapplied. The court of appeals bases its majority-vote verdict on the **appeal** primarily on the **briefs** submitted by the attorneys for both parties; oral arguments are limited.

The pinnacle of the federal court system is the U.S. Supreme Court, consisting of one chief justice and eight associate justices. Its jurisdiction is almost entirely appellate, from lower federal or state supreme courts. For example, if a

appeal
Taking a case to a higher court.

brief
Written summary submitted by one side giving relevant facts, laws, and precedents.

state supreme court declares a federal statute unconstitutional, it is likely that the U.S. Supreme Court will hear the case. Unlike a court of appeals, however, it is not obliged to hear every case and accepts only a small fraction of the petitions that it receives. The Court will generally not hear a case unless it involves a substantial constitutional question, a treaty, or some significant point of federal law. Often, the Court hears a case to resolve differing opinions across two or more circuit courts. Because the U.S. system is based on precedent, the Court's ruling *is* national law.

precedent
Legal decisions based on earlier decisions.

canon law
Laws of the Roman Catholic Church, based on Roman law.

THE STATE COURT SYSTEM   Each of the fifty states has its own court systems, and those court systems handle perhaps 90 percent of the nation's legal business. Most of their cases are civil, not criminal. Generally, state trial courts operate at the county level and have original jurisdiction in all civil and criminal cases. In rural areas, justices of the peace try minor matters. In urban areas, magistrate's or police courts do the same. These local courts operate without juries (serious cases go to state courts), and most of their penalties are fines or short jail sentences.

Case Studies

Common Law versus Code Law

The English common law started with the customary usages of Germanic tribal law of the Angles and Saxons who took over England in the third to the fifth centuries. This law stressed the rights of free and equal men and developed on the basis of **precedent** set by earlier judges; it is thus called "judge-made law." After the Normans conquered England in 1066, they decided the local, decentralized nature of this law hindered governance of the country as a whole and set up central courts to systematize the local laws and produce a "common" law for all parts of England. They also added new features, such as trial by jury.

In administering justice, English judges and courts were forced to improvise. Most had a church education and were familiar with **canon law**. Accordingly, when royal law was inadequate, the judges applied canon law. If these were not applicable, they used common sense and the common practices of the English people. Over the centuries, a substantial body of common law developed—an amalgam of Roman law, Church law, and local English customs.

Common law has three distinctive features. First, it is *case* law; that is, it is based on individual legal decisions rather than on a comprehensive code of statutes. Second, common law was made by *judicial decision* and thus has great flexibility. Judges can reinterpret or modify previous rulings and principles to fit new cases. Third, common law relies heavily on *stare decisis* ("let the decision stand"), or precedent. Because no two cases are exactly alike, a judge can point to difference to break precedent. In this way, common law retains a marvelous flexibility. With the rise of Parliament as a dominant institution in seventeenth-century England, *statute* law supplemented and then supplanted much of the common law. Today, when the two conflict, statute law always takes precedence.

Common law has declined in importance but still has influence in England (but not Scotland), the United States (but not Louisiana), Canada, Australia, New Zealand, and a number of former British colonies. Much of statute law is the formal enactment of old common-law provisions. Common law shaped the development of English society and politics and imparted distinctive political habits to America.

The legal systems of continental Europe (France, in particular) developed very differently. As French kings were overturning feudalism in favor of absolutism, legal scholars revived **Roman law** to bolster central government and encourage commerce. French jurists saw the value of Roman law; it was universal, written, worked well for the ancient world, and already known through canon law.

Codifying the law was Napoleon's lasting contribution to French justice and, eventually, to much of the world. His *Code Napoléon* of 1804, the first modern codification of European law, discarded feudal laws and broke civil law away from religious influence. It preserved many of the gains of the French Revolution, such as elimination of torture and arbitrary arrest and imprisonment, civil liberty, and civil equality. Napoleon conquered most of Europe and brought the code with him; Europe's legal systems are still based on it. It is also in use in Louisiana and Asia, Africa, and Latin America. The centralization of French life even to this day is a reflection of its basic philosophy.

Today, much of the world lives under some form of the *Code Napoléon*. Most **code law** is detailed, precise, comprehensive, and understandable by laypersons. Judges are not expected to "make" law, merely to apply it. Precedent carries less weight. The judiciary is not independent of the executive as in the American system. Therefore, its powers of judicial review are limited—either shared with the legislative branch or assigned to a special constitutional court, which most European countries now have, a relatively new feature.

The differences between the common law and code law are marked. The former is general and largely judge-made, and it relies on precedent and custom. The latter is specific and is largely the product of legislation. Both systems developed to serve the needs of modernizing and centralizing monarchs—Henry I and II in England and Louis XIII and Napoleon in France. The two systems, however, are becoming more and more alike. As the volume of statute law increases in the English-speaking nations, the importance and relevance of common law decreases. In both systems, administrative agencies increasingly fill in the details of legislative enactments, producing regulations that are now part of legal systems.

Judges

FEDERAL JUDGES   Federal judges are nominated by the president and must be approved by the Senate. To free them from executive and political pressure, they may serve for life unless impeached. Some federal judges owe their appointments to party affiliation, but most are well qualified. The attorney general lists eligible candidates; as vacancies occur, the president selects a few names from that list. The president considers the reputation-based ratings of prospective judges by the American Bar Association (ABA). Bush 43 discontinued the practice, believing the ABA was too liberal, but Obama resumed it. The FBI checks out each candidate. Senate approval used to be routine but is now highly political. There is also a tradition known as senatorial courtesy where a president defers to a senator's choice from his party when there is an opening for a judicial district in the senator's state. The opposition party accuses the president of trying to fill the **bench** with incompetent partisans and often tries to block confirmation. Under Clinton and Obama, many federal judgeships went unfilled because Senate Republicans rejected nominees as too liberal. In between, Senate Democrats tried to block Bush's choices as too conservative.

Roman law
System based on codes of ancient Rome.

code law
Laws arranged in books, originally updated Roman law.

bench
The office of judgeship.

Some presidents wanted a federal judiciary that was nonpartisan, or at least bipartisan. Eisenhower, for example, appointed some Democrats to the federal bench (including Supreme Court Justice William J. Brennan) and sought a kind of balance. Presidents now, however, appoint judges of their own political party who share their judicial philosophy. President Johnson, for example, appointed Thurgood Marshall—the Court's first African American and a liberal who believed that the Court should take an active role in promoting social justice—to the Supreme Court. President Nixon, in contrast, appointed four conservative justices who believed that the Warren Court of the 1950s and 1960s went too far in protecting the rights of suspects and hampered law enforcement. President Reagan followed the Nixon example with the appointment of conservative Sandra Day O'Connor, the first female on the Court (who later became the Court's moderate swing vote). Five conservative justices really mattered when the Supreme Court refused five to four to prolong Florida vote recounts and thus gave the 2000 presidential election to George W. Bush. Bush 43 appointed conservatives as several vacancies occurred on the Supreme Court. In this way, his conservative legacy lived long after his presidency. President Obama appointed two liberal women justices in an attempt to counterbalance the conservative tilt. Partisan polarization has thus entered even the judicial branch.

STATE JUDGES   State judges are either popularly elected or appointed, for terms ranging up to fourteen years. Both parties often nominate the same slate of judges so that the judicial elections have become largely nonpartisan. California justices are appointed but later have to be confirmed by voters. In Florida, the governor appoints judges from a list given by a bipartisan nomination commission; later, they are subject to a retention vote after they have been on a bench a number of years. Some argue that elected state judges turn into crowd-pleasing politicians with shaky judicial skills. Others counter that appointed state judges can be the governor's political pals. Florida's system tries to balance merit selection with responsiveness to the public.

Comparing Courts

14.3 **Contrast the conduct of Anglo-American and European trials.**

What role should judges play? Should they act as umpires, passively watching the legal drama, just ruling on disputed points of procedure? Or should they actively direct the trial, question witnesses, elicit evidence, and comment on the proceedings? The second pattern strikes Americans as strange and dangerous because we have been raised in the common-law tradition of passive judges. Yet in code-law countries, judges play just such an active role.

The Anglo-American Adversarial and Accusatorial Process

English and American courts are passive institutions that do not look for injustices to correct or lawbreakers to apprehend. Instead, they wait until a law is challenged or a defendant is brought before them. The system operates on an **adversarial** and **accusatorial** basis. In the adversary process, two sides (plaintiff and defendant) compete for a favorable decision from an impartial court. Courts do not accept a case that does not involve a real conflict of interest; the plaintiff must demonstrate how and in what ways the defendant has caused damage. During the trial, the judge acts as an umpire. Both parties present their evidence, call and cross-examine witnesses, and try to refute each other's arguments. The judge rules on the validity of evidence and testimony, on legal procedures, and on disputed points. After both sides have presented their cases, the judge rules on the basis of the facts and the relevant law. If a jury is hearing the case, the judge instructs its members on the weight of the evidence and relevant laws and then almost always accepts the jury's verdict.

> **adversarial**
> System based on two opposing parties to a dispute.
>
> **accusatorial**
> Like *adversarial* but with a prosecutor accusing a defendant of crimes.

In criminal cases, the police investigate and report to a public prosecutor, often a county's district attorney, who must decide whether to prosecute. The actual trial proceeds like a civil one, but the government is the plaintiff and the accused the defendant. Unless a jury has been waived, the jury determines guilt under instructions from the judge on laws and facts. One weakness of the adversarial system—especially when applied in poor, developing countries—is that the decision often goes to the side that can hire the best attorney. Thus, money may tilt the scales of justice. The same is not unknown in the United States, where even though the accused are guaranteed the right to an attorney under the Sixth Amendment to the Constitution, court-appointed public defenders are often overworked and underprepared.

British Courts

Britain's court system was established by the Judicature Act of 1873 and largely continues common-law traditions. It is divided into civil and criminal branches.

SELECTION AND TENURE OF JUDGES British judges are nominally appointed by the monarch, but the choice is really the prime minister's, based on recommendations of the lord chancellor, who presides over the House of Lords and is usually a cabinet member. British judges have lifetime tenure and are above politics. Britain used to have no judicial review but by adopting the European Convention on Human Rights in 2000 finally got a bit of judicial review. Now British judges can review statutes and police conduct using the European Convention as the equivalent of the U.S. Bill of Rights, a major step.

The British judiciary—like most countries' judiciaries, a part of the executive—is not supposed to be a coequal branch of government.

THE LAWYER'S ROLE   The United States and Britain share a common legal heritage but with important differences. One is that in Britain the Crown—meaning the government—hires lawyers to prosecute crimes. There are no professional prosecutors like U.S. district attorneys. American lawyers may take on any type of legal work, in or out of the courtroom, but British *solicitors* handle all legal matters except representing clients in court. That is reserved for a few specialized lawyers called *barristers*.

European Court Systems

Based heavily on the French system—the pattern for much of the world because of the influence of the Code Napoléon—European courts, unlike British courts, do not have separate criminal and civil divisions. Instead, most European countries maintain separate systems of regular and administrative courts. European judges sit as a panel to rule on points of law and procedure, but at the conclusion of the trial they retire with a jury to consider the verdict and the sentence. Obviously, the lay jurors often go along with the superior—or at least professional—knowledge and wisdom of the judges. In some systems, such as the German, a judge either sits alone or with two "lay judges."

investigating judge
In European legal systems, judicial officer who both gathers evidence and issues indictments.

THE EUROPEAN INQUISITORIAL PROCESS   In code-law countries, judges play a more active role than in common-law countries. The prosecutor (French *procureur*, German *Staatsanwalt*) is an official who forwards evidence to an **investigating judge** (*juge d'instruction, Ermittlungsrichter*), a representative of the justice ministry who conducts a thorough inquiry (*enquête*), gathering evidence and statements. Unlike the Anglo-American system, these European magistrates first make a preliminary determination of guilt *before* sending the case to trial. In practice, a U.S. district attorney does much the same in deciding whether to go to trial. French and Italian investigating judges have become heroes by going after corrupt officials. In European criminal procedure, the decision to **indict** is made not by a district attorney but by a judge, and the weight of evidence is not controlled by the adversaries (plaintiff and defendant) but by the court, which can take the initiative in acquiring needed evidence.

indict
Pronounced *in-dite*; to formally charge someone with a crime.

In the U.S. system, the accused is presumed innocent until proven guilty; in Europe, the assumptions are nearly reversed. In an American or British court, the burden of proof is on the prosecution, and the defendant need not say one word in his or her defense; the prosecutor must prove guilt "beyond a reasonable doubt." In code-law countries, the accused bears the burden of having to prove that the investigating judge is wrong.

THE LAWYER'S ROLE   Unlike a British or American trial lawyer, the French *avocat* or German *Rechtsanwalt* does not question witnesses; the court does that. Instead, he or she tries to show logical or factual mistakes in the opposition's argument or case and sway the lay jury in the summation argument. For the most part, the role of the European lawyer is not as vital or creative as that of the American lawyer, for the court takes the initiative in discovering the facts of the case.

Courts in Russia

Russia's post-Communist legal system has continued much of the Soviet legal structure because most personnel were trained under the Communists. Now Russia is struggling to build "rule of law," including "bourgeois" concepts, such as property law and civil rights. In 1991, a Constitutional Court with fifteen justices was established, the first independent tribunal in Russian history. It can theoretically rule on the constitutionality of the moves made by the president and the State Duma. In practice, Russian presidents have so much power—including power over selection of justices—that the court is no counterweight to the executive. Crime is rampant in Russia. Newly rich *biznesmeny* and *siloviki* (strong men) hire *keelers* to remove anyone in their way, including members of parliament, journalists, and the competition. "The only lawyer around here is a Kalashnikov," despaired one Russian, referring to the assault rifle.

The basic concepts of Soviet law and the workings of the Soviet judicial process were quite different from those of the Western democracies, even though

Classic Works

Marbury v. Madison

President John Adams, a Federalist, appointed William Marbury to the post of a Washington justice of the peace shortly before leaving office. For some unknown reason, however, Secretary of State John Marshall did not deliver the commission to Marbury. Marshall's successor, the Republican James Madison, refused to deliver the commission. Marbury brought suit in original jurisdiction before the Supreme Court, asking the Court to issue a writ of *mandamus* commanding Madison to deliver the commission.

This presented the Court with a dilemma. If Chief Justice Marshall and the Supreme Court issued the writ and Madison refused to deliver the commission, the prestige and authority of the Court would be dealt a severe blow. If, however, Marshall refused to issue the writ, he would in effect call into question the legitimacy of the hasty judicial appointments

given to Federalists in the final days of the Adams administration.

Marshall's solution was brilliant, for it not only criticized Madison and Jefferson but also established the principle of judicial review. On the one hand, Marshall ruled that Marbury was entitled to his commission and that Madison should have given it to him. On the other hand, he stated that the Supreme Court had no authority to issue a writ of *mandamus* in a case brought to it in original jurisdiction and that Section 13 of the Judiciary Act of 1789, "an act of the legislature repugnant to the Constitution[,] is void." The decision infuriated President Jefferson, for he understood how cleverly Marshall had escaped the trap and asserted the authority of the Court. He realized that the precedent for judicial review had been laid and called it "both elitist and undemocratic."

they were similar in strictly criminal—as opposed to political—matters. Soviet law started with Marx's idea that law serves the ruling class. Capitalists naturally have bourgeois laws designed to protect private property. Proletarians, theoretically in power in the Soviet Union, had socialist law to protect state property, which belonged to all society. Especially after the relaxation of Stalin's climate of fear, theft of state property became the norm for Soviet economic life and helped bring down the system. Almost nothing was said of private property, which scarcely existed. Another part of Soviet law dealt with sedition and subversion, areas of minor importance in the West. Soviet citizens could receive harsh sentences to Siberia for "antistate activities" or "slandering the Soviet state."

Apolitical cases were generally handled fairly under Soviet law. Prosecutors gathered evidence and brought cases to court but sometimes took into account mitigating social factors and asked for lighter sentences. Defense attorneys were permitted, but they merely advised their clients on legal points and did not challenge the prosecutor's evidence. There were no jury trials. All Soviet judges were Communist Party members.

Some political cases never came to trial. Obedient Soviet psychiatrists diagnosed dissidents as "sluggish schizophrenic" and put them in prisonlike hospitals without trial. (With the Soviet collapse, the disease disappeared.) Nobel Prize-winning writer Alexander Solzhenitsyn was simply bundled onto a plane for Germany in 1974 with no trial. Likewise, dissident physicist Andrei Sakharov was banished to a remote city in 1980 to get him away from Western reporters. The Committee on State Security (KGB) was powerful and often acted independently of courts. The KGB was succeeded by the Federal Security Service (FSB in Russian) and, staffed by old KGB officials, continues the KGB's primary aim: to make sure those in power stay in power. Regime opponents are shot or poisoned, and practically no one is convicted. President Putin graduated in law, served as a KGB officer and head of the FSB, and appointed ex-KGB agents to top positions. Putin used legal-looking procedures to get rid of opponents, who were charged with embezzlement or tax evasion and sent to prison for decades. Rule of law was never established in Russia, and democracy died. The two are closely connected.

The Role of the Courts

14.4   **Explain judicial review and how it originated in the United States.**

Judicial review is more highly developed in the United States than in any other country, and Americans expect more of their courts than do other peoples. In no other country is the "courtroom drama" a television staple because few other countries have our dramatic courtroom clashes.

Court structures in other Western democracies parallel the U.S. system, but they do not do as much. In Switzerland, for example, cases from the cantonal (state) courts may come before the Federal Tribunal, which determines whether a cantonal law violates the Swiss constitution. However, the tribunal does not review the constitutionality of laws passed by the Swiss parliament. The German Constitutional Court reviews statutes to make sure they conform to the Basic Law (the German constitution). The court, located in Karlsruhe, was included in the Basic Law partly on American insistence after World War II; it was a new concept for Europe. It consists of sixteen judges, eight elected by each

scattergram
Graph showing position of items on two axes.

outlier
Item that deviates from its expected position.

Methods

Scattergrams

To show that your numbers form a pattern, you can move beyond a cross-tab and build a **scattergram**, or scatterplot, which turns items into dots on a graph and can make your argument clear. If you have found something worthwhile, these dots will form a pattern—never perfect—showing more clearly than a cross-tab a relationship between two variables. If, on the other hand, the dots scatter randomly over the graph, they demonstrate that there is no pattern or relationship.

The Corruption Perceptions Index (CPI) from Transparency International (TI), a Berlin research group, is a compilation of surveys of international business people asking how much corruption they encounter. It is subjective and imperfect, but objective measures are impossible, as few officials admit to taking bribes. TI rates countries from 100 (squeaky clean) to 1 (totally corrupt). The scattergram in the figure below displays

per capita GDP on the X (horizontal) axis and the CPIs on the Y (vertical) axis.

Your computer can draw a "line of best fit" (sometimes curved). In this case, it runs about from Haiti to Canada. Most dots are not too far from the line, demonstrating that, very generally, the wealthier a country, the less corrupt it tends to be. However, there are some **outliers**, countries far from the line. Chile, with a third of the income per capita of rich countries, is unusually clean. Italy, Japan, and France—where scandals are standard—are more corrupt than their wealth suggests they ought to be. And the biggest outlier might be the United States. To explain the outliers, you would study their histories, institutions, and political cultures. For example, how does the extreme localness of U.S. governance—as in the powers of counties and school boards—contribute to corruption in America? The outliers frequently tell the most interesting stories.

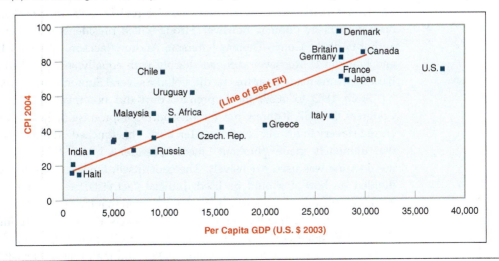

house of parliament, who serve for nonrenewable twelve-year terms. The court decides cases between states, protects civil liberties, and outlaws dangerous political parties. Its decisions have been important. In the 1950s, it found that both neo-Nazi and Communist parties wanted to overthrow the constitutional order and declared them illegal. It found the 1974 abortion bill was in conflict with the strong right-to-life provisions of the Basic Law. Because Germany's Constitutional Court operates within the more rigid code law, its decisions do not have the impact of U.S. Supreme Court decisions, which under the common law are literally the law of the land.

The U.S. Supreme Court

The U.S. Supreme Court's power to review the constitutionality of federal legislative enactments is not mentioned specifically in the Constitution and has been vehemently challenged. Judicial review was first considered and debated at the Constitutional Convention of 1787. Delegates suggested that, when in doubt, legislators might call on the judges for an opinion on a proposed law's constitutionality. James Madison stated that a "law violating a constitution established by the people themselves would be considered by the judges as null and void." However, those who feared that such a power would give the Court a double check and compromise its neutrality challenged this position. Others felt it would violate the separation of powers. Elbridge Gerry (who, in 1812, originated the gerrymander) stated that it would make "statesmen of judges," a prophetic remark. At the close of the convention, judicial review had not been explicitly provided for.

Alexander Hamilton, however, argued in *The Federalist* No. 78 that only the courts could limit legislative authority. John Marshall, chief justice of the Supreme Court from 1801 to 1835, agreed with this position; in fact, he went on record in favor of it nearly fifteen years before *Marbury v. Madison* (1803), the landmark decision establishing judicial review. The doctrine has never been universally popular, however. Strong-willed presidents have resisted the authority of the Court. Thomas Jefferson, Andrew Jackson, Abraham Lincoln, and Franklin D. Roosevelt differed sharply with equally strong-willed judges. Barack Obama made clear that he did not like several Supreme Court decisions.

From 1803 to 1857, the Supreme Court did not invalidate any act of Congress. In 1857, it threw out the Missouri Compromise of 1820, which had barred slavery in the old Northwest Territory. This touched off a political storm that ultimately made Abraham Lincoln president. In the twentieth century, the doctrine was used extensively. The court itself, however, has always been divided on how it should be used. Judicial "activists," led by Hugo Black, William O. Douglas, and Earl Warren, have argued that the Supreme Court must be vigilant in protecting the Bill of Rights. Advocates of judicial "restraint," such as Oliver Wendell Holmes, Felix Frankfurter, and Warren Burger, have argued that only Congress should make public policy and that, unless a legislative act clearly violates the Constitution, the law should stand. The Warren Court (1953–1969), named after its chief justice, was markedly activist, issuing decisions in the areas of racial segregation, reapportionment, and rights of the accused that had great impact on U.S. society. The courts that followed have been more cautious, reflecting the fact that most of their members were appointed by conservative Republicans. In recent years, conservative justices have mostly favored restraint, though that was not always true.

The Supreme Court's Political Role

14.5 Review the changes brought about by the Warren Court.

In this country, the Supreme Court's rulings often become political issues, rarely the case in other countries. When the Supreme Court of Franklin Roosevelt's day ruled that many New Deal laws were unconstitutional, FDR referred to the justices as "nine tired old men." Richard Nixon in the 1968 campaign charged that the Warren Court's liberal decisions had worsened crime and endangered society. The U.S. Supreme Court plays an important political role, and the appointment of just one new justice changes split decisions from five to four against to the same number for. Personal beliefs and ideology loom large in their decisions, raising the question of whether the Court can be an impartial dispenser of justice.

The Views of Justices

Clearly, justices' personal convictions influence their decisions. Historically, Supreme Court justices used to be **WASP** upper- or upper-middle-class males. Radical critics claimed that such judges could not appreciate the situation of the poor or oppressed. That picture has greatly changed. The first woman justice was appointed only in 1981; now there are three. The current court has six Catholics and three Jews. (Some suggested quotas for white Protestant males.) The relatively recent arrival of African Americans and women to the high bench has not necessarily overturned conservative tendencies, for such justices can be conservative in their own right. Justice Clarence Thomas, the second African American ever on the Court, said he reached conservative conclusions by thinking for himself.

WASP
White, Anglo-Saxon, Protestant.

    Other factors affect the justices' rulings. They are older, averaging close to 70. Southern jurists have usually been more conservative on racial matters, though one of the strongest champions of civil rights was Alabama's Hugo L. Black, who had been a member of the Ku Klux Klan in his youth. Former corporation lawyers may be more sympathetic to business problems. Some justices, like Louis D. Brandeis (one of six Jewish justices) and Thurgood Marshall (the first African American justice), were active in reform and civil rights causes and brought their liberalism to the bench. Others who have served on state courts believe that states' rights should be strengthened.

The two most important influences on voting, however, seem to be party affiliation and the justice's conception of the judicial role. Democratic justices are more likely to support liberal stands than are Republican justices and to see the Supreme Court as a defender of minorities and the poor. They are more likely to distrust states and to favor federal authority while also seeking to protect individual rights under the Fourteenth Amendment. Republicans are more likely to uphold state authority within the federal system and are less likely to accept the Bill of Rights as a blanket guarantee. There are many exceptions. When President Eisenhower appointed California Governor Earl Warren in 1953, he thought he was picking a good Republican moderate as chief justice. Later, Eisenhower called the choice "the biggest damned-fool mistake I ever made."

Many justices see the Court's role as standing firm on certain constitutional principles, despite public opinion. Justice Jackson put it this way: "One's right to life, liberty and property, to free speech, a free press, freedom of worship and assembly, and other fundamental rights may not be submitted to vote; they depend upon the outcome of no election."

But changing public attitudes also influence Supreme Court justices. In the 1936 election, after the Court had struck down several important laws designed to alleviate the Depression, President Roosevelt was given the greatest mandate in the nation's history. In 1937, he submitted legislation to expand the Supreme Court to fifteen members and encourage justices 70 or over to retire. The plan failed because many felt that FDR was attacking the constitutional principle of an independent judiciary, but it did force the Court to look beyond its narrow world and accept change. The election of 1936 and the controversy over "court packing" led to the Court's becoming more restrained in dealing with New Deal legislation. As one jokester put it, "A switch in time saves nine."

Another influence is colleagues' opinions. Chief Justices John Marshall, Earl Warren, and currently John Roberts were able to convert some of their colleagues to their judicial philosophies by force of personality and their judicial reasoning. Many factors—not all of them knowable—influence decisions. The fact that Supreme Court justices are appointed for life may be the most important of all. They are independent and immune to congressional, White House, and private-interest pressures. This factor changes them—and in unpredictable ways. Liberals turn into conservatives, activists into restrainists, and vice versa. The seriousness of their position and the knowledge that their votes alter American life make justices think deeply and sometimes change views. The office in part makes its occupant.

The Supreme Court's Political Impact

Warren Court
The liberal, activist U.S. Supreme Court under Chief Justice Earl Warren, 1953–1969.

Our legal system poses a basic conflict. Justices are expected to be impartial, but the importance of the Court gives them political power. In the twentieth century, this power increased. The **Warren Court** was active and controversial in three key areas—civil rights, criminal procedure, and legislative reapportionment—where it rewrote constitutional law. In the opinion of some, as ninety-six Southern members of Congress put it, the Court overturned "the established law of the land" and implemented its "personal political and social philosophy."

CIVIL RIGHTS The Supreme Court's decision in *Brown* (1954) triggered a revolution in American race relations—an area Congress had been unwilling to touch. In a unanimous ruling, the Court accepted the sociological argument of Thurgood Marshall (then attorney for the NAACP) that segregated public school facilities were "inherently unequal" because they stigmatized African American children and deprived them of the Fourteenth Amendment's guarantee of equal protection. A year later, in *Brown II* (1955), desegregation of public schools was ordered "with all deliberate speed." Southern whites vowed massive resistance.

African Americans, encouraged by this legal support, sought equal treatment in other areas and by 1963 engaged in confrontation with the white establishment. In *Lombard v. Louisiana* (1963), the Warren Court supported the **sit-in**, ruling that African Americans who had refused to leave a segregated lunch counter could not be prosecuted where it appeared that the state was involved in unequal treatment of the races. The Court relied on the Fourteenth Amendment that no state may deny any person the equal protection of the laws. The sit-in became a major weapon in the civil rights struggle. In 1964, Congress followed the Court's lead and passed the Civil Rights Act, which barred segregation in public accommodations such as hotels, motels, restaurants, and theaters. The Court led Congress.

sit-in
Tactic of overturning local laws by deliberately breaking them, as at segregated lunch counters.

CRIMINAL PROCEDURE The Warren Court's rulings in criminal procedure included *Mapp v. Ohio* (1961), wherein the Court ruled that evidence police seized without a warrant was inadmissible in a state court. In 1963, in *Gideon v. Wainwright*, the Court held that **indigent** defendants must be provided with legal counsel. In *Escobedo v. Illinois* (1964), in a five-to-four decision, the Court ruled that a suspect could not be denied the right to have a lawyer during police questioning and that any confessions so obtained could not be used in court. One of the Court's most controversial rulings came in 1966 in *Miranda v. Arizona*. The majority (five to four) ruled that arrested persons must immediately be told of their right to remain silent and to have a lawyer present during police questioning.

indigent
Having no money.

LEGISLATIVE REAPPORTIONMENT Equally important was the Warren Court's mandating of equal-population voting districts. Until 1962, many states had congressional districts that overrepresented rural areas and underrepresented cities. In a series of decisions in 1962 and 1964, the Court found that unequal representation denied citizens their Fourteenth Amendment (equal protection) rights. The Court ordered that state legislatures apply the principle of "one person, one vote" in redrawing electoral lines, which many now must do after every census.

Not all loved these decisions. Some felt they had been hurt: segregation-ists who refused to share schools or accommodations with African Americans, police who felt hampered in dealing with suspects, and rural people who wanted a more-than-equal vote. Billboards shouted "Impeach Earl Warren," and in 1968 Nixon ran as much against the Supreme Court as against Hubert Humphrey. The Warren Court overthrew **Jim Crow** laws, rewrote the rules for criminal procedure, and redrew legislative maps. With the possible exception of the Marshall Court, it was the most active, groundbreaking Court in U.S. history.

Jim Crow
System of segregationist laws once standard in the U.S. South.

THE POST-WARREN COURTS The Burger Court (1969–1986) and the Rehnquist Court (1986–2005) were sometimes characterized as conservative, an effort to roll back the Warren Court. Actually, their decisions were not so clear-cut. Overall, there was a conservative drift but an unpredictable one. The most controversial ruling of the century declared abortion was protected by the right to privacy in *Roe v. Wade* (1973), which came from the "conservative" Burger Court (with the chief justice concurring). The Burger Court in the 1978 *Bakke* case found that reserving quotas for African American applicants to medical school violated equal protec-tion for whites. The next year, however, in *Weber*, it found that quotas to help African American workers attain skilled positions were constitutional. In criminal law, the Burger Court issued some hard-line decisions. In 1984, it added a "good faith exception" to the *Mapp* rule, which excluded wrongfully seized evidence. If the police with a warrant to look for a particular piece of evidence stumble on another, it may be used as evidence. This modified but did not overturn *Mapp*. In 1976, the Burger Court found that capital punishment was not necessarily "cruel and unusual" if the rules for applying it were fair.

The Rehnquist Court both pleased and alarmed conservatives. In 1988, in a move that stunned the Reagan administration, the Court upheld the constitu-tionality of independent federal prosecutors, something the White House said interfered with the powers of the executive branch. The Court also ruled that burning the American flag could not be outlawed because it is a form of free speech. This ruling brought a mass outcry and a new federal statute outlawing flag burning. In 2003, the court upheld campaign-finance reform, university affirmative-action programs to promote diversity, and other liberal causes. The Rehnquist Court mostly modified rather than repudiated the Warren Court.

The Roberts Court, which began in 2005, was markedly conservative but not uniformly. The Bush 43 appointments of Chief Justice John Roberts and Associate Justice Samuel Alito gave the Court an unprecedented Catholic major-ity, five of the six conservatives. In 2013, the Court ended the special burdens the 1965 Voting Rights Act placed on Southern states, a setback to African American voting registration. In 2008, the Roberts Court decided five to four that a gun in the home is an individual right. The Court, however, required the Pentagon to accord terrorist suspects certain rights, including habeas corpus, what many called a "liberal" decision. The Court narrowly upheld the constitutionality of the Affordable Care Act ("Obamacare" to its critics) to the dismay of conservatives.

The 2002 McCain-Feingold Act, validated by the Court in 2003, attempted to curb the influence of big money by limiting contributions to political campaigns. But in the 2010 *Citizens United* case, one of its most important recent decisions, the Court ruled that individuals, corporations, and unions could contribute unlimited funds to so-called "super-PACs" on the theory that money is a form of speech and PACs provided information and education. Soon, McCain-Feingold was irrelevant as billionaires contributed millions to super-PACs, which assumed a major role in TV advertising (mostly negative) in the 2012 election. Republicans initially celebrated *Citizens United*, but they were bruised as super-PACs made their presidential primaries unusually long and bitter and did not lead to a Republican victory in the general election.

Perhaps the most conservative shift of the Roberts Court was that it took notably fewer cases than before, a reversal of the liberal tendency to use the Court as a back-up legislature. One of the problems with evaluating the thrust of Court decisions is the definition of *conservative*. The term may be applied to the substance of decisions, such as giving minorities special treatment, or it may be applied to the maintenance of existing institutions. Often the two coincide, as when the Court says states can pass laws limiting abortion. That would be both conservative on substance and conservative on the powers of states. But sometimes the two diverge, as when the Roberts Court upheld the right of habeas corpus for terrorist suspects. Although called a "liberal" ruling, it also upheld Article I, Section 9, of the Constitution, which says habeas will not be suspended, so it was actually "conservative." What the mass media and public opinion call "conservative" plays little role in the Court, which is intent only on constitutionality. Although a staunch conservative, Justice Antonin Scalia at times sides with liberals. "Liberal" and "conservative" are simplified labels used by the mass media and politicians; they are not mentioned in Supreme Court decisions.

The U.S. federal courts are an integral part of the policymaking apparatus—not just mechanical interpreters of law. Judicial decisions influence and are influenced by politics. Groups whose welfare depends on the court's decisions will try to influence the court to adopt their point of view; groups that do not succeed with the president or Congress hope they will have better luck with the courts. Some have called the U.S. judicial system a back-up legislature or parliament of last resort, for it can take on issues the other branches fear. Without Supreme Court decisions leading the way, Congress would not have passed civil-rights bills and presidents would not have enforced them. An autonomous and coequal judicial branch is one of America's great contributions to governance. Very slowly, this approach to judicial power is growing worldwide, contributing to rule of law and stable democracy.

Review Questions

1. Why is the U.S. political system so dependent on the courts?

2. What are the differences between natural and positive law?

3. What are the differences between common and code law?

4. Can you describe the U.S. court system?

5. How are European trials quite different from ours?

6. What does Germany have that resembles the U.S. Supreme Court?

7. How did an 1803 case give the Supreme Court vast powers?

8. In what major cases did the Warren Court make new law?

9. Have subsequent courts reversed Warren Court decisions?

Key Terms

accusatorial p. 277
adversarial p. 277
appeal p. 273
bench p. 275
brief p. 273
canon law p. 274
civil law p. 271
code law p. 275
common law p. 271
consistency p. 272

constitutional law p. 271
higher law p. 272
indict p. 278
indigent p. 285
investigating judge p. 278
Jim Crow p. 286
law p. 270
natural law p. 272
outlier p. 281

plaintiff p. 270
positive law p. 270
precedent p. 274
reciprocity p. 272
Roman law p. 275
scattergram p. 281
sit-in p. 285
Warren Court p. 284
WASP p. 283

Further Reference

Bach, Amy. *Ordinary Justice: How America Holds Court*. New York: Holt, 2010.

Barber, Sotirios A., and James E. Fleming. *Constitutional Interpretation: The Basic Questions*. New York: Oxford University Press, 2007.

Baum, Lawrence. *Judges and their Audiences*. Princeton, NJ: Princeton University Press, 2008.

Belsky, Martin H., ed. *The Rehnquist Court: A Retrospective*. New York: Oxford University Press, 2002.

Bingham, Tom. *The Rule of Law*. London: Allen Lane, 2010.

Breyer, Stephen. *Active Liberty: Interpreting Our Democratic Constitution*. New York: Knopf, 2005.

Calvi, James V., and Susan Coleman. *American Law and Legal Systems*, 7th ed. New York: Longman, 2011.

Carp, Robert A., Ronald Stidham, and Kenneth Manning. *Judicial Process in America*, 9th ed. Washington, DC: CQ Press, 2013.

Carter, Lief H., and Thomas F. Burke. *Reason in Law*, 9th ed. New York: Longman, 2012.

Dworkin, Ronald. *The Supreme Court Phalanx: The Court's New Right-Wing Bloc*. New York: New York Review of Books, 2008.

Feldman, Noah. *Scorpions: The Battles and Triumphs of FDR's Great Supreme Court Justices*. New York: Twelve Books, 2010.

Greenhouse, Linda, and Reva Siegel. *Before Roe v. Wade: Voices that Shaped the Abortion Debate Before the Supreme Court's Ruling*. New York: Kaplan, 2010.

Howard, Philip K. *Life Without Lawyers: Liberating Americans from Too Much Law*. New York: Norton, 2009.

Jenkins, John. *The Partisan: The Life of William Rehnquist*. New York: PublicAffairs, 2012.

Murphy, Bruce Allen. *Scalia: A Court of One*. New York: Simon and Schuster, 2915.

Shesol, Jeff. *Supreme Power: Franklin Roosevelt vs. the Supreme Court*. New York: Norton, 2011.

Sunstein, Cass R. *A Constitution of Many Minds: Why the Founding Document Doesn't Mean What It Meant Before*. Princeton, NJ: Princeton University Press, 2009.

Sweet, Martin J. *Merely Judgment: Ignoring, Evading, and Trumping the Supreme Court*. Charlottesville, VA: University of Virginia Press, 2010.

Tribe, Laurence, and Joshua Matz. *Uncertain Justice: The Roberts Court and the Constitution*. New York: Holt, 2014

Tushnet, Mark. *In the Balance: Law and Politics on the Roberts Court*. New York: Norton, 2014.

Part V
What Political Systems Do

Ch. 15 Political Economy Political economy is a broad term covering the interactions of the economy and government. Even conservatives demand a government role to stabilize the economy. Some would do this through Keynesian counter-cyclical spending while others advocate raising or lowering the money supply through interest rates. The United States has suffered through recurring problems of inflation, tax hikes or cuts, budget and trade deficits, oil shocks, and burst bubbles. Because there is never enough money for everything, the United States must continually reconsider its massive entitlement programs (Social Security and Medicare) that all receive as opposed to welfare aimed at the poor (food stamps and Medicaid).

Ch. 16 Violence and Revolution Political violence is a symptom of system breakdown, something almost every country has experienced. We can distinguish several types of violence: primordial, separatist, revolutionary, and coup. Terrorism uses violence to weaken a hated political authority. Change and rising expectations may fuel violence. Vietnam was less guerrilla warfare than "revolutionary political warfare." Revolutions sweep out old elites and tend to follow a cycle Crane Brinton discerned long ago—regime decay, a takeover by moderates, another takeover by an extremist reign of terror, and finally a Thermidor or calming. Iran fits this pattern. Revolutions tend to end badly—the Arab Spring offers recent examples—but preventing them is difficult because the ruling class refuses to give up any of its wealth or power.

Ch. 17 International Relations International relations (IR), because it is anarchic, is different from and wilder than domestic politics, where a sovereign attempts to preserve order. Instead, power and national interest determine much of IR. National interest is often hard to tell until years later. The causes of war can be divided into micro and macro theories, misperception, and balances (or imbalances) of power. Various plans to curb war have been urged, ranging from world government to collective security to expanding democracy. Functionalism proposes getting countries to cooperate first on small, practical problems. Diplomacy, sometimes by third-party mediation, followed by peacekeeping operations may calm conflicts. Some suggest the concept of sovereignty may be slipping, allowing supranational bodies, such as the UN or NATO, to intervene. Economic factors—such as globalization, currency parities, and oil—now loom large. U.S. foreign policy tends to alternate between interventionism and isolationism. Americans must get used to living in a chaotic, dangerous world.

Chapter 15
Political Economy

Learning Objectives

15.1 Explain the connections between politics and the economy.

15.2 Review the many U.S. economic problems since the 1960s.

15.3 Contrast entitlements and welfare.

15.4 Argue for expanding or cutting U.S. entitlement and welfare programs.

15.5 Discuss Americans' contradictory impulses toward welfare programs.

In 2008, the U.S. economy suffered a gaping wound as several trillion dollars were ripped out of it. It was no ordinary recession, something that comes every few years and is quickly overcome. Some economists called it a "contraction," worse and longer-lasting than a recession. It was led by collapsing home prices, and the standard policies for fighting recession barely budged the flat economy. It is not clear if government programs or the mere passage of time slowly revived the economy.

bailout
Emergency government loan to save firm from collapse.

The heated debate over how to overcome the slump illustrates the close connection between politics and the economy. Most American economists said **bailouts** were necessary; without them, the world might have plunged into a new depression. Governments the world over—even in China—took similar steps. The worst was avoided, but conservatives charged that government deficits were so huge that they would bring inflation and even currency collapse. Hesitation over bailing out Europe's weaker economies raised questions over the future of the new euro currency and even of the European Union. Most European governments practiced **austerity**, but their economies stayed flat. The U.S. federal government avoided austerity, and the U.S. economy slowly recovered. Republicans demanded austerity, but most U.S. economists warned that it would repeat the mistakes of the 1930s Depression. As some economists say, the content of politics is economics. Most really big quarrels are over economics.

austerity
Cutting government spending.

What Is Political Economy?

15.1 Explain the connections between politics and the economy.

political economy
Influence of politics and economy on each other; what government should do in the economy.

Political economy is an old and flexible term. The classical economists of the late eighteenth and nineteenth centuries—Adam Smith, David Ricardo, John Stuart Mill, and Karl Marx—all wrote on what they called the **political economy**. In doing this, they were taking a leaf from Aristotle, who viewed government, society, and the economy as one thing. The old political economists also had normative orientations, prescribing what government should do to promote a just prosperity. In the late nineteenth century, as economists became more scientific and numbers-based, they dropped "political" from the name of their discipline and shifted to empirical description and prediction.

Recently the term has revived, with partisan overtones. Radicals use the term "political economy" instead of Marxism (which is a hard sell these days) to describe their criticisms of capitalism and the unfair distribution of wealth among and within nations. Conservatives use the term to try to get back to the pure market system advocated by Adam Smith. We will avoid taking ideological sides and use the term to mean the interface between politics and the economy. And it is a very big interface.

public policy
What a government tries to do; the choices it makes among alternatives.

Economics undergirds almost everything in politics. Politicians get elected by promising prosperity and reelected by delivering it. Virtually all **public policy** choices have economic ramifications, and these can make or break the policy. A policy designed to boost favored industries but that costs a great deal may not last. Congress, for example, mandated that ethanol (alcohol from grain) be added to gasoline and subsidized it heavily even as criticism grew that the program was an unnecessary subsidy to corn growers that diverted corn from food to fuel in a time of drought and high corn prices.

With a growing economy, a country can afford new welfare measures, as the United States did in the booming 1960s. With a slow economy, an administration has to run massive deficits and devise policies to spur economic growth. Whatever the issue—health care, environment, energy, or welfare—it will be connected to the economy. Some of the worst policy choices are made when decision makers forget this elementary point. Candidates often promise new programs without specifying how to pay for them. Economic policy should take priority over all other policies. Every political scientist should be to some degree an economist. As candidate Bill Clinton constantly reminded himself during the 1992 campaign, "It's the economy, stupid!" And he was right; the economy matters most. Low inflation and low unemployment made most Americans reasonably content with the Clinton presidency.

Nowadays, few thinkers, not even many conservatives, expect the government to keep its hands off the economy. Everyone wants the government to induce economic prosperity, and if it does not, voters may punish the administration at the next election, as happened in 2008. McCain lost in part because voters (perhaps unfairly) blamed the Republican administration of Bush 43 for the financial meltdown. Perhaps luckily for Obama in 2012, the U.S. economy was starting to come out of its long slump.

Earlier in the twentieth century, many European governments as well as Washington followed "classic liberal" doctrines and generally kept their hands off the economy. With the outbreak of the Great Depression in 1929, however, the hands-off policies tended to make things worse, and people demanded government intervention.

A 1936 book by British economist John Maynard Keynes proposed to cure depressions by dampening the swings of the **business cycle**. During bad times, government would increase "aggregate demand" by "countercyclical spending" on public works and welfare to make **recessions** shorter and milder. An economy growing too fast—with risks of speculative bubbles and inflation—should be cooled by raising taxes. Believers in the classic Adam Smith version of the free market were horrified at "deficit spending," but Keynes argued that we just owe the money to ourselves, and, "In the long run, we'll all be dead." Some say the "Keynesian revolution" brought us out of the Depression. Others say FDR's New Deal never seriously applied Keynesianism; only the massive defense spending of World War II did that. Still others doubt that the New Deal achieved anything lasting except debt and **inflation**.

After World War II, conservative economists such as Friedrich Hayek and Milton Friedman sidelined Keynesianism with a "neoclassical" theory based

business cycle
Tendency of economy to alternate between growth and *recession* over several years.

recession
Period of economic decline; a shrinking GDP.

inflation
A general, overall rise in prices.

Case Studies

How High Are U.S. Taxes?

Compared with other advanced industrialized countries, U.S. taxes are low. In 2013, countries paid the following percentages of their GDPs in total taxes, including state and local. Americans complain their taxes are too high—they would complain if taxes were zero—but we tax relatively little because the United States is not much of a welfare state (although it delivers a lot in *tax expenditures*—see box later in chapter). Most Europeans, figuring they get a good deal from the system (including medical plans), complain less about taxes.

The question is how much and what programs are Americans willing to cut to bring taxes even lower? Defense? Social Security? Medicare? Besides, some of the "cuts" in federal programs are just tax burdens shifted to the state and local level or deferred to later years. The debate over the appropriate level of taxes balanced with the appropriate level of government activity is one of the enduring political debates. American public opinion demands both low taxes and a high level of government service—an impossibility over the long term.

Denmark	49
France	45
Germany	37
Britain	33
Canada	31
Japan	30
United States	25

SOURCE: OECD

Federal Reserve Board

"The Fed"; U.S. central bank that can raise and lower interest rates.

on the original supply and demand of Adam Smith. Government regulation of the economy was out; the free market was in. Then the 2008 financial meltdown hit—something only a handful of economists had predicted—and many economists quickly rediscovered Keynes. Even Republicans—such as President Bush in 2008—favored pumping billions of federal dollars into shaky banks and firms, a Keynesian effort. Because Congress is so slow, much of the fight to smooth the business cycle shifted to the **Federal Reserve Board**, which, by controlling interest rates, can raise or lower economic activity much faster than Congress can by raising or lowering taxes or delivering emergency funding. Fed chairpersons are closely watched as they struggle to prevent the U.S. economy from falling into depression or experiencing high levels of inflation.

Government and the Economy

15.2 Review the many U.S. economic problems since the 1960s.

What are some of our leading economic problems and government responses to them? Consider the approximate sequence of events the United States has gone through since the 1960s, and notice how the problems reoccur. Many are with us today.

Inflation

Until 1965, the U.S. inflation rate was low, but as President Johnson escalated the Vietnam War in 1965, it kicked up. War spending pumped some $140 billion (now worth more than six times that, after adjusting for inflation) into the U.S. economy but not a corresponding amount of goods and services to buy with it. Too many dollars chased too few goods—the classic definition of demand-pull inflation. The Vietnam War brought an inflation that took on a life of its own and lasted into the 1980s. Johnson thought he could win in Vietnam quickly and cheaply, before the war made much economic impact, but the policy failed. Many economists say we could have avoided the worst of the inflation if LBJ had been willing to raise taxes at the start of the war.

Tax Hike

President Johnson was reluctant to ask for a tax increase to pay for Vietnam for two reasons. First, he had just gotten a tax cut through Congress in 1964; it would have been embarrassing to reverse course the following year. Second, he did not want to admit that he had gotten the country into a long and costly war. By the time Johnson and Congress had changed their minds and introduced a 10 percent tax surcharge in 1968, it was too late; inflation had taken hold. The lesson was that in war, you must increase taxes to mop up the increased government spending. Bush 43 ignored the lesson and, like LBJ, both cut taxes and took us to war. Dangerous "asset inflation" (of homes and stocks) followed—speculative bubbles that popped in 2008.

Balance of Payments

Starting in the late 1950s, the United States spent more abroad than it sold. With the war-induced prosperity of the 1960s, America sucked in imports without exporting enough to cover them. American industries "offshored," and Americans enjoyed bargain prices on imported goods. Large **balance-of-payments** deficits grew. The too-high value of the dollar in relation to foreign currencies meant it was cheaper to buy foreign goods but harder to sell U.S. goods in foreign markets. Japanese and later Chinese products took a large share of the U.S. market. American dollars flooded the world; they were too plentiful.

balance of payments
The value of what a country exports compared with what it imports.

Floating the Dollar

In an effort to correct this imbalance, in 1971 President Nixon cut the link between the dollar and gold, a **fixed exchange rate** that had been in place since 1944. The Bretton Woods agreement—which priced an ounce of gold at $35 and fixed other currencies in relation to the dollar—had been the basis of postwar recovery. But

fixed exchange rate
Dollar buys set amounts of foreign currencies.

the inflation of U.S. dollars worldwide made our stock of gold way too cheap, so Nixon said no more gold and let the dollar "float" to a lower level in relation to other currencies. This **floating exchange rate** devalued the dollar by about one-fifth. Over time, however, U.S. trade and payment deficits soared even higher.

floating exchange rate
Dollar buys varying amounts of foreign currencies, depending on market for them.

Wage-Price Freeze

At the same time, Nixon froze wages and prices to knock out inflation. The 1971 wage-price freeze was popular at first, but soon many complained that there was no corresponding freeze on profits so that businesses benefited unduly. A bigger problem with wage-price freezes, however, is that when they are removed, pent-up demand pushes inflation higher than ever. Many economists think Nixon's eighteen-month freeze just set the stage for greater inflation. Some (mostly liberal) economists supported the idea of wage and price controls—called "incomes policy"—but now few economists of any stripe want to try them again.

Oil Shocks

International oil deals, like most international trade arrangements, were made with U.S. dollars. The dollar's loss in value meant that the oil exporters were getting less and less for their black gold. The price of oil in the 1960s was ridiculously low. As a result of the 1973 Mideast war, the members of the Organization of Petroleum Exporting Countries (OPEC) were able to implement what they had been itching to do: quadruple oil prices. In 1979, in response to the revolutionary turmoil in Iran, they increased prices again. Altogether during the 1970s, world oil prices soared from $2.50 to $34 a barrel, which now looks cheap. In 2008, oil briefly hit $147 a barrel but by 2015 had fallen to below $50. Increased supply (from "fracking" and oil sands) boosted U.S. oil production while world demand slumped. Oil prices plunge with even a small oversupply but soar with even a small shortage. Oil prices are likely to rebound but unlikely to hold steady.

Stagflation

The manifold increase in petroleum prices produced inflation everywhere while simultaneously depressing the economy. During the 1970s, a new word appeared— **stagflation**—to describe inflation with stagnant economic growth. Previously, economists had seen a connection between economic growth and inflation; as one went up, so did the other. In the 1970s, this connection was broken. Inflation hit double-digit levels (10 percent or higher), but the economy shrank and joblessness increased. Since 1973, average Americans, after inflation, have had little or no income growth. The biggest single culprit is believed to be the massive increase in oil prices that affect every corner of the economy, from agriculture and transportation to manufacturing and construction. The United States was especially hard hit, for Americans had gotten used to cheap energy and had based their industry and lifestyle on it. Low fuel prices boosted the U.S. economy in 2015.

stagflation
Combination of slow growth plus inflation in the U.S. economy in the 1970s.

Interest Rates

President Jimmy Carter attempted to stimulate the economy, but this made inflation worse; in 1980, it was 13.5 percent and probably cost him reelection. Fed members are appointed by the president for fourteen years and cannot be fired; the Fed chair is appointed for four-year terms. The Fed finally stemmed inflation by boosting interest rates to record levels, at one point higher than 20 percent. This brought slower economic growth and curbed inflation but also brought the greatest rate of unemployment (more than 10 percent) since the Depression. No one wants interest rates like that again. Americans became aware of how important the Fed is in our economic life.

Tax Cuts

Again trying to stimulate the economy, President Reagan turned to an approach called "supply-side economics," which focuses on investment and production rather than on consumer demand, as Keynesian policy does. The inspiration of supply-siders was the Kennedy idea that lowering tax rates stimulates economic growth and ultimately generates more tax revenue. Conservatives argue that too-high taxes discourage effort and investment. Congress bought Reagan's proposal and cut income taxes 25 percent over three years. Actually, this scarcely offset the "bracket creep" that American taxpayers had suffered as a result of inflation; their purchasing power had stayed the same, but they found themselves in ever-higher tax brackets. Congress responded to Reagan's calls for spending cuts, leading to large budget deficits. Bush 43, using the same rationale, cut taxes again in 2001 and 2003, again without corresponding spending cuts and again resulting in budget deficits.

Budget Deficits

Presidents Reagan and Bush 43 had presented Congress with budgets that featured both tax cuts and major increases in defense spending. Reagan figured this would force Congress to cut domestic and welfare spending drastically. But Congress cut little, and the U.S. federal budget reached record **deficits**. By issuing Treasury bills, the federal government borrowed the money, which raised interest rates. Because U.S. interest rates were high, foreigners invested heavily in the United States, so in effect much of the U.S. budget deficit was covered by foreign investment. The deficits acted like a gigantic vacuum cleaner that swept in both goods and capital from around the world. This could go on only as long as foreigners trusted the dollar. When Obama ran a $1.3 trillion annual budget deficit in 2011 (about 8.7 percent of GDP; some other countries were worse), many feared the dollar would plunge in value. For a while, during the financial meltdown, the dollar did fall in relation to the euro and other currencies, which helped boost U.S. exports. A "strong dollar" is not always a good thing. By 2015, the deficit fell to around a third of a trillion, and the dollar strengthened again.

deficit
Spending more in a given year than you take in.

Methods

Maps

Maps are often underutilized, but they are essential for studies with territorial components. They are also easy for readers to understand. Like cross-tabs and scattergrams, maps can relate two variables, sometimes suggesting patterns you overlooked. A study of the 1996 Perot vote in Pennsylvania showed it was biggest in the rural counties along the state's northern border, a depressed region where voters have much resentment and low turnout. A map suggested that the Perot vote came from alienated people who typically do not vote.

The basic technique is to shade in territorial components (states, provinces, counties, or electoral districts) to show variation in voting for a certain party. You might take the overall vote for the German Social Democratic party (SPD). In those German Länder (states) where the SPD got more than 5 percent below the national average, color them light blue. In those states where the SPD won from 5 percent under to 5 percent over the national average, color them medium blue. In those states where the SPD got more than 5 percent over the national average, color them dark blue. At a glance,

German Social Democratic Vote by State

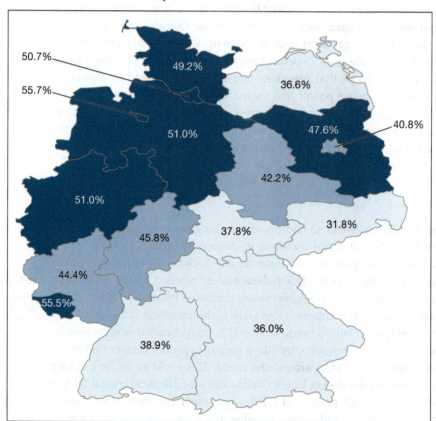

you'll have a picture of German voting by region. Most countries show regional voting patterns.

For your second variable, you might take religion, coloring on the same basis in which states Protestants are either at, below, or above Germany's overall percentage of Protestants. You notice that the two maps are similar, as German Catholics tend to vote Christian Democrat and Protestants SPD. Such maps show a rough fit between religion and voting.

U.S. Congressional and state legislative districts have an advantage in drawing up maps that show urban-rural voting differences. By law, U.S. districts for lower houses must have the same number of residents, adjusted after every census. Because territorially large districts are rural and small districts urban, viewers can tell relative population density among districts. Districts of medium size suggest they are suburban. Coloring in Democratic districts in blue and Republican in red will likely show that rural districts went Republican, cities Democrat, particularly true of recent elections. States and counties, of course, were never designed to have equal numbers of residents.

Percent Protestant by State

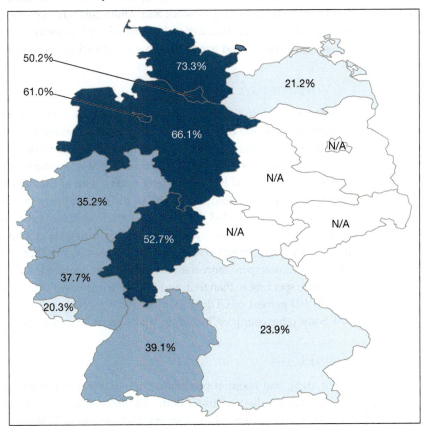

Trade Deficits

The United States for several decades has consumed more than it produced and imported much more than it exported. U.S. imports now top exports by some half a trillion dollars each year, around 3 percent of the GDP. The foreign-trade deficit makes the United States the world's greatest debtor nation. This in turn leads to the buying up of American assets by foreigners. Americans dislike this, but it is really no problem. If foreigners want to invest in America, it simply makes us more prosperous. Off and on, our trading partners bid down the value of the dollar, and the value of the **euro** climbs, briefly touching $1.60 in 2008. This in effect devalued the dollar and made U.S. products cheaper, something Europeans do not want. Some economists argue that the U.S. trade deficit is irrelevant because the U.S. economy is sufficiently strong and foreign creditors know they will be repaid. With increasing urgency, however, others caution that too much hangs on confidence in the dollar; if it collapses, the world would have no standard "reserve" currency to do business with, leading to global recession. In addition to the fluctuations caused by the changing value of the dollar, the U.S. trade deficit shrinks when the economy is weak and Americans have less money to spend—not a good thing. The U.S. deficit has also shrunk recently because of reduced imports of foreign oil and natural gas due to increasing domestic supplies.

euro
Since 2002, common EU currency used in most of West Europe; value fluctuates but now worth around $1.10.

Government Debt

Republican gains on Capitol Hill bring determined efforts to trim government spending and end the chronic budget deficits, which every year are added to the national **debt**. President Clinton went along with the effort, and the federal budget ran a surplus from 1997 to 2000. The surpluses were less the result of cuts—some of which simply shifted burdens to later years—than of the high-tech and investment boom, which boosted the wealth of the few and thus got more taxes from them. Then recession ended the surplus—both from lower tax revenues and from increased federal spending—and federal budget deficits climbed. The Bush 43 administration had projected a decade of surpluses, so the Republican administration and Congress spent more than ever. Then the Obama administration, fearing a depression, spent more than that, and in 2012 government debt topped $15 trillion, equal to 100 percent of GDP. (It had been 109 percent in 1946 and 24 percent in 1974. Some other countries, including Japan, are at 200 percent.)

debt
The sum total owed by the federal government.

Fiscal Cliff

Deficit, debt, and taxation problems came together at the start of 2013 in what was popularly called a "fiscal cliff." In 2012, as a goad to close the big gap between taxes and spending, Obama and the Republicans agreed that without a compromise on the budget, Bush's tax cuts would expire and government spending—even the Defense Department's—would be cut automatically across the board—a step called "sequestration." Many feared the sudden tax increases and simultaneous spending cuts would produce a "double-dip" recession in 2013 just as we were coming out of recession. The Republicans demanded drastic spending cuts and renewal of Bush's tax cuts, but Obama held out for some spending cuts and a tax hike on the wealthiest 1 percent—those with incomes greater than $450,000 a year. We never went over the fiscal cliff, but the compromise to avoid it satisfied few and "kicked the can down the road" for likely repeats every few years.

Inequality

Since the 1970s, Americans' incomes have grown less equal and the middle class smaller. The rich get a bigger slice of the nation's economic pie; the poor and much of the middle class get smaller pieces. Those with the right education and skills may do well, but those with a high-school education or less do poorly. **Offshoring**, much of it to newly industrializing Asia, cuts the number and pay of American blue-collar manufacturing jobs. Unions declined to 7 percent of the private-sector workforce (during the early 1950s, some 40 percent of the U.S. workforce was unionized). Top executives and money managers are compensated extravagantly, and Republican tax cuts favored the rich. In 1970, the richest 1 percent of American households got 9 percent of the nation's pretax income; in 2012, they got 20 percent (about the same as the bottom half of all Americans). The average CEO makes more than two hundred times what a wage worker does. (In the 1950s, it had been twenty times.) Americans who lived off wages saw them stagnate or decline, offset only by wives working. The growth of inequality fuels political anger. Proclaimed placards at Occupy Wall Street in 2011: "We are the 99 percent," a phrase that stuck. In 2016, even the Republicans turned to the challenge of inequality.

offshoring
U.S. firms producing overseas.

Bubbles

Financial markets tend to produce "**bubbles**," fast growth in investments that let people ignore risk—until the bubbles pop. Some economists blame alternating **manias** and **panics**, both heavily psychological, what Keynes called the "animal spirits" of investor irrationality. He urged government intervention to dampen both. One stock-market bubble ended with the 1929 Crash. The savings-and-loan bubble of the 1980s, the dot.com bubble of the 1990s, and the housing bubble of the 2000s likewise burst. Asia has experienced similar bubbles in finance and housing. The big underlying problem with all: Government policy promoting homeownership encouraged banks and investors to lend recklessly and to believe there was little risk, and this encouraged high levels of debt. With easy credit, everyone was encouraged to use their credit cards and home equity to borrow more and more.

bubble
Market that has gone too high.

manias
Periods of market boom in which greed trumps fear.

panics
Periods of market collapse in which fear trumps greed.

This brought the home-mortgage crisis. Lenders collected fat fees as they shoveled out risky mortgages to homebuyers who could not repay them. The theory was that home prices only go up, so everyone would be safe. Complex financial "derivatives"—investments that no one could understand—masked the losses so that no one could accurately evaluate assets. When the wave of home foreclosures began, giant institutions literally did not know their own worth, so their shares tumbled and several went bankrupt or were taken over. Economist Robert Shiller called it "the bursting of the largest bubble in history."

What is Poverty?

15.3 Contrast entitlements and welfare.

Defining poverty can be tricky. What's "poor" currently might have been "comfortable" in previous eras. Find out how your great-grandparents fared during the Depression. A U.S. Labor Department statistician devised a formula in 1963 that became standard, although many argue it is out of date. She found that families spent about one-third of their incomes on food, so a "poverty line" is three times a minimal food budget for nonfarm families of four. Using this definition, the percentage of Americans below the poverty line fell from 17.3 percent in 1965, when President Johnson's War on Poverty started, to 11.7 percent in 1973. In 2014, it was 15 percent. African American and Hispanic rates are much higher, and more than one-fifth of America's children are below the poverty line.

Liberals complain that the poverty line—in 2014 it was $23,550 for a family of four—is set much too low; it can take two to three times that to survive in big cities, as rent and child care are now bigger items than food. Washington has considered updating the poverty line to match modern conditions, including a new category of the "near poor," whose numbers swelled in the aftermath of the 2008 contraction. Conservatives point out that poverty figures do not include *noncash* benefits transferred to the poor by government programs—food stamps, for example. Taking such benefits into account raises some poor families above the poverty line.

Before we conclude that the War on Poverty was a success or failure, we must look at the poverty rate in longer perspective. In 1950, some 30 percent of the U.S. population was classified as below the poverty line, and the rate dropped. One of the fastest decreases occurred between 1960 and 1965, *before* the War on Poverty programs were enacted. The U.S. economy expanded from 1950 to 1965, especially during the early 1960s. Jobs were plentiful, and food became cheaper. It is hard to tell if the further drop in the poverty rate from 1965 to 1973 was the result of government programs or of an economy heated by Vietnam War spending.

By the same token, when the poverty rate began to go up again in the mid-1970s, cutbacks in antipoverty spending were only partly to blame; also responsible were the recessions caused by high oil prices and interest rates discussed earlier. Some blame the increase of poverty and homelessness on offshoring, taking the jobs of many middle-class Americans and pushing them down the socioeconomic ladder. With the disappearance of modestly paying factory jobs, they faced either low-paid service jobs ("flipping hamburgers") or unemployment and welfare. Antipoverty programs cannot offset massive unemployment caused by long-term trends in the U.S. economy.

Democracy

Poverty and Ideology

The U.S. debate about poverty is passionately ideological. Although it can get shrill, as in the 2016 election, it is an important part of our democracy. Conservatives want to limit antipoverty programs, liberals expand them. The policy analyst must cast ideology aside and gather factual answers to questions such as the following:

Are we talking about welfare or entitlement?

The two categories overlap, but the essence of a welfare program is that it is "means tested": Recipients must demonstrate that they are poor according to certain criteria (how much income and how many children). If the program is a pure entitlement, such as Social Security or Medicare, can it realistically be cut without incurring electoral wrath?

Do welfare programs have negative consequences?

The great conservative claim is that welfare programs offer incentives for unemployment, illegitimacy, and drug use. Can this be proved or disproved? New York City, with its extensive welfare programs, has a high incidence of poverty. But so does Mississippi, with its weak and underfunded welfare programs. As usual, causality is terribly difficult to prove. Would a massive, nationwide cessation of all welfare programs force the indolent to work? This raises the next question.

Is poverty an unfortunate circumstance or a character defect?

Are people poor because they cannot find work or because they do not want to work? In other words, are the poor really different from you and me? Do they have a "culture of poverty" that instills a "radical improvidence," an indifference to providing for their families and futures? If poverty is a character defect, as most conservatives maintain, then little can be done. If it is the product of unfortunate

circumstances, as most liberals maintain, then policies that change those circumstances might get people out of poverty.

How much poverty is simply a lack of good jobs?

Do the jobs available to poor people pay enough for them to support their families? In most of America, people are willing to take jobs not much above minimum wage, even though a single mother earning that falls far below the poverty line. Good factory jobs are hard to find because many have moved overseas. Those who would drastically cut welfare should demonstrate there are sufficient jobs with adequate pay. But are poor people generally qualified for decent-paying jobs, or do they lack the skills?

Can we train people out of poverty?

Job training and retraining have long been part of poverty-fighting programs. But do they work? Some who have completed job training still find no work. Can we take people with poor reading and math skills and in a few months make them into skilled technicians? The deeper, underlying problem is the lack of proper education in K–12, which creates an illiterate and innumerate workforce. But is the lack of proper education in the United States the fault of schools and teachers or of families and attitudes? For a long time, liberals blamed schools while conservatives blamed families. Either way, how do you fix the U.S. education system?

What is the international context of domestic poverty?

How much poverty is due to the export of American jobs to low-wage countries? Note how many of your recent purchases were made in Asia. While lowering costs to consumers, offshoring has closed thousands of American factories. Is U.S. poverty, then, the natural result of an open world economy in

(continued)

(contiuned)

which many countries have much lower labor costs? Should we close our borders to such commerce in order to boost domestic employment? If we did, Americans would live less well—their clothing and electronics would cost more, so they would buy fewer of them—but other Americans would exit poverty through new factory jobs. Our trading partners in other lands would retaliate by keeping out U.S. products, so other U.S. factories would close. On balance, trade protectionism hurts more than it helps.

These are some of the questions we must ask. Simple ideological approaches, either liberal or conservative, often deal with consequences rather than causes. Where ideology reigns, reason has difficulty making its voice heard.

Welfare versus Entitlements

The federal budget is divided into two general categories: discretionary and mandatory. The former can be raised or lowered from year to year. Congress, for example, may decide to increase defense spending and cut highway spending. Mandatory spending—which now runs twice as much as discretionary—cannot be so easily changed; it is what the federal budget is stuck with from previous statutory commitments. Mandatory spending in turn is divided into interest payments on the national debt (now about 6 percent of the budget) and **entitlements**; together they are around half of the federal budget. Interest payments are totally untouchable; if they were cut, future offerings of bonds and treasury notes would have no credibility or customers. And with security commitments in several parts of the world, Defense Department demands rise. There is not much wiggle room in the U.S. federal budget.

entitlement
U.S. federal expenditure mandated by law, such as Social Security and Medicare.

Entitlements are extremely difficult to cut because people are used to them and expect them as a right. They are payments to which one is automatically entitled by law: When you turn sixty-five, you are entitled to Medicare, sixty-six (and rising to sixty-seven) for full Social Security. There is no annual cap on entitlement spending; it grows as more people are entitled, what is called "uncontrollable" spending. The only way to change entitlement expenditures is to change the law, a difficult task in the face of strong interests groups fighting to protect the entitlement. Social Security should be solvent until 2033, but Medicare, under heavy pressure as baby boomers (those born between 1946 and 1964) retire, will turn insolvent in a few years. These two programs go to seniors, who get eight times what children get from the federal budget. Children don't vote, oldsters do.

Only a small fraction of federal payments is traditional "welfare" spending; more than 85 percent of spending goes to the middle classes in the form of Social Security, Medicare, government retirement plans, and farm price supports. What goes to poor families includes Medicaid, food stamps, and Supplemental Security Income. With political realities in mind, what can be cut of the first category—middle-class entitlements? Some people argue that if we eliminated "welfare" spending we could cut taxes, but "welfare" makes up such a small share of the budget that government spending would be affected very little and cuts would inflict hardship on society's most vulnerable members, especially children. Entitlements are where real savings could be found, but politicians pretend otherwise because they fear the wrath of the middle class who want their entitlement benefits just as much or more than they want their tax cuts—plus they vote.

How did the U.S. welfare system come about? In the mid-1960s, President Lyndon Johnson launched his War on Poverty, aimed at creating a Great Society. Johnson, who had been the powerful Senate majority leader, got Congress to deliver almost everything he wanted. Then the Vietnam War, with its rising costs and acrimony, seemed to cut down the War on Poverty in its infancy. There wasn't enough money for the growing programs, and the Great Society became discredited. Many of its programs were substantially trimmed or ended. Some say the Great Society was never given a chance. Conservatives hold that the undertaking was inherently infeasible, a waste of money that often did more harm than good, locking recipients into **welfare dependency** and encouraging a subculture of drugs and crime. Some poverty specialists, however, say the Great Society

tax expenditures
Government subsidies through tax breaks.

welfare dependency
Stuck on welfare with no incentive to get off.

Case Studies

Welfare Spending versus Tax Expenditures

American politicians often contrast the relatively parsimonious U.S. welfare system with highspending European welfare states. Republicans accused Obama of being a "European socialist," something close to a swearword in U.S. politics. They proudly note that U.S. welfare spending, as a percentage of GDP, is about half that of Europe and claim that this is the basis of America's dynamic economy.

Critics on both the right and left say look again. U.S. welfare expenditures are indeed low for an advanced industrialized democracy, but **tax expenditures** do the same thing: deliver government money to certain groups. The current tax expenditure is around $1 trillion a year. We subsidize through tax breaks that largely escape public and media attention.

The tax code, for example, classifies the earnings of hedge-fund managers as "carried interest," making them a type of capital gains and taxed at a lower rate. This enables some very wealthy Americans, such as Warren Buffet and Donald Trump, to pay a much lower percentage than ordinary people who earn wages and salaries. Certain industries are allowed "accelerated depreciation" on their assets. In place of public

healthcare insurance, the tax code lets firms deduct their contributions to employee healthcare plans, a major tax expenditure.

The Earned Income Tax Credit, a Republican idea, since 1975 lets low-income workers get back much of what has been withheld from their paychecks for federal taxes. First proposed as a "negative income tax" by conservative economist Milton Friedman, it is considered one of the most efficient welfare measures ever devised. Instead of giving the working poor subsidies, as in Europe, you give them a tax break. A further political advantage is that it is not counted as welfare spending, so few complain.

By the time you add U.S. tax expenditures to open spending, you have a "hidden welfare state" approximately the same size as Europe's, but much of it goes to individuals and firms that are already rich. European welfare states aim more precisely at the poor and working class. Increasingly, thinkers of both major U.S. parties urge a drastic cleanup and simplification of the massive and unintelligible tax code to eliminate tax expenditures. Then, if you want welfare spending, pass it openly, like in Europe.

programs generally did succeed and lowered the U.S. poverty rate. Conservatives, they say, have exaggerated the inefficiency and misuses that accompany any welfare program and have understated the very real accomplishments.

The Costs of Welfare

15.4 **Argue for expanding or cutting U.S. entitlement and welfare programs.**

Food Stamps

Begun as a modest trial program under Kennedy in 1961, the Food Stamp program was implemented nationwide under Johnson in 1964. Renamed the Supplemental Nutrition Assistance Program (SNAP), it has grown significantly, and in 2015 some fifty million Americans (15 percent) got an average of $134 a month per person. One-third of families headed by women receive food stamps.

The Carter administration simplified the program in 1977 by eliminating the provision that recipients *buy* the stamps at a discount with their own money. This policy had meant that the absolutely destitute could get no food stamps. Congress changed the law to eliminate the cash payment and the number of recipients expanded. Reagan, citing an apocryphal story of a young man who used food stamps to buy vodka, tightened eligibility requirements in an effort to eliminate fraud and misuse.

What should be done? The Food Stamp program became bigger than expected, but fraud and waste have not been major factors. Only a few recipients sold food stamps at 50 cents on the dollar to buy liquor and drugs, and all food stamps are now debit cards, which fights the fraud problem. Cash grants, considered by Carter as a replacement for food stamps, could easily be misused. Direct delivery of surplus commodities, as was done on a small scale in the 1950s and episodically in the 1980s to get rid of government cheese stocks (the result of price supports for dairy farmers), was clumsy and spotty.

Welfare Reform

In 1996, President Clinton signed a major welfare reform to "end welfare as we know it." This ended the old Aid to Families with Dependent Children (AFDC) that had begun as part of the 1935 Social Security Act. AFDC had provided federal matching funds to the states to help the poor; most of it went to single mothers. Many accused AFDC of promoting fatherless children and welfare dependency. Because many recipients were nonwhite, the issue became connected with the struggle for racial equality.

The 1996 reform replaced entitlement-type welfare payments with block grants to the states to spend fighting poverty as they saw fit. Recipients had five years to get off welfare. Many states developed **workfare** programs that

workfare
Programs limiting the duration of welfare payments and requiring recipients to work or get job training.

required recipients to either take jobs or training. Workfare, which has been tried for years, does not always work and initially costs more than traditional welfare programs because it must provide both welfare and training for a while. Some recipients who took jobs were still quite poor because for every dollar they earned, they lost around 40 cents in "ancillary benefits," which include food stamps, child day care, and Medicaid. The federal earned income tax credit (EITC), a Republican idea, helps low-paid workers cut their income taxes and even gives some additional cash. Some analysts call EITC the best welfare program because it encourages people to work their way out of poverty.

The 1996 reform came when the U.S. economy was excellent, and most people bumped off welfare found jobs. The unemployment rate for single mothers fell from around 48 percent during the 1980s and early 1990s to 28 percent in 1999. The total number of welfare recipients dropped from 12.2 million in 1996 to 5.8 million in 2000, a decline that does not necessarily mean they got out of poverty; they just got off welfare. The real test of welfare reform is how it holds up during recession. With some 9 percent unemployed in 2010 and 2011, more needed help. How long they should be helped sharply divided Republicans and Democrats.

Healthcare Reform

The Democrats' healthcare reform, the Affordable Care Act, was watered down and barely passed in 2010. It does not go nearly as far as most European and Canadian medical insurance and lacks a "public" option; it operates mostly through private insurers. Critics, not all of them Republicans, worry that the plan is too long, too complex, and too expensive. Some charge that the Affordable Care Act does not sufficiently control the ballooning costs of health care, which are inching up to one-fifth of the nation's GDP with poorer results in Americans' health than other western democracies. And, the program came at a time when U.S. budget deficits were already swollen from the Iraq and Afghanistan wars and the financial bailouts.

Some say the giants Medicare and Medicaid—the first an entitlement, the second welfare—both enacted in 1965, offer warnings of how medical costs escalate. Medicare, a federally funded program for older people, now covers about half their healthcare costs for a federal expenditure of more than half a trillion dollars a year. Medicaid combines federal and state funds for poor people and grew, as it expanded coverage for the uninsured under Affordable Care Act. Both Medicare and Medicaid grew so rapidly that benefits had to be limited and eligibility requirements tightened. As 78 million baby boomers started to reach sixty-five in 2011, Medicare costs began to climb. Who will pay for it?

At least two factors induce exponential growth in medical assistance: More people become eligible and medical costs soar. Medicare is especially expensive, for all get it upon reaching age sixty-five, even rich people. The proportion of older people in American society is increasing steadily, and they are by far the biggest consumers of medical care. Many Americans consume most of their lifetime medical expenses in the last few years of life.

Hospitals and doctors, once they are assured of payment, have no incentive to economize. When in doubt, they put the patient in the hospital—at $1,000 and more a day—and order expensive tests. Some hospitals expanded into medical palaces, and some physicians got rich from Medicare and Medicaid. (Ironically, the powerful American Medical Association had for years lobbied against such "socialized medicine.") Medical costs consume nearly 18 percent of the U.S. gross domestic product, most of it paid through government and private health insurance. Other advanced countries pay less and have healthier populations. Their laws set maximum fees that are often a fraction of U.S. costs.

Washington tried various ways of tightening up, but medical costs continued to climb. Recipients were required to contribute bigger "copayments" to hold down overuse. Hospitals and doctors were monitored on costs and on how long they kept patients hospitalized. Hospices—nursing homes for the terminally ill—were made allowable under Medicare, as such care is cheaper than hospital care. Competitive bidding began in some states, and patients were assigned only to low-bid hospitals. Fees for each type of disorder were established, and overruns were not reimbursed. Every time insurers tighten medical assistance, patients, families, doctors, and hospitals complain bitterly, and they form a powerful lobby. Any "end of life" decision—at what point to pull the plug—raises howls of "death panels." But if you never pull the plug, health costs climb even higher. Even conservatives had to admit that the current patchwork of U.S. medical plans was slowly crashing and that something had to be done. People were being shoved out of their private insurance plans for either having "preexisting conditions" or by big hikes in their premiums. Health care and how to pay for it will be a major U.S. political quarrel for decades.

How Big Should Government Be?

15.5 Discuss Americans' contradictory impulses toward welfare programs.

Americans have the funniest ideas about where their tax dollars go. Many think most of the federal budget goes for welfare, which is not at all the case. Angry talk-show hosts suggest it goes to welfare and Medicaid fraudsters, but this percentage too is small. As noted earlier, the bulk of federal spending goes not to welfare for the poor but to entitlements for the middle class; it is impossible to repeal or seriously cut most middle-class programs. A Congress dominated by Republicans in 2003 added an expensive prescription-drug benefit to Medicare; otherwise, they would have ceded the hot issue to Democrats. The complexity of the program angered many elderly. Fumed one oldster: "It's like the IRS run by FEMA!" Politicians are wary about limiting Social Security or Medicare expenditures. It can cost them votes. If you want to cut taxes and deficits, just what programs are you prepared to cut?

The American welfare state is small compared with that of other advanced industrialized countries. Should it get bigger? The American answer, rooted in its political culture, is to keep government small and to suspect and criticize the expansion of government power. But we also recognize that we need government intervention in the economy, education, energy planning, environmental protection, and health care. We have trouble making up our minds about how much government we want. Americans demand various forms of government intervention, but scarcely is the ink on new laws dry before we begin to criticize government bungling. Not understanding where Medicare comes from, many oldsters exclaim, "Don't let the government get its hands on Medicare!" Europeans and Canadians generally do not suffer from this kind of split personality; they mostly accept that government has a major role to play and do not complain as much about their higher taxes.

Americans were in a quandary over the federal government's role in the 2008 financial crisis. In principle, they disliked rescue packages. Both borrowers and lenders should pay for their mistakes, not taxpayers. If government assumes the **moral hazard** of bad loans, firms will just be encouraged in their risky behavior. But the prospect of national economic collapse sobered many into recognizing that government bailouts are sometimes necessary. Even many conservative economists agreed that some firms are "too big to fail" because they would bring down the entire economy. Scary circumstances turn conservatives into liberals.

moral hazard
Shielding firms from the risky consequences of their behavior.

The general reluctance to expand government's role, however, may redound to America's long-term advantage. Government programs tend to expand, bureaucracy is inherently inefficient, and ending an entitlement program is all but impossible. Government programs become so sprawling and complex that officials don't even *know* what is in operation, much less how to control it. As political scientist Ira Sharkansky put it, "All modern states are welfare states, and all welfare states are incoherent." Accordingly, it is probably wise to act with caution in expanding government programs.

Review Questions

1. What policy choices do we now face that are not economic?

2. What was Keynes's solution to the Depression?

3. What started the U.S. inflationary spiral in the 1960s?

4. Are U.S. taxes too high? Compared to what?

5. What went wrong with the U.S. economy in 2008?

6. Why has income inequality grown in the United States?

7. How do entitlements differ from welfare?

8. How does ideology influence our views on poverty?

9. Which U.S. programs can realistically be cut?

10. Why do medical costs tend to escalate?

Key Terms

Further Reference

Backhouse, Roger E., and Bradley W. Bateman. *Capitalist Revolutionary: John Maynard Keynes.* Cambridge, MA: Harvard University Press, 2011.

Bartlett, Bruce. *The Benefit and the Burden: Tax Reform—Why We Need It and What It Will Take.* New York: Simon & Schuster, 2012.

Bernanke, Ben S. *The Courage to Act: A Memoir of a Crisis and Its Aftermath.* New York: Norton, 2015.

Blinder, Alan S. *After the Music Stopped: The Financial Crisis, the Response, and the Work Ahead.* New York: Penguin, 2013.

Conn, Steven. *To Promote the General Welfare: The Case for Big Government.* New York: Oxford University Press, 2012.

Deaton, Angus. *The Great Escape: Health, Wealth, and the Origins of Inequality.* Princeton, NJ: Princeton University Press, 2013.

Edelman, Peter. *So Rich, So Poor: Why It's So Hard to End Poverty in America.* New York: New Press, 2012.

Emanuel, Ezekiel J. *Reinventing American Health Care.* New York: PublicAffairs, 2014.

Freeland, Chrystia. *Plutocrats: The Rise of the New Global Super-Rich and the Fall of Everyone Else.* New York: Penguin, 2012.

Johnson, Simon, and James Kwak. *White House Burning: The Founding Fathers, Our National Debt and Why It Matters to You.* New York: Pantheon, 2012.

Katznelson, Ira. *Fear Itself: The New Deal and the Origins of Our Time.* New York: Liveright, 2013.

Krugman, Paul. *End This Depression Now!* New York: Norton, 2012.

Picketty, Thomas. *Capital in the Twenty-First Century.* Cambridge, MA: Belknap/Harvard, 2014.

Madrick, Jeff. *Age of Greed: The Triumph of Finance and the Decline of America, 1970 to the Present.* New York: Knopf, 2011.

Putnam, Robert. *Our Kids: The American Dream in Crisis.* New York: Simon & Schuster, 2015.

Sachs, Jeffrey D. *The Price of Civilization: Reawakening American Virtue and Prosperity.* New York: Random House, 2011.

Scheiber, Noam. *The Escape Artists: How Obama's Team Fumbled the Recovery.* New York: Simon & Schuster, 2012.

Starr, Paul. *Remedy and Reaction: The Peculiar American Struggle over Health Care Reform.* New Haven, CT: Yale University Press, 2011.

Stiglitz, Joseph E. *The Price of Inequality: How Today's Divided Society Endangers Our Future.* New York: Norton: 2012.

Wapshott, Nicholas. *Keynes Hayek: The Clash That Defined Modern Economics.* New York: Norton, 2011.

Wilkinson, Richard, and Kate Pickett. *The Spirit Level: Why Greater Equality Makes Societies Stronger.* New York: Bloomsbury, 2010.

Chapter 16
Violence and Revolution

 ## Learning Objectives

16.1 Explain the relationship of legitimacy to system breakdown.

16.2 Review the several types of violence and what causes them.

16.3 Define and give examples of terrorism.

16.4 Explain the stages revolutions are likely to go through.

16.5 Analyze the present era, whether it is revolutionary or postrevolutionary.

Recent mass upheavals in Tunisia, Egypt, Libya, Yemen, and Syria let political scientists analyze revolutions as they unfolded. They found some similarities. The old regimes had suffered from weak *legitimacy* for decades; people knuckled under to them but did not respect them. Most of their population was young, under thirty, a "demographic bulge" that had some education but few jobs. Corruption, long standard, became intolerable as economic growth multiplied the need for government permits. New mass media—satellite television, the Internet, and the hand-held social media—spread worldwide. A possible trigger was a global increase in food prices that hit poor countries especially hard. These factors—we do not know which were the most important—deepen our understanding of revolution.

Revolutions tend to end badly. Of the above, only Tunisia established democracy. Egypt slid back to military dictatorship. The last three spiraled into civil war. To prevent revolution, could the old regimes have carried out gradual reforms? Few authoritarian regimes voluntarily give up their wealth and power. Eventually, however, an impasse develops that the regime cannot bribe its way out of, and the frightened regime promises reforms, but by then its opponents sense weakness and see no reason to compromise.

System Breakdown

16.1 Explain the relationship of legitimacy to system breakdown.

Some decades ago, political scientists paid little attention to violence and revolution. They constructed theories of political systems as machines that never broke down. But in the late 1960s, with violence and revolution all around, political scientists began criticizing the status-quo orientation of their discipline and discovered breakdown and upheaval. The inner-city riots of 1965–1968 forced academics to look at violence in America. Some eventually suggested, along with black militant H. Rap Brown, that "violence is as American as cherry pie." Europeans were shocked when the nationalities of ex-Yugoslavia slaughtered each other in the 1990s. That was supposed to be long past in Europe.

system breakdown
Major political malfunction or instability.

coup
From the French *coup d'état*, hit at the state; extralegal takeover of government, usually by military.

Political systems break down. Indeed, most countries have suffered or are suffering from **system breakdown**, marked by major riots, civil wars, terrorism, military **coups**, and authoritarian governments. Dictatorships are rarely the work of small bands of conspirators alone; they are usually the result of system decay and collapse, which permits small but well-organized groups—often the military—to take over. We denounce cruel military regimes in Argentina, Chile, and Guatemala, which killed thousands on suspicion of leftism. But why did these coups happen? Why does system breakdown recur repeatedly in some countries? These are the deeper questions that must be asked to understand these horror stories.

Breakdown starts when legitimacy erodes. Legitimacy is citizens' feeling that the regime's rule is rightful and should be obeyed. Where legitimacy is high, governments need few police officers; where it is low, they need many. In England, for example, people are mostly law-abiding; police are few and hardly any carry firearms. In Northern Ireland, until recently, terrorists killed with bombs and bullets, for a portion of the population saw the government as illegitimate. Here the police are armed, and British troops patrolled with automatic weapons and armored cars. The civil war in Northern Ireland cost some 3,600 lives.

Legitimacy erodes as the regime shows it is unfair and ineffective in running the country. Uncontrollable inflation, blatant corruption, massive unemployment, or defeat in war demonstrate that the government is ineffective.

Violence as a Symptom

Violence by itself does not indicate that revolution is near. Indeed, the most common response to serious domestic unrest is military takeover. Violence is symptomatic of political decay, the government's loss of effectiveness and legitimacy. Sometimes new leadership can calm unrest and begin to deal with the problems, as Franklin D. Roosevelt did in the 1930s. But if the government is clumsy, if it tries to simply crush and silence discontent, it can make things worse. In 1932, the "Bonus Army" of World War I veterans seeking benefits in the Depression was dispersed by army troops under General Douglas MacArthur. Public revulsion at the veterans' rough treatment helped turn the country decisively against President Herbert Hoover in that fall's election.

Domestic violence is both deplorable and informative. It tells that not all is going well, that there are certain groups that, out of desperation or conviction, are willing to break the law to bring change. A government's first impulse is to crush unrest and blame a handful of "radicals and troublemakers." Instigators may deliberately provoke incidents, but the fact that some people support angry groups should signal that something is wrong. At the 1968 Democratic convention, Chicago police attacked Vietnam War protesters—as well as many passersby. The convention ignored the protesters and nominated President Johnson's vice president, Hubert Humphrey, who lost, largely because of his equivocal position on the war. The riot showed that the Democratic Party had lost touch with important elements of its constituency, which only four years earlier had voted for Johnson because he vowed to keep the country out of war. The Democrats should have been listening to, instead of ignoring, the protesters.

In some cases, violence serves a purpose. The United States as a whole and Congress in particular paid little attention to the plight of inner-city African Americans until a series of riots ripped U.S. cities in the late 1960s. The death and destruction were terrible, but there seemed to be no other way to get the media's, the public's, and the government's attention. The rioting in this case "worked"; that is, it brought a major—if not very successful—effort to improve America's decaying cities. When America "forgot" about its inner cities, new rioting reminded us of the problems still there.

The white minority government of South Africa arrested or killed black opponents, but the fact that thousands of young, black South Africans were willing to take up arms against the whites-only regime should have told the Pretoria government something. The ruling whites-only National Party had imagined for decades that Africans (75 percent of the country's population) would simply keep their place (on 13 percent of the land). Pretoria engaged in no dialogue with the country's Africans; it expected them merely to obey. Finally, growing violence persuaded the government to begin a dialogue leading to the release of Nelson Mandela from prison in 1990, the political enfranchisement of the black majority, and a government elected by all citizens in 1994. South Africa held a peaceful revolution in order to avoid a violent one.

China currently experiences thousands of "mass incidents" a year in which citizens gather to protest corrupt local officials, the seizure of farmland, toxic factories, or police cover-up of crimes. The regime responds with warnings and sometimes tear gas and gunfire. The message to Beijing is clear: Institute reforms to clean up the corruption and misuse of power before widespread anger explodes. The regime hopes that showy corruption arrests, economic growth, rising living standards, and nationalism will buy off or deflect discontent. It may be mistaken.

Types of Violence

16.2 Review the several types of violence and what causes them.

Violence has been categorized in several ways. Political scientist Fred R. von der Mehden sees five general types of violence.

Primordial

primordial
Groups people are born into, such as religions and tribes.

Primordial violence grows out of conflicts among the basic communities—ethnic, national, or religious—into which people are born. Fighting between Sunni and Shia in Iraq, Russians in Ukraine, Tibetans and Chinese in Tibet, and Hutus and Tutsis in Rwanda (which killed some 800,000 in the mid-1990s) are examples of **primordial** violence. It also can appear in developed countries such as Quebec, the Basque country of Spain, and Northern Ireland, where Protestants and Catholics conducted a nearly tribal feud.

Separatist

Separatist violence, sometimes an outgrowth of primordial conflict, aims at independence. Tamils in northern Sri Lanka fought from 1983 to 2009 to break away; more than sixty thousand were killed. The Ibos tried to break away from Nigeria with their new state of Biafra in the late 1960s, but they were defeated in a long and costly war. But the Bengalis did break away from Pakistan with their new state of Bangladesh in 1971. Croatia and Bosnia fought Serbia

Methods

Thinkpieces

Sometimes instructors want you to play with ideas rather than concentrate on theses, evidence, and endnotes. They may want you to consider how logically things might unfold, to anticipate events. This is called a **thinkpiece**, and it is quite useful in political science, where we often lack important data but still need an informed estimate of what is likely to happen.

Thinkpieces are often justifiable because we know that many data are flawed. Statistics from developing countries are mostly estimates. Some data are partly subjective, such as the Corruption Perceptions Index. Top decisions are made behind closed doors, even in democracies, leaving us with anecdotal evidence about who influenced whom. All data are historical; none come from the future. How then can we discuss the possibilities for democracy in China or Egypt? Scholars who gathered much evidence failed to anticipate the collapse of the Soviet Union. Why? Because it hadn't happened yet, so there were no data.

To counteract this kind of learned helplessness, we turn to logic and construct an "if-then" essay: If A is repeatedly the case, then logically A will appear in similar situations. For example: Countries that modernize and grow their per capita GDP to about $10,000 mostly turn into democracies, as happened in Taiwan and South Korea. Does this mean China will turn democratic in a few years? We have no firm data for this, just an **analogy** drawn from the pattern of the region.

Reasoning by analogy, of course, is often mistaken, as no two situations are exactly alike. China is quite different from Taiwan and South Korea. We can get into trouble with false analogies. One infamous analogy compared the giveaway of Czechoslovakia to Hitler at Munich in 1938 with the challenge the United States faced in Vietnam in 1965. Intelligent Americans said "No more Munichs" in plunging us into the Vietnam War. But a good thinkpiece corrects for mistaken analogies by pointing out the **dysanalogy** between the two situations.

If political scientists are unwilling to do thinkpieces, what good are we on the great questions of the day, questions for which data are missing, mistaken, or incomplete? Do we have to wait until all the facts are in before making such statements as "Russia has long possessed Ukraine and will strive to get it back"? A thinkpiece is not wild speculation; it is grounded in evidence but does not shy away from carrying it to a logical outcome. Some of the most interesting political science articles are thinkpieces.

---

in order to separate from Yugoslavia in the early 1990s. Ethnic Russians in eastern Ukraine fight to separate from Ukraine.

Revolutionary

Revolutionary violence aims at overthrowing or replacing an existing regime. Castro's ouster of Batista in Cuba, the fall of the shah of Iran, and Naxalite guerrilla warfare in India are examples of revolutionary violence. We tended to think of revolutionary movements as largely Marxist, but in our day several are Islamist. The murderous Boko Haram in Northern Nigeria aims to not only overthrow Nigeria's government but take over neighboring countries. ISIS is the most extreme; it prepares for the apocalypse by slaughtering all who do not believe precisely as they do, including other Muslims.

Von der Mehden includes in this category "counterrevolutionary" violence, the efforts of conservative groups to block revolutions—for instance, the killings

thinkpiece
Essay based on logic rather than on firm evidence.

analogy
Taking one thing as the model for another.

dysanalogy
Showing that one thing is a poor model for another.

carried out by Colombian "self-defense forces." The crushing of anti-Communist movements in Hungary in 1956, Czechoslovakia in 1968, and Poland in 1970 and 1980 also come under this heading, with the ironic twist that here the Communists were the counterrevolutionary force.

Coups

Coups are usually aimed against revolution, corruption, and chaos. Coups are almost always military, although the military is usually supported by key civilian sectors, as in the Brazilian coup of 1964 or the Egyptian coup of 2013. Most coups involve little violence, at least initially. The army forces the president to resign and go into exile, and a general takes over as president. When the military senses opposition, though, it can unleash legalized murder. Some 30,000 Argentines "disappeared" following the military takeover of 1976, many dumped alive at sea. The Chilean military killed nearly 3,000 following its 1973 coup. For decades after the 1954 coup, the military in little Guatemala murdered 200,000 on suspicion of leftism. In Latin America, the counterrevolutionary terror that follows some coups is far bloodier than anything the revolutionaries have done.

praetorianism
From the Praetorian Guard in ancient Rome; tendency of military takeovers.

Coups tend to repeat. Some countries get stuck in **praetorianism**. Egyptian officers pulled coups in 1952, 2011, and 2013. Since 1932, Thailand has had nineteen constitutions and nineteen coup attempts, twelve of them successful. The last coup, in 2014, was over the return of a demagogic former prime minister. Pakistan, wracked by Islamist extremists, has had four coups since independence in 1947, the latest in 1999; many fear another one. Coups generally occur because the civilian institutions of government—parties, parliaments, and executives—are weak, corrupt, and ineffective, leaving the military the choice of taking over or chaos.

Issues

Some violence does not fit any category. Violence over particular issues is generally less deadly. Protests against globalization, strikes by Greeks protesting austerity, and Turkish riots triggered by police beating youths are examples of issue-oriented violence. Egyptian secularists, alarmed by President Mohamed Morsi's turn to Islamist dictatorship, protested until the army ousted him in 2013 after only one year in office. Chinese villagers turn riotous at local officials who invent fake "taxes" and sell farmers' lands to developers. In 1976, black students in South Africa's Soweto township protested against having to learn Afrikaans in school; police shot down several hundred. Issue-oriented violence can turn revolutionary if the issue is serious and police repression brutal.

All of these categories are arbitrary. Some situations fit more than one category. Some start in one category and escalate into another. The complaints of ethnic Albanians in Kosovo against their second-class status led successively to

Albanian political parties, protests, underground groups, violence, and armed rebellion that broke Kosovo away from Serbia in 1999. No country, even a highly developed one, is totally immune to violence.

Change as a Cause of Violence

Many find the underlying cause of unrest in the changes societies go through as they modernize. Traditional societies with old authority patterns and simple economies are relatively untroubled by violence. People live as their ancestors lived and expect little. Likewise, modern, advanced societies with rational authority and productive economies have mostly minor types of violence. The in-between stage, as modernization upsets traditional societies, sees the most violence. Such societies have left traditional stability, but have not yet entered into modern stability. Everything is changing in such societies—the economy, religious views, lifestyle, and the political system—leaving people worried, confused, and ripe for violent actions. Much of this can be seen in the Middle East today.

Economic change can be the most unsettling. Improvement can be as dangerous as impoverishment. The great French social scientist Alexis de Tocqueville observed that "though the reign of Louis XVI was the most prosperous period of the monarchy, this very prosperity hastened the outbreak of the Revolution of 1789." Why should this be? When people are permanently poor and beaten down, they have no hope for the future; they are miserable but quiet. When things improve, when people are less *misérable*, they start imagining a better future; their aspirations are awakened. They want improvement fast—faster than even a growing economy can deliver. Furthermore, some people get rich faster than others, arousing jealousy. Certain groups feel bypassed by the economic growth and turn bitter; Marxists call this "class antagonisms." Revolutionary feeling, however, typically does not arise among the poor but among what Crane Brinton called the "not unprosperous people who feel restraint, cramp, [and] annoyance" at a government that impedes their right to greater wealth.

The underlying problem, as Ted Robert Gurr emphasized, is not poverty itself but **relative deprivation**. The very poor seldom revolt; they're too busy feeding their families. But once people have a full belly, they start noticing that others are living much better than they are. This sense of relative deprivation may spur them to anger, violence, and occasionally revolution. Gurr's findings match those of Tocqueville and Brinton: Revolutions come when things are generally getting better, not when they're getting worse. China should take careful note.

relative deprivation
Feeling of some groups that they are missing out on economic growth.

Other changes spur unrest. Anthropologist Eric R. Wolf argued that the shift from simple subsistence farming to cash crops dependent on markets, landlords, and banks impoverishes many peasants and turns them from quietude to revolution. The economic modernization of agriculture in Mexico, Russia, China, Vietnam, Algeria, and Cuba paved the way for successful peasant-based revolutions in those countries, according to Wolf. Rapid population growth is also associated with civil strife. One study found that 80 percent of civil conflicts

Theories

Rising Expectations

One way of looking at what economic growth does to a society is to represent it graphically. Here the solid line represents actual economic change in a modernizing society—generally upward. The broken line represents people's expectations. In a still-traditional society—at the graph's left—both actual performance and expectations are low. As growth takes hold, however, expectations start rising faster than actual

improvement. Then may come a situation that produces a downturn in the economy—bad harvests, a drop in the price of the leading export commodity, or too much foreign indebtedness—and expectations are frustrated. A big gap suddenly opens between what people want and what they can get. In the words of Daniel Lerner, the "want:get ratio" becomes unhinged, producing a "revolution of rising frustrations."

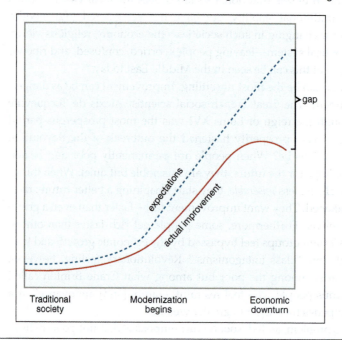

from 1970 to 2000 came in countries where at least 60 percent of the population was under 30 years of age, standard in the Middle East. Unemployed young males are naturally restless.

The political system may be stuck in the past, based on inherited position with no mass participation. As the economy improves, educational levels rise. People learn abstract ideas such as "freedom" and "democracy." Especially among educated people, there is growing fury at despotic rulers. Peasants may hate the system for squeezing them economically, but urban **intellectuals** hate it for suppressing rights and freedoms. It is the confluence of these two forces, argued Samuel P. Huntington—the "numbers" of the peasants and the "brains" of the intellectuals—that makes revolutions.

intellectuals
Educated people who think deeply about things.

Terrorism

16.3 **Define and give examples of terrorism.**

The attacks of September 11, 2001, brought terrorism to the United States. Basically, terrorism is a strategy to weaken a hated political authority. Related to guerrilla or underground warfare, it is not a new thing. The Irish Republican Army (IRA) and Internal Macedonian Revolutionary Organization (IMRO) go back more than a century. Political, ethnic, nationalistic, religious, economic, and ideological grudges fuel terrorist activity. **Terrorism** is a strategy of groups with grudges.

The governments that terrorists hate are usually corrupt and repressive, which unfortunately is standard in the Middle East. Muslim terrorists hate the United States for supporting these governments. Because their foe is more powerful, **jihadis** choose tactics calculated to surprise and horrify. They put bombs in cars, trucks, and boats and strap them on their own bodies. On 9/11, they used tons of jet fuel to collapse skyscrapers. The only advice: "Expect the unexpected."

Terrorists are not insane; they are highly calculating. They aim to panic their enemies, to gain publicity and recruits, and to get the foe to overreact and drive more people to side with the terrorists. Osama bin Laden and his followers were calm and rational in their pursuit of political goals that strike outsiders as mistaken and evil. "One man's terrorist," an old saying goes, "is another man's freedom fighter." Basques, Kurds, Palestinians, and Tamils desire their own state. Spain, Turkey, Israel, and Sri Lanka, respectively, do not want them to have their own state and repress their movements. Thus were born, respectively, the ETA, PKK, PLO, and Tamil Tigers. There's always a reason behind every terrorist movement. In these cases, it's national liberation. Al Qaeda and its offshoots, such as the Islamic State proclaimed in Syria and Iraq (also known as ISIS or ISIL), aim not to liberate separate peoples but to unite Muslims into a new caliphate, a Muslim empire based on a strict reading of the Koran.

Terrorism is group activity, the work of committed believers in political causes. Lone gunmen such as John Hinkley, who shot President Reagan in 1981, are deranged. Currently, the Middle East breeds much terrorist activity, for both material and psychological reasons. High birth rates produce many unemployed youth attracted to the simplistic lessons of *Islamism*, which has made the United States an object of hate. Al Qaeda recruited Sunni Muslims everywhere and bonded them into a religious goal, to make all Muslim countries fundamentalist, remove U.S. influence from the Middle East, and destroy Israel. Ultimately, only the modernization of Muslim societies—a long task they must do themselves— can end Islamist terrorism.

Many experts fear terrorists could get a nuclear device or fissile material. Worldwide, there are already more than thirty thousand nuclear warheads plus fissile material (highly enriched uranium or plutonium) for another two hundred forty thousand. Much of this material, especially in ex-Soviet lands, is

terrorism
Political use of violence to weaken a hated authority.

jihadi
From *jihad* (holy war); Muslim holy warrior.

poorly secured and easily stolen. A nuclear device in a shipping container would not have to be an advanced or compact model.

All nations officially denounce terrorism but some—such as Syria, North Korea, and Iran—engage in "state-sponsored terrorism." The 1981 attempt to kill Pope John Paul II clearly traces back to the Kremlin. The Turkish gunman, an escaped convict, got his money, forged passport, and gun from Bulgarian

Case Studies

Revolutionary Political Warfare in Vietnam

Many people speak of "guerrilla warfare," but this is a misnomer and a redundancy, for *guerrilla* is simply Spanish for "little war," what Spaniards practiced against Napoleon. It is not really about ambushes and booby traps but the accompanying political action. The two combined equal *revolutionary political warfare*, which political scientist Bernard Fall (1926–1967) described as the struggle "to establish a competitive system of control over the population." Fall, an expert on Vietnam who died when he stepped on a land mine there, emphasized *administration* as the crux of revolutionary warfare. "When a country is being subverted it is not being outfought; it is being outadministered. Subversion is literally administration with a minus sign in front."

Fall discovered, both under the French in North Vietnam during the early 1950s and under the Americans in South Vietnam during the early 1960s, that the Communists were collecting taxes throughout most of the country under the very noses of the regimes they were overthrowing. The occupying power, whether French or American, deceived itself by being able to drive through villages in armored convoys; this does not indicate administrative control, which may be in the hands of the insurgents. The emphasis on military hardware is a big mistake, argued Fall, for it detracts from the administrative element.

The Vietnamese insurgents were able to outadminister the regime for several reasons. In the first place, they could identify closely with the population, something the French and Americans could never do. Indeed, the fact that the anti-Communist side in both Vietnam wars was connected with white foreigners gave the kiss of death to the effort. There was no

political package the French or Americans could sell to the locals. Even the Saigon rulers lacked legitimacy among their countrymen. The Diem and subsequent Saigon governments were run by Central and North Vietnamese urban Catholics who looked down on the largely Buddhist rural South Vietnamese. The Saigon officials were city dwellers who disdained assignments in the provinces and working with the peasants, which was precisely the Communists' strong point.

Terror, to be sure, plays a role in revolutionary political warfare. The Vietcong murdered many Saigon officials and government-appointed village headmen. But the villagers were not uniformly horrified at such terror because it was selective and targeted at people who were outsiders anyway. To many peasants, the Vietcong executions seemed like extralegal punishment for collaborators. When the Americans made whole villages disappear, that was terror. There's nothing selective about napalm.

While the insurgent is patiently building a network to supplant the regime, the occupier or government is impatiently trying to substitute firepower for legitimacy. The killing of civilians produces more sympathizers and recruits for the guerrillas. The government's overreliance on firepower erodes its tenuous moral claims to leadership of the nation. Some critics wonder if the American people and leadership ever understood what we were up against in Vietnam and repeated the mistakes in Iraq and Afghanistan. We fought a military war while our opponents fought a political war, and in the end the political mattered more. Said one American officer as he surveyed the smoking ruins of a South Vietnamese town, "Unfortunately, we had to destroy the town in order to save it."

security police, who were supervised by the Soviet KGB. Terrorists need bases, money, arms, and bombs, usually supplied by the intelligence services of one country that wants to inflict harm without direct responsibility. Iranian intelligence founded, funds, and arms the Lebanese Hezbollah, which blew up the U.S. embassy and Marine barracks in Beirut and a Jewish center in Buenos Aires.

Does terrorism work? Rarely, and seldom alone. A touch of violence on top of massive political and economic pressures persuaded whites to abandon their power monopoly in South Africa in the early 1990s. In most cases, however, especially after civilians have been killed, terrorism just stiffens the resolve of the target country. Israelis, attacked by suicide bombers, grew less willing to compromise with Palestinians. The 9/11 attacks united Americans to eliminate al Qaeda. But the U.S. occupation of Iraq fostered more terrorism—including ISIS—and taught Washington the difficulties of building stable democracy amid chaos.

U.S. agencies, even with the new Department of Homeland Security, are not well prepared to fight terrorism. The FBI and CIA had trouble communicating with each other, even less with the cop on the beat. Terrorism is tricky to fight because it falls between war and crime. Like war, it has big stakes, but like crime it is extremely diffuse. Fighting it as a "war" is too simple because it is not a country and cannot be invaded like one. It requires skilled and mobile special forces, such as the SEAL team that killed Osama bin Laden in Pakistan in 2011. Drones may enrage target populations and create more enemies.

Islamist terrorism will likely fade. Muslim clerics denounce its violence, especially for killing Muslims, its chief victims. Several Arab states, including Jordan and Egypt, wage war on ISIS. Islamic terrorism is divided: Sunnis despise and kill Shias, and Shias, including Iran, fight them. Curiously, Iran and the United States are natural allies against ISIS. Islamism has no economic plan for putting food on the table, as Iranians have discovered. Several former activists have turned against and denounced al Qaeda and ISIS. Time may solve the problem.

Revolutions

16.4 Explain the stages revolutions are likely to go through.

A **revolution** is a quick, dramatic system change that throws out the old regime and its elites. A small or moderate change that essentially leaves the system intact is reform, not revolution. Some regimes, to quiet mass discontent, claim they are making a revolution, but the changes may be cosmetic. If the old elites are still in power, there has been no revolution. In a radical revolution, the new elite eliminate the old by guillotine, firing squad, and exile. Revolution is not necessarily bloody, however. In 1989, most East European countries changed systems without bloodshed (exception: Romania). South Africa negotiated a revolution in the early 1990s.

Frustration and unrest by themselves may not make a revolution. People may be unhappy, but with no organization to focus their discontents, little will

revolution
Sudden replacement of an old system by a new one.

happen. In a study of Brazilian political attitudes under the 1964–1985 military dictatorship, Peter McDonough and Antonio Lopez Pina found "a substantial amount of unchanneled dissatisfaction with the authoritarian regime," but it was "free-floating" resentment not especially directed against the government. They suggest that "in the absence of organizational alternatives, resistance is most likely to take the form of apathy and indifference," current characteristics of most Chinese. Beijing tries to keep it that way by outlawing autonomous media, churches, and labor unions, which can focus discontent.

Intellectuals and Revolution

utopia
An imagined and idealized perfect system.

Intellectuals often provide the organization that leads to revolution. Many educated people become the spark plugs of upheaval because they articulate ideas, some of them **utopian**. Preachers, teachers, lawyers, journalists, and others who deal with ideas often criticize the system as bitter outsiders. Prime example: Lenin, who lived to bring down the tsarist regime.

Some intellectuals develop what Librarian of Congress James Billington (1929–) called a "revolutionary faith" that the current system can be replaced with something much better, a "fire in the minds of men." Common folk, ordinary workers and peasants, are seldom interested in abstract ideologies; they want improved material conditions. Intellectuals' idealistic convictions provide the cement that holds revolutionary movements together, the goals they aim for, and leadership.

Most twentieth-century revolutionary movements were founded and led by educated people. Lenin, although kicked out of university, taught himself and passed the law exam with top marks. Mao Zedong helped found the Chinese Communist Party while a library assistant at Beijing University. Fidel Castro and most of his original guerrilla fighters were law school graduates. Che Guevara, who was killed in 1967 while trying to foment revolution in Bolivia, was a medical doctor. The leader of Peru's Shining Path guerrillas was a philosophy professor. The leaders of Iran's revolution against the shah were either religious or academically trained intellectuals. Libya's first prime minister after the 2011 revolution had a U.S. doctorate and taught engineering in the United States. (He lasted only a year.)

The Stages of Revolution

In his 1938 *The Anatomy of Revolution*, Harvard historian Crane Brinton (1898–1968) theorized that all revolutions pass through similar stages, like a human body passing through the stages of an illness. In the English revolution of the 1640s, the American Revolution of 1776, the French Revolution of 1789, and the Russian Revolution of 1917, Brinton found the following rough uniformities.

THE OLD REGIME DECAYS Administration breaks down, and taxes rise. People no longer believe in the government; in fact, the government doubts itself. Intellectuals become alienated from the regime and turn to a proposed ideal system. All this is happening while the economy is generally on the upgrade, but this provokes discontent and jealousy.

THE FIRST STAGE OF REVOLUTION   Committees, networks, cells, or conspiracies form, dedicated to overthrowing the regime. People refuse to pay taxes. A political impasse arises that cannot be solved because lines are too deeply drawn. The government calls in troops, which backfires because the troops desert and the people are further enraged. The initial takeover is easy; the old regime has effectively put itself out of business. Popular exultation breaks out.

AT FIRST, MODERATES TAKE OVER   People who opposed the old regime but were connected with it by background or training assume command. They initiate nonradical reforms, which are not enough for real revolutionaries who accuse the moderates of compromising. The moderates are "nice guys" and not ruthless enough to crush the radicals, who form a parallel government.

shah
Persian for king.

ayatollah
Top cleric in Shia Islam.

Case Studies

The Iranian Revolutionary Cycle

The Iranian revolution closely followed Brinton's pattern of previous revolutions. The Iranian economy boomed, especially with the quadrupling of oil prices in 1973–1974, but economic growth was uneven. Some people got rich fast, provoking jealousy. Corruption and inflation soared. Many educated Iranians opposed the shah's dictatorship; students especially hated the **shah** for his repression of freedoms. Networks of conspirators formed, rallying around the figure of exiled **Ayatollah** Khomeini and using mosques as their meeting places. Major riots broke out in 1978, but the use of troops to quell riots simply enraged more Iranians. Soldiers began to desert. Always disdainful of democracy and mass participation in politics, the shah had relied on his dreaded SAVAK secret police, but even they could no longer contain the revolution. In January 1979, the shah left and Khomeini returned to Iran.

Before he left, the shah named a moderate revolutionary, Shapour Bakhtiar, to head the government. But the very fact of being chosen by the shah ruined Bakhtiar, and the newly returned ayatollah, who instantly became the de facto power in Iran, replaced him with Mehdi Bazargan, another moderate, but one never connected with the shah. Bazargan's government didn't count for much, though, because real power resided with Khomeini's Revolutionary Council. In November 1979, radical Islamic students, angered over the shah's admission into the United States, seized the U.S. Embassy and began the famous "hostage crisis" that lasted more than a year. Bazargan, realizing he was powerless, resigned.

Muslim extremists devoted to Khomeini took over and purged anyone they did not control. Firing squads worked overtime to eliminate suspected "bad" people, including fellow revolutionaries who had deviated. Tens of thousands of young Iranians, promised instant admission to heaven, threw their lives away in repelling Iraqi invaders. Strict Islamic standards were enforced—no alcohol or drugs, veils for women, and hatred of America.

After Khomeini died in 1989, the Iranian revolution gradually calmed and stabilized. There was not one single event to mark a Thermidor, but moderates have won the presidency with promises of greater freedom and economic improvement. Reforms are blocked because real power stays in the hands of the religious elite, which many Iranians now hate. We may not have seen the last upheaval in Iran.

THE EXTREMISTS TAKE OVER   More ruthless, better organized, and with a radical program, the extremists oust the moderates and drive the revolution into a frenzy, throwing out everything old. People are required to be "good" and obey the new, idealistic society. "Bad" people are punished in a reign of terror. Even revolutionary comrades can be executed. As French revolutionary Danton reflected at his trial: "The revolution devours its children." The entire society appears to go mad in what Brinton likened to a high fever during an illness.

A "THERMIDOR" ENDS THE REIGN OF TERROR   Eventually, the society can take no more revolution. People, even revolutionaries, become exhausted from the frenzy and want some normalcy. This leads to a **Thermidor**—so named after the French revolutionary month during which the extremist Robespierre was guillotined—which Brinton described as a convalescence after a fever. Often a dictator resembling the tyrants of the old regime takes over to restore order, something most welcome.

Thermidor
Summer month of French revolutionary calendar that marked end of revolutionary extremism.

Another Harvard scholar, sociologist Theda Skocpol, emphasized the role of the state. Revolutions do not simply bubble up from below but start at the top, from governments caught in situations they cannot manage, "state crises." International pressures such as war and fiscal strain can lead to *elite* divisions and mass mobilization. As Russia was losing to Germany in World War I, the tsarist state collapsed, giving Lenin's small Bolshevik party a chance to grab power. Japan's conquest of China in World War II ruined the effectiveness of the Nationalists and let the Communists win the Chinese Civil War. Without war, it is doubtful that Communism would have taken over Russia or China.

After the Revolution

16.5   **Analyze the present era, whether it is revolutionary or postrevolutionary.**

Revolutions tend to replace one form of tyranny with another. In little more than a decade, the French kings had been replaced by Napoleon, who crowned himself emperor and supervised a police state far more thorough than anything previous. The partial despotism of the tsars was replaced by the perfect despotism of Stalin. Fidel Castro threw out the crooked Batista regime, and Cuban freedom and economic growth declined abruptly.

It was fear of the "Arab Spring" revolutions falling under extremists that made the United States hesitate before backing them. Some revolutionaries were radical Islamists, even al Qaeda affiliated. Khomeini's Islamists had been a minority in the 1979 Iranian revolution but, through better organization, took over and set up a militant, theocratic state that eliminated all opposition (see box on page 323). The same, some worry, could happen in several unstable Arab lands.

Egypt, for example, was the birthplace (in 1928) and home of the original Islamist movement, the Muslim Brotherhood, which the Egyptian government suppressed. Many Brothers were hanged, but the Brotherhood continued underground. President Hosni Mubarak (ruled 1981–2011) won U.S. support and aid by claiming that only he could prevent an Islamist takeover. He was no democrat but, Washington figured, better than the alternative. After his largely nonviolent overthrow—only his security police practiced violence against demonstrators—and Egyptian elections that fall, the Muslim Brotherhood emerged as the largest party, but it showed an extremist side in drafting an Islamist constitution and electing Mohamed Morsi in 2012, who soon gave himself authoritarian powers. Educated, secular Egyptians cried in despair that they had ousted one dictator only to get another. In a year, amid rioting, a military coup ousted Morsi, and a general took power and kept it. Brinton would not have been surprised.

Many other revolutions also work out poorly. Some observers were tempted to despair with Simon Bolivar, the liberator of South America, who said, "He who aids a revolution plows the sea." In general, revolutions end badly. (As soon as you can accept that statement, you have become to some degree a conservative.)

But what about the United States? We call our 1776–1781 struggle with Britain the Revolutionary War, but some say it was not really a revolution, for it did not remake American society. Indeed, most of its leaders were wealthy and prominent figures who wanted simply to get rid of British rule. It was a war of independence rather than a revolution, some argue, and extremists never seized control. Others point out that there was revolutionary violence, directed at America's Tories, colonials who remained pro-British, some one hundred thousand of whom fled in fear to Canada with the phrase, "Freedom wears a crown."

Political philosopher Hannah Arendt (1906–1975) argued that the American struggle was perhaps history's only complete revolution, for it alone ended with a new foundation of liberty instead of the tyranny that came after other revolutions. American revolutionaries did not have to wrestle with the difficult "social question" of how to help the poor that obsessed the French revolutionaries, she noted. America was prosperous, and wealth was distributed rather equally. The American struggle was not sidetracked by the poverty problem, so it could focus on establishing a just and durable constitution with balanced powers and political freedom. America needed no guillotine, for there was no aristocratic class to behead. It had no demagogues of the Robespierre stripe because there was no rabble to rouse. The French Revolution, trying to correct social injustice, became a bloody mess that ended in dictatorship. In Arendt's terms, the French Revolution failed because it did not end with the constituting of liberty, as the American Revolution did.

In France, the Revolution is still controversial more than two centuries later. Few celebrate it uncritically, and many French conservatives hate it. Most French are proud of its original idealistic impulses—"liberty, equality, fraternity"—but many admit that it went wrong, that it turned to bloodshed and dictatorship. The big question here is whether this was avoidable or inevitable. Some argue that it was an accident that the Revolution fell into the hands of extremists and fanatics. Others argue that the revolutionary process itself made it, in the words of François Furet, "skid out of control." Most scholars accept the inevitability thesis.

In Russia, this question is asked about the 1917 Bolshevik Revolution. Lenin, an intelligent and sophisticated man, died in 1924. Had he lived, would communism have taken a more humane and less brutal path? Some blame Stalin for betraying the revolution by turning it into his personal dictatorship. More recent scholarship has shown that Lenin was also ruthless and willing to exterminate all opposition. Some now admit that Lenin was wrong from the start.

Revolution, popular in the 1960s, developed a bad reputation in the 1970s. By the 1980s, many radical countries were trying to back out of their revolutionary systems. There were simply no positive examples of revolutions that had worked out well. The Soviet Union and China, earlier the models for many revolutionaries, admitted that they were in economic difficulty and tried to change to a more open, market system. In 1989, the Communist lands of Eastern Europe simply walked away from communism. Then communism collapsed in the Soviet Union at the end of 1991. In Africa, the revolutionary Communist lands of Angola, Mozambique, and Ethiopia liberalized and begged for aid from the capitalist West.

The worst revolutionary horror was Cambodia. In the late 1970s, the Khmer Rouge (Red Cambodia) murdered an estimated 1.7 million of their fellow citizens. The nonfiction movie about these massacres of all educated people, *The Killing Fields*, shocked the world. And Vietnam, united by the Communists in 1975 after its fierce war with the United States, turned itself into one of the poorest countries in the world. Tens of thousands of Vietnamese "boat people" risked the open sea and Thai pirates to leave their starving land. Sadly, few countries wanted them. In 1995, Vietnam and the United States established diplomatic relations, and the Vietnamese economy turned to the world market with excellent results. In Cuba, Fidel Castro continued to proclaim his regime revolutionary, but most Cubans tired of the shortages and restrictions. Under his brother Raúl since 2006, Cuba has made some free-market reforms and resumed diplomatic relations with the United States. Nicaragua's free election in 1990 voted out the revolutionary Sandinistas and replaced them with a democratic coalition.

velvet revolution
Relatively nonviolent mass uprisings that ousted Communist regimes.

Case Studies

Violent versus Velvet Revolutions

Historically, most revolutions have been violent and bitter, as enraged sectors of the population rose up against hated regimes. They swept clean, leaving none of the old elites with power or wealth. But scholars note that recently a new "velvet" revolution has become common, starting with the overthrow of Communist regimes in Eastern Europe in 1989 and the Soviet Union in 1991. These revolutions are largely nonviolent mass outpourings that reject corrupt, bungling regimes. The old elites lose power but are not executed or exiled. Communist parties, for example, broadened themselves into moderate and democratic Socialist parties and ran in free elections.

Some scholars say these **velvet revolutions** are not revolutions at all because they lack the ferocious qualities of violent revolutions. But if, as we argued, revolution means sweeping system change, especially the ouster of the ruling elite, the overthrow of Communist regimes was also revolutionary. The impulses are the same as in other systems: injustice and corruption. Promised a socialist utopia for generations, citizens tired of the failure to deliver. Actually, Soviets generally enjoyed rising living standards, but their expectations, fanned by party propaganda, rose faster. Soviets were aware that a privileged party elite enjoyed special apartments, food shops, medical care, and vacation cottages. Much of the consumer economy ran on the basis of special deals. Desirable products never made it to the store shelf; they were sold through the back door for big profits. Intellectuals deplored the repression of critical views. The same resentments that smoldered in non-Communist countries smoldered in Communist countries.

As in earlier revolutions, the most dangerous time in the life of a Communist regime is when it tries to reform itself, which is as difficult as in traditionalist countries, for Communist elites also have a lot to lose in terms of power and privilege. In their system, the Communist Party elites become the conservatives who live well and block reforms. When conditions so deteriorate that reforms have to come, it is too late. Things were bad in the Soviet Union under Brezhnev, but mass unrest came only when Gorbachev instituted major reforms. By admitting that things were wrong, he gave the green light to restive workers, intellectuals, and nationalities to demand more than any had dared mention a few years earlier. By asking for support and patience, Gorbachev also showed he was running scared, a further incitement to revolution. By letting in more Western media, he showed the Soviets how well Americans and West Europeans lived. Soon the pressure for massive change became explosive.

Halfway reform does not suffice and often makes things worse. The Communist regimes of Eastern Europe promised reforms and brought in fresh, new leadership. But few were fooled; they recognized that the reforms basically left defective systems intact and that the new leaders were still party bigshots. In Czechoslovakia in 1989, for example, the rapidly growing Civic Forum movement jeered down a new cabinet that the frightened Communist regime presented. The "new" cabinet, still dominated by Communists, looked like the old one. After massive street protest, Civic Forum won a cabinet of non-Communists, some of whom had been in jail only two weeks earlier. Czech President Vaclav Havel, using a phrase coined earlier, called it the "velvet revolution," and the term stuck. When an unpopular regime begins by offering "reforms," it may end by putting itself out of business.

Faced with this prospect, some regimes attempt to crush mass demands with military force. An example is the bloody 1989 crackdown in China. Hundreds of protesting students were gunned down in Beijing's Tiananmen Square because the elderly party elite feared what they called a "counterrevolutionary revolt." Deng Xiaoping had attempted economic reform only to find that it awoke demands for democracy. Partial reform of a corrupt dictatorship is difficult because, as soon as you let people criticize it, they want to replace it. Give them a free-speech inch and they demand a democratic mile. That, of course, would mean ousting the Communist elite, which then fights tenaciously for its power and privileges. But by digging in their heels and refusing to institute major reform, the rulers just build up a head of steam for a later and greater explosion. The party can crush political opponents, but it cannot produce the economic growth necessary to feed and house the people, who just get angrier. Ironically, Communist countries, which always claimed to be "revolutionary," indeed led the way to revolution.

Currently, there are few major revolutionary movements. In Colombia, Peru, and India, Marxist armies still wage guerrilla warfare and terrorism. In Muslim countries, Islamists bomb and assassinate in an effort to overthrow corrupt governments, but their brutality has alienated most Muslims. Currently, Washington debates how deeply to get involved fighting them.

Notice the difference between countries before and after revolutions. Before, revolutionary movements are still idealistic and convinced they will bring a better society. Revolutions are based on the belief that, by seizing state power, a truly committed regime can redo society, making it just, fair, and prosperous. This feeling grows in societies that are unjust and miserable. But after seizing power, the revolutionary regime discovers it's hard to make an economy work. Disillusionment and bitterness set in; many people would like to get rid of the revolutionary regime, which stays in power by blaming capitalist holdouts and imperialist saboteurs. To control these alleged plotters, regimes use draconian police powers.

But things get worse. Farmers do not plant unless they get a decent price for their crops. Workers do not work without something to buy. Unable to admit it is mistaken after having killed so many people, the revolutionary regime locks itself into power through police controls. After some time of hardship and poor growth, a new generation may come to power and admit that the system needs to loosen up. Embarrassment may be a factor here. Comparing itself with free countries, the revolutionary country sees itself falling behind. Chinese in the 1970s could note with regret that on China's rim—in Singapore, Hong Kong, and Taiwan—Chinese prospered, but not in China. Under Deng Xiaoping, China turned to capitalist industry and foreign investment, and the economy set growth records. This also increased inequality and corruption, which Chinese increasingly hate. New Chinese upheavals are likely.

The crux of radical revolutionary thinking is that it is possible to remake society. With the discovery that remaking society leads to terrible difficulties and poor results, the revolutionary dream dies. Does this mean that we will not see another major wave of revolutions? Not necessarily. There is plenty of injustice in the world, and this brings rage. Rage, as Hannah Arendt pointed out, is the fuel of revolution. The greatest cause of rage is the massive corruption now found in the developing lands, including the U.S. clients of Iraq and Afghanistan.

What can be done to head off radical revolutions? The answer is simple but difficult to carry out: reforms to end the injustices and corruption. Land reform in Peru and the Philippines and elected parliaments in Muslim lands could curb corruption and dampen revolutionary movements. The Middle East has the world's highest unemployment rates, recruiting young males to Islamic revolution. The rulers around the Persian Gulf fear the loss of their wealth and power if they democratize, and they have a good argument that liberalizing at this time would just let radicals take over. If Saudi Arabia held free and fair elections, someone like Osama bin Laden could win. The solution: slow and gradual reform that eliminates corruption.

Governments in much of the developing world hate to admit that their corrupt officials siphon off economic growth—especially petroleum revenues—into their own pockets while mass resentment grows. Reforms are hard to apply because the class in power has much to lose and strongly resists. In South

Vietnam in the early 1960s, for example, the United States urged the Saigon regime to carry out sweeping land reform to win the peasants away from Communist guerrillas. But landowners, many of whom collected exorbitant rents from tenant farmers, blocked land-reform bills. If they had given up their land, they might have saved their country; instead, they lost both. The message is to institute reforms before revolutionary feeling takes root—to head off the problem *before* it becomes dangerous.

Review Questions

1. What causes political systems to break down?
2. What purposes can violence serve?
3. Which types of violence are most prevalent today?
4. How can modernization lead to unrest?
5. How can you tell if there has been a revolution?
6. Why are intellectuals prominent in revolutions?
7. What are Brinton's stages of revolution?
8. Do all revolutions end badly? Why?
9. How did the 2011 "Arab Spring" work out?

Key Terms

analogy, p. 315
ayatollah, p. 323
coup, p. 312
dysanalogy, p. 315
intellectuals, p. 318
jihadi, p. 319
praetorianism, p. 316
primordial, p. 314
relative deprivation, p. 317
revolution, p. 321
shah, p. 323
system breakdown, p. 312
terrorism, p. 319
Thermidor, p. 324
thinkpiece, p. 315
utopia, p. 322
velvet revolution, p. 326

Further Reference

Benjamin, Daniel, and Steven Simon. *The Next Attack: The Failure of the War on Terror and a Strategy for Getting It Right.* New York: Henry Holt, 2006.

Goldstone, Jack A., ed. *Revolutions: A Very Short Introduction.* New York: Oxford University Press, 2014.

Greene, Thomas H. *Comparative Revolutionary Movements,* 3rd ed. Englewood Cliffs, NJ: Prentice Hall, 1990.

Heymann, Philip B. *Terrorism, Freedom, and Security: Winning Without War.* New York: Cambridge University Press, 2003.

Katz, Mark N., ed. *Revolution: International Dimensions*. Washington, DC: CQ Press, 2000.

Laqueur, Walter. *No End to War: Terrorism in the Twenty-First Century*. New York: Continuum, 2004.

Parsa, Misagh. *States, Ideologies, and Social Revolutions: A Comparative Analysis of Iran, Nicaragua, and the Philippines*. New York: Cambridge University Press, 2000.

Rand, Dafna Hochman. *Roots of the Arab Spring: Contested Authority and Political Change in the Middle East*. Philadelphia, PA: University of Pennsylvania Press, 2013.

Rapoport, David C., and Leonard Weinberg, eds. *The Democratic Experience and Political Violence*. Portland, OR: Frank Cass, 2001.

Roberts, Adam, and Timothy Garton Ash, eds. *Civil Resistance and Power Politics: The Experience of Non-Violent Action from Gandhi to the Present*. New York: Oxford University Press, 2011.

Spindlove, Jeremy R., and Clifford E. Simonsen. *Terrorism Today: The Past, The Players, The Future*, 5th ed. Upper Saddle River, NJ: Prentice Hall, 2013.

Whittaker, David J. *Terrorism: Understanding the Global Threat*, rev. ed. New York: Longman, 2007.

Wright, Lawrence. *The Looming Tower: Al-Qaeda and the Road to 9/11*. New York: Knopf, 2006.

Chapter 17
International Relations

 ## Learning Objectives

17.1 Contrast domestic politics and international relations.

17.2 Explain why national interests are often disputed.

17.3 Evaluate the economic factor in international relations today.

17.4 Review the several theories on the causes of war.

17.5 Review the several approaches to keeping peace.

17.6 Argue that the trend is now away from absolute sovereignty.

17.7 Evaluate the present era of U.S. foreign policy in terms of interventionism.

The rising hostility of both Russia and China toward the United States marks what some fear is a new Cold War. The original Cold War ended not with a nuclear bang but with an economic whimper as the inefficient Soviet economy fell further behind and Mao damaged China's economy with his permanent revolution. In the old Cold War, the Soviet Union and China were ideological, aiming at global revolution under their leadership. Their ideological and global motives have disappeared, replaced by nationalistic rage and control of resources. Economics and patience won us the original Cold War—and will again.

escalation
Tendency of wars to become bigger and fiercer.

Moscow's snarling at Washington over Syria and Beijing's across the China Seas could spiral into a dangerous **escalation**. Americans—after fourteen years of fighting in Afghanistan and eight in Iraq, the longest wars in U.S. history—were not eager for new conflict. Instead, they are of two minds about the role they should play in world affairs. Many wanted the United States to lead the world, arguing that we have both a moral and a security duty to foster peace and democracy. If we don't lead, no one else will. Perhaps an equal number—in some cases, the same people—did not want Americans dying to bring peace and democracy to regions that appeared unready for either. In the final analysis, what good had we gotten out of involvement in Afghanistan and Iraq?

This is a very old debate: Should America's defense start on the near or far side of the oceans? The Founding Fathers, worried that the small, new United States could get involved in wars that were not hers, urged a close-to-home defense, a theme echoed by isolationists in the twentieth century (and Rand Paul in the twenty-first). By the 1898 Spanish-American War, however, the muscular United States was ready to fight across the oceans, but not all Americans supported it. Whether to go to war far across the seas is an ongoing debate that you will be part of. You should start equipping yourself by understanding international relations.

What Is International Relations?

17.1 Contrast domestic politics and international relations.

domestic politics
Interactions within states.

international relations (IR)
Interactions among states.

International relations differs from the **domestic politics** we have been studying: There is no world sovereign power over the nations to get them to obey laws and preserve peace. Compared with domestic politics, **international relations (IR)** is wilder and more complex. Sovereignty means being boss on your own turf and is the dominant force within a country. Criminals, rebels, and breakaway elements are, in theory, controlled or crushed by the sovereign, who now, of course, is no longer a monarch but the national government. Sovereignty also means that foreign powers have no business intruding into your country's affairs. Their reach—again in theory—stops at your borders.

So much for theory. In practice, nothing is so clear-cut. Just because a nation is legally sovereign does not necessarily mean it really controls its own turf. Witness Ukraine recently: Ethnic Russian fighters with Russian arms seized Crimea and eastern Ukraine. European and U.S. threats did not dissuade Russia. Was Ukraine still "sovereign"? Europe, on the other hand, peacefully came together first in the Common Market and now the European Union (EU). Its members give up some of their sovereignty to form an economic and political union, which could eventually (but not soon) turn into a United States of Europe. Sovereignty is not a simple yes or no but a question of degree.

Further, the idea that sovereignty precludes outside intervention doesn't hold up. Small, weaker countries are routinely dominated and influenced by larger and more powerful countries. Eastern Europe during the **Cold War** was under Soviet control, and the small countries of Central America were under the watchful eye of the United States. Some Canadians claim that U.S. economic and cultural penetration erodes their sovereignty. What meaning does sovereignty have in a *failed state* that cannot govern anything?

Cold War
Armed tension and mistrust between U.S. and Soviet camps, 1946–1989.

Still, the term has some utility. Where established, national sovereignty does bring internal peace, and most countries can claim to have done this. In dealing with other nations, countries still mostly do what they want. When North Korea tests its nuclear bombs, there is nothing that the rest of the world can do to stop it, although many protest. North Korea does what it wishes on its territory. When the United States urges the economic isolation of Russia and Iran, many countries ignore the calls and make trade and oil deals with them. The U.S. Congress cannot pass laws for other countries. Most countries sign treaties to combat global warming, land mines, germ warfare, and exporting weapons, but not the United States, which claims that the treaties are flawed and that it has a sovereign right to ignore them. Other countries cannot make the big, powerful United States conform to these treaties.

Within a sovereign entity, there is—or at least there is supposed to be—law. If you have a grievance against someone, you do not take the law into your own hands. You take the person to court. In international relations, nearly the opposite applies: Taking the law into your own hands—by the threat or use of force—is quite normal. Often there is no other recourse; no universally recognized authority exists to resolve disputes.

This important difference between domestic and international politics sometimes exasperates skilled practitioners of one when they enter the realm of the other. President Johnson was a master of domestic politics; he got whatever he wanted from Congress. But he could not make skinny little Ho Chi Minh back down, for Ho was boss on *his* own turf, Vietnam. What worked domestically for Johnson—deals, threats, persuasion—flopped internationally. Some suggest that it was Nixon's use of the "dirty tricks" of IR in domestic politics that launched Watergate and his subsequent resignation. Nixon was a clever statesman; he simultaneously improved ties with the Soviet Union and China. But his deviousness tripped him up in a delicate domestic problem. International politics is not just domestic politics writ large.

Power and National Interest

17.2 **Explain why national interests are often disputed.**

Lacking sovereignty, IR depends a lot on *power*: A gets B to do what A wants. Hans Morgenthau (1904–1980) held that power is the basic element of international politics that idealists ignore at their peril. Without sufficient power, a country cannot survive, let alone prevail, in a tumultuous world. Power is not necessarily evil or aggressive; it may be simply persuading an aggressor to "Leave me alone!"

Power is not the same as force. Force is the specific application of military might; power is a country's more general ability to get its way and includes military, economic, political, cultural, and psychological factors. The best kind of power: rational persuasion. Power is tricky to calculate. Whole departments of the CIA spend millions trying to figure out how much power various countries have. Some elements of power—such as a country's geography, natural resources, population, and economy—are tangible or calculable. Some of the most important factors, however—such as a country's military capability, the quality of its political system, and its determination—can only be estimated until it is involved in a war. The war then shows, at a terrible price, which side had more power.

national interest
What's good for the nation as a whole in world affairs.

In this situation, countries generally pursue their **national interest**, and this makes IR partly intelligible. If you know a country's national interest—from its history, geography, economy, and current politics—you can understand much of

---

Methods

Avoid "They"

Beware of collective pronouns like "they," which often paint with too broad a brush. When you use "they," always explain who it represents. Grammatically, "they" refers to the previous plural noun. Many new students of international relations use "they" as if an entire national population is making decisions and actions that are the work of a handful of top decision makers. The leaders of France are often critical of U.S. policy. Some Americans then say that "the French" are against us. Actually, 99.99 percent of French people either have no interest in or no input into foreign policy. And many like the United States.

To guard against the overgeneralization that comes with "they," either specify who is taking the action—the president of France, the foreign minister,

or the Quai d'Orsay (French foreign ministry)—or use the name of the capital to stand for the top decision makers—"Paris" for France's foreign-policy elite, "Moscow" for Russia's, and "Beijing" for China's.

There isn't even much of a "we" in U.S. foreign policy. Most Americans have no views or weak views on foreign affairs, and few have any input into foreign-policy decisions. Many do not support administration policies. Even "inside the beltway" (around the District of Columbia), every policy provokes conflicting views. In such situations, instead of the term "Washington," use the person's name and/or organization espousing the viewpoint: "Secretary of State John Kerry sometimes was at odds with Secretary of Defense Ashton Carter." Specific is better.

its behavior. Russia held a security belt to its south and west for centuries and hated when it broke away in 1991. Accordingly, Moscow saw its national interest in using military force to control Georgia and Ukraine, even though the outside world protested. When it comes to their national interests, nations rarely behave like saints.

Countries see their national interests through different eyes. Most of the world sided with the United States after 9/11 and supported the U.S. overthrow of the Taliban regime in Afghanistan. NATO forces helped to try to stabilize the country because many European countries had a national interest in fighting al Qaeda, which had headquarters in Afghanistan. With Iraq in 2003, however, few saw a national interest, and several countries warned against destabilizing Iraq. These were different situations and different perceptions of national interest.

The diplomat's work is in finding and developing complementary interests so that two or more countries can work together. (Listening to diplomats' warnings against invading Iraq could have saved the United States much grief.) Often, countries have some interests that are complementary and others that are

Theories

Types of National Interest

National interests may be divided into four categories:

1. Vital versus secondary
2. Temporary versus permanent
3. Specific versus general
4. Complementary versus conflicting

A vital, or core, interest is one that potentially threatens the life of your nation, such as Soviet missiles in Cuba. When a country perceives a threat to its vital interests, it may go to war. A secondary or peripheral interest is usually more distant and less urgent. The United States, for example, has an interest in calming the troubled Middle East. Nations are more inclined to negotiate and compromise over their secondary interests.

A temporary interest is one of fixed duration, as in U.S. support for Iraq during its 1980s war with Iran. U.S. diplomacy had trouble understanding that, as soon as that war was over, their complementary interests vanished. A permanent interest lasts over centuries, as in the U.S. interest in keeping hostile powers out of the Western hemisphere.

A specific interest focuses on a single problem, such as Chinese export subsidies that cost U.S.

jobs. A general interest might be universal respect for human rights.

When nations have some important goals in common, their interests are *complementary*, which happened in the 1991 Gulf War as several Arab countries sided with the West. Complementary interests are what make alliances. When interests conflict, as when the Moscow government saw no Russian national interest in joining with the United States and West Europe to oust Syria's dictatorship, countries pull apart.

Two countries, even allies, seldom have identical national interests. The best one can hope for is that their interests will be complementary. The United States and Iraqi Kurds, for instance, had a common interest in opposing Saddam's genocidal campaign (which included poison gas) against Kurds, but the U.S. interest was a general, temporary, and secondary one concerning human rights and regional stability. The Kurdish interest was a specific, permanent, and vital one of forming an independent Kurdistan that includes oil-rich Mosul and Kirkuk. Our interests may run parallel for a time, but we must never mistake Kurdish interests for U.S. interests.

conflicting, as when NATO members cooperated to block the Soviet threat but clashed over who was to lead the alliance. The French–U.S. relationship can be described in this way. Where interests totally conflict, of course, there can be no cooperation. Here it is the diplomat's duty to say so and find ways to minimize the damage. Do not despair; national interests shift, and today's adversary may be tomorrow's ally. Few guessed in the 1960s that Communist Vietnam would be friendly to the United States today. The two countries have parallel interests in opposing Chinese claims to almost all of the South China Sea.

Defining the national interest may be difficult. Intelligent, well-informed people may come up with opposite definitions of the national interest. Hawks in the 1960s, for example, claimed a Communist victory in Southeast Asia would harm U.S. interests. Others claimed Vietnam was of little importance to us. Neoconservatives in the Bush 43 administration claimed taking out Saddam Hussein in Iraq was urgent, to prevent him from building **weapons of mass destruction (WMD)**. Critics countered that it was an unnecessary war. In 2010, Secretary of State Hillary Clinton said freedom of navigation in the South China Sea is a U.S. national interest, something China took as a threat. How can you tell when a genuine national interest is at stake? One way is feasibility; power is the connecting link. An infeasible strategy—where your power is insufficient to carry out your designs—is a mistake. If the type of power is wrong for the setting (for example, helicopters and artillery against terrorists; air power to stop a civil war), you are undertaking an infeasible strategy.

Foreign policy is inherently an elite game, and elites usually define the national interest. Unless facing a war or major threat, most people pay little or no attention to foreign policy, which, before 9/11, was nearly absent in U.S. elections. In a democracy, the masses may influence foreign policy—as angry Americans did over the Vietnam and Iraq wars—but only long after the basic decisions have been made in secrecy. Foreign-policy decisions, even in democracies, are made by perhaps a dozen people. Notice how, even in the United States, presidents and a few advisors make foreign policy and then announce it to the American people and to Congress, which usually goes along with it. In late 2001, President Bush decided to invade Iraq, but only a few knew. Only years later did the United States get a real debate on the wisdom of U.S. military involvement in Iraq.

weapons of mass destruction (WMD)
Nuclear, chemical, and bacteriological weapons.

The Importance of Economics

17.3 Evaluate the economic factor in international relations today.

Economics now looms large in IR, perhaps the biggest single factor. The big flaw in the Cold War bipolar model was that it all but left out economics, the very factor that brought down the Soviet Union. In the words of Columbia economist Jeffrey Sachs, "Markets won." But will markets stay the winner? Historically, countries tend to control, regulate, or own their industries. Perhaps the most free-market economy is that of the United States. The Europeans construct large and expensive welfare states whose controls and taxes work against starting new enterprises. In East Asia, the state guides key industries, aimed at rapid growth and dominance of certain markets. Many say Adam Smith's ideas on a free economy are just theories, and few totally practice them.

In recent decades, controlled economies got a jolt from British Prime Minister Margaret Thatcher's attack on the welfare state and her promotion of capitalism. "Thatcherism" spread to many countries, leading to freer markets. Some countries—in large part because domestic interest groups strongly objected—resisted the encroachments of free markets; they tended to hide behind **tariffs** or **quotas**. And a few countries simply prohibit certain foreign imports; Japan, for example, taxes imported rice at nearly 800 percent. Many domestic interest groups have sufficient clout to block foreign goods.

tariff
A tax on an import.

quota
A numerical limit on an import.

The World Trade Organization (WTO) aims at freer trade by cutting tariffs and other barriers. It has some powers of judicial settlement of disputes. Its predecessor before 1995, the General Agreement on Tariffs and Trade (GATT), did the same thing but without enforcement powers. GATT and WTO have done much good. Tariffs are at an all-time low, and most goods flow over the globe, but now nontariff barriers increasingly block trade, many of them concerning nonindustrial products. Several countries (including Canada and France) limit U.S. movies and TV shows, arguing that they replace local productions and endanger cultural and national identities. Some countries (including Japan and China) keep out U.S. banks and online services, arguing that such vital areas belong under national control. Americans argue that if entertainment and online technology are what we do best, our products should flow wherever there are customers. Keeping world trade open is a never-ending task, for new industries are always developing, and countries continually come up with excuses to keep out the new foreign products. The recent global contraction threatened a new wave of **protectionism**, as one country after another worried about keeping jobs at home.

protectionism
Policy of keeping out foreign goods to protect domestic producers.

If the WTO system were to break down and the world returned to protected markets, we could see another depression. The very high Hawley-Smoot tariff, which the United States introduced in 1930 to protect U.S. manufacturers from foreign competition as the Great Depression began, brought retaliation from our trading partners, making the Depression deeper, longer, and worldwide. The Depression was the biggest factor that led to the rise of Hitler and thus to World War II.

Some argue that **globalization** is the big trend. Most countries participate in the world market, a largely capitalistic competition where goods, money, and ideas flow easily to wherever there are customers. The motto of a globalized system: "Make money, not war." The few countries that don't play, such as Cuba and North Korea, live in isolation and poverty. But there are problems with globalization. Is it a cause or a consequence of peace? Are the two intertwined? If so, what happens to one when the other is disrupted? Predictions that economic interdependency would prevent war, widely believed before World War I, have proved false. The British-led globalization of the nineteenth century collapsed

globalization
Free flow of commerce across borders, making the world one big market.

with World War I. It revived, led by the United States, after World War II. Now some say globalization is reversing: "de-globalization."

Prosperity does not necessarily bring peace. Indeed, newly affluent countries often demand respect, resources, and sometimes territory. As China got richer, for example, it combed the globe for oil and mineral deals and defined its borders grandly, reaching far out into the South and East China Seas. And globalization creates resentments, especially in Muslim and other lands with proud and different cultures, at the American and capitalist culture of a globalized system: "McWorld." Some cultures and religions do not wish to become like America.

The prosperity offered by globalization does not reach everyone equally. Often, new jobs go to poor countries to make products to sell to rich ones. But those poor countries do not have protections for their workers such as safe working conditions and minimum wages—which is why it is so cheap to make products there. Are those workers better off because they have jobs? Or worse because globalization exploits them economically? What happens when a country tries to protect its jobs and workers from foreign competition? Or when workers begin to notice their relative deprivation discussed in Chapter 16? The massive growth of China in the world economy raises such questions.

Why War?

17.4 **Review the several theories on the causes of war.**

Very broadly, theories on the cause of war divide into two general camps, the *micro* and the *macro*—the little, close-up picture as opposed to the big, panoramic picture.

Micro Theories

micro theories
Focus on individuals and small groups.

Micro theories are rooted in biology and psychology. They might explain war as the result of genetic human aggressiveness that makes people fight. In this, humans resemble other mammals. Most anthropologists reject such biological determinism, arguing that humans exhibit a wide variety of behavior—some are aggressive and some not—that can be explained only by culture, that is, learned behavior. Psychologists explore leaders' personalities, what made them that way, and how they obtained their hold over the masses and brought them to war.

Biological and psychological theories offer some insights but fall far short of explaining wars. If humans are naturally aggressive, why aren't all nations constantly at war? How is it that countries fight a long series of wars—the Russian-Turkish struggle or the Arab-Israeli wars—under different leaders? Under what circumstances do humans become aggressive? The answer: when they think they are being attacked. For that, we turn to politics.

Macro Theories

Macro theories are rooted in history and geography and concentrate on the power and ambitions of states. States, not individuals, are the key actors, argue macro theorists. Where they can, states expand, as in Russia's push into the Caucasus, the U.S. "manifest destiny," and the growth of the British Empire. Only countervailing power may stop the drive to expand. One country, fearing the growing power of a neighbor, will strengthen its defenses or form alliances to offset the neighbor's power. Much international behavior can be explained by the aphorisms *Si vis pacem para bellum* ("If you want peace, prepare for war") and "The enemy of my enemy is my friend." Political leaders have an almost automatic feel for national interest and power and move to enhance them, argue IR theorists. Does the pursuit of power lead to war or peace? Again, there are two broad theories.

macro theories
Focus on nations, geography, and history.

BALANCE OF POWER   The oldest and most commonly held theory is that peace results when several states use national power and alliances to balance one another. Would-be expansionists are blocked. According to **balance-of-power** theorists, the great periods of relative peace—between the Peace of Westphalia in 1648 and the wars that grew out of the French Revolution (1792–1814), and again from 1815 to the start of World War I in 1914—have been times when the European powers balanced each other. When the balances broke down, there was war. Fighting in Bosnia calmed in 1995 only after power there roughly balanced. When the Serbs were ahead, they had no motive to settle; when they were on the defensive, they decided to settle. Many thinkers consider the Cold War a big and durable balance-of-power system that explains why there was relative peace—at least no World War III—for more than four decades.

balance of power
System in which major nations form and reform alliances to protect themselves.

HIERARCHY OF POWER   Other scholars reject the balance-of-power theory. Calculations of power are problematic, so it is impossible to know when power balances. Often periods of peace occurred when power was *out* of balance, when states were ranked hierarchically in terms of power. Then nations knew where they stood on a ladder of relative power. In transitional times, when the power hierarchy is blurred, countries are tempted to go to war. A big war with a definitive outcome brings peace because then relative power is clearly displayed.

Misperception

Weaving micro and macro approaches together, some thinkers focus on "image" or "perception" as the key to war. It's not the real situation (which is hard to know) but what leaders perceive that makes them decide for war or peace. They often misperceive, seeing hostility and threats from another country, which sees itself as merely defensive. JFK portrayed a Soviet "missile gap" over the United States and increased the U.S. missile program. It turned out that the Soviets were actually behind the United States, and they perceived the American effort as a threat they had to match. The misperceptions led to the 1962 Cuban missile crisis—the closest we came to World War III. Iraq's weapons of mass destruction (WMD) were dismantled under UN supervision in the 1990s, but Bush 43 was convinced Iraq had revived its WMD programs and went to war in 2003 to remove a nonexistent threat. In the emotional and patriotic climate after 9/11, America was angry and suspicious. Intelligence data were skewed to show what the administration wanted to show. Misperception can count for more than reality.

In misperception or image theory, the psychological and real worlds bounce against each other in the minds of political leaders. They think they are acting defensively, but their picture of the situation may be distorted. In our time, it is interesting to note, no country ever calls its actions anything but defensive. The Americans in Vietnam and Iraq saw themselves as defending freedom; the Russians in Georgia and Ukraine saw themselves as defending their country. Leaders often use ideology and mass media to work citizens into anger and then march to war. Under rabidly nationalistic leadership, most Germans and Japanese in World War II saw themselves as defending their countries against hostile powers. Once convinced they are being attacked, otherwise rational people will commit atrocities.

A hopeful trend has appeared after the Cold War: The number and ferocity of wars have declined. The mass media show a lot of fighting—"if it bleeds, it leads"—but careful counts by scholars show a world of less violence. Prehistoric skeletons reveal that our ancestors chiefly died violently. The Mongols, Thirty Years War, Taiping Rebellion, and two world wars killed tens of millions, but nothing so bad has happened since 1945 and even more so since 1989, the fall of the Berlin Wall and end of the Cold War. U.S. interventions are less bloody—60,000 Americans killed in Vietnam as compared to 4,500 in Iraq. Some thinkers suggest the world really is getting more civilized. The spread of democracy (see box) works against war.

Classic Works

Kennan's Dinosaur Analogy

In a famous and oft-reprinted 1950 lecture, diplomat-historian George F. Kennan (1904–2005) compared American democracy to a pea-brained dinosaur sitting contentedly in a swamp unmindful of threats around him. Once harmed by an adversary, though, he erupts into a violent rage that not only destroys the foe but wrecks his own habitat. Kennan concluded: "You wonder whether it would not have been wiser for him to have taken a little more interest in what was going on at an earlier date and to have seen whether he could not have prevented some of these situations from arising instead of proceeding from an undiscriminating indifference to a holy wrath equally undiscriminating." Kennan had U.S. entrance into World War I in mind, but his advice fits many more recent instances of blind American rage. Pay attention earlier. In 2002 at age 98, Kennan warned that the U.S. conquest of Iraq would leave a difficult and chaotic aftermath.

Keeping Peace

17.5 Review the several approaches to keeping peace.

Whatever its causes, what can be done to prevent or limit war? Many proposals have been advanced; none has really worked.

World Government

The real culprit, many claim, is sovereignty itself. States should give up some of their sovereignty—the ability to go to war—to an international entity that would prevent war much as an individual country keeps the peace within its borders. But what country would give up its sovereignty? Certainly not the United States. North Korea does not heed UN calls to open its nuclear sites to international inspection. Without the teeth of sovereignty, the United Nations becomes a debating society, useful for diplomatic contact but little more.

Collective Security

The United Nations' predecessor, the League of Nations, tried **collective security**. Members of the League (which did not include the United States) pledged to join in economic and military action against any aggressor. If Japan, for example, invaded China, every other power would break trade relations and send forces to defend China. Aggressors would back down. It was a great idea on paper, but when Japan conquered Manchuria in 1931, the League merely studied the situation. Japan claimed the Chinese started it (a lie), and the other powers saw no point in entering a distant conflict where they had no interests. The League had no mechanism to make the other countries respond, and the same happened when Italy invaded Ethiopia in 1935. Japan, Italy, and Germany withdrew from the league to practice more aggression, and the League collapsed with World War II.

collective security
An agreement among all nations to automatically counter an aggressor.

Functionalism

Another idea related to world organizations is to have countries work together first in specialized or "functional" areas so they see that they accomplish more by cooperation than by conflict. Increasingly able to trust each other, gradually they will work up to a stable peace. **Functionalism** should produce a "spillover" effect. Dozens of UN-related agencies now promote international cooperation in disease control, food production, weather forecasting, civil aviation, nuclear energy, and other areas. Even hostile countries are sometimes able to sit together to solve a mutual problem in specialized areas.

functionalism
Theory that cooperation in specialized areas will encourage overall cooperation among nations.

But there is no spillover effect; they remain hostile. Sometimes, the specialized organization becomes a scene of conflict, as when the developing nations group expelled Israel and South Africa from the UN Educational, Scientific, and

Cultural Organization (UNESCO) and the United States quit UNESCO over alleged Soviet dominance. Even offers of the UN-related International Monetary Fund (IMF) to bail out distressed economies generate controversy, as the recipient country often claims that economic reforms mandated by the IMF interfere with its sovereignty. The functionalist approach has brought some help in world problems but has not touched the biggest problem, war.

Third-Party Assistance

third party
A nation not involved in a dispute helping to settle it.

One way to settle a dispute is to have a **third party** not involved in the conflict mediate between the contending parties to try to find a middle ground. Third parties carry messages back and forth, clarify the issues, and suggest compromises, as the UN's Ralph Bunche did between Arabs and Israelis in 1949, President Carter did with Begin and Sadat at Camp David in 1978, and Richard Holbrooke did at Dayton over Bosnia in 1995. Third parties can help calm a tense situation and find compromise solutions, but the contenders have to *want* to find a solution. If not, third-party help is futile.

Diplomacy

The oldest approach to preserving peace is through diplomatic contact, with envoys sent from one state to another. A good diplomat knows all the power factors and interests of the countries involved and suggests compromises that leave both parties at least partly satisfied. This is crucial: There must be willingness to compromise. This can be hard because countries often define their vital, nonnegotiable interests grandly and are unwilling to settle for less. After years of intensive negotiations presided over by the United States, Israelis and Palestinians could not compromise on what they saw as their vital interests.

treaty
A contract between nations.

If successful, diplomats draw up **treaties**, which must be ratified and observed. If one country feels a treaty harms it, there is nothing to stop it from opting out, as Bush did in 2002 with the 1972 Anti-Ballistic Missile Treaty with Russia. Countries enter into and observe treaties because it suits them. Some observers say the United States and Soviet Union, both relative newcomers to the world of great-power politics, were unskilled at diplomacy and too unwilling to compromise. The climate of mistrust between them was one of the hallmarks of the Cold War.

Peacekeeping

Related to diplomacy is the use of third-party military forces to support a cease-fire or truce to end fighting. Wearing the blue berets of the UN, they helped calm and stabilize truces between Israel and its Arab neighbors and between Greeks and Turks on Cyprus. Such forces cannot "enforce peace" by stopping a conflict that is still in progress. The only way to do that would be to take sides in the war, and that would be the opposite of **peacekeeping**. It was therefore inherently unrealistic to expect **UNPROFOR** (the UN Protective Force) to separate and calm the warring parties in Bosnia in the 1990s. UNPROFOR, given an impossible mission, covered itself with shame. The **IFOR** (Implementation Force) that took over from UNPROFOR was different and successful because it came after the three sides—Bosnia, Croatia, and Serbia—agreed to a U.S.-brokered peace in Dayton. The U.S. forces in IFOR were also equipped and instructed to destroy attackers; these robust **rules of engagement** dissuaded rambunctious elements, something UNPROFOR was unable to do. Some propose the IFOR model for future peacekeeping, but such actions work only if a peace agreement has been reached beforehand.

Beyond Sovereignty?

17.6 **Argue that the trend is now away from absolute sovereignty.**

The end of the Cold War and of a violent century brought into question the basic point of international politics, sovereignty—namely, is sovereignty slipping? Increasingly, the world community is acting in ways that infringe on the internal workings of sovereign states. For some decades, the International Monetary Fund has been able to tell countries that wanted loans to stop their profligate economic policies. The recipients of such advice often fume that the IMF is infringing on their sovereignty, but if they want the loan, they take the advice, as Greece had to do. The United States, Britain, France, and other NATO allies provided air cover to help Syrian rebels against the dictator Assad, who got Russian help. Most of the world understood that in some cases sovereignty must be infringed upon.

Starting with the Nuremberg War Crimes Trials in 1945–1946, international law increasingly discounts sovereignty as a cover for mass murder. The 1946 Tokyo War Crimes Tribunal and 1961 Eichmann trial in Israel reinforced the Nuremberg precedent. Mass murderers in Bosnia and Rwanda were tried before international tribunals. (Saddam Hussein was tried before an Iraqi court but with strong international support.) Nothing like this happened before World War II. International law is slowly eating into sovereignty.

After a broad, U.S.-led coalition booted Iraq out of Kuwait in 1991, UN inspectors combed through Iraq looking for the capacity to build WMD. The Baghdad dictatorship screamed that Iraq's sovereignty was being infringed upon. Indeed it was, and most of the world was glad of it. Should the international community stand back while a tyrant develops the power to annihilate neighboring countries? By the same token, should the civilized world stand by while the Syrian government shoots its own people? Should the rest of Europe

peacekeeping
Outside military forces stabilizing a cease-fire agreement.

UNPROFOR
UN Protective Force; ineffective peacekeeping effort in Bosnia in early 1990s.

IFOR
Implementation Force; effective NATO-sponsored peacekeeping effort in Bosnia following 1995 Dayton Accords.

rules of engagement
Specify when military forces can shoot.

act as if Balkan massacres were none of its concern? A new doctrine, the "responsibility to protect" (R2P), is growing and could someday override sovereignty.

The world seems to be changing, willing to move beyond sovereignty and toward some kind of order. The trouble is no one knows what kind of order. President Bush 41 used the term "new world order" in building a coalition against Iraq, but he dropped the expression just as debate on it was starting. Few wanted the United States to play world cop, but most understood that if there was to be leadership, only America could provide it. Could **supranational** (above-national) entities take on some of the responsibilities held previously by individual sovereign nations? A new class of "world-order" issues has emerged, such as climate change, that no country can handle on its own. Are any organizations able to play such a role?

supranational
A governing body above individual nations (such as the UN).

The United Nations

The United Nations comes quickly to mind, and indeed the UN functioned better after the Cold War than during it. But it still has problems. As permanent members of the Security Council, Russia and China have the power to veto anything they dislike, such as leaning on Syria to stop killing its own citizens. Russia did nothing against Serbia, long regarded as a Slavic little brother. The UN has sent many peacekeepers to observe truces, as in the Middle East and Balkans, but these few and lightly armed forces from small countries were in no position to enforce peace. The bloodthirsty Khmer Rouge in Cambodia repeatedly kidnapped UN peacekeepers, knowing they would do nothing. Without enforcement powers and fragmented into blocs, the UN remained largely a "talking shop."

The North Atlantic Treaty Organization

NATO was arguably the best defensive alliance ever devised. The former Communist countries of Eastern Europe were happy to join after the Soviet bloc collapsed; NATO assured their freedom and security. Since 1949, NATO coordinated Western Europe and North America to act as a single defender under unified command in the event of Soviet attack. But the North Atlantic Treaty is limited in scope—that an attack on one member in Europe or North America be treated as an attack on all—and does not apply anywhere else, not in the Middle East, Africa, the Balkans, or the Caucasus, which are "out of area." NATO members can, to be sure, volunteer to serve in Afghanistan and Libya, but they cannot be counted on.

There is no organization that can seriously calm and stabilize world trouble spots. Should there be one, or should the civilized world put together a series of ad hoc arrangements, as the United States did in Afghanistan in 2001? Either way, the United States will have to take a leading role if anything is to be done effectively.

Democracy

The Democratic Peace

Can you name any cases where two democracies have fought each other? Some say the U.S. Civil War, but the South was not really a democracy. When Argentina and Britain fought over the Falklands in 1982, Argentina was a military dictatorship. India fought four wars with Pakistan, but Pakistan has been mostly ruled by generals. No two democracies have ever gone to war with each other. The theory of the democratic peace is robust.

Why, logically, should democracy bring peace? Democracy renders leaders accountable, so they tend to be cautious and follow Friedrich's famous "rule of anticipated reactions." They think, "If I take the country to war, how will voters react? Hmm, I guess I better not." When President Johnson ignored such caution in Vietnam—because he thought voters would hold it against him if the Communists won—he lost support and could not stand for a second term. Bush 43 and

the Republicans suffered similarly from the Iraq War. Dictators have no such inhibitions and may be inclined to reckless misadventures, as when Brezhnev invaded Afghanistan in 1979 or Saddam Hussein invaded Kuwait in 1990.

Democracies, because they are better informed through free media, cannot easily demonize other democracies. (They do demonize non-democracies.) The French and Americans are periodically irritated at one another, but neither portrays the other as an enemy. Dictatorships, through their control of the media, can convince their people that hostile powers threaten. North Korea tells its hungry citizens that they have a high standard of living that the Americans want to take away. With little outside information, many North Koreans believe it. The cause of peace is served by the spread of democracy.

U.S. Foreign Policy: Involved or Isolated?

17.7 Evaluate the present era of U.S. foreign policy in terms of interventionism.

The Cold War created a **bipolar** system that was clear but dangerous: the Western allies against the Soviets. Many describe the current system as **multipolar**, a more complicated system, one that reawakened an old question: Should the United States defend its interests on the near or far side of the oceans? For most of America's history, it was assumed that we should generally stay on our own shores, that little overseas really concerned us. Americans, some say, are natural-born isolationists. With Pearl Harbor in 1941, however, isolationism was rejected in favor of massive involvement in world affairs, first in winning World War II and then the Cold War. Isolationism was not an option. Is it one now?

With the Cold War over and facing budgetary constraints, U.S. armed forces shrank. Presidents Bush 41 and Clinton used them little overseas. After 9/11, Bush 43 plunged U.S. forces into Afghanistan and Iraq until they were

bipolar
System of two large, hostile blocs, each led by a superpower, as in the Cold War.

multipolar
System divided among several power centers.

stretched thin. Few suggest returning to a draft, which would take an act of Congress. More than 70 percent of Americans supported the 2003 Iraq War, but by 2006 the same percentage thought it had been a mistake. Public opinion is volatile.

Cycles of U.S. Foreign Policy

foreign policy
Interface of domestic and world politics; in Lippmann's phrase, "the shield of the Republic."

interventionism
Policy of using military force overseas.

isolationism
U.S. tendency to minimize importance of outside world.

unilateralism
Doing things our way against the wishes of allies.

U.S. **foreign policy** tends to swing between **interventionism** and **isolationism**. Can we find a stable and moderate middle ground? Many scholars think not; they see a pendulum swing between overinvolvement and underinvolvement. Stanley Hoffmann discerned "the two *tempi* of America's foreign relations," alternating "from phases of withdrawal (or, when complete withdrawal is impossible, priority to domestic concerns) to phases of dynamic, almost messianic romping on the world stage." Hans Morgenthau saw U.S. policy moving "back and forth between extremes of indiscriminate isolationism and an equally indiscriminate internationalism or globalism." Getting more specific, historian Dexter Perkins divided American foreign relations in cycles of "relatively pacific feeling," followed by "rising bellicosity and war," followed by "postwar nationalism," and then back to "relatively pacific feeling." If Perkins is right, in which phase of the cycle are we now?

Some argue that since the 2003 Iraq War we have practiced **unilateralism**, losing allies and rejecting treaties that most countries want (against global warming, germ warfare, land mines, and other issues). The neoconservatives prominent in the Bush 43 administration despised most of our European allies as cowardly. If we practice unilateralism long enough, however, we may alienate our allies and isolate ourselves. Exercising too much U.S. power could actually lose us the power to influence others. Remember that power is the ability of one country to get another to do something.

Theories

Klingberg's Alternation Theory

A *behavioral* political scientist, Frank L. Klingberg, using such indicators as naval expenditures, annexations, armed expeditions, diplomatic pressures, and attention paid to foreign matters in presidential speeches and party platforms, discovered alternating phases of "introversion" (averaging twenty-one years) and "extroversion" (averaging twenty-seven years). Klingberg added: "If America's fourth phase of extroversion (which began around 1940) should last as long as the previous extrovert phases, it would not end until well into the 1960s." Writing about 1950 and making no reference to Vietnam, Klingberg virtually predicted the impact of the Vietnam War, for it was precisely in the late 1960s (1940 plus twenty-seven years) that the U.S. public and Congress tired of the Vietnam War and intervention in general, an amazingly accurate prediction. Are we now in a new period of extroversion, or are Americans again cautious about sending troops overseas?

Because isolationism connotes ignorance, some prefer the term **noninterventionism**, a reluctance to use U.S. forces overseas. From the birth of the Republic until the 1898 war with Spain, the United States intervened rarely overseas, focusing instead on its own continent. World War II and the Cold War brought massive U.S. overseas intervention. For two decades after Vietnam, we used few U.S. forces abroad and with caution, a "risk-averse" strategy. This suggested that the United States was not completely happy about a world leadership role. 9/11 changed that, but as the Iraq and Afghanistan wars became the two longest wars in U.S. history, Americans shied away from further military involvement. The U.S. public, Congress, and Obama administration were divided and hesitant over further intervention in the Middle East. Many did not want even modest U.S. airpower used in Libya or boots on the ground to fight ISIS in Iraq. Should the United States intervene overseas to stop horrors that do not directly affect U.S. national interests?

noninterventionism
A policy of not sending troops abroad.

The United States in a Dangerous World

Foreign policy is one of the most difficult areas of governance because we have to take into account not only our own abilities and preferences but also those of dozens of other states. We can make two opposite errors (and often do), both related to the problem of *misperception* (discussed previously). First, we can underestimate the dangers we face. In the late 1930s, as the clouds of World War II gathered, we supposed that the oceans were our two great moats, shielding us from the war. Pearl Harbor jolted Americans out of isolation.

During the Cold War, however, we often overestimated the importance of a region, supposing that all areas of the globe were of equal and urgent importance to our national security. On this basis we plunged into Vietnam, with unhappy results. Ironically, a decade and a half after the Communists took over South Vietnam, we won the Cold War largely due to the economic inefficiency of communism. American firms, taking advantage of low Vietnamese wages, now manufacture clothing and footwear there, and the U.S. Navy makes courtesy calls at Vietnamese ports.

U.S. foreign policy faces a twin problem: (1) a messy outside world that often defies our influence and (2) an American people and government little interested in or equipped for putting this world in order. There is no simple solution. Wise practitioners of foreign policy such as George Kennan (see box on page 340) urge calm, reason, and patience. Avoid emotion and extremes. Military power is sometimes necessary but should be used sparingly, as the aftermath of wars is often a power vacuum. Politicians, however, often like to sound decisive and bold in advocating military solutions.

We have recently been in a time of emotion and anger in our foreign affairs. This has led to oversimplifications and unanticipated consequences. Whichever side you take in a foreign-policy debate, panic or despair is seldom justified. Our generation lived through the fears of the Cold War and sometimes overreacted. We now realize that we were always going to win, that communism was

Classic Works

Thucydides on War

The terrible Peloponnesian War (431–404 B.C.) destroyed Athens. A cashiered Athenian general, Thucydides, turned into a historian who reflected on what had gone wrong. "War became inevitable," he wrote, "with the growth of Athenian power and the fear this caused in Sparta." The long and brutal war deranged both sides. Greek civilization took a big step backward and never fully recovered. Political discourse became debased:

> What used to be described as a thoughtless act of aggression was now regarded as courage ..; to think of the future and wait was merely another way of saying one was a coward; any idea of moderation was just an attempt to disguise one's unmanly character; ability to understand a question from all sides meant that one was totally unfitted for action. Fanatical enthusiasm was the mark of a real man.... Anyone who held violent opinions could always be trusted.... Society became divided into camps in which no man trusted his fellow.

Any resemblance to more recent situations?

an unworkable system that was eventually going to collapse. Current threats are not trivial, but we must not panic over Islamist extremism, which will fade because, like communism, it cannot put food on the table.

The biggest long-term problem now is a rapidly rising China. Already the world's largest exporter and second-largest economy, China demands respect. Some IR theorists argue that rising powers must collide with other powers, usually resulting in war. That is true of the Athenian, Roman, Arab, British, German, Japanese, and several other empires. The United States too emerged on the world stage through a series of wars. The rising Portuguese and Spanish empires, though, never fought each other; they agreed to let Spain dominate in Latin America and Portugal in Asia. The trick seems to be to make an agreement in advance over who has what.

China historically never expanded overseas, although it easily could have. Currently Beijing defines its national interest as economic growth and is reluctant to do anything that disrupts it. This explains why China claims Taiwan but has not invaded it, why it is cautious about letting its currency rise, and why it lines up energy and raw-materials deals around the globe. Things could go wrong, however. Strong nationalism simmers in China, which is constructing a major fleet and claims most of the South and East China Seas and areas disputed with India. And China's leaders tend to deflect domestic discontent onto alleged threatening foreign powers, namely the United States.

The great task for your generation will be to define U.S. and Chinese national interests in compatible ways. Beware of misleading *analogies* that equate China to Imperial Japan or the Soviet Union. China is neither of these. Handled with calm and reason, the world can live in peace with a rising China. We made it through the Cold War; you will make it through the twenty-first century, which, with the spread of democracy, may turn out to be a relatively peaceful one.

Review Questions

1. How do domestic and international politics differ?

2. Why does *power* loom so large in international relations?

3. What are the several types of national interest?

4. Which theory of war is the most satisfactory?

5. Are democracy and peace related? How?

6. Is there any effective way to prevent war?

7. What was the Cold War? Why did it begin and end?

8. Which supranational organizations do the most good?

Key Terms

balance of power, p. 339
bipolar, p. 345
Cold War, p. 333
collective security, p. 341
domestic politics, p. 332
escalation, p. 332
foreign policy, p. 346
functionalism, p. 341
globalization, p. 337
IFOR, p. 343

international relations (IR), p. 332
interventionism, p. 346
isolationism, p. 346
macro theories, p. 339
micro theories, p. 338
multipolar, p. 345
national interest, p. 334
noninterventionism, p. 347
peacekeeping, p. 343
protectionism, p. 337

quota, p. 337
rules of engagement, p. 343
supranational, p. 344
tariff, p. 337
third party, p. 342
treaty, p. 342
unilateralism, p. 346
UNPROFOR, p. 343
weapons of mass destruction
    (WMD), p. 336

Further Reference

Bacevich, Andrew J. *Washington Rules: America's Path to Permanent War*. New York: Metropolitan Books, 2010.

Brzezinski, Zbigniew. *Stratgic Vision: America and the Crisis of Global Power*. New York: Basic Books, 2012.

Cashman, Greg, and Leonard C. Robinson. *An Introduction to the Causes of War: Patterns of Interstate Conflict from World War I to Iraq*. Lanham, MD: Rowman & Littlefield, 2007.

Chollet, Derek, and Samantha Power, eds. *The Unquiet American: Richard Holbrooke in the World*. New York: PublicAffairs, 2011.

Chua, Amy. *Day of Empire: How Hyperpowers Rise to Global Dominance—and Why They Fall*. New York: Knopf, 2009.

Dunne, Tim, Milya Kurki, and Steve Smith, eds. *Theories of International Relations: Discipline and Diversity*. New York: Oxford University Press, 2007.

Gallarotti, Giulio M. *The Power Curse: Influence and Illusion in World Politics*. Boulder, CO: Lynne Rienner, 2010.

Kagan, Robert. *The World that America Made*. New York: Random House, 2012.

Kennedy, Paul. *Parliament of Man: The Past, Present, and Future of the United Nations.* New York: Random House, 2006.

Little, Richard. *The Balance of Power in International Relations: Metaphors, Myths, and Models.* New York: Cambridge University Press, 2007.

Mahbubani, Kishore. *The New Asian Hemisphere: The Irresistible Shift of Global Power.* New York: PublicAffairs, 2008.

Mazower, Mark. *Governing the World: The History of an Idea.* New York: Penguin, 2012.

McWilliams, Wayne C., and Harry Piotrowski. *The World Since 1945: A History of International Relations,* 8th ed. Boulder, CO: Lynne Rienner, 2014.

Morgenthau, Hans J., Kenneth W. Thompson, and David Clinton. *Politics among Nations,* 7th ed. Burr Ridge, IL: McGraw-Hill Higher Education, 2005.

Parent, Joseph M. *Uniting States: Voluntary Union in World Politics.* New York: Oxford University Press, 2011.

Sachs, Jeffrey D. *Common Wealth: Economics for a Crowded Planet.* New York: Penguin, 2008.

White, Hugh. *The China Choice: Why We Should Share Power.* New York: Oxford University Press, 2013.

Zakaria, Fareed. *The Post-American World, Release 2.0.* New York: Norton, 2012.

Glossary

absolutism   Post-feudal concentration of power in monarch.

accusatorial   Like adversarial but with a prosecutor accusing a defendant of crimes.

administration   Executives appointed by U.S. president, equivalent to European "government."

adversarial   1) Inclined to criticize and oppose, to treat with enmity. 2) System based on two opposing parties to a dispute.

AFL-CIO   American Federation of Labor-Congress of Industrial Organizations, the largest U.S. union federation.

aggregate   Thing or population considered as a whole.

amicus curiae   Statement to a court by persons not party to a case.

anachronism   Something out of the past.

analogy   Taking one thing as the model for another.

anarchy   Absence of government.

anecdotal   Recounting the views of a few respondents.

anglophone   An English speaker.

anticlericalism   Movement in Catholic countries to get Church out of politics.

apartheid   System of strict racial segregation formerly practiced in South Africa.

apolitical   Not interested or participating in politics.

apparatchik   Russian for "person of the apparatus"; full-time Communist party functionary.

appeal   Taking a case to a higher court.

appropriation   Government funds voted by legislature.

attentive public   Those citizens who follow politics, especially national and international affairs.

austerity   Cutting government spending.

authoritarian   Nondemocratic government but not necessarily totalitarian.

autonomías   Spanish regions with devolved powers.

ayatollah   Top cleric in Shia Islam.

backbencher   Ordinary member of parliament with no leadership or executive responsibilities.

bailout   Emergency government loan to save firm from collapse.

balance of payments   The value of what a country exports compared with what it imports.

balance of power   System in which major nations form and reform alliances to protect themselves.

bandwagon   Tendency of frontrunners to gain additional supporters.

bar graph   Stand-alone data points comparing categories.

Basic Law   (German *Grundgesetz*) Germany's constitution since 1949.

behavioralism   The empirical study of actual human behavior rather than abstract or speculative theories.

bench   The office of judgeship.

bicameral   Parliament having two chambers, upper and lower.

bimodal   A distribution with two large clusters at the extremes and a small center.

bipolar   System of two large, hostile blocs, each led by a superpower, as in the Cold War.

blog   Short for "Web log"; online free magazine, often partisan and idiosyncratic.

bourgeois   Adjective, originally French for city dweller; later and current, middle class in general. Noun: *bourgeoisie.*

brief   Written summary submitted by one side giving relevant facts, laws, and precedents.

bubble   Market that has gone too high.

Bundesrat   Upper, weaker chamber of German parliament.

Bundestag   Lower, more important chamber of German parliament.

bureaucracy   The *career* civil service that staffs government executive agencies.

bureaucratic politics   Infighting among and within agencies to set policy.

business cycle   Tendency of economy to alternate between growth and *recession* over several years.

cabinet   Top executives who head major ministries or departments.

cadre   In Asian Communist systems, party members serving as officials.

cadre party One run by a few political professionals and only intermittently active.

canon law Laws of the Roman Catholic Church, based on Roman law.

Capitol Hill Home of U.S. Congress. (Note the spelling: -*ol*.)

career Professional civil servant, not political appointee.

caste Rigid, hereditary social class or group.

catchall Large, ideologically loose parties that welcome all.

center Nation's capital and its powers.

center-fleeing Parties become extremist, ignoring voters in center.

center–periphery tension Resentment of outlying areas at rule by nation's capital.

center-seeking Parties become moderate to win the many votes in center of political spectrum.

centralization Degree of control exercised by national headquarters.

centrifugal Pulling apart.

chancellor Germany's prime minister.

charismatic Having strong personal drawing power.

civil disobedience The nonviolent breaking of an unjust law to serve a higher law.

civil law Noncriminal disputes among individuals.

civil rights Ability to participate in politics and society, such as voting and free speech; sometimes confused with but at a higher level than human rights.

civil society Humans after becoming civilized. Modern usage: associations between family and government.

class action Lawsuit on behalf of many persons acting together.

class voting Tendency of a given social class to vote for a party that promotes its economic interests.

classic liberalism Ideology founded by Adam Smith to keep government out of economy; became U.S. conservatism.

coalition Multiparty alliance to form a government.

code law Laws arranged in books, originally updated Roman law.

coherence Sticking together to make a rational whole.

Cold War Armed tension and mistrust between U.S. and Soviet camps, 1946–1989.

collective security An agreement among all nations to automatically counter an aggressor.

common law "Judge-made law," old decisions built up over the centuries.

communism Marxist theory merged with Leninist organization into a totalitarian party.

confederation Political system in which components override *center*.

conservatism Ideology of keeping systems largely unchanged.

consistency Applying the same standards to all.

constituency The people or district that elects an official.

constituency casework Attention legislators pay to complaints of people who elect them.

constituent assembly Legislature convened to draft new constitution.

constitution Basic rules that structure a government, usually written.

constitutional law That which grows out of a country's basic documents.

constitutionalism Degree to which government limits its powers.

constructed Something widely believed as old and hallowed but actually recent and artificial.

corporatism The direct participation of interest groups in government.

coup From the French *coup d'état*, hit at the state; extralegal takeover of government, usually by military.

covariance How much two factors change together, indicating how strongly they are related.

critical election A single election which proves to result in a realignment.

cross-pressured Pulled between opposing political forces; said to produce apathy.

culture Human behavior that is learned as opposed to inherited.

cynical Untrusting and suspicious, especially of government.

deadlock In presidential systems, executive and legislative branches blocking each other (current term: *gridlock*).

dealignment Major, long-term decline in party ID.

debt The sum total owed by the federal government.

decentralization Shifting some administrative functions from central government to lower levels; less than *devolution*.

deficit Spending more in a given year than you take in.

demagogue Politician who whips up masses with extreme and misleading issues.

democracy Political system of mass participation, competitive elections, and human and civil rights.

democratic peace   Theory that democracies do not fight each other.

departement   French first-order civil division.

dependent variable   The factor that changes under the impact of the *independent variable*.

descriptive   Explaining what is.

devolution   Shifting some powers from central government to component units.

devotee party   One based on a single personality.

Diet   Japan's national legislature.

discipline   A field of study, often represented by an academic department or major.

dissolve   Send a parliament home for new elections.

domestic politics   Interactions within states.

dysanalogy   Showing that one thing is a poor model for another.

economic issues   Questions relating to jobs, income, taxes, and welfare benefits.

economic rights   Guarantees of adequate material standards of living; the newest and most controversial rights.

efficacy   The feeling that what one does can make a difference.

Electoral College   U.S. system of weighting popular presidential vote to favor smaller states.

electoral system   Laws for running elections; two general types: single-member district and proportional.

electromagnetic spectrum   The airwaves over which signals are broadcast.

elite media   Highly influential newspapers and magazines read by elites and the attentive public.

elites   The "top" or most influential people in a political system.

empirical   Based on observable evidence.

entitlement   U.S. federal expenditure mandated by law, such as Social Security and Medicare.

environmentalism   Ideology to save an endangered nature through regulation and lifestyle changes.

escalation   Tendency of wars to become bigger and fiercer.

Estates General   Old, unused French parliament.

euro   Since 2002, common EU currency used in most of West Europe; value fluctuates but now worth around $1.10.

face-to-face   Communication by personal contact.

failed state   One incapable of even minimal governance, with essentially no national government.

fall   In parliamentary system, a cabinet is voted out or resigns.

fascism   Extreme form of nationalism with elements of racism, socialism, and militarism.

Federal Reserve Board   "The Fed"; U.S. central bank that can raise and lower interest rates.

federalism   Balancing of power between a nation's capital and autonomous subdivisions, such as U.S. states.

feminism   Ideology of psychological, political, and economic equality for women.

feudalism   System of political power dispersed among layers.

first-order civil divisions   Countries' main territorial components, such as U.S. states or Spanish provinces.

Five-Year Plans   Stalin's plans for rapid, centrally administered Soviet industrial growth.

fixed exchange rate   Dollar buys set amounts of foreign currencies.

floating exchange rate   Dollar buys varying amounts of foreign currencies, depending on market for them.

foreign policy   Interface of domestic and world politics; in Lippmann's phrase, "the shield of the Republic."

framing   A news story's basic direction and interpretation.

franchise   The right to vote.

francophone   A French speaker.

functionalism   Theory that cooperation in specialized areas will encourage overall cooperation among nations.

fusion of power   Executive as an offshoot of the legislature.

gender gap   Tendency of American women to vote more Democratic than do men.

generalize   Explaining the causes of consequences of a whole class of events.

general will   Rousseau's theory of what whole community wants.

gerrymander   To draw electoral district boundaries so as to favor one party.

glasnost   Gorbachev's policy of media openness.

globalization   Free flow of commerce across borders, making the world one big market.

government   In Europe, a given cabinet, equivalent to U.S. "administration."

Great Society   President Johnson's ambitious program of social reforms.

gross domestic product (GDP)   Sum total of goods and services produced in a given country in one year, often expressed per capita (GDPpc) by dividing population into GDP.

habeas corpus   Detainee may protest innocence before a judge.

hierarchy   Organized in a ranking of power from top to bottom, as if on a ladder.

higher law   That which comes from God.

honeymoon   High support for presidents early in their terms.

human rights   Freedom from government mistreatment such as arrest, torture, jail, and death without due process.

hypothesis   An initial theory a researcher starts with, to be proved by evidence.

ideologue   Someone who believes passionately in an ideology.

ideology   Belief system that society can be improved by following certain doctrines; usually ends in *ism*.

IFOR   Implementation Force; effective NATO-sponsored peacekeeping effort in Bosnia following 1995 Dayton Accords.

if-then statement   Says that two variables are linked: Where X happens, so does Y.

illiberal democracy   Regimes that are elected but lack democratic qualities such as civil rights and limits on government.

immobilism   Getting stuck over a major political issue.

impeachment   President indicted by the House and tried by the Senate.

imperialism   Amassing of colonial empires, mostly by European powers; pejorative in Marxist terms.

inchoate   Not yet formed.

incumbent   Official who already occupies the office.

independent variable   The factor you think influences or causes something to happen.

indict   Pronounced *in-dite*; to formally charge someone with a crime.

indigent   Having no money.

inference   Accepting the opinions of a sample as reflecting those of a whole population.

inflation   A general, overall rise in prices.

instability   Frequent changes of cabinet.

institutionalize   To make a political relationship permanent.

institutions   The formal structures of government, such as the U.S. Congress.

integration   Merging subcultures into the *mainstream* culture.

intellectuals   Educated people who think deeply about things.

intensity   The firmness and enthusiasm with which an opinion is held.

interest aggregation   Melding separate interests into general party platforms.

interest group   An association that pressures government for policies it favors.

international relations (IR)   Interactions among states.

interventionism   Policy of using military force overseas.

introspective   Looking within oneself.

investigating judge   In European legal systems, judicial officer who both gathers evidence and issues indictments.

irrational   Based on the power to use fear and myth to cloud reason.

Islamism   Muslim religion turned into a political ideology.

isolationism   U.S. tendency to minimize importance of outside world.

jihadi   From *jihad* (holy war); Muslim holy warrior.

Jim Crow   System of segregationist laws once standard in the U.S. South.

judicial activism   Judges' willingness to override legislatures by declaring certain statutes unconstitutional.

judicial restraint   Judges' unwillingness to overturn statutes passed by legislatures.

judicial review   Ability of courts to decide if laws are constitutional; not present in all countries.

Junker   (Pronounced: YOON-care) Prussian state nobility.

KGB   Soviet Committee on State Security, powerful intelligence and security agency.

kleptocracy   Rule by thieves, used in derision and jest.

Knesset   Israel's 120-member unicameral parliament.

laissez-faire   French for "let it be"; economic system of minimal government interference and supervision; capitalism.

Land   German federal first-order civil division; plural *Länder*.

law   That which must be obeyed under penalties.

legitimacy   Mass feeling that the government's rule is rightful and should be obeyed.

libertarianism   U.S. ideology in favor of shrinking all government power in favor of individual freedom.

life cycle   Theory that opinions change as people age.

life peer   Distinguished Briton named to House of Lords for his or her life, not hereditary.

likely voters   Population of adults likely to vote in an upcoming election based on their voting history or intention.

line graph   Connection of data points showing change over time.

lobbying   Interest-group efforts to sway legislators.

log rolling   Legislators mutually supporting each other to get pork-barrel bills passed.

longitudinal   Studying how something changes over time.

Lords   Upper, weaker chamber of British parliament.

macro theories   Focus on nations, geography, and history.

mainstream   Sharing the average or standard political culture.

majoritarian   Electoral system that gives more than half of seats to one party.

majority   More than half.

mandarin   Official of imperial China, schooled in Confucianism.

mandate   A representative carrying out the specific wishes of the public.

manias   Periods of market boom in which greed trumps fear.

Maoism   Extreme form of communism, featuring guerrilla warfare and periodic upheavals.

marginalized   Pushed to the edge of society and the economy, often said of the poor and of subcultures.

margin of error   Range around sample's results within which the population's opinions likely fall.; usually written "+/− 3%".

mass media   Modern means of communication that quickly reach very wide audiences. (The word *media* is plural; *medium* is the singular form.)

mass party   One that attempts to gain committed adherents; usually has formal membership.

media event   News incident planned to get media coverage.

merit civil service   One based on competitive exams rather than patronage.

METI   Japan's Ministry of Economy, Trade, and Industry; formerly MITI, Ministry of International Trade and Industry.

micro theories   Focus on individuals and small groups.

minister   Head of ministry, equivalent to U.S. departmental secretary.

ministry   Major division of executive branch; equivalent to U.S. *department.*

minority   Subgroup distinct by background, viewpoint, or practice within the larger society.

minority government   Cabinet lacking firm majority in parliament.

MITI   Japan's Ministry of International Trade and Industry (now METI).

mixed-member   Hybrid electoral system that uses both single-member districts and proportional representation.

mobilization   Rousing people to participate in politics.

modern liberalism   Ideology favoring government intervention to correct economic and social ills; U.S. liberalism today.

modernization theory   Economic growth fosters a large, educated middle class that demands democracy.

monarchy   Hereditary rule by one person.

moral hazard   Shielding firms from the risky consequences of their behavior.

MP   British member of Parliament, namely, the House of Commons.

multicausal   Several factors making something happen.

multipolar   System divided among several power centers.

NAM   National Association of Manufacturers, a major federation of U.S. industrial executives.

nation   Population with a historic sense of self.

National Assembly   Lower, more important chamber of French parliament.

national interest   What's good for the nation as a whole in world affairs.

nationalism   A people's heightened sense of cultural, historical, and territorial identity, unity, and sometimes greatness.

nationalization   Putting major industries under government ownership.

natural law   That which comes from nature, understood by reasoning.

neoconservatism   U.S. ideology of former liberals turning to conservative causes and methods.

neo-institutional theory   Institutions take on lives of their own, sometimes disconnected from electorates.

nomenklatura   Lists of top Soviet positions and those eligible to fill them, the Soviet elite.

noneconomic issues   Questions relating to patriotism, religion, race, sexuality, and personal choice.

noninterventionism   A policy of not sending troops abroad.

nonpaternalism   Not taking a supervisory or guiding role.

normative   Explaining what ought to be.

offshoring   U.S. firms producing overseas.

oligopoly   A few big firms dominate a market.

ombudsman   Swedish for "agent"; lawyer employed by parliament to help citizens wronged by government.

opinion leaders   Locally respected people who influence the views of others.

opportunists   Persons out for themselves.

opposition   Those parties in parliament not supporting the government.

outlier   Item that deviates from its expected position.

overt socialization   Deliberate government policy to teach culture.

panics   Periods of market collapse in which fear trumps greed.

paradigm   A model or way of doing research accepted by a discipline.

parliament   National legislature; when capitalized, British Parliament, specifically House of Commons.

parliamentary systems   Those with election of parliament only, which in turn elects the prime minister.

parochial   Narrow; having little or no interest in national politics.

participatory   Interest or willingness to take part in politics.

partisan identification (party ID)   Enduring psychological attachment to a party, often from childhood socialization.

party system   How parties interact with each other.

peacekeeping   Outside military forces stabilizing a cease-fire agreement.

personalistic   Based on personality of a strong ruler.

petrostate   Country based on oil exports, such as Saudi Arabia.

plaintiff   The person who complains in a law case.

pluralism   Theory that politics is the interaction of many groups.

plurality   The most, even if less than half.

polarization   Opinion fleeing the center to form two hostile camps.

polarize   To drive opinion into a *bimodal* distribution.

polarized pluralism   System in which parties become more extremist.

Politburo   Russian for "political bureau"; the ruling committee of a Communist party.

political action committee (PAC)   U.S. interest group set up specifically to contribute money to election campaigns.

political appointment   Government job given to non–civil servant, often as reward for support.

political competence   Knowing how to accomplish something politically.

political culture   The psychology of the nation in regard to politics.

political economy   Influence of politics and economy on each other; what government should do in the economy.

political efficacy   Feeling that one has at least a little political input (opposite: feeling powerless).

political generations   Theory that great events of young adulthood permanently color political views.

political institution   Established and durable pattern of authority.

political party   Group seeking to elect office-holders under a given label.

political power   Ability of one person to get another to do something.

population   All people a poll is meant to represent.

pork barrel   Government projects aimed at legislators' constituencies, also called earmarks.

portfolio   Minister's assigned ministry.

positive law   That which is written by humans and accepted over time—the opposite of natural law.

positivism   Theory that society can be studied scientifically and incrementally improved with the knowledge gained.

postbehavioral   Synthesis of traditional, behavioral, and other techniques in the study of politics.

postmaterialism   Theory that modern culture has moved beyond getting and spending.

praetorianism   From the Praetorian Guard in ancient Rome; tendency of military takeovers.

pragmatic   Using whatever works without theory or ideology.

precedent   Legal decisions based on earlier decisions.

prefect   Administrator of a French department.

prefecture   Japanese first-order civil division.

premier   France's and Italy's prime ministers.

president   In U.S.-type systems, the chief political official; in many other systems, a symbolic official.

presidential systems   Those with separate election of executive (as opposed to symbolic) president.

prime minister   Chief political official in parliamentary systems.

primordial   Groups people are born into, such as religions and tribes.

productivity The efficiency with which goods or services are produced.

proletariat Marx's name for the industrial working class.

proportional representation Elects representatives by party's percent of vote.

protectionism Policy of keeping out foreign goods to protect domestic producers.

public financing Using tax dollars to fund something, such as election-campaign expenses.

public opinion Citizens' reactions to current, specific issues and events.

public policy What a government tries to do; the choices it makes among alternatives.

quantify To measure with numbers.

quasi Nearly or almost.

Question Hour Time reserved in Commons for opposition to challenge cabinet.

quota A numerical limit on an import.

rally event Occurrence that temporarily boosts presidents' support.

rational Based on the ability to reason.

realignment Major, long-term shift in party ID.

realism Working with the world as it is and not as we wish it to be; usually focused on power.

recession Period of economic decline; a shrinking GDP.

reciprocity Mutual application of legal standards.

red scare Exaggerated fear of Communist subversion, as in World War I and McCarthy periods.

referendum A mass vote on an issue rather than for a candidate; a type of direct democracy.

regionalism Feeling of regional differences and sometimes breakaway tendencies.

regions Portions of a country with a sense of self and sometimes cultural differences.

relative deprivation Feeling of some groups that they are missing out on economic growth.

religiosity Degree of commitment to one's religion; often affects political beliefs.

representative democracy One in which the people do not rule directly but through elected and accountable representatives.

republic A political system without a monarch. In Communist Soviet Union and Yugoslavia, federal first-order civil division.

responsible party government Voters electorally reward or punish governing party for its policies.

retrospective voting Voters choosing based on overall incumbent performance.

revisionist Changing an ideology or view of history.

revolution Sudden replacement of an old system by a new one.

Riksdag Sweden's parliament.

Roman law System based on codes of ancient Rome.

rule of anticipated reactions Politicians form policies based on how they think the public will react.

rules of engagement Specify when military forces can shoot.

salience Literally, that which jumps out; the importance of given issues in public opinion or the characteristics of the public holding various opinions.

sample Persons selected to be surveyed, usually representative of the whole.

scandal Corruption made public.

scattergram Graph showing position of items on two axes.

scholarship Intellectual arguments supported by reason and evidence.

secular Not connected to religion.

secular realignment A slow, gradual shift in party ID.

sedition Incitement to public disorder or to overthrow the state.

separation of powers U.S. doctrine that branches of government should be distinct and check and balance each other, found in few other governments.

shah Persian for king.

simple random sample Subset of population chosen by random chance.

single-issue group Interest association devoted to one cause only.

single-member districts Electoral system that elects one person per district, as in the United States and Britain.

sit-in Tactic of overturning local laws by deliberately breaking them, as at segregated lunch counters.

skewed A distribution with its peak well to one side.

social class A broad layer of society, usually based on income and often labeled lower, middle, and upper.

social contract Theory that individuals join and stay in civil society as if they had signed a contract.

social democracy Mildest form of socialism, promoting welfare measures but not state ownership of industry.

social mobility The rise and fall of people into another social class.

socialism Economic system of government ownership of industry, allegedly for good of whole society; opposite of capitalism.

socialization The learning of culture.

socioeconomic status Combination of income and prestige criteria in the ranking of groups.

soft money Campaign contributions to parties and issue groups so as to skirt federal limits on contributions to candidates.

source Whom or where a news reporter gets information from.

sovereignty A national government's being boss on its own turf, the last word in law in that country.

stagflation Combination of slow growth plus inflation in the U.S. economy in the 1970s.

Standing Committee Top governing body of Chinese Communist Party.

state Government structures of a nation.

state In Europe, all branches of the national political system; what Americans call "the government."

State Duma Russia's national legislature.

state of nature Humans before civilization.

statism Economic system of state ownership of major industries to enhance power and prestige of state, a precapitalist system.

status quo Keeping the present situation.

statute An ordinary law passed by a legislature, not part of the constitution.

strong state Modern form of government, able to administer and tax the entire nation.

structured access Long-term friendly connection of interest group to officials.

stump To campaign by personally speaking to voters.

subculture A minority culture within the *mainstream* culture.

subject Feeling among citizens that they should obey authority but not participate much in politics.

subprime Risky mortgage made to unqualified borrower.

suffrage The right to vote.

Sullivan Short for *New York Times v. Sullivan*, 1964 Supreme Court decision protecting media against public officials' libel suits.

supranational A governing body above individual nations (such as the UN).

survey A public-opinion poll.

swing Percentage of voters switching parties from one election to the next.

system breakdown Major political malfunction or instability.

tariff A tax on an import.

tax expenditures Government subsidies through tax breaks.

Tea Party Very conservative Republicans.

tendency Finding that two variables are linked but not perfectly.

terrorism Political use of violence to weaken a hated authority.

Thermidor Summer month of French revolutionary calendar that marked end of revolutionary extremism.

thesis A main idea or claim, to be proved by evidence.

thinkpiece Essay based on logic rather than on firm evidence.

third party A nation not involved in a dispute helping to settle it.

Third World The developing areas: parts of Asia, Africa, and Latin America.

Titoism Moderate, decentralized, partially market form of communism.

Tory Nickname for British Conservative.

totalitarian Political system in which the state attempts total control of its citizens.

transparency Political money and transactions open to public scrutiny.

treaty A contract between nations.

trustee A representative deciding the public good without a specific mandate.

turnout Percent of eligible voters who vote in a given election.

two-plus party system Country having two big and one or more small parties.

unforeseen consequence Bad or counterproductive result when laws or policies do not work as expected.

unicameral Parliament with one chamber.

unilateralism Doing things our way against the wishes of allies.

unimodal A single, center-peaked distribution; a bell-shaped curve.

unitary system Centralization of power in a nation's capital with little autonomy for subdivisions.

UNPROFOR UN Protective Force; ineffective peace-keeping effort in Bosnia in early 1990s.

utopia An imagined and idealized perfect system.

values Deeply held views; key component of political culture.

velvet revolution   Relatively nonviolent mass uprisings that ousted Communist regimes.

vice minister   Civil servant who directs a Japanese ministry.

volatility   Tendency of public opinion to change quickly.

vote of confidence   Vote in parliament to support or oust government.

voting bloc   Group with a marked tendency.

Warren Court   The liberal, activist U.S. Supreme Court under Chief Justice Earl Warren, 1953–1969.

WASP   White, Anglo-Saxon, Protestant.

weak state   One unable to govern effectively, corrupt and penetrated by crime.

weapons of mass destruction (WMD)   Nuclear, chemical, and bacteriological weapons.

welfare dependency   Stuck on welfare with no incentive to get off.

welfare state   Economic system of major government redistribution of income to poorer citizens.

Weltanschauung   German for "worldview"; parties that attempt to sell a particular ideology.

whig democracy   Democracy for the few, typical of early stages of democracy.

whip   Legislator who instructs other party members when and how to vote.

wire service   News agency that sells to all media.

workfare   Programs limiting the duration of welfare payments and requiring recipients to work or get job training.

X axis   The horizontal leg of a graph.

Y axis   The vertical leg of a graph.

Zeitgeist   German for "spirit of the times"; Hegel's theory that each epoch has a distinctive spirit, which moves history along.

Index